Jesus Christ as Ancestor provides an engaging analysis of different genres of ancestor Christology in African theological discourse. Readers will find fresh insights into the phenomenon of ancestral mediation in African thought and also the varying ways some Christian theologians have appropriated it for their Christian contexts. Though it is tailored for African evangelical communities, *Jesus Christ as Ancestor* will appeal to theologians interested in African Christian theology.

Victor I. Ezigbo, PhD
Professor of Biblical and Theological Studies,
Bethel University, St Paul, Minnesota, USA

The book is well written, and clearly articulates the issues in contention with deep insight. As a valuable resource for teachers and students of theology, the book provides a useful background to ongoing christological discussion by providing the conversation on the subject in the early church and modern African theological input.

Rev Musa Gaiya, PhD
Professor of Church History,
University of Jos, Nigeria

Dr Reuben Turbi employed a theological method which enabled him to do a historical, biblical and systematic study of all the major players in the ancestor theology discourse. Engaging and critiquing major and primary scholars in a field of study is always very fundamental in serious scholarly discussion. Though a very broad and wide subject, the author subjected all the major proponents of the ancestor Christology models to a historical, biblical, theological, evangelical and well-grounded theological summation. This important section alone sets up and prepares the ground for articulating his important contribution to the field of study.

The major contribution of this highly exciting book is an "African Linguistic Affinity Christology that uses the Greek Yesus to formulate *Yesu/Jesu* Christology in Africa." *Yesu* or *Jesu* as used in many African languages captures the real essence and meaning of Jesus Christ and is to be preferred to the ancestral Christology. This proposal as Dr Turbi has vigorously and persuasively done will find acceptance not only among grassroots believers, but will provide food for thought in theological and academic discussions.

In my mind, Dr Turbi has contributed immensely in providing yet another addition to the search for a contextualized theology that sticks very close to the inspired Scriptures. Congratulations!

Rev Samuel Waje Kunhiyop, PhD
Head, Postgraduate School,
South African Theological Seminary, Bryanston, South Africa
Author, *African Christian Ethics* and *African Christian Theology*

Jesus Christ as Ancestor

A Theological Study of Major African Ancestor Christologies in Conversation with the Patristic Christologies of Tertullian and Anthanasius

Reuben Turbi Luka

MONOGRAPHS

© 2019 Reuben Turbi Luka

Published 2019 by Langham Monographs
An imprint of Langham Publishing
www.langhampublishing.org

Langham Publishing and its imprints are a ministry of Langham Partnership

Langham Partnership
PO Box 296, Carlisle, Cumbria, CA3 9WZ, UK
www.langham.org

ISBNs:
978-1-78368-716-9 Print
978-1-78368-717-6 ePub
978-1-78368-718-3 Mobi
978-1-78368-719-0 PDF

Reuben Turbi Luka has asserted his right under the Copyright, Designs and Patents Act, 1988 to be identified as the Author of this work.

All rights reserved. No part of this publication may be reproduced, stored in a retrieval system or transmitted, in any form or by any means, electronic, mechanical, photocopying, recording or otherwise, without the prior written permission of the publisher or the Copyright Licensing Agency.

Requests to reuse content from Langham Publishing are processed through PLSclear. Please visit www.plsclear.com to complete your request.

All Scripture quotations, unless otherwise indicated, are taken from the Holy Bible, New International Version®, NIV®. Copyright ©1973, 1978, 1984, 2011 by Biblica, Inc.™ Used by permission of Zondervan.

Scripture quotations marked RSV are from Revised Standard Version of the Bible, copyright © 1946, 1952, and 1971 National Council of the Churches of Christ in the United States of America. Used by permission. All rights reserved.

Scripture marked NASB taken from the New American Standard Bible®, Copyright © 1960, 1962, 1963, 1968, 1971, 1972, 1973, 1975, 1977, 1995 by The Lockman Foundation. Used by permission.

British Library Cataloguing-in-Publication Data
A catalogue record for this book is available from the British Library

ISBN: 978-1-78368-716-9

Cover & Book Design: projectluz.com

Langham Partnership actively supports theological dialogue and an author's right to publish but does not necessarily endorse the views and opinions set forth here or in works referenced within this publication, nor can we guarantee technical and grammatical correctness. Langham Partnership does not accept any responsibility or liability to persons or property as a consequence of the reading, use or interpretation of its published content.

Dedication
In loving memory of my dear Father, Pa Luka Turbi Tagwai
(27 June 1900 – 3 October 1997)

Contents

Foreword xi
Acknowledgments xiii
Abstract xvii
List of Abbreviations xix

Chapter 1 1
   Introduction
      Background to the Study 1
      Statement of the Research Problem 22
      Purpose and Contribution of the Study 23
      Research Methodology 29
      Summary 34

Chapter 2 37
   Jesus as an Ancestor: A Paradigm Shift in African Christology and Theological Method
      Introduction 37
      Colonial and Missionary Invasion of Africa between the Eighteenth and Twentieth Centuries: Setting the Stage for the Emergence of Ancestor Christology 41
      African Theology and the Cult of the Ancestors: The Problem of Definition, Terminology, Language and Historical Trends 47
      Major African Schools of Thought on Christ's Ancestorship 55
         I. Abbé Marc Ntetem – Christ the Ancestor par Excellence 55
         II. Bénézet Bujo – Christ the Proto-Ancestor 61
         III. Charles Nyamiti – Christ the Brother and Greatest Ancestor 68
      The Problem with the Ancestorship Emblem 79
      Summary 85

Chapter 3 89
   Historical and Theological Foundations of Christology: Conversing with the Christologies of Tertullian and Athanasius
      Introduction 89
      Jesus in the Life and Thought of the First-Century Church 97
      Apostolic Proclamation of Christ 100
      The Issues Inherent in the Apostolic Christology: African Apologists Defending Apostolic Christology 104
         I. Tertullian of Carthage: The Ray of God Foretold in Ancient Times in His Birth Became God and Man United ...110

  II. Athanasius of Alexandria: The Word Prepares a Body in
    the Virgin as a Temple unto Himself 118
  III. Greek Metaphysics and the African Ancestor Realm 134
  IV. Biblical and Theological Models of Christ in the Thoughts
    of Tertullian and Athanasius and the Contemporary African
    Projection of Christ as an Ancestor: An *Apologia* 139
 Summary 145

Chapter 4 147
 African Ancestor Christological Interpretation and Formulation as Rooted
 in African Worldview and Traditional Belief: Connecting Christ to Africa's
 Pre-Christian Category
  Introduction 147
  Man in African Cosmology 148
  Death in African Cosmology: The Journey to *Ghi Dhen Derrhe*
   (The Hereafter) 155
  The Perceived Role of an Ancestor 159
  Factors for Change: From African Ancestors to Christ as Ancestor ... 165
  Connecting the Communion of the Dead Saints in Christian
   Tradition with Africa's Ancestral Cult 170
  Summary 176

Chapter 5 179
 Theological Sources of African Ancestor Christologies: Exploring Inculturation
 and Contextualization as Theological Methods
  Introduction 179
  Church and Missions in Global Christianity: The Quest for
   Contextual Theology 180
  Motivation from Pre-Vatican II Ecclesial Declarations 190
   I. Pius XII – *Evangelii Praecones* (1951) and *Musicae Sacrae*
    Disciplina (1955) 191
   II. John XXIII – Allocution to African Writers and Artists
    (1959) 196
  Vatican II and Its Aftermath: A Turning Point in Global
   Christian Movement – Toward Inculturating Christianity in
   the Various Cultures of the World 198
   I. Paul VI – *Africae Terrarium* (1967), SECAM, Kampala
    (1969) and *Evangelii Nuntiandi* (1975) 199
   II. John Paul II – The Gospel and African Culture,
    Inculturating and Africanizing Evangelization (1980),
    and Inculturating Christianity in Africa (1982) 202
   III. Francis Arinze and M. I. Fitzgerald – Pastoral Attention
    to African Traditional Religion (1988) 206

  Contextualization and Inculturation as Contextual Theological
   Methods 208
  The Theological Framework of Vatican II, Church Magisterium
   and Inculturation and African Ancestor Christology 214
    I. *Aggiornamento* 217
    II. *Instrumentum Laboris* 219
    III. Code of Canon Law 221
  African Symbols and Christian Beliefs: Towards Comparing
   African Pre-Christian Model of Ancestor and Christian Model
   of Christ 223
  Inculturating Christian Faith through the Ancestor Model:
   Church Magisterium and Vatican II and the Theological
   Implications of Inculturating Christian Model through the
   Ancestor Model 226
  Summary 231
Chapter 6 233
Theological and Biblical Interpretations of African Ancestor Christologies:
Exploring African Linguistic Affinity Christology
  Introduction 233
  Presuppositions of the Ancestorship of Christ 233
  The Significance of Ancestors in African Cosmology 239
  Ancestors as the Channel of Interacting with the Supreme Being 243
    I. African Traditional Notions about the Potency of
     Divinities and Spirit Beings 244
    II. Ancestor as Powerful Intercessors 245
    III. Ancestors as a Way of Understanding the Acts and
     Powers of Jesus Christ 248
  The Cult of the Ancestors as a Theological Meeting Point for
   Christianity and African Indigenous Religions 251
    I. The Cult of Ancestors as the Heart of African Primal
     Tradition and Culture 252
    II. Incarnation as Impetus to Ancestor Christology 254
  Ancestors in the Jewish Worldview: An Overview of the Adamic
   Covenant of Redemption and the Abrahamic Covenant of
   Promise 257
    I. Adam: The Crown of God's Creation and the Mysterious
     Figure in the Garden 258
    II. The Origin of Ancestors in Jewish Religious Context 263
  The Relationship between the Role of Jewish Ancestors and the
   Role of African Ancestors 268
    I. Jewish Ancestorship and African Linguistic Affinity
     Christology 268

    II. African Ancestorship Is Rooted in General Revelation 273
    III. Both Jewish and African Ancestors Anticipated the
    Fulfillment of the Adamic Redemptive Covenant and the
    Abrahamic Covenant of Promise 276
  Summary 278

Chapter 7 279
Towards Yesu/Jesu Christology: Conversing with Ancestor Christology and Some Christological Models in the New Testament

  Introduction 279
  Background and Theological Significance of New Testament
  Christological Models...281
    I. Christ the Promised Messiah 283
    II. Christ the Mediator 299
    III. Christ the High Priest 305
  Relationship between African Pre-Christian Models and New
  Testament Christological Models: Biblical Mediation and
  African Primal Traditions 309
  God and the African Ancestors: The Theological Significance of
  the Being and Otherness of God 316
    I. God Is Transcendent..317
    II. God Is Immanent 320
    III. God, the First and Second Commandments and
    Ancestor Worship..321
      God and Theological Language – Anthropomorphism..............329
  African Ancestors and Biblical Eschatology: Christ and Time
  and the State of the Dead 336
  Exploring The Theological Implications of Ancestor Christology
  in the Light of Contemporary Voices on the Identity of Jesus
  Christ..339
  Summary 356

Chapter 8 359
General Summary and Conclusion

  Summary of the Study 359
  Pertinent Observations Derived from the Study............................363
  Recommendations for Further Research..366

Bibliography...369
Index of Names..397
Index of Subjects..399

Foreword

The book, *Jesus Christ as Ancestor: A Theological Study of Major African Ancestor Christologies in Conversation with the Patristic Christologies of Tertullian and Athanasius* is a critical study of African Christologies and theology and specifically Jesus Christ as Ancestor. African theologians and scholars have proposed how Jesus could be addressed within the African context and worldview. This search for an African name for Jesus to replace the Hebrew and Greek names for Jesus is the heart of the book. The major question is: How successful are African theologians and scholars in finding an African replacement name? The main emphasis of this book is that they have not succeeded in finding the correct christological substitute, apart from linguistic correlations of names and attributes of Jesus to some designated African substitutes, such as the ancestor, the elder, the brother, the healer, etc.

Since African ancestors did not have the revelation of Jesus, it would be incorrect to say that they named *Jesus* as *God*. The God of the ancestors has been an established fact in African traditions, but this does not include Jesus. In order to address this issue adequately and biblically, the author used the method of African Linguistic Affinity Christology as means of resolving the African Christology and nomenclature of Jesus. In the words of the author, this method is a study of Jesus "in Africa in the light of the Adamic covenant of redemption in Genesis 3:14–19, alongside God's covenant of promise, made to Abraham in Genesis 12:2–3 that culminated in the incarnation of the Son of God whose generally accepted given name in Christendom is Jesus (Ἰησοῦς – Greek and *Yesu/Jesu* in most African tribal groups) in Matthew 1:21–23. A befitting nomenclature for this new approach is African Linguistic Affinity Christology methodology which identifies Jesus Christ in Africa as *Yesu/Jesu*."

The author used this method to formulate "a universally accepted name for Jesus in the continent that seeks to be faithful to the Bible and also aligns with Yahweh's promises and covenants made to the Jewish patriarchs, Abraham, Isaac, Jacob, and Moses, in the Old Testament that have been fulfilled in the New Testament."

The case study of some African theologians and scholars was done considering the biblical data and its confirmation and theologization by the African patristic fathers, Tertullian and Athanasius. This is the basis of the author's critique of some African theologians and scholars for naming Jesus the "ancestor." It is interesting to read the African Christologies as propounded by some African theologians and scholars and their criticisms by the author. This fact raises a new level of theological discourse in Africa on who Jesus is and how Africans should address or name him.

The book is insightful, innovative, creative, contextual and critical as it makes the Bible and the African patristic church fathers central to christological formulation in Africa. The choice of African Linguistic Affinity Christology as a worthy tool in addressing Jesus Christ as an Ancestor is biblical, historical and deliberate, because of its value and significance in creating a new approach to the African christological debate. To this end, this book provides fodder to enrich biblical, linguistic, historical and theological discourse in Africa. This book will interest African theologians and scholars as it has drawn the battle lines for serious African christological debates and formulations.

Yusufu Turaki, PhD
Professor of Theology and Social Ethics
Jos ECWA Theological Seminary, Jos, Nigeria

Acknowledgments

This study on *Jesus Christ as Ancestor*, has been to my mind a melting and turning point in my academic pursuit since it stretched my academic muscles and opened new horizons in academic circles. For this reason, my journey into this world of academics at JETS has been quite eventful. In light of this, I sincerely admit and bow to the kind help and guidance of my gracious God – the Father of my Redeemer, Lord and Saviour Jesus Christ who has graciously raised erudite scholars that helped shaped my thought to give this work an expected end.

My interest and desire to undertake this study was kindled and fanned into flames after reading of Professor Yusufu Turaki's *The Unique Christ for Salvation: The Challenge of the Non-Christian Religions and Cultures* (2001) and Professor Victor Ifeanyi Ezigbo's *Re-Imagining African Christologies: Conversing with the Interpretations and Appropriations of Jesus in Contemporary African Christianity* (2010). The contact with the mentioned works placed a responsibility on me to sincerely thank these great minds, whose ideas greatly shaped my thought and inspired me to embark upon this project. Because God's ways are amazing, he divinely and graciously ordained Professor Victor Ifeanyi Ezigbo, whose works I initially read from a very far distance, to eventually come close to the extent of becoming my amiable and dependable supervisor, while Professor Turaki was always there for me. For this, I am most grateful to God and them. Ezigbo's kind words to me will always resound, "Reuben, I am stretching you so that you produce your best." Where I failed to be elastic, he came in to complement. Sir, I am most grateful. You believed I could do it and here today doubt has been transformed into dance.

I also would like to express my gratitude to the Provosts past and present and faculty and staff members of ECWA Theological Seminary, Kagoro and

Jos, for their love to me. Professor Zamani Buki Kafang and Professor Sunday Bobai Agang (Kagoro), and Professor and Dr Mrs Galadima, Professor Bauta Motty, and Professor Morphé Randee-Ijatuyin (JETS) not only served as Provosts but much more like parents to me. Sirs, thank you very much. Professor Cephas Tushima, thank you for your kind smiles and encouraging words that served as a balm to my hurting heart during the tough moments of my research work. Dr Joseph Dyaji (Bingham University, Abuja) thank you for guiding the initial stage of this study.

Permit me to especially appreciate the kind treatment all the doctoral students got from the Dean of Doctoral Programme, Academic Dean and the Secretary past and present for their concern and commitment to ensuring that our dreams turned to diamond. The above named prayed continuously with us, monitored our progress of work, and reminded us always that we cannot afford to fail. Sirs, your desire to have us succeed has yielded tremendous results.

The most important figures second only to my supervisor Professor Victor – my second reader and external examiner – please accept my heartfelt gratitude for your wonderful insights and criticisms that further enriched this study. The minuses and pluses that you made helped give a defining shape to the entire work. Sirs, thank you so much.

To my fellow PhD students, our word has always been, "It is difficult but not impossible, so, we will do it!" Yes! Yes!! To study at this level locally is tortuous but the Lord was there for us. To this end, I encourage you to keep the keeping on. Thank you for praying for me to succeed and please do not give up the race. Worthy of mention is Pastor David and his lovely wife Debbie Colvin who helped edit some chapters of this work at a time they needed rest and adjustment, having retired from the Seminary in Kagoro and gone back to the UK, but they painstakingly helped in this respect. May God bless your ministry back home. Dr Philip Hayab (JP) of the College of Education, Gidan Waya, thank you very much for accepting to do the grammatical editing as well as doing the preliminary formatting of this work. Mr Emmanuel Kure of JETS, thank you for taking the pains to do the final formatting that satisfied JETS's style of writing and formatting.

Acknowledgments

My heart goes out to Dr and Mrs Denis Shelly for continually helping me to order for books overseas in my research area. My coworkers in the vineyard, your efforts have paid off, thank you.

Professor Gorge Janvier cannot be forgotten for his fatherly love and kind support in the course of this study. May the good Lord bless you bountifully with quality retirement life. I must also thank Mr and Mrs Siman Yakubu Jibji who had helped financially and prayerfully in the first two years of this study. Mr and Mrs Danjuma M. Jatau, I cannot fail to thank you. Despite your schoolwork, you have always been around to give me a push. Friends, thank you. Engineer and Mrs Bala Usman, Mr and Mrs Charles Garba, and Pastor and Mrs Joseph Andrew Musa, thank you for coming in at the most needed times.

To the DCCs and individual churches that have helped financially to make these studies a success, I say may God bless you all. To my pastor friends, Reverend Sunday Naggeh (of blessed memory – one who was like a brother), Reverend Lucky Osaghakhoe, Reverend Isaac Ambi, Reverend Musa Kwari, Reverend Nuhu Ghijebet, Reverend Jacob Tanimu, Reverend Yusufu Maikuranda, Reverend Peter Dantata, Bishop Musa Mwin Tula, and Reverend Seth Makama (very much like a son to me), Reverend Felix Gugong, Reverend Dogo Daura, Reverend Iliya Kure, Reverend Yahaya Bodam, Reverend Inuwa Sambo, Reverend Joseph Anda, Reverend Joel Waide, Reverend Samaila Musa, Reverend Fika Asaba Jen and host of others, thank you for your love. Below in rank to these ministers worth appreciating are Pastor Nuhu Danladi Chawai, Daniel Dogo, Julius Jatau, and Benjamin Zani. My pastors past and present at ECWA Good News Jenta Mangoro Jos and all the elders past and present, thank you for your prayers and support. Elder James Kpanto deserves a special thanks for always being there to fix my computer for free. Sir, thank you.

My appreciation will be incomplete if it is not extended to the many students at the two seminaries – Kagoro and JETS – who sat under me and encouraged me to persevere in the midst of a seemingly futile exercise. The relationship with some of you went beyond lecturer-student to prayer partners together with whom we spent hours at the foot of the cross. Two of these students – Lieutenant Andy Simon and Mrs Joseph Doyin – ended up becoming part of my very family members. Brothers and sisters, thank you for being the Aaron and Hur who helped hold my two academic hands to victory.

Finally, I'd like to principally appreciate my backbone and caring wife, Margaret Reuben Luka Turbi, who poured out herself to ensure the excellent finishing of this work. Gimbee, may God bless you. Our seven lovely children: Dorcas, Deborah, Daniel, Zipporah, Seth, Carter and Miracle, and my two grandchildren, Tamar and Frederick Turbi, deserve special thanks for their patience and prayers during this long and solitary journey. May God bless all of you.

Abstract

A current christological trend in African theological discourse is built around the notion that Jesus Christ is an Ancestor. African theologians who formulate ancestor Christology draw their inspiration from the African cult of the ancestors which is found in the primal beliefs of Africa and the debate for or against this view seems unending in evangelical and Roman Catholic circles. Two main theological methods are used in this discourse: contextualization among evangelicals and inculturation among Roman Catholics. Both of these methods seek to present Jesus Christ as an ancestor or otherwise as, in both camps, there are those for and those against Christ's ancestorship.

In this study, both sides are examined and investigated against the backdrop of apostolic and traditional Christology derived from the New Testament and the early church's teaching on Christ. The study examined three select New Testament christological concepts and how they evolved in Christian circles to clarify and validate the assertions of African theologians on the subject. Along with this, the researcher conducted two critical surveys using two different sets of masters and undergraduate students from various African countries at the Jos Evangelical Church Winning All (ECWA) Theological Seminary and the ECWA Theological Seminary in Kagoro, in 2016. The preceding was done to test and establish the ground adduced for or against the ancestor Christology.

To achieve this aim, the ancestor Christologies of three African theologians was reviewed: Abbé Marc Ntetem, Bénézet Bujo and Charles Nyamiti against the backdrop of the Christologies of Tertullian and Athanasius in the third and fourth centuries. As a solution, ancestor Christology was compared and contrasted with the Christologies of Tertullian and Athanasius against heterodox Christologies of the early church and calls for the formulation of Christology in Africa in the light of the Trinitarian and incarnational Christologies of these Roman North-African scholars.

Regarding the current quest to contextualize and inculturate Christology, this study proposes an alternative approach dubbed, "African Linguistic Affinity Christology." This new methodology explores a universally accepted name for Jesus in Africa that resonates with God's covenants made to the Jewish patriarchs Abraham, Isaac, Jacob and Moses. Thus, the theological meaning of Jesus the Christ is explicitly brought out and retained. By so doing, this approach maintains continuity with Old Testament prophecies that found fulfilment in the New Testament through the birth of Jesus Christ whose African name is *Yesu/Jesu*, the Lamb of God who redeemed humanity from sin and condemnation (Matt 1:21–23).

List of Abbreviations

AIC	African Independent Churches
ATR	African Traditional Religion
CUEA	University of East Africa
ECWA	Evangelical Church Winning All
ETSK	ECWA Theological Seminary Kagoro
FESTAC	Festival of Art and Culture
IFES	International Fellowship of Evangelical Students
INEC	Independent National Electoral Commission
JETS	Jos ECWA Theological Seminary
NABIS	Nigerian Association for Biblical Studies
NBTE	National Board for Technical Education
NUC	National University Commission
SECAM	Symposium of Episcopal Conferences for Africa and Madagascar
SIM	Sudan Interior Mission
TCNN	Theological College of Northern Nigeria

CHAPTER 1

Introduction

Background to the Study

In the traditional African belief, "those who are dead are never gone,"[1] they die only to form a consortium of ancestors, which John S. Mbiti pertinently calls "the living-dead."[2] While Mbiti calls the ancestors the living-dead, I call them the living-memories since they exist only in the psyche and memories of their surviving relations. The living-dead were, therefore, living-memories "believed to have survived death."[3] As Emmanuel Bolaji Idowu argues, in Africa "death does not write 'finish' to life."[4] Life is a continuum and cyclically shrouded in what Bénézet Bujo dubbs "memorative-narrative-soteriology."[5]

Thus, the dead are never to be forgotten; their living kin "were expected to perpetuate and immortalised [sic] their memories"[6] through memorial rites provided by the traditional religious institution. For this reason, life in the primal belief of Africa does not end with physical death but crosses over in the next life and what carries your life across is your good name, which

---

1. John V. Taylor, *The Primal Vision: Christian Presence amid African Religion* (London: SCM, 1994), 152.

2. John S. Mbiti, *African Religions and Philosophy*, 2nd rev. ed. (Oxford: Heinemann, 2006), 25.

3. E. G. Parrinder, *African Traditional Religion*, 3rd ed. (London: Sheldon, 1974), 58.

4. E. Bolaji Idowu, *African Traditional Religion: A Definition* (London: SCM, 1973), 186.

5. Ndubisi Innocent Udeafor, *Inculturation: Path to African Christianity* (Nigeria: Snaap Press Limited, 1994), 142.

6. Patrick Ryan, ed., *Inculturation in the South African Context* (Nairobi, Kenya: Paulines Publications Africa, 2000), 37.

often is immortalized in the memory of the surviving kith and kin. The German-South African Klaus Nürnberger is right to assert that "Ancestors notoriously depend on the recognition and remembrance of their progeny for their survival."[7]

Memorials that celebrate antiquity, such as mosaic paintings, sculptures, pictures and graveyard inscriptions are a wonderful means of retrospect whereby the dead are remembered, celebrated and immortalized. For instance, the most important feature of the fourteenth-century renaissance movement was the cult of antiquity, which drew its inspiration from, and celebrated, the past. Thus, Leonardo da Vinci in one of his most famous paintings captured the memory of the Last Supper.[8] The cenotaph of the soldier at the Plateau State secretariat roundabout in Jos, Nigeria, like Leonardo da Vinci's painting, reminds Nigerians of those who lost their lives and limbs during Nigeria's military *coup d'état* and counter-coups in the 1960s and 1970s, as well as the Nigerian Civil War, so that peace can reign in the nation today.[9]

Similarly, the magnificent towering cenotaph of the Martin Luther King Jr memorial, in Washington, DC, remembers the life and work of the American civil rights leader.[10] The captivating portrait of the three Sudan Interior Mission (SIM) pioneers: Walter Gowans, Thomas Kent and Roland

---

7. Klaus Nürnberger, *The Living Dead and the Living God: Christ and the Ancestors in a Changing Africa* (Pietermaritzburg: Cluster, 2007), 15.

8. Stewart C. Easton, believes that the renaissance was a curious look to the past of antiquity for inspiration. The past was remembered in the present through the work of architectural designs, mosaic paintings and sculptural arts etc. In addition to Leonardo da Vinci another specialist who excelled in painting human figures during the renaissance period was Botticelli. For more on the renaissance and those who did much to showcase its ideals, see Stewart C. Easton, *A Survey of Ancient, Medieval, and Modern History* (New York: Barnes & Noble, 1965); Paul Oskar Kristeller, *Renaissance Thought: The Classic, Scholastic, and Humanist Strains* (New York: Harper & Row, 1961).

9. The Cenotaph of the veteran soldier at the Plateau State Secretariat Roundabout in Nigerian-West Africa was built in 1999 during the Nigerian Armed Forces Remembrance Day by the then Military Administrator, Colonel Musa Sheikh Shehu. For thorough investigation of this issues, see Government of Plateau State "Armed Forces Remembrance Day and Emblem Appeal Week Launching," circular to government boards and parastatals, ref no. MSDYS/ASS/294/550 of 8 January, 1999; Max Siollun, *Oil, Politics and Violence: Nigeria's Military Coup Culture (1966-1976)* (New York: Algora, 2009); Chinua Achebe, *There Was a Country: A Personal History of Biafra* (London: Penguin Books, 2012).

10. "Visiting the Martin Luther King, Jr. Memorial in Washinton, DC," Washington DC, https://washington.org/visit-dc/martin-luther-king-jr-memorial.

V. Bingham, conspicuously displayed at the reception of the International Headquarters of Evangelical Church Winning All (ECWA) in the Jos Plateau State celebrates and immortalizes the memory of the founding fathers of the denomination. The argument of Nürnberger invites us to reflect the important place memories occupy in human psychology. He writes, "Memories . . . are dynamic entities that do not simply reproduce historical facts but change, grow or diminish."[11]

In time past, memories of historical events – fictional or real – that seemed not to have mattered are these days not only being celebrated but are enjoying global acceptance. The story behind the Trojan Horse, for instance, believed to have been used by the Greeks to smuggle their soldiers into the city of Troy and conquer it, has in recent times "become part of every educated person's memory, whether from repeated reference in the media," as acted in the movie, *The Odyssey*, "or in books, and possibly from reading Homer's Iliad."[12]

The growing interest in wanting to preserve memories of either the dead or historical events is universal, demonstrated, for example, in the concrete blocks or "stellae" that memorialize the lives of Jewish Holocaust victims, in Berlin, Germany.[13] At the continental level, the African Renaissance Monument (Monument de la Renaissance Africaine) in Dakar, Senegal, is another contemporary example. This monument – a bronze statue of a man, woman and child emerging from a volcano, situated on a 100-metre-high

---

11. Nürnberger, *Living Dead*, 26.

12. Modern archaeological excavation has proven the historical fact behind the Trojan War and the Greek's construction of the Trojan Horse through the work of the German excavator Heinrich Schliemann. For detail investigation of this historical event, see Virgil, "The Aeneid Book," trans. A. S. Kline, *Poetry in Translation*, accessed 10 August 2012, *https://www.poetryintranslation.com/PITBR/Latin/VirgilAeneidII.php#highlightaeneid*; Michael, John Anderson, *The Fall of Troy in Early Greek Poetry and Art* (New York: Oxford University Press, 1997), 22–23; Jacques Barzun and Henry F. Graff, *The Modern Researcher* (Belmont, CA: Thomson/Wadsworth, 2004), 9, and http/www.encyclopedia.com/Troy.aspxpp, accessed 28 July 2015.

13. The stellae in Berlin, Germany, were erected to commemorate the gruesome murder of the six million Jews by General Adolf Hitler during World War II. The gory experience of World War II led to the establishment of the United Nations' peace pact during which time member nations signed a global peace treaty. For more details on the marble stellae, see Jackie Craven, "About the 2005 Berlin Holocaust Memorial: A Memorial to the Murderd Jews of Europe," Thoughts Co., https://www.thoughtco.com/the-berlin-holocaust-memorial-by-peter-eisenman-177928.

hill – was inaugurated at a ceremony on 3 April 2010, to celebrate the fiftieth anniversary of an Independent Senegal and to be a symbol of a modern and independent Africa.[14]

In almost every culture, there is the belief that the dead, while being the community's departed loved ones, should never be forgotten. Rather, they must in some way – no matter how mundane – be remembered and honoured, which is sometimes done out of respect or from a fear of ghostly retribution. In some cultures and religious traditions, there are holidays set aside specifically to commemorate the dead. In the Roman Catholic Church, for instance, All Saints' Day and All Souls' Day are two ceremonies meant to honour unknown saints and martyrs, and to commemorate the saints believed to be in purgatory. In Japan, the Buddhist faithful honour and commemorate dead ancestors during the Bon Festival. Similarly, the Koreans' Chuseok festival is celebrated to give thanks to their ancestors for an abundant harvest. In North Korea, Chuseok is climaxed with a visit to the ancestral graveyard, especially that of their former leader Kim Jong-il. Chuseok resonates with Gai Jatra, a memorial festival in Nepal in which a light-hearted celebration of death is held. In China, Qingming Festival, also known as Tomb-Sweeping Day, is a festival meant to pay homage to people who died during significant events in China's history. In Hindu religious tradition, Pitru Paksha, or fortnight of the ancestors, is celebrated to remember and to pay homage to their ancestors. El Día de Muertos, the Day of the Dead is not only a Mexican festival in which the dead are celebrated, this festival also finds its counterpart in the Philippines and in the United

---

14. Historically, the unveiling of monument De La Renaissance Africaine by the Senegalese President Aboulaye Wade was to mark fifty years of independent Senegal. During this ceremony, the President remarked that he "hopes the public monument will attract tourists to the West African country," and defended the public monument in writing, stating "[t]his African who emerges from the volcano, facing the West . . . symbolizes that Africa which freed itself from several centuries of imprisonment in the abyssal depths of ignorance, intolerance and racism, to retrieve its place on this land, which belongs to all races, in light, air and freedom." For detail examination of the historical background and significance of Monument De LaRenaissance Africaine, see Mark John, "Senegal Unveils 'African Renaissance' Statue," *Reuters*, 4 April 2010; Ofeibea Quist-Arcton, "For Many in Senegal, Statue Is a Monumental Failure," NPR (1/5/2010) quoted in "The African Renaissance Monument in Dakar, Senegal," Black History Heroes, http://www.blackhistoryheroes.com/search?q=renaissance+monument.

Introduction   5

States. Among the Malagasy of Madagascar, Famadihana is celebrated to commemorate the memory of the dead.[15]

In Africa, one of the richest cultural heritages bequeathed to our forefathers through which the departed ancestors are remembered and celebrated by their living kin is the ancestral cult. The ancestors are believed to be the "source of life."[16] More than anyone else, they are believed to be largely responsible for the welfare of the society and of every one of its achievements. The crowning glory of ancestral achievement in society is peaked in the religious festival of memorials through which the memories of the departed are immortalized in sacrifices offered and libation poured to appease the wrath of the ancestors and also secure their protection and blessings.

With the advent of Christianity to Africa, and the teaching that Jesus Christ is the source of life and means of protection and blessing analogous to the traditional African belief about the role of the ancestors, some African theologians who see the need to preserve Africa's pre-Christian religious heritage have interpreted Jesus Christ in light of the traditional concept of ancestors. For example, Charles Nyamiti persuasively argues "indeed, in Christ, the African will find a true and faithful—but immeasurably more perfect—image of His brother ancestors."[17] Interpreting and appropriating the person, work, and significance of Jesus Christ in light of the ancestral cult was in some ways an attempt by African Christian scholars to Christianize some African religious ideas and beliefs. While some African theologians assert that a valid way in which Jesus Christ can adequately be presented and apprehended on the continent is through the exploration of the ancestor model, this study differs from such a christological configuration since such appropriation of christological titles and methodology (e.g. gap and

---

15. Memorial services and festivals meant to remember the dead are not restricted to certain cultures particularly in Africa but are practices wherever man is found in time and space. For more on festivals, see Sumitra, "Famadihana – Dancing with the Dead in Madagascar," OddityCentral, posted on 4 April 2012, accessed 1 August 2015, http://www.odditycentral.com/pics/famadihana-dancing-with-the-dead-in-madagascar.html; Carissa MacDonald, "10 Festivals that Honor the Dead," Listverse, posted on 19 January 2013, accessed 1 August 2015, https://listverse.com/2013/01/19/10-festivals-that-honor-the-dead/.

16. Charles Nyamiti, "African Christologies Today," in *Faces of Jesus in Africa*, ed. Robert J. Schreiter (Maryknoll: Orbis Books, 2005), 5.

17. Charles Nyamiti, *Christ as our Ancestor: Christology from an African Perspective* (Gweru, Zimbabwe: Mambo Press, 1984), 69.

fulfillment theory) stems from African Traditional Religion as opposed to meaningful engagement with biblical sources and Christian theology.[18]

In this study, I will validate, or invalidate as the case might be, the argument of the gap and fulfillment theory proponents who use the Roman Catholic inculturation methodology to formulate theology that does not truly engage the Bible and Africans but engages African ideology of traditional theology to formulate Christian theology, as Ntetem, Bujo, and Nyamiti have demonstrated. Furthermore, research has shown within the Roman Catholic circle that the inculturation model employed by the proponents of ancestor Christology to formulate theology has not truly provided a meeting point between Christianity and African traditions.

In his PhD dissertation entitled, "The Theological Analysis of *Ikpu-Ala* as a Social Justice Value in Igbo Catholic Church (Nigeria)," Okey Jude Uche robustly argues, "There is strong evidence that the Igbo Catholic Church, in matters of inculturation, has been paying lip service to inculturation efforts. In many areas of doctrinal importance, such as burial ceremonies, marriage, *ozo* title taking, *ikpu-ala/aru*, and a lot of others, the Church has not made any serious efforts but has ended up creating 'dual observance.'"[19]

For example, Uche has maintained that after over one hundred years of Catholicism in Igbo land, most Igbo Catholics still perform the second burial of their fathers and grandfathers. According to him, evidence also exists that most of those who perform this ritual derive more satisfaction from the celebration of the second burial. In matters concerning morality, especially with regard to abominable acts such as murder, incest, disputes, and settlements, Uche notes that his fieldwork shows that many respondents were bold enough to share that despite the confessions and advance absolutions, most Igbo Christians find the traditional *Ikpu-ala/aru* and *igbu oriko* as popular with both Christians and traditionalists as ever.[20]

---

18. Part II: *Challenge and Response in the 1980s and '90s*; taken from Ian Ritchie, "African Theology and Social Change: An Anthropological Approach," (Phd diss), digitool.library.mcgill.ca/thesisfile41148.pdf, 11.

19. Okey Jude Uche, "The Theological Analysis of Ikpu-Ala as a Social Justice Value in Igbo Catholic Church (Nigeria)," (PhD diss., South African Theological Seminary, June, 2016), 285.

20. Uche, "Theological Analysis of Ikpu-Ala," 285.

Having established the fact that the inculturation methodology has failed to provide for meaningful engagement between Christian theology and African primal traditions, Uche keenly notes, "Therefore, there is need to try another method or model rather than inculturation."[21] For him, "It is clear that inculturation has not been working because the discussions have been one-sided and the Igbo traditional religious rituals have not been treated with respect and accorded the dignity they deserve. The inculturation process in the Igbo Church has rather been a means of confrontation, condemnation, and intimidation."[22]

Against the backdrop of inculturation methodology's failure to bridge the lacuna between Christian theology and African primal traditions, this study proposes an African Linguistic Affinity christological methodology that seeks to make sense of the Trinitarian and incarnational Christologies of the Roman North African theologians Tertullian and Athanasius, who in the third and fourth centuries engaged with the Bible to formulate normative Christian theology that had set the pace for the formulation of standard Christian Christology the world over through their pioneering works against heretics. This researcher is also convinced, as are other contemporary African scholars today (see ch. 7), that Africans have a far better way of presenting and, at the same time, appropriating the mystery of the incarnation of the Son of God. The notion of incarnation as developed in Jewish literature reveals that Jesus, the Word of God in the Old Testament, became the Son of God in the New Testament, which is known theologically as the Word becoming flesh in the man Jesus of Nazareth (Isa 7:14; John 1:14). The process by which God became human is through incarnation, and incarnation is the work of the Spirit of God (in the OT) and the Holy Spirit (in the NT).

The incarnation is the leitmotif of Christology, with Christology being understood as discourse about Jesus Christ who took human flesh to fulfil God's promise about the coming Messiah for human redemption. With the right notion of incarnation and Christology, Jesus in Africa could be understood in a more explicit theological and biblical manner than in the local pre-Christian category of an ancestor. Noone who thinks straight will

---

21. Uche, 286.
22. Uche, 286.

dispute the obvious fact that the Bible remains the key source from which Christian theology can be derived and formulated in any context. Since, therefore, the communities of African theologians cannot name Christ personally without going to the Bible or Catechism, they do just the opposite and attribute to Christ the traditional title of an ancestor that they would like to see him given in the communities.[23]

To the researcher, this approach, of course, casts a dark shadow on the true and real biblical identity and theological meaning of Jesus Christ, because Africans at the grassroots perfectly know Jesus Christ as the long-awaited Messiah promised to the Jewish ancestors. For this reason, African Christians prefer to call him by a name which conveys a sense of the fulfilled prophecies and promises found in the Old Testament which also locates their redemption in the one promised to the Jews. The name African Christians have for Jesus Christ at the grassroots is derived from the Bible and that name is *Jesu* or *Yesu*. Timothy C. Tennent buttresses this position and points out that "Many African Christians prefer to utilize biblical images that are explicitly used of Christ in the Scripture."[24]

This study therefore proposes a theological approach to the study of Jesus Christ in Africa in terms of his ontological and redemptive work, similar to Tertullian's and Athanasius's ontological Christologies since within the Godhead, these scholars were able to show distinction in persons. Thus, God the Father is not the same as God the Son, and God the Holy Spirit is different from God the Father. In this light, the work calls for the study of Jesus Christ in Africa in light of God's covenant of redemption to Adam in Genesis 3:14–19 alongside God's covenant of promise made to Abraham in Genesis 12:2–3.

The promises were fulfilled in the birth of Jesus (Matthew 1:21–23). The etymology of this name Jesus derives from God's prophecies, promises, and covenants in the Old Testament (Gen 3:15; Isa 7:14; 9:7; Mic 5:2), as fulfilled in the New Testament (Matt 1:21) is the Hebrew name Yeshua.

---

23. Part II: *Challenge and Response in the 1980s and '90s*; taken from Ritchie, "African Theology," 11.

24. Timothy C. Tennent, *Theology in the Context of World Christianity: How the Global Church Is Influencing the Way We Think About and Discuss Theology* (Grand Rapids, MI: Zondervan, 2007), 131.

The Old Testament Yeshua has been transliterated into the New Testament Greek as Ἰησοῦς. Furthermore, Yeshua is also transliterated into Arabic as *Issah*. The transliteration of the Hebrew Yeshua into the two languages became the norm by which African Christians followed and also did their own transliteration of the Hebrew, Greek and Arab name for Jesus, so that not only the theological meaning of Jesus the Christ is retained but so it would also has a connection and continuity with the Abrahamic covenant. Hence Yeshua or Ἰησοῦς is universally transliterated into most African languages as *Yesu* or *Jesu*.

For the above reason, Ἰησοῦς in most African tribes is called *Jesu* or *Yesu*. Therefore, a befitting methodology and nomenclature with which to formulate Christology in Africa is an African Linguistic Affinity christological methodology that unanimously presents Jesus Christ as *Jesu/Yesu* in Africa, hence *Jesu/Yesu* Christology.[25] I used African Linguistic Affinity christological methodology to mean, Christology formulated in Africa that explores a universally accepted name for Jesus in the continent that seeks to be faithful to the Bible and also aligns with Yahweh's promises and covenants made to

---

25. The notion of African Linguistic Affinity methodology which identifies Jesus Christ as *Yesu/Jesu* was born while interacting with Victor I. Ezigbo's work. Ezigbo developed the idea of "Revealer Christology Model" in his, *Re-Imagining African Christologies: Conversing with the Interpretations and Appropriations of Jesus in Contemporary African Christianity* (Eugene, OR: Pickwick, 2010), 145. His work inspired me to seek a suitable christological model for Africa in my work. This idea became full blown when reading through the works of Yusufu Turaki and O. Palmer Robertson. In his *The Unique Christ for Salvation: The Challenge of the Non-Christian Religions and Cultures* (Nairobi: International Bible Society, 2001), 142, Turaki maintains that "Christ came as a divine fulfillment of both the law and the Prophets," while Robertson in his *The Christ of the Covenants* (Phillipsburg, NJ: P & R, 1980), 127 and 157, talk about "Abraham: The Covenant of Promise" and "The New Testament Fulfillment of the Old Testament Symbol." The ideas of these scholars have helped not only to shape my thought but also opened my horizon to chart a new course in my research work. Equipped with their ideas, I gave two separate essays to thirty-three masters of theology students in the 2016 summer school at the Jos ECWA Theological Seminary (JETS) and a two-page essay to fifteen international students during the first semester of 2016 between August and December, on the appropriate African name for Jesus in their culture or ethnic groups. The findings were breathing taking since most ethnic groups call Jesus "*Yesu*" or "*Jesu Kristi*" which to my mind is not only more biblically inclined compared to Jesus as ancestor but it does convey the sense of his ontological being and his redemptive purpose as Jesus the Christ confessed by the apostle Peter in the New Testament. It is the argument of this work that African Linguistic Affinity methodology which identifies Christ as "*Yesu/Jesu*" matches naturally with the literal Graeco-Roman name and perception of Jesus the Christ in the first five centuries of the Christian church.

the Jewish patriarchs Abraham, Isaac, Jacob, and Moses in the Old Testament that have been fulfilled in the New Testament.

African Linguistic Affinity Christology is, in the opinion of this researcher, a better method of presenting a genuine view of Jesus Christ to the traditional ancestor religious cult which characterized African theological discourse, since it vividly brings out the theological meaning of Jesus the Christ and also maintains affinity and continuity with Old Testament prophecies, covenants and fulfilment (see chs. 6 and 7 for details). In a three page essay (see ch. 7) I gave to thirty-three Masters of theology students during the 2016 summer school (between May and July, at the Jos ECWA Theological Seminary [JETS]), and another two page essay given to fifteen international students, comprising of both Masters and undergraduate students at JETS, in the first semester of 2016 (between August and December), on what name Jesus is called among their people group, the first survey showed that 99.8 percent of African tribes prefer to identify Christ with the transliterated name *Jesu/Yesu* and in the second survey 99.6 percent of African languages call Jesus *Yesu/Jesu*.[26]

Among the Swahili people of East Africa for instance, Jesus is perceived as *Jesu*. This same nomenclature resonates with the name of Jesus among the Chawai people of north-central Nigeria, in West Africa, whose name for Jesus is also *Jesu*. Among the Akan of Ghana, Jesus is called *Yesu*, the Yoruba of Nigeria address Jesus as *Jesu*, the Tshwane of South Africa call Jesus *Jesu* and among the Igbo of Enugu-Nigeria he is *Jisos Kristi*.[27] From the responses

---

26. As each student submitted a 3–5 page essay on the subject they have not been included as appendicies due to space. Throughout the text "essay" and "survey" are used interchangeably to refer to their responses.

27. In a survey work done among the Akan AIC of Ghana that sought to find out the ideal vernacular name for Jesus in 2011, Clifton Clarke distributed a questionnaire which respondents gave the answers as follows: Saviour – 1867 (74.6 percent), Messiah – 1551 (62 percent), Lord – 1444 (57.7 percent), Healer – 1382 (55.2 percent), God – 724 (28.9 percent), Conqueror – 334 (13.3 percent), Chief – 76 (3 percent), Brother – 61 (2.4 percent) and Ancestor – 60 (2.4 percent). From the two essays I gave the two separate classes in 2016 and the investigation of Clarke, the responses gathered on the appropriate African name for Jesus among the various ethnic groups in Africa, it is evident that most African ethnic groups are more inclined with biblical titles for Jesus Christ than the traditional religious titles given to him by the ivory tower ancestor theologians and biblical scholars. It is on this ground that this researcher proposes and undertakes an African Linguistic Affinity methodology that argues that Africans are more comfortable with calling Jesus either "*Yesu*" or "*Jesu*." These findings make for *Yesu/Jesu* Christology far acceptable than ancestral Christology. For more on

gathered from the two surveys, this study discovered that African Christians are far more comfortable calling Jesus Christ by his transliterated biblical name *Yesu* or *Jesu*. This discovery, therefore, further strengthens all the more the concern of this work to propose and undertake an African Linguistic Affinity Christology methodology which identifies Jesus as *Jesu/Yesu*.

In what Clifton Clarke calls, "the orality that characterises the Akan AIC practice of prayer,"[28] an Akan Christian prays; "Lord, I have come to hear what you have to say to me. I have been waiting and praying for a long time . . . I have come today, and my heart is very heavy. *Yesu Kristo*, you rose from the dead to give us life. Your blood gives us power and heals us . . ."[29]

From the other oral prayer in which the petitioner invokes the name *Yesu Kristo*, about Jesus he admits, "you rose from the dead . . . your blood gives us power and heals us." The above point means that when African Christians say *Yesu* or *Jesu* they mean Jesus the Christ, beyond just a literal interpretation of that biblical name but its theological import. By calling Jesus Christ *Yesu* or *Jesu*, African Christians have in view his ontological being, which was revealed in the incarnation of our redemption. In light of the above, the study argues that African Linguistic Affinity Christology methodology, which names Jesus *Yesu* or *Jesu*, captures the entire essence of Christ – his otherness as in his transcendent and immanent nature. As the concept further defines Christ's person, deity, and his soteriological work it is no doubt an improved model for presenting Christ in the African context than the ancestor model, which only serves to portray Jesus's functional role as ancestor in Africa in relation to the African engagement with the spirit world without, however, any connection to the theological meaning of Jesus or link with Yahweh's promises and covenants with the Jewish patriarchs.

No doubt, presenting Christ as an ancestor in Africa is not without its cultural merits, since in Africa name is synonymous with life and life in Africa is living, eternal, and salvation. The preceding explains why Africans believe that when your enemies have your name, they have your life and

---

Jesus as "*Yesu*" or "*Jesu*," see Deji Ayegboyin, "Li Oruko Jesu: Aladura Grass-roots Christology," *Journal of African Christian Thought* 8, no.1 (June 2005): 11–19; Clifton R. Clarke, *African Christology: Jesus in Post-Missionary African Christianity* (Eugene, OR: Pickwick, 2011).

28. Clifton R. Clarke, "Towards a Post-Missionary Oral Christology among African Indigenous Churches in Ghana," *Journal of African Christian Thought* 8, no.1 (June 2005): 5.

29. Clarke, "Towards a post-Missionary," 5.

can take it. For this reason, Africans are taught not to answer a call from a strange voice they do not know since that is capable of receiving life.

I have established the fact that ancestor Christology has its cultural merits in Africa; we must, however, ask with Gerald O' Collins, "What sources provide the appropriate material for our systematic account of Jesus Christ's identity and function? Where can we learn about Jesus Christ and find what Christians have believed about him and done because of their faith in him?"[30]

These are valid questions that undergird the overriding interest of this research endeavour. As I am convinced, "there are some privileged sources like the New Testament and the christological confessions from the early centuries of the Church's history,"[31] which should be our fundamental sources for articulating a valid model for the understanding of the person, work, and significance of Jesus Christ that is both African and universal.

We must not, in our passionate attempt to do so, fall prey to the same criticism we have all along hurled against the West of theological hegemony. The tendency is the likelihood for the West to construe African christological discourse as recolonizing Christian theology. To offer a compelling picture of Jesus Christ to Africans in tandem with universal Christian tradition, and upon which Tertullian and Athanasius built their Christologies; we must fall back to the question of Jesus Christ to his disciples. Doing this is critical because, even though christological models were formulated employing Western categories, the early church in all its ecumenical councils had, however, unanimously accepted such groups as the *sine qua non* and canon for the formulation of universal standard christological models and the norm of Christian belief and practice.

The question of who Jesus Christ is to an African Christian today is urgent, especially in the midst of global terrorist threats like Isis and Al-Qaeda, and Boko Haram in Africa. Along with that, there is also the influence of cultural revivalism, which didn't exist five decades ago when Gabriel C. Setiloane first asked the question that is accepted as the sprout of the seed of African christological formulation, in which he roused African theologians' and biblical scholars' consciousness to the christological question. At that

---

30. Gerald O' Collins, *Interpreting Jesus* (London: Mowbray, 1992), 5.
31. Collins, *Interpreting*, 5.

time, as it is quite known, Christianity on the continent was generally at its infant stage.[32]

With Christianity now overshadowing virtually every other religious belief on the continent, the question of Jesus Christ's identity becomes all the more pressing. For example, Timothy Tennent argued that "at the turn of the twentieth century the Christian Church was predominantly white and Western. By 1900, there were over 380 million Christians in Europe and less than 10 million on the entire continent of Africa."[33] Today, Timothy Tennnent asserts, there are over 367 million Christians in Africa, comprising of one-fifth of the whole of the Christian church.[34] Amazingly, he argues that throughout the twentieth century, an average net gain of 16,500 people were coming to Christ every day in Africa.[35] Craig Ott and Harold A. Netland buttressed Timothy Tennent's argument and wrote,

> The growth of Christianity in Africa has been especially dramatic . . . with Africa firmly under colonial rule, there were 8.7 million Christians, about 9 percent of the total population of 107.86 million (2003, 14-15). "In 1962 when Africa had largely slipped out of colonial control, there were about 60 million Christians" . . . in 1970 there were 120 million Christians [in Africa] estimated; in 1998 the figure jumped to just under 330 million; and in 2000 to 350 million.[36]

This phenomenal growth in the number of Christians on the African continent calls for not only a celebration but also a new way of doing theology that while remaining faithful to the Bible should as well be able to address

---

32. In a contribution in 1979 entitled, "Where are we in African Theology?" Gabriel C. Setiloane lamented the dearth of African christological discourse and remarked, "the next task of African theology is seriously to grapple with the question of Christology – who is Jesus . . . what does Messiahship or Christos become in the African context?" This provocative call from Setiloane gave impetus to the current trend for African christological formulation with ancestor Christology standing taller. For more on Setiloane's lament, see Gabriel C. Setiloane, "Where Are We in African Theology?" in *African Theology en Route*, ed. Kofi Appiah-Kubi and Sergio Terres (Maryknoll, NY: Orbis Books, 1979), 64.

33. Tennent, *Theology in the Context*, 8.

34. Tennent, 8.

35. Tennent, 8.

36. Craig Ott and Harold A. Netland, eds., *Globalizing theology: Belief and Practice in an era of World Christianity* (Grand Rapids, MI: Baker Books, 2006), 24.

our problems as Africans. The reasoning explains why the question of Jesus Christ's identity is resurrected and many leading African theologians of our day voice the opinion that the classical answers articulated by Tertullian and Athanasius, against heretics during the ecumenical councils in the patristic period, are inadequate and that new solutions must be sought.[37]

Jesus Christ asked his disciples a similar question. Even though shades of solutions were given, nevertheless, the apostle Peter gave a defining response, "You are the Messiah." (Mark 8:29).

From the other disciples and Peter's answer to Jesus's question, it is clear that from the beginning of Christianity Jesus of Nazareth was understood in quite a broad spectrum of faces. Veli-Matti Kärkkäinen alluded to this when he maintained that "the New Testament itself contains several complementary interpretations of Jesus Christ."[38] Jerome H. Neyrey, also held that in the New Testament there is diversity in the way Jesus is portrayed.[39] This submission is valid for nowhere else, other than the Christian Bible, do we have comprehensive and reliable information about Jesus Christ. Jesus's self-consciousness and the disciples' perception of him, together with what John and Paul believed and taught, are fundamental to a real knowledge of the person and deity of Jesus Christ in the life and thought of the early church.

The early church believed that Jesus Christ is the image of the invisible God, who made himself known through the Holy Scriptures, and they saw themselves as heralds of that mystery, which for decades had been concealed. They first had to interpret the content of that mystery and in turn translate it "through the apostolic traditions, and finally received its fixed record in the written Scripture."[40] Ever since then, the church has come to believe and teach that Jesus Christ is the God-Man; as such an object of worship:

> Although the worship of the community proclaimed that Jesus Christ was the God-Man and thus the subject of worship and adoration, the specifics of what this entailed was not quite set

---

37. Klass Runia, *The Present-day Christological Debate* (Leicester: Inter-Varisty Press, 1984), 9.

38. Veli-Matti KärKKäinen, *Christology: A Global Introduction* (Grand Rapids, MI: Baker Academic, 2003), 10.

39. Jerome H. Neyrey, *Christ Is community: The Christologies of the New Testament* (Collegeville, MN: Liturgical Press, 1990), 7.

40. Collins, *Interpreting*, 5.

forth in any detail leading the Church into the Christological controversies of the fourth and fifth centuries which caused havoc and dissension for a very long time. The question was simply what did it mean that Jesus was a man, but he was also God. This is an antinomy which countless leaders of the early Church wrestled with and finally concluded in a great part by determining what this did not mean.[41]

This narrowing down to a definition, however, required that many people had to put forth ideas that were rejected as heresy by the leaders of the church. Thus, Arius's view that the Father alone is underived while the Father begets the Son was countered by Athanasius who maintained that the Son is not any less God, the way the Father is God. It is on the basis of this narrowing down that Arius's error was rejected by the fathers of the church,[42] and the real divinity and real humanity of Christ was established as Catholic doctrine.[43] As a result, the council declared that there is; "One Lord, Jesus Christ . . . very God of very God, begotten not made, consubstantial (*homoousios*) with the Father, by whom all things were made."[44]

This definitive declaration which is understood as the establishment of the biblical canon, "Christian theology, in the form of the classical creeds of Nicea [*sic*] in the fourth century and Chalcedon in the fifth century, attempted to formulate a definitive understanding of Christ in light of the existing cultural milieu."[45]

---

41. Patrick Oden, "The Christologies of Apollinaris of Laoicea and Theodore of Mopsuestia," Dual Ravens, accessed 17 June 2014, http://www.dualravens.com/fullerlife/christologies.htm.

42. Obviously, during the Nicene christological debate in AD 325, the metaphysics of the Son of God undergirded Athanasius's Christology. Hence he argued that if the divinity of the Son of God is strictly immutable as Arius contends, then, the problem would be, how could such an immutable being become united with human existence in any real ontological way? In this way Athanasius saw an imminent problem that would make impossible the salvation of man. Since only God can save, if the Son is not truly God the same way God the father is, then, there is no way the Son being man like unto us could save fellow human beings. For detail treatment of this christological debate, see Francis M. Young, *From Nicaea to Chalcedon: A Guide to the Literature and Its Background* (Philadelphia: Fortress, 1983), 58–64.

43. Henry Bettenson, ed., *Documents of the Christian Church*, 2nd ed. (New York: Oxford University Press, 1967), 44.

44. Alan Richardson, *Creeds in the Making: A Short Introduction to the History of Christian Doctrine* (London: SCM, 1961), 52.

45. Kärkkäinen, *Christology*, 10.

As we examine the theological terrain of subsequent decades, the belief that Jesus Christ is the God-Man became a norm. Hence, during the Medieval and Reformation periods, the classical questions of Jesus Christ's humanity and divinity were again debated and consolidated. The Reformers, in particular, in their attempt to defend the humanity, deity, and work of Christ emphasized the concept of *Communicato Idiomatum* and held that there is no splitting of persons in Christ. For them, Christ is the God-Man; God's Son or *Logos* became a person in the man Jesus of Nazareth.

The classical christological proclamation and formulation from the early church to the patristic period are now being challenged in twentieth-century Africa, through the African ancestor Christologies of Abbé Marc Ntetem, Bénézet Bujo and Charles Nyamiti, who wish to immortalize the memories of the ancestors since we admitted that in Africa name is life and eternal. Ntetem, for instance, maintained that "acceptance of the Christian faith does not involve a complete break with African tradition, for it has its source in God, and thus finds its fulfilment in Christianity."[46] Bujo raised a similar, but more subtle, question thus, "could not the recognition of the place which the ancestors and elders occupy in the life of Africans stimulate theologians to construct something new?"[47] Nyamiti climaxes the issue by asking, "Is there an ancestral relationship in God?"[48] These questions all led to one conclusion; that Jesus Christ is an ancestor *par excellence*, or brother and greatest ancestor or proto-ancestor respectively. Such ancestor Christology of gap and fulfilment methodology is the Afrocentric fabricated version of African worldview and cultural ideology. The term Afrocentric is derived from "Afrocentrism," which dates back to 1961/1962 following social changes in the United States and Africa, due both to the end of slavery and the decline of colonialism that resulted in independence for most African countries.[49] With independence,

---

46. Abbé Marc Ntetem, "Initiation, Traditional and Christian," in *A Reader in African Christian Theology*, ed. John Parrat (London: SPCK, 2001), 99.

47. Bénézet Bujo, *African Theology in Its Social Context* (Kenya: Paulines Publications Africa, 2003), 72.

48. Charles Nyamiti, *Studies in African Christian Theology*, vol. 1, *Jesus Christ the Ancestor of Humankind: Methodological and Trinitarian Foundations* (Nairobi: CUEA, 2005), 70.

49. Thomson Gale, "Afrocentrism," Encylopedia of African-American Culture and History, Encyclopedia.com, https://www.encyclopedia.com/history/biographies/historians-canadian-biographies/afrocentrism.

Africans began to think independently, a new wave of doing things had dawned. Intellectually, Africans began to articulate independent selfhood and ways of educating themselves. Politically, Africans formulated their political systems; culturally, they referred to ancient times before colonialism.[50] To that end, the so-called black race convened in Lagos, Nigeria to celebrate its cultural emancipation tagged, "FESTAC" in 1977.[51]

The twentieth century, which also marked the advent of modern and postmodern periods, witnessed a post-missionary Christianity with their attendant reaction against Western theological hegemony. The inevitable consequence of modern and postmodern negative responses to Western theological articulation was the birth of Afrocentrism in Africa. The postmodern African theologians work against the foundation already laid in the early church by Tertullian and Athanasius formulated within the contextual christological paradigms in the light of their pre-Christian cultural categories under the pretext that "Christianity is an incarnational religion,"[52] thus, Christology by the same token must be contextualized or enculturated. Consequently, "Christian theology must, therefore, be informed by the contextual milieu and the culture of its target audience in such a way that the Word will become flesh among the people."[53] While the method in which one's culture becomes the source for the formulation of Christian

---

50. Gale, "Afrocentrism."

51. When African nations got their independence, it was believed that a new day has dawn. This dawn brought about the emerging trends in Africa's political life, social life, economic life, and a new theological way of articulating our Africanness. Consequently, Africans expressed their independent selfhood in quite a number of important fronts: due to apartheid, liberation hermeneutics was born in South Africa, feminist or womanist theology and cultural hermeneutics emerged in the entire continent giving rise to the current trends in Afrocentric biblical hermeneutics in which some African theologians interpret Scripture employing African spectacles. For detail analysis of Afrocentricism, refer to David T. Adamo, *Africa and the Africans in the Old Testament* (Benin City, Nigeria: Justice Jeco Press & Publishers, 2005) and *Reading and Interpreting the Bible in African Indigenous Churches* (Benin City, Nigeria: Justice Jeco Press & Publishers, 2005).

52. This view seems to be the generally accepted opinion of most African theologians' and biblical scholars' hermeneutics since they hold that incarnation is the baptism and healthy wedding between invading beliefs with the existing host's cultural belief systems of a given context. For detail examination of Afrocentric biblical hermeneutic scholars' arguments, see Osadolor Imasogie, *Guidelines for Christian theology in Africa* (Achimota: African Christian Press, 1993), 14.

53. Osadolor Imasogie, *Guidelines for Christian Theology in Africa* (Achimota: African Christian Press, 1993), 14.

theology "is an eminently true and valid way of doing theology in a particular context,"[54] Stephen B. Bevans, however, fears that such a methodology carries with it "the danger of making theology to fall into a kind of a cultural romanticism and popular religiosity which do not represent the current trends of the host culture."[55]

The approach of making the host culture as the source for the formulation of Christian theology marked a drastic shift from the christological proclamation and elaboration of Tertullian and Athanasius to the present quest for reformulation and re-interpretation employing social philosophies and worldviews. Hence, christological discourse became fundamentally reactionary, contextual and inculturation christological formulations that paint the picture of Christ from the sociocultural and sociopolitical point of view. New Christologies that emerged during this time saw Christ as a cultural, social, and political figure. This era marked the quest for global contextual Christologies like Christ the liberator in Latin America and Africa, and Christ the ancestor in Africa.

The methodology in which Jesus Christ is presented as a social and political liberator and cultural ancestor, advocated by the proponents of African ancestor Christology, is grounded in the gap and fulfilment presupposition. For this reason, this work argues that the gap and fulfilment presupposition is problematic since it arose mainly from African traditional religious categories and concepts as a theological meeting point for Christianity and indigenous religions, as against the Orthodox christological configuration of Tertullian and Athanasius in response to heretics in the patristic era.[56]

The ancestor Christology approach is, in the estimation of this writer, not only a thorn in the flesh of the defenders of orthodox Christology, but is also revealing of the fact that the Christ who was presented to us in the Bible by the Western missionaries has not been well understood, let alone meet our dire spiritual needs. Nürnberger is well articulated in suggesting that the Christ Africans came to know through the message of the missionaries, subsequent indigenous leaders, even their reading of the Bible, does not

---

54. Stephen B. Bevans, *Models of Contextual Theology* (Maryknoll, NY: Orbis Books, 2011), 25.

55. Bevans, *Models of Contextual Theology*, 25–26.

56. Victor Ifeanyi Ezigbo, *Re-Imagining African Christologies*, 26.

seem to have covered their most pressing spiritual needs.[57] For this reason, he robustly argued that where Christ is irrelevant, a severe spiritual vacuum can be expected to open up in the consciousness of Christians, which is quite naturally filled with authority, power, and presence of the ancestors, who have always been around.[58] For me, the ancestor Christology method propounded by some African theologians compromises the Christ presented to us in the Bible by missionaries. Byang H. Kato, whose telescopic eyes saw this, had earlier entertained fear on this methodology as he warned African theologians and biblical scholars in the 1970s to beware of the tendency of Africanizing Christ and Christianity under the cloak of contextualization; he thus described such an approach as universalism.[59]

The hermeneutical approach which makes Jesus Christ to look like one among other African ancestors, is questionable and raises a lot of doubts, since it arose mainly from an advocacy spirit, in which the marginalized, the oppressed, and the colonized of the so-called third world nations seek to have, through cultural identity, a voice in the global theological enterprise. No doubt, the voices of Abbé Marc Ntetem, Bénézet Bujo and Charles Nyamiti (see ch. 2) are speaking louder. For them, the christological answer articulated by the apostle Peter and the entire New Testament teaching on Christ, alongside the conciliar definitive christological formulations by the church fathers and the early African apologists (Tertullian and Athanasius), is at best anachronistic and incompatible with Africa's pre-Christian religious conceptions. With this understanding, African theologians began to articulate theology in the light of African thought using local concepts to make Christianity revant to Africans.

The above case is to be expected because Christian confessions and doctrines are shrouded in metanarrative with a universal message about Jesus Christ for all cultures and people groups. Consequently, African theologians argue that the search for Jesus Christ in contemporary African theological discourse should some what be addressed contextually.

---

57. Nürnberger, *Living Dead*, 40.

58. Nürnberger, 40.

59. Byang H. Kato, *Biblical Christianity in Africa: A Collection of Papers and Addresses* (Achimota, Ghana: African Christian Press, 1985), 15

In a penetrating analysis of the images of Christ through the centuries in *Images of Jesus: How Jesus is perceived and portrayed in Non-European Cultures*, Anton Wessels examined the religious and cultural projections of Christ in Judaism, Islam, Spanish, Suriname, Indian, Asian, Latin America and Africa, and concludes with a breathtaking question that borders on the relation of Jesus to the various cultures of the world.[60]

The proliferation of intercultural Christology literature in Africa – mainly from Catholic and Protestant circles that portray the image of Jesus Christ from a political and pre-Christian cultural heritage – is not without ecclesial backing, majorly from Vatican II and some sacerdotal pronouncements on the need to inculturate Christianity into different mindsets. Of course, one of the common statements of Pope John XXIII, and later the documents of the Vatican Council II, was "know the signs of the times," summarized by the term *aggiornamento* (see ch. 5). In this same spirit of knowing the sign of the times, earlier on in 1951, Pope Pius XII asserted, "Let not the Gospel on being introduced into any new land destroy or extinguish whatever its people possess, that is naturally good, just or beautiful."[61] Similarly, Pope Paul VI in his address to the African Bishops at the closing of the 1st Plenary Assembly of the Symposium of Episcopal Conferences of Africa and Madagascar (SECAM) in Kampala, Uganda on 31 July 1969 remarked,

> From this point of view, a certain pluralism is not only legitimate but desirable. An adaptation of the Christian life in the field of pastoral, ritual, didactic and spiritual activities is not only possible;the Church favours it . . . And in this sense, you may, and must have an African Christianity, indeed, you

---

60. In this work, Anton Wessels traveled great vistas to survey the various portraits of Jesus Christ among peoples group in non-European settings and his finding are really alarming. For detail review of his investigation, see Anton Wessels, *Images of Jesus: How Jesus Is Perceived and Portrayed in Non-European Cultures* (Grand Rapids, MI: Eerdmans, 1991); see also Volker Küster, *The Many Faces of Jesus Christ* (Maryknoll: Orbis Books, 2001); Robert Schreiter, ed., *Faces of Jesus in Africa* (Maryknoll: Orbis Books, 2005); Vinay Samuel and Chris Sugden, eds., *Sharing Jesus in the Two Thirds World* (Grand Rapids, MI: Eerdmans, 1983); and José Míguez Bonino, ed., *Faces of Jesus: Latin American Christologies* (Maryknoll, NY: Orbis Books, 1984).

61. Pope Pius XII, *Evangelii Praecones (1951)*, translated as *The Popes and Missions: Four Encyclical Letters* (London: Sword of the Spirit, 1990), 66–70. See also Teresa Okure and Paul van Thiel, eds., *32 Articles Evaluating Inculturation of Christianity in Africa* (Eldoret, Kenya: AMECEA Gaba Publications, 1990), 3.

possess human values and characteristics forms of culture which can rise to perfection, such as to find in Christianity, and for Christianity, a trulysuperior fullness, and prove to be capable of a richness and experience all of its own, and genuinely African.[62]

This famous speech, along with the spirit of nationalism, gave impetus to an inculturation approach to theology, in which African theologians began to deconstruct Western belief. In Africa, the dominant socio-religious, contextual and inculturation christological discourse in modern and postmodern periods is built around the idea that Jesus Christ is an ancestor. This study is an investigation and critical re-evaluation of the African ancestor christological formulation in light of historical and theological developments in the New Testament and the patristic age, as fashioned in the thoughts of Tertullian and Athanasius the African apologists of that period. The study presents a survey of the christological formulations in the New Testament to the patristic era as a prelude to the discussion on the African ancestor Christology.

The above point is not to conclude prematurely that this thesis is going the same direction of other works on the subject followed. Instead, the survey provides the platform upon which the research would unveil the significant presuppositions (see ch. 6) of the proponents of African ancestor Christology as a fertile ground for the apologetical arguments of Tertullian and Athanasius (see ch. 3) which this thesis seeks to present. The survey is therefore foundational for a thoroughly comparative re-evaluation of the African ancestor Christology vis-à-vis apostolic and traditional Christian Christology. In other words, this study attempts to get to the root of ancestor Christology through a review of the previous images of Jesus Christ in the life of the early church in the light of modern times. The intention here is not only to ascertain whether African ancestor christological formulation is in tandem with the apostolic and patristic Christology, but also to demonstrate that the African ancestor Christology is not congenial with the biblical Christ presented by the New Testament evangelists and early

---

62. J. M. Waliggo, A. Roest Crollius, T. Nkeramihigo, and J. Mutiso-Mbinda, *Inculturation: Its Meaning and Urgency* (Kampala, Uganda: St Paul Publications, 1986), 75–76; Okure and van Thiel, *32 Articles Evaluating*, 14.

church fathers as well as African apologists together with Africa's grassroots perception of Jesus Christ.

Statement of the Research Problem

The research problem explored in this study is that Abbé Marc Ntetem, Benézét Bujo and Charles Nyamiti in their quest for contextual and inculturation christological methodology have diminished the deity of Christ at the altar of ancestor Christology. By so doing, their Christologies have also failed the test of full divinity and full humanity expressed in apostle John's and apostle Paul's christological proclamation and the early church's creedal formulations. Consequently, initial research utilizes gap and fulfilment theory[63] to create christological paradigms from African traditional religious concepts that are not congenial with biblical Christology.[64] The leading thoughts and aspirations of Tertullian and Athanasius in the early church became the primary sources for articulating Christology as derived from Scripture, history and the apostles' testimony of Jesus Christ.

---

63. In his witty and apt display of academic prowess, Victor I. Ezigbo gives the background and elaborate exploration of gap and fulfillment presupposition. Accordingly, he notes that the gap and fulfillment presupposition is one of the oldest apologetic tools that some African theologians have employed to engage with the theological tension that emerges as they try to set out a theological meeting point for Christianity and the indigenous religions. Of course, the tension that arose as a result of the encounter between African primal tradition and Christian belief necessitated a dialogue. For this reason, Ezigbo has shown succinctly that the gap and fulfillment exponents argued that there are gaps in the indigenous religious understandings of God's revelatory activities that need to be filled if African people must make sense of God's purpose and salvific history, and also to appreciate the purpose and limits of their God-given cultures and traditions since as they believed, the indigenous religions contain only some fragments of divine truth, and as such, are incomplete and are in dire need for a supreme and definitive fulfiller. To that end, Jesus does not need to destroy all the core values and beliefs of the indigenous religions of Africa. For more on the arguments of the proponents of gap and fulfillment view, see Ezigbo, *Re-Imagining African Christologies*, 26–35.

64. By biblical Christology I mean the apostolic kerygmatic proclamation of Jesus Christ in the early church that laid the foundation for the appropriation of the person and work of Jesus Christ. It is upon the testimony or witness of the apostles that the apostolic fathers and apologists consolidated and formulated orthodox Christology that has become the norm for Christian belief and confession universally. To this end, biblical Christology means the apostles' and the early church's understanding and presentation of the Christ event. This Christology is derived from Scripture, history and the apostles' testimony of Jesus Christ.

Purpose and Contribution of the Study

The primary concern of this study is to examine the ancestor Christologies of Abbé Marc Ntetem, Bénézet Bujo and Charles Nyamiti that are grounded in the gap and fulfilment methodology. By using African primal traditions and worldview, Charles Nyamiti was more inclined to an adoptionist method in his christological formulation.[65] The foregoing view is vividly illustrated in his Trinitarian Christology in which he overtly undermined the divinity and equality of Jesus with God the Father by calling God the Father "Ancestor to Jesus Christ his Son,"[66] over against Tertullian's Trinitarian formulation in the third century, who argued that Jesus Christ the Son is one with God the Father, and Athanasius's portrayal of Christ as being of one substance with the Father in the fourth century. The theological implication of Nyamiti's assumption is that the Son is a creature while God the Father is his progenitor. For in traditional African belief, an ancestor is one who originates the family, clan and tribe. To call God, therefore, an ancestor to Jesus Christ would imply in our vocabulary and worldview that through consanguineous relationship God begot Christ or the Father of Christ who now becomes a descendant in that family lineage. This view is not any better than the position of Bediako Kwame whose approach is inclusive. It is with this mindset that he comfortably made a case for the universality of Jesus and argued that there is continuity between Christianity and Africa's pre-Christian beliefs.[67] While Kwame was somewhat reluctant to bring the God of Abraham, Isaac and Jacob to near the same class with African ancestors, Bujo saw nothing wrong in doing that. His dogmatic view is stated in explicit terms that the Christian God can also be worshipped via the

---

65. Adoptionism is one of the false teachings in the early church propounded by the dynamic Monarchian party. The basic point at issue with dynamic monarchians was the relationship of the Father to the Son. For them, the problem could be solved by thinking of the divinity of the Son as being merely derived. They therefore taught that impersonal divine power was active in the man Jesus. Therefore, Christ was adopted as the Son of God because of his obedient life. This view resonates with Nyamiti's assertion that God the Father became the ancestor of Jesus in the Trinitarian relationship. For detail exploration of this heresy, see Bernard Lohse, *A Short History of Christian Doctrine* (Philadelphia: Fortress, 1980), 42.

66. Nyamiti, *Studies in African Christian Theology*, vol. 1, 74.

67. Keith Ferdinando, "Christian Identity in the African Context: Reflections on Kwame Bediako's Theology and Identity," *Journal of the Evangelical Theological Society* 50, no. 1 (March 2007): 124.

ancestor. He says, "When Africans honour the ancestors they are at least implicitly, also honouring God."⁶⁸ What Bujo had failed to tell us is whether Africans are at liberty to substitute one for the other since, as his contention goes, the two seem to play complementary roles. He has also failed to educate us on whether "honouring" and "worship" are bedfellows that can be employed interchangeably in offering a solution to the Christian God and the African ancestors. Nyamiti and Bujo are blunt in their approach in associating God with African ancestors, it is, however, Abbé Marc Ntetem who, until his stance is viewed critically, the tendency to quickly give it a pass on the ground of orthodoxy is very high. Thus for him, Jesus Christ is ancestor par excellence. What his attempt as Tersur Aben posits is a clever way to "strip African Christianity of all foreign categories and to replace them with African religious categories."⁶⁹

While the proponents of ancestor Christology find it convenient to configure a Christology that tends to make Jesus Christ analogous to African ancestors in their works, this study presents a theological and contextual Christology that seeks to resonate with Athanasius's and Tertullian's view on the person, deity and work of Christ. For this reason, the work proposes an African Linguistic Affinity Christology methodology which uses biblical names with theological meaning for Jesus Christ. To be successful in this quest, the research will explicate three christological models derived from the Bible. These three christological models: Christ the Messiah, Christ the mediator, and Christ the high priest, presented in the New Testament are the climax of the Adamic covenant of redemption and the Abrahamic covenant of promise made in the Old Testament.

In other words, these old covenantal promises find fulfilment in the person and the redemptive work of Christ. The redemptive-historical method is adopted to analyse that even though Tertullian and Athanasius models from Greco-Roman philosophy and worldview to project a meaningful description of the person and work of Christ. The approach offers a biblical, contextual, and evangelical perspective on the deity of Christ in tandem with Tertullian's

---

68. Bujo, *African Theology*, 23.

69. Tersur Aben, "Ntetem on the Ancestorship of Christ," *TCNN Research Bulletin* 38 (August 2002): 32–38. For a detailed examination of Marc Ntetem's argument, see Ntetem, "Initiation, Traditional and Christian," 99.

Trinitarian Christology and Athanasius's apologetic Christology that rhyme with traditional Christian faith. The view point is engaged to demonstrate how African ancestor theologians failed to understand that Jesus's mission on earth was far beyond just social and cultural interests. Consequently, in their quest to make Jesus Christ a social and cultural emancipator, African theologians have failed to properly contextualize Tertullian's and Athanasius's christological themes as a frame of reference to critique their presuppositions and christological formulation as this work seeks to develop.

The contribution of this work to scholarship is that it proposes the study of Christ in Africa in the light of the Adamic covenant of redemption in Genesis 3:14–19, alongside God's covenant of promise, made to Abraham in Genesis 12:2–3 that culminated in the incarnation of the Son of God whose generally accepted given name in Christendom is Jesus (Ἰησοῦς – Greek, and *Yesu/Jesu* in most African tribal groups) in Matthew 1:21–23. A befitting nomenclature for this new approach is African Linguistic Affinity Christology which identifies Jesus Christ in Africa as *Yesu/Jesu*. *Yesu/Jesu* Christology is, in the opinion of this researcher, a way of presenting an antithetical position to the subjective way African theologians have reduced Christ to an ancestor in their theological discourse.

It has been shown in this study that among the Swahili people of East Africa Jesus is perceived as "*Jesu*." This same nomenclature resonates with the name of Jesus among the Chawai of Northern-central Nigeria, the Akan of Ghana, the Yoruba of Nigeria, the Tshwane of South Africa and the Igbo Nigeria.[70]

From the preceding, this work argues that when you mention *Yesu* or *Jesu* in the midst of any tribe in Africa, they will pause and think you speak the same language and share the same culture with them. Since no accessible work, as far as we know, has been carried out on African Linguistic Affinity Christology which identifies Christ as *Yesu/Jesu* in Africa, the researcher, therefore, offers this methodology as his major contribution to scholarship and hopes that twenty-first-century African theologians would be more comfortable to use the already accepted transliterated nomenclature of Jesus which is at home in almost all African ethnic groups. As this researcher

---

70. See footnote 27 for Clifton Clarke's research results. Also for Jesus as "*Yesu*" or "*Jesu*," see Ayegboyin, "Li Oruko Jesu," 11–19; Clarke, *African Christology*.

believes, African cultural nomenclature is more entrenched in the Bible than other cultures in the world. It is with this name *Yesu/Jesu* that most African Christians experience Jesus as their saviour from sin and eternal condemnation (see chapter 7).

Therefore, far from viewing the passion of Christ in terms of what a deceased African ancestor has achieved for his living kin, and is thus remembered and immortalized, the research contends that the finished work of Christ on the Cross at Calvary should instead be adequately understood as fulfilling the Adamic covenant of redemption through his seed (Gen 3:14–19), and the Abrahamic covenant of promise through which all nations of the world have been blessed and saved (Gen 12:2–3 cf. Rev 7:9). By this understanding, the study argues that Christ did not die the same way African ancestors die, Jesus's death was the fulfilment of the laws and prophecies spoken through the mouths of the prophets of the God of Abraham, Isaac and Jacob. By his death, Jesus has not only fulfilled but replaced the ancestors and any role they were known to perform in any given African society. And by his resurrection, Jesus did not only become the Creator and Saviour of our ancestors but also their benefactor.

Furthermore, the research also argues that nowhere in Jewish society do we have evidence that their ancestors ever served as mediators, the work of mediation in Judaism was strictly that of the Aaronic priesthood. One wonders then, how Jesus could be viewed by African theologians and biblical scholars as an ancestor who mediates even as Abraham himself, the receiver of the covenant of promise and foundation of the patriarchs, looked forward to the coming of the Christ the fulfiller of the laws and prophets for his salvation (Rom 8:19–25).

Other significant contributions of this work to scholarship are that it has also examined how the African ancestor christological discourse has been influenced by Greek metaphysics, particularly, platonic idealism, Greek dualism and biblical eschatology. The Christian Bible, we know carries "history" and history we proposed is his-story. History is the story of Jesus contained in revelation – the invasion into time and space of God in the flesh for our redemption. Redemptive history is thus the salvation story of God from the Garden of Eden embedded in his Son, Jesus Christ, and is progressively moving to its consummation in Christ the seed of Adam. The ultimate fulfilment of God's salvation history culminates human history and earthly existence and introduces a heavenly realm wherein dwell the righteous. But Christ is God, and God is transcendent, immanent and incomparable. Thus, human language regarding metaphor and analogy cannot adequately capture the essence of Christ as the survey of the christological debates of the first five centuries would reveal in chapter three of this work.

Six critical research questions undergird this study: (1) What theological precedence undergirds the formulation of African ancestor christological discourse which the proponents of ancestor Christology take as their point of departure in theologizing? (2) What christological methodology are African theologians seeking to offer to the church in Africa and how has such a method helped give adequate knowledge of Christ to the Africans in tandem with Tertullian's Trinitarian Christology, in the third century, and Athanasius's apologetic Christology, in the fourth century? (3) Why do the proponents of ancestor Christology find it appealing to describe Christ with Africa's pre-Christian traditional religious category? (4) Moreover, the ancestor model in most African tribal groups call Jesus *Yesu* or *Jesu*, which carries a sense of his ontological being and salvific work that would have helped to throw more light in the understanding and acceptance of Christ in Africa than portraying him in the classroom African traditional religious concept of an ancestor? (5) Are the inculturation and contextualization methodologies employed by the leading proponents of the ancestor Christology adequate for making Jesus Christ relevant to the church in Africa without at the same time diminishing his divinity? (6) What are the basic arguments of the exponents of African ancestor Christology and how have they meaningfully engaged the Bible in the christological reflections, vis-à-vis God's covenant of redemption to Adam after the fall and God's covenant of promise to Abraham – both of which captures the soteriological and eschatological role of Christ as the Messiah and mediator of a new covenant, which function supersedes the one performed by African ancestors before the advent of Christ?

In the Akan African Indepent Church (AIC) oral prayer (found on page 11),[71] the petitioner prays; "Lord, I have come to hear what you have to say to me. I have been waiting and praying for a long time . . . I have come

---

71. Clarke, "Towards a Post-Missionary," 5.

today, and my heart is very heavy. *Yesu Kristo*, you rose from the dead to give us life. Your blood gives us power and heals us."[72] We have argued in this study that when the petitioner invokes the name "*Yesu Kristo*," he had in view Jesus's ontological being which was revealed in the incarnation for the redemption of humanity. In light of the above, could African Linguistic Affinity Christology methodology – which identifies Christ as *Yesu/Jesu*, which captures the entire essence of Jesus Christ (his otherness as in his transcendent and immanent nature), which further defines his person, deity and his soteriological work – be a better model for presenting Christ in the African context than the ancestor model which only serves to portray Jesus's functional role as ancestor in Africa in relation to the African engagement with the spirit world?

These thought-provoking questions will serve as the pillar upon which this work towers. They are meant not only to challenge the methodology of the proponents of ancestor Christology to rethink their notion of Jesus Christ, but as well disclose the faulty foundation upon which their assertions hang, since, as we believe, such a portrayal of Jesus Christ has a dearth of sound biblical and theological backing.

Bible-believing Christians with a good grasp of biblical eschatology know, and rightly so, that when God in Christ climaxes history and ushers in the new heaven, there can't be any independent realm for African ancestors. Biblically, the dead do not partake in anything that happens under the sun (Ecc 9:6). Furthermore, the Bible says they know nothing, and their memories are forgotten (Ecc 9:5). Because the dead know nothing, this work argues that they cannot mediate for their living kin who are far better than they.

Employing a presuppositional apologetical method, the work maintains that the transcendent, immanent and incomparable Christ whom the evangelists present in the New Testament as the Messiah, mediator and high priest (visible image of the invisible God) is an eschatological figure whose redemptive work fulfills the Adamic covenant of redemption (Gen 3:14–19) and Abrahamic covenant of promise (Gen 12:2–3) which extends to African ancestors as their Lord and saviour (Matt 1:21–23). This approach will, therefore, help in presenting a more biblically centred work on African

---

72. Clarke, 5.

ancestor Christology since most works on this subject lack treatment on biblical eschatology and christological models that seeks to resonate and fulfil the Adamic covenant of redemption and the Abrahamic covenant of promise which this work develops.

A significant landmark in this work is its critical examination of the religious, political, social, economic and cultural factors in Africa that informed the formulation of contextual and inculturation Christologies in our continent against the backdrop of the traditional Christian Christology formulated in the apostolic era down to the Reformation period.

Research Methodology

This research work proposes an African Linguistic Affinity Christology methodology from an evangelical perspective using the framework of historical method. E. O. Akuezuilo opines that historical research describes what was and it represents and analyzes past events.[73] E. C. Osuala investigated the etymology of the word and traced its origin back to the Greek "Historia." Historia was understood among the Greeks as "a searching to find out."[74] Osuala notes that "Historical research interprets past trends of attitude, event, and fact. History is any integrated narration or description of past events or facts written in a spirit of critical inquiry for the whole truth."[75]

This research follows a historical-theological approach: it investigates available written documents/sources, the historical root and the development of African ancestor Christology belief and also the general African beliefs about ancestors within African Cosmology, which laid the foundation over time for the postulated image of Jesus Christ as an ancestor. To that end, the available sources will be studied, and the various opinions of African theologians on the ancestorship of Jesus Christ will be compared and contrasted, analysed and evaluated theologically using the Christologies of Tertullian and Athanasius as a frame of reference. From the African Linguistic Affinity Christology and historical, methodological paradigms, the first chapter of

---

73. E. O. Akuezuilo, *Research Methodology and Statistics* (Abba: NuelCenti Publishers, 1993), 7.

74. E. C. Osuala, *Introduction to Research Methodology*, 3rd ed. (Onitsha, Nigeria: Africana First, 2005), 162.

75. Osuala, *Introduction to Research*, 162.

this work addresses the statement of the research problem, the purpose of the study and contribution of the study to scholarship which will be developed in chapters 6 and 7.

Chapter 2 examines the factors that gave rise to the formulation of contextual and inculturation Christologies. It will consider in a top-down treatment the context that informed the re-interpretation and reformulation of christological models by African theologians. The chapter contends that the foundation upon which African ancestor christological building is standing tall has its origin in Africa's social, religious and political encounter with Western missionaries and colonial masters of the past. We cannot in this sense, formulate a qualitatively meaningful theology in Africa without at the same time referring to our past historical context. African history is the story of the struggle for liberation in all its ramifications. The issue of freedom which prevailed in Africa in the early decades of this century leading to the emergence of contextual African Christian theology which metamorphosed to the ancestor Christology paradigm as a response to colonialism and imperialism was a prevailing ideology. Too, of all the Christologies framed in Sub-Saharan Africa, ancestor Christology receives more significant attention. In establishing the fact, the chapter examines the Christologies of Abbé Marc Ntetem, Bénézet Bujo and Charles Nyamiti, which foundation has been laid in the one hand on the encounter of Africa with the Western superpowers in pre-independent Africa and the other; the method derives its inspiration from the motivation of Vatican II.

Up until the enlightenment that subsequently ushered in modernism and postmodernism, traditional Christian theology was never challenged. The enlightenment became a thorn in the flesh of orthodox Christology and scholars began to view Christ regarding scientific innovation and human reason. Hence liberalism made its appearance in theological circles in the nineteenth century giving rise to post-missionary Christianity consequence of which new christological paradigms emerged as a response to colonialism and modern and postmodern philosophical and ideological influences.

I wish to state that from the incarnational Christology of the apostle John and the transcendent Christology of the apostle Paul in the New Testament, the formulation of Christology by Justin Martyr and Ignatius of Antioch and the defence of Christology by Tertullian and Athanasius up to the

Reformation period, Christology against all the odds has been classic. With the eighteenth-century enlightenment confidence in human ability associated with Africa's struggle for independent selfhood and cultural emancipation, Christology was challenged, thereby laying the foundation for modern and postmodern African christological formulation evaluated in this work.

Chapter 3 lays the foundation for a biblically contextual Christology. It will examine the context that informed the proclamation and formulation of christological models by the apostles and patristic fathers of the early church. The chapter is intentionally arranged to facilitate a healthy conversation between the assertions of proponents of African ancestor christological discourse and the christological formulation of two select African apologists; Tertullian of Carthage and Athanasius of Alexandria who reflected and formulated a normative Christology to preserving the Orthodox Christology of the apostolic church.

Chapter 4 concentrates on a detailed examination of African cosmology, worldview and cosmogony. The study argues that the building block of African ancestor Christology rests firmly on African primal belief on the ancestors and the desire to remember and immortalize the dead.

The fifth chapter of this study examines the theological sources that are antecedent to the current literature on African ancestor christological themes and their implications for African Christianity. Fundamentally, the church's quest for Afrocentric biblical hermeneutical methods through inculturation to present an acceptable Christianity accounts mostly for the need to have an African Christ.

Chapter 6 discusses the theological and biblical interpretations of ancestorship from the perspective of Old Testament Adamic covenant of redemption through his seed in Genesis 3:15 which was climaxed with the Abrahamic covenant of promise in Genesis 12:2–3 and traditional African belief. This exercise is essential, for, at first sight, the tendency to project Jesus Christ as an African ancestor is excellent. But in a typical Jewish setting, the Jews have never for once even likened Abraham the father of the patriarchs with Jesus Christ. Instead, Abraham who received the covenant promised in furtherance of the Adamic covenant looked with eager expectations to the coming of the fulfiller of the promise inaugurated with Adam's fall. The section concludes that African cult of the ancestors was the channel of interacting with the supreme being. With the advent of Christianity, some African theologians believe there should be a healthy contextualization and inculturation between biblical christological categories with African pre-Christian models. Hence, the ancestral cult is viewed as a theological point of contact for Christianity and African beliefs.

Chapter 7 of the study is the heart of the study. In it, an analysis of main christological passages from three selected christological models: Christ the Messiah (2 Sam 19:22; Isa 61:1;1 Kings 19:16; Sirach 48: 8; Mark 8:29–31; John 1:41; 4:25, 42) , Christ the mediator (see 1 Tim 2:5; Heb 6; 8:6; 9:5; 10:5–14; 12:24; Rom 8:3), and Christ the high priest (Deut 5:24; Ps 110:4; Heb 7:27, 10:5–14, 12:24; Lev 9:7; Rom 8:34; 1 John 2:1) is done.

The explication of these models serves as prelude to the prepositional apologetic argument of this work which contends that a biblically contextual approach that presents an African Linguistic Affinity Christology methodology that identifies Jesus Christ as *Yesu/Jesu* in fulfillment of the Adamic redemptive covenant (Gen 3:15–19) – "the first declaration of the covenant of redemption contains in seed form which God reveals in a most balanced fashion the various elements constituting his commitment to redeem his fallen creation,"[76] climaxed in the covenant of promise God made with "Abraham the Father of the Jews of the coming Seed. 'I will make you a great nation; I will bless you and make your name great, and you shall be a blessing. I will bless those who bless you, and I will curse him that curses you; and in you, all the families of the earth shall be blessed' (Genesis 12:2–3)."[77] And not ancestor Christology should be formulated in Africa. Rather than re-imaging Christ as ancestor as way of preserving and immortalizing memories, African theologians should articulate an African Linguistic Affinity christological paradigm and prophetic-fulfillment Christology in tandem with God's redemptive covenant made to Adam and Abraham's covenant of promise through which all nations of the world, by virtue of the death and resurrection of *Yesu/Jesu Kristi*, have already been blessed. The blessedness of the African state does mean that our ancestors have become benefactors and also inheritors of the covenant of Adam and

---

76. O. Palmer Robertson, *The Christ of the Covenants* (Philipsburg, NJ: P & R, 1980), 93.

77. Turaki, *Unique Christ*, 142.

Abraham and members of the multiracial community of Christ, whose resurrected power inaugurated it when he defeated death by resurrecting triumphantly. His resurrection and present reign over the entire cosmos transcends national, tribal, clan and familial solidarity. Yusufu Turaki warns, "It is certain that the Holy Scriptures set Jesus the Messiah apart. For this reason, He cannot be domesticated to join the ancestors."[78] Furthermore, the section argues that God is transcendent, immanent and incomparable. Thus, the anthropomorphic language shrouded in the metaphor and the analogy of African theologians about Jesus Christ cannot adequately capture nor express the full essence of the Triune God.

On the aspect of projecting Christ as an ancestor who performs the role of mediation, the section argues that in the Jewish religious context the ancestors were never mediators, the part of conciliation was strictly the function of the Aaronic priesthood. The above outlook brings us to the heart of the apologetics of the study where African ancestors are considered regarding biblical eschatology that portrays the state of the dead. The debate on whether ancestors are venerated or worshipped is also highlighted against the backdrop of the first two commandments on idol worship in the Bible. The section argues that the theological-exegetical significance of Christ as the Messiah, mediator and high priest is invariably grounded first on the *protevangelium* in Genesis 3:15 which envisages a global harvest of the redeemed people of God and second, on the Abrahamic covenant of promise in Genesis 12:2–3 that through this kind of faith; all nations of the world will be blessed. This blessing is through the salvation brought by *Yesu/Jesu Kiristi* on the cross. He and no one else consummated all the previous covenants made to Adam and Abraham. On this note, Palmer O. Robertson writes, "The heart of this consummative realisation consists of a single person. As fulfiller of all the messianic promises, he achieves in himself the essence of the covenantal principles: 'I shall be your God, and you shall be my people.' He, therefore, may be seen as the Christ who consummates the covenant."[79] How Jesus Christ has consummated the covenants, Paul Peter Enns keenly explains;

---

78. Turaki, 140.
79. Robertson, *Christ of the Covenants*, 272–273.

> Although Adam and Eve had sinned, incurring death, and God moved to resolved man's dilemma by pointing to a feature saviour who would eliminate death, restore believing man to fellowship with God, and consummate history with Messiah's reign on earth to restore all that Adam lost . . . even though Adam lost considerable authority with his kingdom rule as God's mediator, Genesis 3:15 looks to the feature when the Messianic Kingdom will be inaugurated, restoring all that Adam lost.[80]

These views articulated by scholars on the redemptive work of Christ, coupled with the apostles' apostolic authority, and an incontrovertible image of Jesus Christ has been presented that cannot be compared with an African ancestor who looked forward to the promised messiah and who is at the same time the firstborn high priest and mediator of a new covenant.

Chapter 8 presents a concise summary of the entire study. This section maintains that the research is not exhaustive, thus written in the light of further investigation. The previous point, therefore, draws the work to a close with a caution that African theologians should be conscious of what we offer to global Christianity in the name of contextualization and inculturation.

Summary

Chapter 1 gives an overview of the entire research work. It discussed how on a worldwide scale ancestors are commemorated and immortalized. The chapter argues that the desire to preserve the primal traditions of Africa, some African theologians believe it is necessary to give room for continuity between African pre-Christian heritage, particularly the ancestral cult, and Christian theology. According to the proponents of ancestor Christology, the ancestral worship provides the best meeting point between African belief and Christian theology. For this reason, the African category of ancestor should be used to formulate Christian theology. The above, of course, is a worthy course in so far as such articulation seeks not only to contribute to the overall Christian theological enterprise but as well attempts to make

---

80. Paul Peter Enns, *The Moody Handbook of Theology* (Chicago, IL: Moody, 1989), 42.

Jesus Christ relevant to Africans. It is, however, the opinion of the researcher that the attempt to make Christ an ancestor is the result of re-reading and re-interpreting Jesus Christ from antiquarian African rather than modern African and Christian worldview. Africans no longer value ancestors today the same way they cherished them some five to six decades ago. Nowadays, in a very solemn mood very few, if at all there is any, Africans who will be comfortable to call Jesus Christ ancestor in the twenty-first century wholeheartedly. Jesus Christ in most African ethnic groups has one renowned name which varies from the context it is called but which rings a belt once it is mentioned. Jesus Christ to most Africans is transliterated either *Yesu* or *Jesu Kiristi*. It is the transliterated Ἰησοῦς that Africans prefer to be associated with, for it gives them not only a sense of belonging to the Adamic and Abrahamic covenants but also speaks of their engraftedness in the overall scheme of God's salvific plan, which culminated in the death of Jesus Christ. The most suitable methodology for the formulation of Christology using the transliterated name of Jesus is African Linguistic Affinity Christology. With this christological method, the theological meaning of Jesus is retained concerning Old Testament promises and prophecies and the apostolic formulation of Christology in the New Testament and early church. This study argues that the African concept of an ancestor is not linked with biblical promises and prophecies to warrant the comparison. The mosaic model introduces the supreme God to the polytheistic and pantheistic religious, and it is within this context that Christology emerged in contrast to the veneration of gods and intermediaries. And Jesus as an ancestor is presented as one of the intermediaries when he is viewed from African spectacle. This has failed to reveal the quintessence of the redemptive work of Christ as opposed to the work of the ancestors presented in African traditional beliefs.

A further argument could be adduced against the ancestor Christology which uses inculturation as a theological model, since research has shown among Igbo Catholics that the inculturation model used in Roman Catholic circles to formulate ancestor Christology has not indeed achieved any milestone. Instead, it further widens the cleavage between Christianity and African primal beliefs and makes the latter more appealing than ever before. Uche pointedly declared, "The most disturbing fact about the Catholic Church in Igbo land is that the Church hierarchy seems to be blind to the reality of the life of Christians in Igbo land. They do not believe that most of their followers are Catholic on Sundays and traditionalists during the week."[81] In fact, Uche sees the inculturation methodology as a slave master from whom the Roman Catholic Church in Igboland needs to be liberated. He writes, "The Inculturation process in the Igbo Church has rather been a means of confrontation, condemnation, and intimidation. Every Igbo religious ritual has been condemned as evil and as paganism and a train therefore to hellfire. Consequently, the Igbo Christian is culturally and theologically handicapped by the present inculturation or adaptation approach. Therefore, every Igbo Christian needs liberation."[82] Uche's position is tenable since rather than making Christianity more acceptable in Africa, the inculturation methodology has only succeeded in creating enmity than dialogue between the two belief systems. On this ground, I concur with him that this method should be discarded and new ones propose and formulated. For this reason, I introduced African Linguistic Affinity christological methodology which best meets the African Christian and theological needs.[83]

---

81. Uche, "Theological Analysis of *Ikpu-Ala*," 286.

82. Uche, 286.

83. In this study, I employ the adjective, "African" to mean anything that pertains to or relates to the people of Africa whose skin colour is Charcolate as opposed to the popularly accepted misnomal notion of "Black skinned people." Thus, African Linguistic Affinity Christology is a theological methodology proposed to be formulated among the multilingual and multicultural African tribes and ethnic groups in tropical Africa, while Africa itself is to be understood as "The second largest continent in the whole world located in the eastern hemisphere south of Europe and joined to Asia by the Sinai peninsula: 11,500.000 square miles." For more on Africa's location and land mass, see *The New International Webster's Comprehensive Dictionary of the English Language*, encyclopedic edition (Naples, FL: Typhoon Media Corporation, 2010), 25.

CHAPTER 2

Jesus as an Ancestor: A Paradigm Shift in African Christology and Theological Method

Introduction

One of the fastest growing and the most likely would be Christian continents in the world today is the post-independence and post-missionary era, Africa.[1] Philip Jenkens accentuates this submission by stating that "The weight of numbers within Christianity is shifting so decisively to the churches of the global south."[2] In 1991 Robert J. Schreiter predicted that by the year 2000, the Christian population in Africa would be 250 million.[3] Amazingly for him, the actual African Christian population in 2000 turned out to be 335 million.[4] For Jenkens, "Between 1900 and 2000, the number of Christians in Africa grew from 10 million to over 360 million, from 10 percent of the population to 46 percent."[5] With this rapid growth in Christian population, Jenkens further argues, "Today, the most vibrant centres of Christian

---

1. Robert J. Schreiter, "Jesus Christ in Africa Today," in *Faces of Jesus in Africa*, ed. Robert J. Schreiter (Maryknoll: Orbis Books, 2005), vii.
2. Philip Jenkens, *The New Faces of Christianity: Believing the Bible in the Global South* (Oxford: Oxford University Press, 2006), 8.
3. Schreiter, "Jesus Christ in Africa Today," vii.
4. "The Explosion of Christianity in Africa," Christianity.com, accessed 7 December 2016, http://www.christianity.com/church/church-history/timeline/2001-now/the-explosion-of-christianity-in-africa-11630859.html.
5. Jenkens, *New Faces of Christianity*, 9.

growth are still in Africa itself."⁶ Elsewhere he predicted, "By 2025, Africa and Latin America will vie for the title of the most Christian Continent."⁷ "Within this continent, it is not uncommon" to borrow Schreiter's epigram; "one finds the full range of questions facing Christianity as a world Church today."⁸ After Africa's political and religious independence, two principal trends emerged: "One was the theological dimension to the struggle for the social and political transformation of the conditions of inequality and oppression in South Africa, and it produced 'black theology.' The other was the theological exploration of the indigenous cultures of African peoples, with particular stress on their pre-Christian religious traditions."⁹ The perspective above resulted in the emergence of African theology the main emphasis of which is ancestor Christology that also seeks to explore the relationship between the emerging Christian faith and the primal religions and cultures of Africa. Some African theologians believe that having brought the gospel to the African continent, the work of Western missionaries is completed, what else we do with what they brought has nothing to do with the West. On this note, John Parratt reports that the Sierra Leone-born theologian Canon Harry Sawyer was of the view that a more promising approach in exploring theology in Africa should be that which seeks a common ground between Christianity and African religious thought, so that the gospel may be meaningfully communicated to Africans.¹⁰ The above-stated goal became the obsessive agenda for the "necessity of peeling away from the gospel the accretions of the centuries, and of Western, white, European, American culture, to get to the kernel of the gospel underneath."¹¹ This obsession was motivated in part by statements from Western missionaries who served in Africa. Vincent J. Donovan, for example, noted: "The task of the missionary is to present the gospel, and the task of the people who respond to it is to express that gospel and its meaning in their language and within their

---

6. Jenkens, 9.
7. Jenkens, 9.
8. Schreiter, "Jesus Christ in Africa Today," vii.
9. Kwame Bediako, "African Theology," in *The Modern Theologians: An Introduction to Christian Theology in the Twentieth Century*, ed. David F. Ford (Malden: Blackwell, 2002), 426.
10. John Parratt, ed., *A Reader in African Christian Theology* (London: SPCK, 2001), 9.
11. Vincent J. Donovan, *Christianity Rediscovered* (Maryknoll: Orbis Books, 2003), 54.

thought forms."[12] The attempt to express the gospel in African thought and cultural categories has become the basis for the formulation of Christian theology in the continent. Central to African theological discourse is the identity of Jesus Christ who is presented in the Bible as the redeemer of humankind. As Wilson Muoha Maina puts it, "the main issue in African Christian theology is developing an African understanding of the gospel and the person of Jesus Christ."[13]

In the first five centuries of the Christian church, it was theologians in the ancient Roman North Africa, notably Tertullian in the third century and Athanasius in the fourth century, who set the pace and shaped the continents of early Christian theology and their insights saved Christian theology from the Trinitarian and Arian heresies of their days. Thomas C. Oden accentuates this fact when he claims that Western Christian legacy germinated and was nursed on the African Christian seedbed. He asserts; "By sea and land, early Africa significantly shaped the basic layers of both Eastern and Western traditions of Christianity."[14]

After several decades of articulating Trinitarian Christology by Tertullian in his response against philosophers and heretics in the third century, and incarnational Christology by Athanasius against the Arian party in the fourth century who laid the foundation for Western theological tradition, African theologians of our day are dissatisfied with the ancient Christian traditions laid by these Roman North African theologians and contend that patristic theological methods are anachronistic and incompatible with current trends in African theological discourse. Thus, they argue that for Christianity to be relevant in the continent, we need to employ African pre-Christian cultural categories to formulate contemporary theology. The current attempt, therefore, to express the gospel in African thought forms is no doubt the result of dissatisfaction with that which our forebears have established, and is definitely counter to their efforts since the ancestor model does not enjoy general acceptance in world Christianity the same way christological models

---

12. Donovan, *Christianity Rediscovered*, quoted by Bevans in *Models of Contextual Theology*, 65.

13. Wilson Muoha Maina, *Historical and Social Dimensions in African Christian Theology: A Contemporary Approach* (Eugene, OR: Wipf & Stock, 2009), 84.

14. Thomas C. Oden, *How Africa Shaped the Christian Mind: Rediscovering the African Seedbed of Western Christianity* (Downers Grove, IL: InterVarsity Press, 2007), 22.

like *Logos*, Trinity etc. are universally accepted in traditional Christian confession. In fact, even within Africa, most African Christians prefer to call Jesus by biblical names only.[15] Thus, this work argues that the inculturation methodology that employs analogy of proportionality to explore Christology by presenting Jesus Christ as one or equal with African ancestors does not satisfy for Christology, since Jesus and African ancestors are not proportionally the same or similar. Furthermore, Turaki adduced that giving African "ancestors a Christological definition by exploring ways that can be incorporated or rehabilitated into African Christianity by describing Jesus in the eyes of Africans or their conceptions does not qualify for Christology."[16] Furthermore, Turaki argues, "we can take and have wonderful research findings, but that does not qualify for Christology. Except if Christology loses its biblical and prophetic meaning."[17] The necessary question that follows is why there is the present dissatisfaction with antiquity that has, at the same time in our day, given rise to the current ancestor christological paradigm?

Often, African theologians appeal to colonialism and Western missionary activities in Africa between the eighteenth and twentieth centuries to justify the claim that the invasion of these Western world powers has denigrated everything African. Consequently, the poor economic, political, religious, and social conditions of Africa today should be blamed on these forces. This chapter argues that to comprehend the theological positions of African theologians, it is expedient to investigate the social, religious, economic, and political larger systemic structures they belong. Given that African theologians and biblical scholars hold the Western world responsible for our present predicaments, we wish to propose that the understanding of the ancestor Christology paradigm cannot be complete without at the same time first understanding the systemic background of these theologians.

The chapter first examines the various factors that led to the emergence of African theology particularly the ancestor Christology paradigm. The examination is preceded by reviewing the writings of Abbé Marc Ntetem,

---

15. Clarke, *African Christology*, 82–93. See also Jørn Henrik Olson, "Contextualised Christology in Tropical Africa?" *Swedish Missiological Theme* 85, no. 3–4 (1997): 247.

16. Yusufu Turaki, "Christianity and African Traditional Religion: A Systematic Examination of the Interactions of Religion," vol. 1 (unpublished manuscript), 95.

17. Turaki, "Christianity and African Traditional Religion," vol. 1, 66–67.

Bénézet Bujo and Charles Nyamiti on the ancestorhip of Jesus Christ in Africa before we conclude. Our intention here is to ascertain the extent to which the ancestor model has shaped Christianity in Africa especially the ways such a cultural category has helped in the evangelization of Africans in the past three decades, since it became a popular christological model within the academic circles in the first quarter of the 1980s.

Colonial and Missionary Invasion of Africa between the Eighteenth and Twentieth Centuries: Setting the Stage for the Emergence of Ancestor Christology

Ancestor Christology is the product of several theological movements in Africa. These movements were due in part to the problem of comprehending Christianity, let alone integrating Christian beliefs with African primal traditional faiths and cultures in such a way that there would be continuity between Christian theology and African primal traditional ideas and customs. Before the advent of Christianity, Africans had always believed that the traditional religion was a channel to reach and worship the supreme being. This belief was challenged by the missionaries who denigrated African culture and religious belief and taught that African traditional religion was pagan. Western missionaries presented what seemed antithetical to the Africans. For their part, African theologians and biblical scholars were faced with the problem of integrating the Christian faith into the traditional African religious beliefs. As Yusufu Turaki argues, "The problem of presenting and transmitting the Gospel of Christ is created by how the African sees, understands, interprets and constructs Christianity within his traditional religious worldview and context."[18] Presenting Christian models in the African traditional religious categories and worldview through inculturation and contextualization has been African theologians' and biblical scholars' response to colonial and Western missionary contempt for African traditional religion and culture.

---

18. Turaki, "Christianity and African Traditional Religion," vol. 1, 33.

Against the backdrop of Western superpowers' invasions Africa, the home of the so-called black race, suffered much from the scourge of Western colonialists and imperialists. In Western estimation, Africa was a "dark continent" wallowing in utter ignorance without hope. Westerners described Africans as "ignorant; people who wander in moral twilight; that 'know not what they do.' Africa is the 'darkest region of the earth' where one encounters the lowest of the low."[19] The Sudan United Mission (SUM) missionary Karl Kumm described Africa as, "a land in this wonderful world, called 'the land of darkness,' . . . dark are the bodies of the people who live there, darker are their minds, and darker still is their souls – of the Sons and daughters of the Dark Continent."[20] These are words of hate rather than love. Perhaps, Albert Schweitzer's critique of Hermann Samuel Reimarus and David Friedrich Strauss that hate "motivated their portrayal of the historical Jesus,"[21] better defines Kumm's slant here albeit purportedly written from a compassionate heart.

Evidence abounds to confirm our argument for low Western esteem for Africa. For example, some missionaries themselves have written confessing their contempt for Africans. Note this; "He (missionary) confessed that he and his colleagues had a secret contempt for the African that was hard to get rid of."[22] Elsewhere they further confess; "One has no use for that spirit that regards an African as a being lower than a dog in the moral scale."[23]

The devastating effect of colonialism and imperialism on Africa is taking its toll on the continent in several areas of human life. For instance, in the last six decades, or thereabouts, almost all the fifty-five African (Morocco included) countries have gained independence from their colonial masters and the continent seems to be marching forward politically, economically, socially, and educationally at an amazing rate of progress. Even when this seems to be so, Africa's growth indexes indicate the opposite. Undoubtedly, African countries that were the colonies of Britain, France, Portugal, Germany, Spain,

---

19. Cited in Jan H. Boer, *Missions: Heralds of Capitalism or Christ?* (Ibadan: Daystar Press, 1984), 35.

20. Boer, *Missions*, 35.

21. Albert Schweitzer, *The Quest of the Historical Jesus: A Critical Study of Its Progress from Reimarus to Wrede* (New York: Macmillan, 1961), 4.

22. Boer, *Missions*, 43.

23. Boer, 43.

Belgium, and Italy, have up to this day fashioned their educational, political, and religious systems after those of these colonial masters.[24] Needless to talk about language diversity since all colonies speak and write the language of their former colonial masters to this day. This diversity in language with a commensurate disjunctive Africa is better captured in the lament of Daniel Etounga-Manguelle that "There is an Arabophone Africa, an Anglophone Africa, a Francophone Africa, a Lusophone Africa, a Hispanophone Africa, not to mention the scores of languages that have no relation to the languages of the European colonizers."[25]

It is true to state that Africa's encounter with colonial and missionary activities of the past defines her dilemma, which has led to an apparent loss of identity and independent selfhood. All African countries without exception had, before the advent of colonial rule, an established traditional system of governance under their headmen – Obas, Chiefs, and Emirs. When the colonial masters arrived, they took over power from the headmen. The consequential loss of power was followed by the scrambling of our land. In his famous apothegm, T. Mofokeng wrote, "When the white man came to our country he had the Bible and we had the land. The white man said to us 'let us pray.' After we opened our eyes, the white man had the land and we had the Bible."[26] The land in question here is not just any land but the very best land belonging to our ancestors. Walter Rodney concurs, "The white settlers took the best land and then tried to create a new world with African labour."[27]

While a non-African may see these words the expression of sentiment, most of Africans see them as the expression of their great loss in the hands of foreign invaders. A Kikuyu white settler, Colonel Grogan, once said;

---

24. Ehiedu E. G. Iweriebor, "The Colonization of Africa," Africana Age, accessed 20 January 2016, http://exhibitions.nypl.org/africanaage/essay-colonization-of-africa.html, 1–10.

25. Daniel Etounga-Manuelle, "Does Africa Need a Cultural Adjustment Program?" in *Culture Matters: How Values Shape Human Progress*, eds. Lawrence E. Harrison and Samuel P. Huntington (New York: Basic Books, 2000), 65–77.

26. T. Mofokeng, "Black Christians, the Bible and Liberation," *Journal of Black Theology in South Africa* 2, no. 1 (1988): 34.

27. Walter Rodney, *How Europe Underdeveloped Africa* (Abuja, Nigeria: Panaf Publishing, 2009), 278.

"We have stolen his land. Now we must steal his limbs."[28] The scramble for Africa was far more intense than the scramble of wild game by ravenous wolves. This dicey situation almost resulted in an inter-imperialist war. To remedy the situation, the German chancellor Otto Von Bismarck convened a diplomatic summit of European powers in the late nineteenth century.[29] This summit which became known as the Berlin West African conference took place between November 1884 and February 1885. Like Mao Zedong's division and hierarchy of the world in which the people of the so-called third world nations did not participate,[30] so also Africans were relegated in the partitioning of their very own continent. The conference, which major articles became known as the Berlin Act, has been summarized by Iweriebor as follows:

1. The principle of Notification (Notifying) other powers of a territorial annexation
2. The principle of effective occupation to validate the annexation
3. Freedom to trade in the Congo Basin
4. Freedom of Navigation on the Niger and Congo Rivers
5. Freedom of trade to all nations
6. Suppression of the slave trade by land and sea.[31]

With this treaty, Africa, the home of dark people, became the home of the white people who swarmed like wild locus in their hundreds and in their thousands across the entire continent and ravaged it over several decades until Africans made a move to regain control of their lands.[32] The end of the colonial rule marked the gradual return of power to Africans with Western education, some of whom did not belong to the defunct ruling class. They were professional politicians that claimed to establish a "government of the people, by the people, and for the people."[33] By taking over of power from

---

28. Rodney, *How Europe Underdeveloped Africa*, 198.
29. Iweriebor, "Colonization of Africa," 2.
30. Virginia Fabella, and R. S. Sugirtharajah, eds., *The SCM Dictionary of Third World Theologies* (London: SCM, 2003), xxii.
31. Iweriebor, "Colonization of Africa," 2.
32. Rodney, *How Europe Underdeveloped Africa*, 271.
33. Pandang Yamsat, *The Role of the Church in Democratic Governance in Nigeria* (Bukuru, Nigeria: Biblical Studies Foundation, 2001), 10.

the colonial masters, African politicians inherited European power tussle which has become the lot of virtually all Africa countries.

It could be argued that what we have today, in post-independence Africa, is not the heritage of Africans before the advent of the colonial era but the tottering movement of the hangover of colonial intoxication and Africans aptly became victims of circumstances.

This work argues therefore that the introduction of a Western type of politics by Western stooges in Africa, whose system – as opposed to Africa's pre-colonial politics – began the reign of terror, vote rigging, and manoeuvring along with arson killing, that seem to have become an essential part of our political life and history. That cases of political killings abound across the continent is no longer news. Istifanus Dafwang, a resident electoral commissioner for Gombe and Benue states, between December 2011 and January 2016, appointed by the Independent National Electoral Commission (INEC) describes the magnitude and worrisome situation of Nigerian politics thus, "During the 2015 elections, some thugs were arrested with AK47 rifles in Benue State."[34] A corollary of weapon possession is killing, which explains why on 4 December 1997, for instance, the bodies of four Liberians, Samuel and Janet Dokie, his sister and bodyguard, were found in their burned-out car on the outskirts of Gbarnga, Liberia.[35] Similarly, Mr Sendashonga, a Rwandese former government minister was shot dead in the Kenyan capital of Nairobi, by the mercenaries of his political opponents on 16 May 1998. On 25–28 January 2011, thirty-five Kalenji were killed in the home at Naishi by Kikuyu political rivals; 12 September 1977 – Steve Biko of South Africa, anti-apartheid campaigner, was murdered during detention; 16 January 2000 – president Laurent Kabila of the Democratic Republic of Congo, was shot by bodyguards; 5 September 1990 – President Samuel Doe of Liberia, was mutilated and killed by rebel leader Prince Johnson.[36]

---

34. Istifanus Dafwang, *Christians are Politicians* (Benue, Nigeria: Vedan Biz Solutions, 2016), 50.

35. Tiawan Gonglo, "Rights and the Politics of Fear and Violence," The Perspective, posted 9 December 2003, http://www.theperspective.org/december2003/gongloe_un.html.

36. Amnesty International, *Inquiry into Assassination of Rwandese Opposition Leader in Exile Urgently Needed*, 18 May 1998, AFR/47/19/98, available at, https://www.refworld.org/docid/3ae6a98540.html.

In Nigeria, the situation seems to be particularly dicey, hopeless, and perplexing as cases of high profile political assassinations are being recorded on almost a daily basis. Take for instance the killings of Mr Anthony Olufunsho Williams, a governorship aspirant in Lagos State on Wednesday 27 July 2006, and Dr Ayodele Dramola, a governorship aspirant in Ekiti State on 14 August 2006. In 2016, a senator violently and brutally took over the politics of his constituency and forcefully became senator with impunity.[37] The abuse of security vote, especially by Chief Executives at State and Federal levels, was headline news on a daily basis in 2015 and 2016.[38] In Jos, the capital of Plateau State, Mr Shie Rinti was murdered in cold blood in 2016, because of his affiliation with a particular party. Each of these deaths takes a momentary centre stage in national discussion and systematically fades away into a reclusive national sub-consciousness. The citizens gaze in confusion and hoped they never happen again. The clouds of uncertainties hang over our head, and there remain more questions than answers.[39] Apart from political killings, corruption is a cancer that is ravaging many countries in Africa[40] For example President Frederick Chiluba of

---

37. Dafwang, *Christians are Politicians*, 50.

38. Dafwang, 84.

39. Uzochukwu J. Njoku, "Reflecting on Assassinations and Destructions in Nigeria's Socio-Political Culture," *African Renaissance* 3, no. 6 (2006): 45–48. Available online at, https://journals.co.za/content/aa_afren/3/6/EJC10240.

40. According to *TELL Magazine*, number 42 of October 24, 2011; four past governors of Nigeria: Gbenga Daniel, Ogun, is alleged to have stolen 62.4 billion Naira between 2004 and 2011, Alao-Akala, former governor of Oyo State; Hosea Agbola, a serving senator and former Oyo State commissioner for local government and chieftaincy matters; and Olufemi Babalola, owner of Pentagon Engineering Service were arraigned before an Oyo high court for defrauding the State of 11 billion Naira during Alao's tenure as governor. In this same edition, former governor Danjuma Goje of Gombe and four others diverted 52 billion Naira between May 2003 and May 2011. The magazine carried; "The money was siphoned from various sources, especially, the Universal Basic Education Commission, the State Universal Basic Education Board and statutory allocations to local governments in the State." Governor Aliyu Akwe Doma formerly of Nassarawa State is not immune to the corruption endemic for he and nine others defraud Nassarawa State of 28 billion Naira during his tenure as governor of the State. See "Trial of Ex-Governors: Another Offensive to Nowhere?" *TELL Magazine*, no. 42, 24 October 2011. For other cases of corruption, see Johnny Danjuma, "Violence in Lafia as Doma is Arraigned," *The Nation*, vol. 7, no. 1918, 19 October 2011; "War against Corruption," Countdown Magazine, vol. 7, no. 1, anniversary edition 2011; "Corruption: The Cankerworm Eating Our Economy," Countdown Magazine, vol .4, no. 2, information edition; "800 killed during post-election riots—Human Rights Watch" *The Punch*, 17 May 2011, vol. 17, no. 208884.

Zambia, on 29 December 1991, repented "of our wicked ways of idolatry, witchcraft, the occult, immorality, injustice and corruption . . . Zambia . . . Christian nation . . . will . . . be governed by the righteous principles of the word of God."[41] Chiluba's declaration may appear to show contrition for his crimes, but history proved him wrong since he was charged years later with 168 counts of theft totalling more than $40 million.[42] The story is not any better with President Olusegun Matthew Aremu who, like President Chiluba, was also accused of mismanagement of funds.[43]

It is argued in this work that colonialism impacted the African continent negatively. For this reason, its political, economic, social, and religious activities and influence have generated and engendered reactions from African theologians and biblical scholars, who in the 1950s began to articulate independent selfhood through the spirit of African nationalism. The acknowledged situation is the context and the factors that gave birth to African theology, whose basic theological agenda is ancestor Christology as the next section reveals. Thus, "When African theology is mentioned, one cannot avoid thinking of colonialism and missionary endeavours. Although there are many developments in Africa today, we cannot ignore the impact of colonialism and missionary work on the continent."[44]

African Theology and the Cult of the Ancestors: The Problem of Definition, Terminology, Language and Historical Trends

African theology has itself been a disputed term – partly because it is not clear if it refers to theology with a specifically African theme or content, or some philosophizing carried out by African theologians. Theologians disagree on what exactly the adjective "African" means. In many cases, the

---

41. Samuel Waje Kunhiyop, *African Christian Ethics* (Kaduna: Baraka Press, 2004), 100–102.

42. "Attorney General of Zambia v. Meer Care & Desai (A Firm) & Ors," Casemine, https://www.casemine.com/judgement/uk/5b46f1f62c94e0775e7ef1bf.

43. Mwangi S. Kimenyi and Nelipher Moyo, "The Late Zambian President Fredrick Chiluba: A Legacy f Failed Democratic Transition," Brookings, https://www.brookings.edu/opinions/the-late-zambian-president-fredrick-chiluba-a-legacy-of-failed-democratic-transition/.

44. Maina, *Historical and Social*, 3.

term "African" refers to the traditional worldview of the people of Africa. Tite Tiénou has noted that "Discussions on the relationship between Christianity and African culture and religion eventually lead into an inquiry about the possibility and legitimacy of African theology."[45] Furthermore, he observes, "In itself, the expression 'African theology' is quite ambiguous . . . It could legitimately be used to describe the reflections about God contained in the various traditions and religious beliefs of African peoples."[46] The seemingly inclusive nature of the term leads Tiénou to argue further: "The term African theology as such bears no specific Christian focus."[47] Harry Sawyer is rather blunt. For him, "the term is misleading,"[48] and "one tends to become increasingly sceptical about the use of the term."[49] John S. Pobee, however, sees no reason to drop the term. He writes, "When we use 'Africa,' we refer to the African people's religiousness in the flux and turmoil of the modern world. And that is no doubt rooted in the past. We wish to hold the past, present and future together."[50]

The basic premise of African theologians is that Christianity came to Africa in a Western garment. Therefore, it is foreign to Africans. For it to be accepted, and at the same time make the African feel at home as he practises his religion, it Western trappings has to be stripped off. For this reason, Gwinyai H. Muzorewa argues for the integration of African traditional life and the Christian faith. He writes, "To be 'at home' is, for the African, to experience continuing between traditional life and the Christian faith."[51]

Muzorewa's argument explains the unwillingness of some African theologians to abandon the primal traditions of the African past. Pobee's call to expurgate Western categories from African Christianity indicates the reluctance of some African theologians and biblical scholars to abandon African

---

45. Tite Tiénou, *The Theological Task of the Church in Africa: Theological Perspectives in Africa* (Ghana: African Christian Press, 1990), 27.

46. Tiénou, *Theological Task*, 27.

47. Tiénou, 27.

48. Harry Sawyer, "What Is African Theology?" in *A Reader in African Christian Theology*, ed. John Parratt (London: SPCK, 2001), 17.

49. Sawyer, "What is African Theology?" 17.

50. John S. Pobee, *Toward an African Theology* (Nashville, TN: Abingdon, 1979), 18.

51. Gwinyai H. Muzorewa, *The Origins and Development of African Theology* (Maryknoll: Orbis Books, 1987), 7.

cultures for Western thought in their theological reflection. "The simple truth is that Christianity, having reached Africa via Europe, came with a European stamp on it. And so in the African context, if there is to be a serious and deep communication and rooting of the gospel of Christ, the African stamp will have to replace the European stamp."[52] Pobee also contends "in order that the gospel may have real encounter with *homo Africanus,* there is need to translate Christianity into genuine African categories. That is what we call African theology. It is the attempt to couch essential Christianity into African categories and thought forms."[53]

Some theologians have argued against uniform traditional beliefs and practices in Africa since it is a continent with diverse ethnic groups and multiple cultural beliefs and practices. To that end, Africa's heterogeneous nature does not allow for a homogeneous theology that captures the plurality of the continent's primal traditions. Osadolor Imasogie pushes the point further, "Africa is a large continent with diverse peoples and cultures. In that case no one may be so presumptuous as to claim to describe African religions and worldviews in singular."[54] With this challenge in having a unified theme for African theology, Tiénou observes that the adjective "African" should be used to qualify "African Christian theology (or theologies) when one intends to treat issues related to the rooting of the Gospel message in African situations since as he believes, unanimity as to source and content would still be difficult to achieve."[55] Moreover, the antecedence to the emergence of African theology hinges on Africa's ancient past and this has helped to explain its most important features. Africa's past history is conveyed in the bias advanced against her by Western colonial anthropologists who first wrote about the continent from a purely Western scientific worldview, and cultural biases that denigrated African primal traditions and cultures. For example Okey Jude Uche quotes Pobee who in 1992 reportedly declared,

> The missionary practice of the *tabula rasa* was employed regularly in the mission field. This was the doctrine that there was nothing in the non-Christian culture upon which the Christian

---

52. Pobee, *Toward an African Theology,* 17.
53. Pobee, 17–18.
54. Imasogie, *Guidelines for Christian Theology,* 53.
55. Tiénou, *Theological Task,* 27.

missionary could build, and as a result every aspect of the traditional non-Christian culture must be destroyed before Christianity could be built up. It was even denied that Africans had religion; their religion was stigmatized as superstition or fetish or even magic (Pobee 1992:10).[56]

The denigration of African primal traditions and cultures provoked reactions from African theologians. The consequential effect of this development led ultimately to the birth of African theology, which is more of advocacy theology that came from the shared experiences of colonial domination and ecclesiastical denigration of the African race, cultures, and persons of the past. Thus, colonialism and imperialism alongside the African reality created the context that gave birth to African theology of which African ancestor Christology is standing taller by exploring a model for Jesus Christ from an African primal tradition to do Christian theology in African Christianity. Diane B. Stinton gives helpful insights by stating that respondents to her PhD research questionnaire articulated answers not only in the light of biblical revelation and Christian tradition but also regarding African realities both past and present.[57] It is true, therefore, that most of what is subsumed under the rubric of "African Christian theology" is the result of a reaction against cultural and ecclesiastical colonialism.[58] African theology is, therefore, the long search for an ideal method that seeks to integrate the Christian faith to the African needs, so that not only Christian theology but Jesus Christ as well may be relevant in the African soil of African traditional religion.[59] Of course, African theologians have long held that for the Jesus of Christian theology to be indeed at home in the continent; he must be domesticated and presented in the local concepts and categories of African pre-Christian

---

56. Uche, "Theological Analysis of Ikpu-Ala," 116.

57. Diane B. Stinton, *Jesus of Africa: Voices of Contemporary African Christology* (Nairobi: Paulines Publications Africa, 2004), 36.

58. Edward Fashole-Luke, ed., *Christianity in Independent Africa* (London: R. Collings, 1978), 364.

59. Samuel G. Kibicho, "The Continuity of the African Conception of God into and through Christianity: A Kikuyu Case Study," in *Christianity in Independent Africa*, ed. Edward Fashole-Luke (London: R. Collings, 1978), 371.

past since the question about him is usually answered contextually. Over time, some contexts have been able to make their answers normative."[60]

The brief overview of the history of African theology necessitates the conclusion that the history of African ancestor Christology cannot be successfully divorced from the history of African theological development. In a PhD dissertation, "Contextualizing the Christ-Event: A Christological Study of the Interpretations and Appropriations of Jesus in Nigerian Christianity," Victor Ifeanyi Ezigbo traces the evolution of African Christology from the 1950s but then concluded that it was John Taylor who, more than anyone else, in 1963 fanned into flames the African christological discourse.[61] History has shown therefore that what has become African theology today took its root in the 1950s when a conference was held in Accra, Ghana, in May 1955 with a concern to bring the African worldview seriously as we practise Christianity. In 1960 a Lutheran missionary to South Africa, Bengt Sundkler, argued that the church in Africa needs to interpret Christ regarding the African experience.

The outlook was when African theologians and biblical scholars saw the apparent need to carve out a befitting methodology that would cater to this quest. In 1971 Charles Nyamiti, a Tanzanian Catholic priest, postulated three methods of African Christian theology which he labelled as; "Pastoral," "Apologetical," and "Pedagogical."[62] Following in Nyamiti's footpaths, Fashole Luke, in 1974, proposed his theme for an African Christian theology and labelled it "ancestors." Luke's proposal culminated in the building and inauguration of an institute for ancestor veneration in East Africa.[63]

---

60. O. Samuel Nichols, "African Christian Theology and the Ancestors: Christology, Ecclesiology, Ethics and Their Implications beyond Africa," *Journal of African Christian Thought* 8, no. 1 (June 2005): 27.

61. For detail investigation into the history of African Christology, see Taylor, *Primal Vision*; Victor Ifeanyi Ezigbo, "Contextualizing the Christ-Event: A Christological Study of the Interpretations and Appropriations of Jesus in Nigerian Christianity," (PhD diss., University of Edinburgh, March 2008); Rosino Gibelini, ed., *Paths of African Theology* (Maryknoll: Orbis Books, 1994); Pobee, *Toward African Theology*; Fashole-Luke, *Christianity in Independent Africa*; Samuel O. Abogunrin, ed., *Decolonization of Biblical Interpretation in Africa* (Ibadan, Nigeria: Association for Biblical Studies, 2005); Valentin Dedji, *Reconstruction and Renewal in African Christian Theology* (Nairobi: Action, 2003); Tiénou, *Theological Task*.

62. Richard J. Gehman, *Doing African Christian Theology: An Evangelical Perspective* (Nairobi: Evangel, 1987), 52–53.

63. Gehman, *Doing African Christian Theology*, 41.

Gabriel Setiloane in 1979 asserted, "the next task of African theology is serious to grapple with the question of Christology–who is Jesus . . . what does Messiahship or Christos become in the African context?"[64]

Setiloane's argument positively impacted John Pobee as he maintained that "Our approach would be to look on Jesus as the Great and Greatest Ancestor-in Akan language *Nana*."[65] Similarly, in 1983, Abbé Marc Ntetem wrote, "Christ [as] the Ancestor *Par Excellence*" and discussed Christ's ancestorship vis-à-vis African rite of initiation.[66] His perspective of Christ inspired Charles Nyamiti's first work, *Christ as Our Ancestor* in 1984. A summary of his thought on Christ as African ancestor culminated in a three-volume work, *Studies in African Christian Theology: Jesus Christ, the Ancestor of Humankind: Methodological and Trinitarian Foundations*, volume 1–3.[67] Restating the thesis of African ancestor Christology in the work, *Jesus in African Christianity: Experimentation and Diversity in African Christology*, edited by J. N. K. Mugambi and Laurenti Megesa in an article in 2003 entitled, "African Christologies today" Charles Nyamiti posited that "Christ is Joto-Ancestor who is the source of life and the fulfilment of the cosmotheandric relationship in the world."[68] Furthermore, the fruit of Nyamiti's thought of Christ influenced many theologians, prominent among them is François Kabasélé whose work, *Christ as Ancestor and Elder Brother*, first appeared in 1986 as an article in French and was later translated into English. In this work, Kabasélé maintained that Jesus's words to Thomas in John 14:6 are reminiscent of Muntu's ancestors' last words but then held that being the child of God; Jesus is the Great Spirit ancestor whose death inaugurates a new equilibrium and new networks of communications among the vessels. To that end, Christ is the culmination of Bantu religious piety and mediation.

---

64. Nichols, "African Christian Theology," 27.

65. Pobee, *Toward an African Theology*, 94. Even though he saw Jesus as the great and greatest ancestor, such terms only portrays hierarchy in African ancestral realm without a true understanding of the ontological essence of Christ.

66. Ntetem, "Initiation, Traditional and Christian," 102.

67. Nyamiti, *Christ as Our Ancestor*; Nyamiti, *Studies in African Christian Theology*.

68. Charles Nyamiti, "African Christologies Today," in *Jesus in African Christianity: Experimentation and Diversity in African Christology*, 3rd ed., ed. J. N. K. Mugambi and Laurenti Magesa (Nairobi: Action, 2003), 19.

Most works that explore the African ancestor and other allied models were compressed in a PhD research conducted by Diane B. Stinton in 2004. In this work, Stinton notes, "Contemporary African Christologies represents a significant landmark in the development of African theology."[69]

Writing in 1995 and 2008, *Christianity in Africa: The Renewal of a Non-Western Religion, and Jesus and the Gospel in Africa: History and Experience*, Kwame Bediako states, "Once Jesus Christ comes, the ancestors are cut off as means of blessing, and we lay our power-line directly."[70] So, "Thus the gulf between the intense awareness of the existence of God and yet also of his 'remoteness' in African Traditional Religion is bridged in Christ."[71]

Since then, these approaches have continued to change in varying degree giving birth to the ancestor Christology debate which this work seeks to develop. All this goes to prove the fact that Africa, between the eigtheenth and twentieth centuries, has been subjected to the influence of unusually two western superpowers that changed the face of our continent dramatically: Western Christianity and European colonialism.[72] The wedding between colonialism and Western missionary endeavour is further attested to by Stephen Neill who argues that, "In West Africa, the progress of discovery and the establishment of Western domination went hand in hand."[73] In a somewhat poetic tone, Neil paints; "Where the explorer had penetrated, it was certain that the missionary would penetrate too; and the missionary would be followed by the trader and the trader by the government official."[74]

For Randee Ijatuyi-Morphé, colonization and slavery are just but two sides of the same coin, with the former being identical to Christianity. He opined that "colonization and slavery may be located in the religious/political world of early Christianity."[75] The link between colonialism and

---

69. Stinton, *Jesus of Africa*, 36.
70. Kwame Bediako, *Christianity in Africa: The Renewal of a Non-Western Religion* (Maryknoll, NY: Orbis Books, 1997), 217.
71. Kwame Bediako, *Jesus in Africa: The Christian Gospel in African History and Experience* (Akropong, Ghana: Regnum Africa, 2000), 25–26.
72. B. J. van der Walt, *The Liberating Message: A Christian Worldview for Africa* (Potchefstroom: University for Christian Higher Education, 1994), 5.
73. Stephen Neill, *A History of Christian Missions* (London: Penguin, 1990), 318.
74. Neill, *History of Christian Missions*, 320.
75. Randee Ijatuyi-Morphé, *Africa's Social and Religious Quest: A Comprehensive Survey and Analysis of the African Situation* (Jos, Nigeria: LogosQuest, 2011), 262.

the missionary movement is remarkably described by David J. Bosch who writes, "Colonial government and the missionaries were indeed ideal allies."[76] Elsewhere he claims, "Mission and Colonialism belong together."[77] J. A Oladunjoye echoes this thesis: "In the early phase of Western expansion the Churches were allies of the colonial process."[78] In the same vein A. Ngindu Mushete does not mince words, he notes, "Evangelization was carried out in tandem with colonisation."[79]

Because colonial domination and the Western missionary movement are a somewhat conjoined twin of the same stock, Neill further affirms; "Thus the Gospel and politics inextricably intertwined in Africa."[80]

In a dramatic portrayal of colonial activities, Yusufu Turaki states; "during the 18th and 19th centuries, European powers abandoned their coastal mercantile activities and imposed their colonising powers through military conquests in America, Africa, Asia, Middle East, Oceania and the Pacific Regions."[81] While the former had as its goal the evangelization of the African continent with the gospel of salvation in Christ, the latter had as its goal the exploration of the African continent and all the two movements came in at almost the same period in the nineteenth century.[82] The nineteenth century, reports Efe M. Ehioghae, marked the zenith of colonialism in Africa. It was this period that most parts of this continent were parcelled out by the European powers.[83] And what we have today as African theology is, in the

---

76. David J. Bosch, *Transforming Mission: Paradigm Shifts in Theology of Mission* (Maryknoll, NY: Orbis Books, 2009), 303.

77. Bosch, *Transforming Mission*, 306.

78. J. O. Oladunjoye, "Decolonizing Biblical Studies: An Opening Address," in *Decolonization of Biblical Interpretation in Africa*, ed. Samuel O. Abogunrin (Ibadan: NABIS, 2005), 4.

79. A. Ngindu Mushete, "An Overview of African Theology," in *Paths of African Theology*, ed. Rosino Gibellini (Maryknoll: Orbis Books, 1994), 11.

80. Neill, *History of Christian Missions*, 319.

81. Yusufu Turaki, *The Theory and Practice of Christian Missions in Africa: A Century of SIM/ECWA History and Legacy in Nigeria 1893-1993*, vol. 1 (Nairobi, Kenya: International Bible Society Africa, 1999), 23.

82. Yusufu Turaki, *Tribal Gods of Africa: Ethnicity, Racism, Tribalism and the Gospel of Christ* (Nairobi: Ethics, Peace and Justice Commission of the Association of Evangelicals, 1997), 78.

83. Efe M. Elioghae, "Decolonizing Jesus in Africa: A Critical Evaluation of the Missionary Influence," in *Decolonization of Biblical Interpretation in Africa*, ed. Samuel O. Abogunrin (Ibadan: NABIS, 2005), 309.

estimation of this writer, Africa's quest for identity as a response to imperialists' treatment of Africans during the colonial and missionary eras of the past.

Major African Schools of Thought on Christ's Ancestorship

This section explores and analyzes the Christologies of Abbé Marc Ntetem, Bénézet Bujo and Charles Nyamiti. The intention here is to test the validity of the inculturation methodology they employ to formulate ancestor Christology against the backdrop of Tertullian's and Athanasius's christological methodologies discussed in the next chapter. It is argued that no theology is Christian if it does not uphold accurate knowledge of God, the teaching of Jesus Christ about God and also the teaching of the apostles on God. As John S. Mbiti once remarked, "The final test for the validity and usefulness of any theological contribution is Jesus Christ. Since his Incarnation, Christian Theology ought properly to be Christology, for Theology falls or stands on how it understands, translates and interprets Jesus Christ at a given time, place and human situation."[84]

Mbiti's call for African Christian theological discourse to be grounded in the biblical concept of the incarnation has generated a positive response from some African theologians who have argued that one of the best ways to express and interpret the mystery of the incarnate God is through the cult of the ancestors. It is in this light that the section will examine how African theologians are handling the data the Christian Bible presents to them on the identity of Jesus Christ, from the vantage point of African ancestor cult before a conclusion is drawn.

I. Abbé Marc Ntetem – Christ the Ancestor par Excellence

Gwinyai H. Muzorewa argues that "Most African theologians who are involved in the development of an African theology find that African traditional religion is one of their chief sources."[85] In the traditional African religion, ancestors occupy a prominent place. "No ancestors, no traditional

---

84. John S. Mbiti, *New Testament Eschatology in an African Background: A Study of the Encounter Between New Testament and African Traditional Concepts* (Oxford: Oxford University Press, 1971), 190.

85. Muzorewa, *Origins and Development*, 7.

beliefs" is a common saying in some African societies. It is on the basis of that belief that Abbé Marc Ntetem predicates his Christology on the ancestorship of Jesus Christ using an analogy.

The Cameroon born Roman Catholic Priest, Abbé Marc Ntetem studied theology and ethnology in Germany. The heart of his argument on the ancestorship of Jesus Christ is found in his book, *Die Negroafrikanische Stammesinitiation*, 1983. An extract of that work is contained in an essay titled, "Initiation, Traditional and Christian," featured in, *A Reader in African Christian Theology*, edited by John Parrat, 2001.[86]

On the topic of his essay, "Initiation, Traditional and Christian," it is natural that Ntetem should trek the path of traditional African belief and worldview. He asserts, "acceptance of the Christian faith does not involve a complete break with African tradition, for it has its source in God, and thus finds its fulfilment in Christianity."[87] He adopts, like many other African theologians and biblical scholars, gap and fulfilment theory; one of the oldest apologetic tools that some African theologians employed to engage with the theological tension that emerges as they try to set out a theological meeting point for Christianity and indigenous religions.[88]

Ntetem's notion of continuity between African primal traditions and Christian faith, resonates with an earlier concern articulated by Edward Bolaji Idowu, who encouraged African Christians to carry with them into the Christian faith their pre-Christian religious heritage. Idowu posits that to be, "at home is, for the African to experience continuity between traditional life and the Christian faith."[89] In the same vein, Ntetem sees a good ground to formulate a theology around the African pre-Christian religious heritage particularly, the traditional cult of the ancestors. He maintains, "Jesus is an Ancestor *par excellence*,"[90] noting that, "When each *muntu* becomes converted by his assent to the faith, he acknowledges that the sovereignty of

---

86. Ntetem, "Initiation, Traditional and Religion," 99.
87. Ntetem, 99.
88. Ezigbo, *Re-Imagining African Christologies*, 26.
89. E. Bolaji Idowu, *Toward an Indigenous Church* quoted by Muzorewa in *Origins and Development*, 7.
90. Ntetem, "Initiation, Traditional and Religion," 100.

God has become a reality in Jesus Christ, who is the ancestor *par excellence*."[91] Once Jesus Christ's sovereignty is acknowledged as the supreme ancestor over *muntu*, a new affinity is established in which *muntu* is engrafted and "assured of a place in the coming kingdom since he is greater than the lineage ancestors."[92] The above reasoning for Ntetem is the hub and also "the real substance of conversion and the overall goal of mission."[93] Ntetem's methodology, like those of most of his contemporaries on the ancestorship of Jesus Christ, is novel and seeks to propel his steering on the wheels of "translating faith in Christ into a new cultural context, and thereby at the same time to interpret it anew."[94]

What exactly is Ntetem attempting to interpret anew in this context? His article, "Initiation, Traditional and Christian" unveils his main aim. Ntetem wishes to bath afresh, the African traditional rites of passage and initiation, in which the initiate undergoes the rigorous processes of circumcision, ritual washing etc., to become a full fletched member of, not only his peer group but also, of the entire community with the soap of Christian conversion whereby a repentant sinner undergoes the process of baptism and at baptism becomes a bonafide member of the church of Jesus Christ here on earth. He states, "If, through the Christianizing of tribal initiation, the essential identity of the Christian faith can be attained without losing its relevance, and at the same time relevance can be attained without the loss of its identity, then indeed the Christian faith will be seen as it really is."[95] What is it that the Christian faith is to him? Ntetem's voice here is not quite explicit and vocal. And one wonders whether he quickly realizes here that he runs the risk of syncretism. While one cannot be overtly dogmatic over this, it is however certain that he operates with a gap and fulfilment theory. For this reason, he continues, ". . . every reality which touches the life of *muntu* would be embraced in Jesus Christ, the ancestor *par excellence*, the one who transforms these realities from within, to make them vehicles of grace."[96] The

---

91. Ntetem, 100.
92. Ntetem, 100.
93. Ntetem, 100.
94. Ntetem, 100.
95. Ntetem, 101.
96. Ntetem, 101.

concern this work raises is whether Ntetem has forgotten that the apostle Paul does not believe that the traditional Jewish rite of circumcision is a means for a Jew to obtain the grace that leads ultimately to God's saving grace. In Galatians 3:26, for instance, Paul argues that "So in Christ Jesus you are all children of God through faith." If saving faith is what qualifies one to become a member of God's family, as Paul argued, and not the Jewish rite of circumcision, we wish to argue that the African rite of circumcision is not a good christological model to make Jesus relevant to Africans. After all, some societies in Africa do not practise circumcision for this model to be attractive to them. We wish to contend further that in Paul's estimation, keeping the traditional Jewish rites of initiation is a weak and miserable principle that enslaves (Gal 4:9). On physical circumcision, the apostle writes, "Neither circumcision nor uncircumcision means anything; what counts is the new creation" (Gal 6:15). If the apostle Paul does not uphold these rites as important vehicles to obtain grace, how could the rites of initiation avail *muntu* the grace to become a member of God's family? After all, Ntetem is quite aware that "The content of Christian salvation is, of course, different from salvation portrayed in such Bantu concepts and ideas. . ."[97] Ntetem also observes that "By contrast, the content of Christian salvation is Jesus Christ. The event of Jesus Christ has absolute primacy in the Christian message. The event of Jesus Christ and nothing else must be preached."[98] What form and shape should preach the event of Jesus Christ take in Africa and what are the valid means of presenting the gospel? Ntetem is blunt, " . . . it must be so presented that it finds a ready response in the hearers, that is, it must be comprehensible, using the ideas, symbols, conceptual values of the hearers; in short, it must be in their language."[99] For Ntetem, African worldview must dictate the tone and tempo in doing theology in the continent otherwise, as he believes, Christian theology in Africa will remain an alien tradition without deep rooting in the hearts and minds of Africans.

Ntetem finds the inspiration for his ancestor Christology permutation from his "paragon,"[100] as Tersur Aben puts it. Arthur Schopenhauer is re-

---

97. Ntetem, 102.
98. Ntetem, 102.
99. Ntetem, 102.
100. Aben, "Ntetem on the Ancestorship," 32.

ported saying, "In every translation, the spirit needs to receive a new body."[101] With Arthur's call for the insertion of a new spirit in the course of translation, a concept which meaning Ntetem denies us, he set out to pursue the same course. Hence, it is noted that "As the ancestor is the true master of initiation, so tribal initiation offers us a point of contact which makes clear to the believing *muntu* that Jesus Christ is the ancestor *par excellence*, and that he has received in the salvation which God gives through Jesus Christ a real and valid, indeed an ultimate, answer to his religious questions and his lost condition."[102] Ntetem has now transformed Arthur's notion of new spirit into the African traditional religious vocabulary of initiation. And with it, his ancestor christological crescendo moves to its climaxes in the following statement, "The new understanding of tribal initiation (that is, about Christian initiation) which results from this can lead us to a deeper understanding of what has been accomplished in Jesus Christ."[103]

We can infer from Ntetem's argument the appeal to African pre-Christian religious categories in which he locates Jesus Christ as master of initiation within the traditional cosmology the same way "the ancestor is the true master of initiation"[104] in some African societies. It seems to us that in Bantu traditional religious worldview, an initiation which is believed to have been performed by their ancestors is the knot that ties the society firmly together. As the religious life of the society revolves around the "position and function of the ancestor in Bantu tribal society,"[105] so Jesus Christ who is analogous to African ancestors should be seen as occupying the same status and also performing the role ancestors are known for among the Bantus. Ntetem believes that the Bantu Christian finds a sense of satisfaction and "true fulfilment" when Jesus is presented as his ancestor.[106] Thus, he finds it very necessary to designate Jesus Christ as "ancestor *par excellence*,"[107] so

---

101. Ntetem, "Initiation, Traditional and Religion," 102.
102. Ntetem, 102.
103. Ntetem, 102–103.
104. Ntetem, 102.
105. Ntetem, 102.
106. Ntetem, 102.
107. Ntetem, 102.

"that they (alien elements) may (be assimilated to) become part of the new wholeness of the life that is Jesus Christ."[108]

Like most of his contemporaries that propose Jesus Christ's ancestorship, Ntetem's Christology hinges on Christology from below, from the humanity of Jesus Christ. It is quite true that Matthew, Mark and Luke presented their Christologies from below, from the existential Jesus of Nazareth; this work argues that African theologians need to also take as their point of departure a high or Christology from above, from the metaphysical being of Jesus Christ the same way the apostle John started. As the case is, with most gap and fulfilment Christologies and also Christologies from below, it is a functional Christology articulated around the role ancestors are known to perform in the religious setting of ancient Bantu society. As Charles Sarpong Aye-Addo once said that John Pobee "engaged some Akan cultural and traditional sources in articulating his Christology,"[109] so, it is obvious that Ntetem also by the same token engages Bantu cultural and traditional sources to articulate his Christology. While we must admit that Ntetem has succeeded in contributing a significant comparative research that draws out elements within the Bantu culture that can contribute to an African Christology, we wish to conclude however that such an approach should be faithful to the Bible.[110] Notwithstanding the effort as Aye-Addo admits, "there are also several issues in his exploration that needs closer examination"[111] that are explored later in this research. At the moment we turn to the Christology of Bénézet Bujo.

---

108. Ntetem, 102.

109. Charles Sarpong Aye-addo, *Akan Christology: An Analysis of the Christologies of John Samuel Pobee and Kwame Bediako in Conversation with the Theology of Karl Barth* (Eugene, OR: Pickwick, 2013), 83.

110. Aye-addo raises the observation that although John Samuel Pobee has succeeded in presenting a significant comparative study of Jesus Christ in Africa thereby contributed immensely in strengthening African scholarship, there are however serious flaws that go with such a methodology. And we strongly believe that this is the general consensus of most theologians whose theological root is founded on the Nicene-Chalcedonian declarations of 325 AD and 451 AD respectively. For detail on Aye-addo's stance, see his work *Akan Christology*.

111. Aye-addo, *Akan Christology*, 83.

II. Bénézet Bujo – Christ the Proto-Ancestor

Bénézet Bujo is also a Roman Catholic theologian from Zaire. He studied in Europe and received his doctorate in moral theology from the University of Würzburg.[112] "As in much recent African Catholic theology, Bujo takes his point of departure from Vatican II's openness to other religions and cultures, which he sees as having special relevance in need of African theology to break away from its present Eurocentrism."[113] In addition to Vatican II's toleration of religious and cultural plurality and inclusivism, "modernity demands that the theologian interpret the Christian message in the light of the contemporary self-understanding of human existence."[114] Consequently, "African theologians are seeking to reinterpret biblical and historical Christological dogma in fresh categories that are both traditional African and at the same time relevant to the Africa of today."[115] To that end, there is today in Africa, an African metaphorical face of Jesus Christ represented among others in the thought of Bujo, whose work is concerned with inculturation. Inculturation in Africa, according to Bujo, has to do with what he calls "ancestral theology."[116] For Bujo, "The inculturation of Christianity, however, should not hide the social relevance of African tradition, but rather challenge the African person to

---

112. John Parratt, *Reinventing Christianity: African Theology Today* (Grand Rapids, MI: Eerdmans, 1995), 122.

113. The Vatican Council Article No 56 "Declaration on the Relation of the Church to non-Christian Religions" (Nostra aetate, 28 October, 1995) subsection 2 declares that
> Throughout history even to the present, there is found among different peoples a certain awareness of a hidden power, which lies behind the course of nature and the events of human life . . . This awareness and recognition results in a way of life that is imbued with a deep religious sense. . . . The religions which are found in more advanced civilizations endeavor by way of well-defined concepts and exact language . . . The Catholic Church rejects nothing of what is true and holy in these religions. The Church, therefore, urges her sons to enter with prudence and clarity into discussion and collaboration with members of other religions. Let Christians, while witnessing to their own faith and way of life acknowledge, preserve and encourage the spiritual and moral truths found among non-Christians, also their social life and culture.

This declaration on religious freedom and appreciation of the value of people's culture by Vatican II gave impetus to contemporary Catholic inculturation theology. Parrat, *Reinventing Christianity*, also made this same comment. See page @@122. For more details on Vatican II position on religious freedom, see Austin Flannery, ed., *Vatican Council II*, vol. 1, *The Conciliar and Post Conciliar Documents* (New Delhi: Rekha Printers, 2013), 653–654.

114. Imasogie, *Guidelines for Christian Theology in Africa*, 30.

115. Jern Henrik Olsen, "Contextualised Christology," 249.

116. Maina, *Historical and Social*, 90.

transform his/her world into a better place."[117] Bujo, therefore, pursues the course of inculturation vigorously, and he sees the African theologians and biblical scholars under the church saddled with this task, as a responsible propagator of the assignment. He notes, "The confidence that the common people demonstrate towards the Churches must urge the latter to pursue the process of inculturation which cannot be limited to the religious sphere but must penetrate all the areas of African life."[118] Based on his conviction that inculturation is ancestral theology; he begins, "In which way can Jesus Christ be an African among the Africans according to their own religious experience?"[119] Furthermore, Bujo opines, "This is the question which a truly African theology must solve. Christology thus understood and taken as a starting point will eventually lead towards a truly African ecclesiology where all the traditional charisms will be given their full rights."[120] Bujo's thesis is predicated on the belief that the "liberating and cultural aspects of theology must be wedded."[121] Therefore, is it necessary "for the African to rediscover roots, and it is to be hoped that this will enable him or her to relate ancestral religion to modern society."[122] The rediscovery of roots is, however, not a task to be taken for granted. For him, "Anyone who wants to construct an African theology must take the basic elements of the African tradition and interpret them in light of the Bible and the Fathers."[123] The fathers Bujo had in mind in this context remains veiled. He has failed to tell us whether the fathers in question are the fathers of the apostolic church or the progenitors of African society. His assertion seems to move from light to obscurity. He has saved the day, however when he rightly admits, "it has to be recognised that in the post-colonial era, many Africans no longer know their traditions. Many of the old African values are simply disappearing."[124] With this admittance that ancient African traditional values are no longer appreciated in modern times one would have expected Bujo, even in

---

117. Maina, 90.
118. Bujo, *African Theology*, 8.
119. Bujo, 9.
120. Bujo, 9.
121. Parratt, *Reinventing Christianity*, 122.
122. Parratt, 122.
123. Bujo, *African Theology*, 63.
124. Bujo, 63.

postmodern era Africa, to quit his ancestor Christology proposal quickly, but he went ahead to say, "African theology, it is plain, must be contextual, that is, it must take into full account the actual African situation."[125] His justification here is that "words, actions and rituals associated with the ancestors, and with the elders in general, have a deep meaning in the life of African people. They constitute a rule of conduct for the living, and they must be continually repeated."[126]

What Bujo is hinting at here is the African community-oriented life at the centre of which is the traditional religion. The cohesive nature of African society is tied firmly together around the religious belief bequeathed to descendants by their ancestors. John Parratt alludes to this when he asserts,

> In traditional society, religion was a force that bound together the community as a balanced whole. The wholeness of society depends upon the concept of life, which pervades the community . . . Bujo sees society as cohering using vital force that flows through that society as a kind of mystical bond.[127] . . . This divine life is conveyed to the living through the channel of the first ancestors of the family, clan, and tribe. . . . The ancestors have bequeathed to their descendants all their wisdom, including custom and law, which serves for the well-being of the society.[128]

It is little wonder that Bujo is so inclined to ancestor Christology since at the centre of ancient African traditional life and society stands conspicuously the ancestors who must not be displaced. African traditional religion then, upon which African theology is obviously standing, is no doubt, anthropocentric: it stands and falls on man.

Even though African primal traditions have been a little bent towards a belief in the supreme being who is acknowledged, as Maina quotes, "not only to transmit life through the elders and ancestors," but life in Africa is

---

125. Bujo, 65.
126. Bujo, 71.
127. Parratt, *Reinventing Christianity*, 123.
128. Parratt, 123.

"a participation in God."[129] This work argues that ancestors should not even metaphorically be considered as equal with the supreme being. The equation of African ancestors with God makes Bujo write that "When Africans honour the ancestors they are at least implicitly, also honouring God."[130]

An ancestor upon whom the society and its religious life are tied together is immeasurably, by this understanding, a divine conduit and invariably one of the channels through which God, as Bujo endeavoured to show, is reached. Above reaching God through the ancestor, Africans have always held that in the traditional society, life is meaningless without the vital force present in one's life, which is a function played out by the ancestor and through whom one feels belonging to the society in an indivisible communion with the mystical body. Bujo notes, "It is above all in the ancestor cults of Africa that we see how people envisage life, for it is above all here that they seek an increase of that life-force which flows through the mystical body to which both they and the ancestors belong."[131] Commenting on the primacy of the ancestral role in ancient African society, Parratt observed, "In such a model the role of the ancestors is of primary importance, and the ancestral cult is the special (though not the only one) place where the increase of the mystical body is sought."[132]

The primacy of African ancestral role has dual purposes; it is eschatological and salvific, covering in its entirety the ultimate goal of human religious piety and devotion. Notwithstanding this however, Africans are also concerned with the present life and the society within which they live. This makes for the living to covet reunion with the long departed ancestors in this earthly life through the oblation one offers. The offer of oblation does not only avail an African the opportunity to commune with the living-dead, as Mbiti calls them and the living-memories as I dubbed them, but it is by and large viewed as the only channel through and by which one's life takes its meaning, finds fulfillment and protection.[133] On the part of the departed

---

129. Maina, *Historical and Social*, 91.
130. Bujo, *African Theology*, 23.
131. Bujo, 23.
132. Parratt, *Reinventing Christianity*, 123–124.
133. John S. Mbiti, describes the living-dead as a person who is physically dead but alive in the memory of those who knew him in his life as well as being alive in the world of the spirits. Because the dead are alive in the memory of those who knew them, I therefore

ancestors, Bujo maintains that there is joy and happiness when they are remembered and celebrated. He writes, "The dead can only be happy when they live on in the affectionate remembrance of the living."[134] Additionally Bujo, quoting Hans Häselbarth, asserts that "the deceased takes part in the common meal, at which he is still accepted as a relative: the clan eats with its dead as well as with its living."[135]

The nature and manner of meal that the ancestors participate in it seems unclear to us, since it is not explicit whether it is the gathering together of a community to celebrate the life of the departed through a communal meal, or it is the coming together by the community eating in the actual physical participation of the deceased whose ghost makes its presence in company of the living during the communal meal. Whatever is it that has prompted Bujo to concede Häselbarth's postulate, it cannot be anything more than just trying to preserve the tradition of African fathers of the past. In fact Bujo himself admits,

> The present is enshrined in the traditions of the Fathers, but it is a past which still lives and is the guarantee of present salvation. Representation of the past in a kind of memorial calendar is no mere pious, ineffective remembrance but a necessary return to the source of life which is essential if men and women are to be able to take a decisive step forward.[136]

Obviously, Bujo's desire not to break with Africa's past is largely responsible for predicating ancestorship on Jesus Christ. Hence, he raises a whole lot of questions; "Would it not be possible to develop a theology . . . which is capable of integrating African culture, and out of which an African Christian ethic could be constructed? . . . could not the recognition of the place which the ancestors and elders occupy in the life of Africans stimulate theologians

---

call the dead the living-memories. For me, the nomenclature "living-dead" is a misnomer since the dead live only in memory and not in actual existential situation. Mbiti further argues that so long as the living-dead is thus remembered, they are in the state of *personal immortality* which is continued through procreation, so that the children bear the traits of their parents and progenitors. For more on Mbiti's notion of the living-dead, see his *African Religion and Philosophy*, 25.

134. Bujo, *African Theology*, 23.
135. Bujo, 24.
136. Bujo, 71.

to construct something new?"¹³⁷ it is possible, Bujo concludes. Thus, African new titles for Jesus Christ for him should hang on the pillar of, "Ancestor par Excellence, or Proto-Ancestor."¹³⁸

But what exactly does Jesus Christ as proto-ancestor mean according to Bujo? His attempt to respond to this question took him through the journey of human virtues. First, he feels that in Africa, some ancestors do not usually live good lives, enough to command the reverence of their living kith and kin. Accordingly, living relations of such bad ancestors who die without evidence of good reputation should allow their memories to go into extinction since, as he believes, their "earthly lives cannot serve to build up, or edify the clan or community."¹³⁹ Second, there is from within the same society, those ancestors who are always the epitome of not only good morals but are to be held in high esteem. Of such ancestors, Bujo writes,

> When we say that we want to use the concept of ancestor as the basis of Christology, we refer only to God-fear ancestors who exercise a good influence on their descendants by showing how the force which is life is to be used as God wishes it to be used. Only in the case of such ancestors can we speak of experiences and examples as truly a "last will and testament" left behind by the ancestors for the benefit of their descendants.¹⁴⁰

Bujo is convinced, as he held, unwaveringly;

> If we look back on the historical Jesus of Nazareth, we can see in him, not only one who lived the African ancestor-ideal in the highest degree but one who brought that idea to an altogether new fulfilment. Jesus worked miracles, healing the sick, opening the eyes of the blind, raising the dead to life. In short, he brought life, and life-force, in its fullness. He lived his mission for his fellow-humans in an altogether matchless way, and,

---

137. Bujo, 72.
138. Bujo, 72.
139. Bujo, 73.
140. Bujo, 73.

furthermore, left to his disciples, as his final commandment, the law of love.[141]

There can be no mistakehere; the direction Bujo is going, he is poised to represent Jesus Christ from traditional African belief on the ancestors who, at the point of death, usually leave behind a word for their family members and the entire clan. On this ground, he gives Jesus a look with African spectacles. As Parratt explains, "Bujo's Christology is securely rooted in the traditional concept of the ancestors."[142] As the good ancestors are believed to be an ideal prototype, so is it proper if Jesus Christ is modelled on them. Bujo affirms, "In his earthly life, Jesus manifested precisely all those qualities and virtues which Africans like to attribute to their ancestors and which lead them to invoke the ancestors in daily life . . . we can perceive the importance of Jesus for Africans regarding ancestor-theology."[143]

Bujo himself, however, has problem predicating ancestorship upon Jesus Christ. As he is certain, placing Jesus Christ in a literal sense along with the ancestors would amount to infringing upon his metaphysical nature as God. He quickly notes, "The term 'ancestor' can only be applied to Jesus in an analogical, or important way since to treat him otherwise would be to make of him only one founding ancestor among many."[144]

Bujo would have to go a step further in trying to look for the ideal mosaic of Jesus Christ that would suit the African context and also rhyme with his novel proposal. Whatever picture of Jesus Christ he comes up with, must, indeed, certainly contain something of the superiority of Jesus Christ's qualities over the normally accepted human standard. Jesus Christ cannot, therefore, be ancestor on par with other African ancestors in the normal sense of the word but "Proto-Ancestor." And he believes that this, "Signifies that Jesus did not only realise the authentic ideal of the God-fearing African ancestors but also infinitely transcended that ideal and brought it to new completion. No other ancestor can be thought of who was capable of such a complete and effective realisation of the ideal."[145]

---

141. Bujo, *73*.
142. Parratt, *Reinventing Christianity*, 128.
143. Bujo, *African Theology*, 74.
144. Bujo, 74.
145. Bujo, 74.

Does all this adequately and comprehensively capture and reflect the biblical data on the identity of Jesus Christ as presented by the evangelists, particularly the apostle John in the New Testament who sees Jesus as God become a man? Bujo feels that this becomes an all the more obvious reason why Jesus should be called proto-ancestor. He speaks, "It will be clear that giving the title of 'Proto-Ancestor' to Jesus Christ is no superficial or whimsical concession to the fashion of the day. It is no mere label, corresponding to nothing in reality. My proposal has to do rather with the very essence of the Word's becoming human."[146] Furthermore, Bujo is convinced that "If Jesus is Proto-Ancestor, the source of life and happiness, our task is to bring to realisation in our lives the memory of his passion, death and resurrection, making of that Saving Event the criterion for judging all human conduct."[147]

To sum up his argument, Bujo returns to the anthropocentric outlook of African society, and he uses this as the basis for the formulation of ancestor Christology. He states, "From all this, it follows that a reading of the gospel shows that the positive elements in African anthropocentrism are thoroughly endorsed in the person of Jesus Christ . . . When Africans narrate the deeds of Christ, they are acting in complete conformity with the biblical and Christian tradition."[148]

Apparently, Bujo has successfully made a significant contribution to African theology by presenting Jesus Christ using African cosmology and tradition as his point of departure. For this reason, we give credit to him for making inroads into the African christological discourse. He did, and his contribution is well appreciated. Before a further comment is made on his inculturation method, we would first consider the work of Charles Nyamiti on Christ the brother and greatest ancestor.

III. Charles Nyamiti – Christ the Brother and Greatest Ancestor

It seems to us that the presentation of the person and work of Jesus Christ from the framework of an African pre-Christian category of an ancestor would seriously be incomplete and undermined, without attention devoted

---

146. Bujo, 75.
147. Bujo, 80.
148. Bujo, 81.

to the insights of Charles Nyamiti on the identity of Christ. More than anyone else, Nyamiti has elaborately discussed the ancestorship of Christ. His underlying conviction is that "Christology is the subject which has been most developed in today's African theology."[149] It is only proper then, as he seems to say, to fittingly construct Christology from the perspective of ancestrology.

Born in 1931 into the family of *Mzee* (old man) Theophilus Chambi Chambigulu and Mama Helen Nyasolo, belonging to the Wanyamwezi of Tanzania, Nyamiti studied systematic/dogmatic theology and graduated with a PhD at Louvain University in Belgium. He also has a certificate in music theory and piano and a second PhD in cultural anthropology and music composition from Vienna.[150] Nyamiti is not only a prime mover and pacesetter in Christian theology; he is, as well, a prolific writer on African theology and also co-founder of the Roman Catholic University of Eastern Africa (CUEA).

The foundation of his theology could be gleaned from the anxiety exercised by some African theologians and biblical scholars concerning the encounter of Christian faith with African primal traditions. One such African biblical scholar, Jean-Marc Éla, expresses his fears this way; "How can we live and express our faith so that it becomes more than an alienating reflection of a foreign world which attacks our religious customs and belief?"[151] He continues, "How can we live our faith so it will not marginalise and discredit our ancestors?"[152]

Some of these questions and concerns are arising from the African preoccupation with the ancestral world and the fear of allowing the memories of the ancestors to go into extinction. As it is said, "In many traditional

---

149. Nyamiti, "African Christologies Today," in *Faces of Jesus*, 3. See also J. N .K. Mugambi and Laurenti Magesa, ed. *Jesus in African Christianity: Experimentation and Diversity in African Christology* (Nairobi: Action, 2003), 17.

150. Nyamiti's biodata is lifted in Patrick N. Wachege, "Charles Nyamiti: Vibrant Pioneer of Inculturated African Theology," in *African Theology: The Contribution of the Pioneers*, vol. 2, ed. Bénézet Bujo and Juvénal Ilunga Muya (Nairobi: Paulines Publications Africa, 2006), 149–151.

151. Jean-Marc Éla, *My Faith as an African* (Maryknoll: Orbis Books, 1989), 14.

152. Éla, *My Faith as an African*, 14.

societies, the cult of the dead is perhaps that aspect of culture to which the African is most attached – the heritage clung to above all else."[153]

What remains to be established is the method Nyamiti would formulate in articulating his theology. Like Ntetem and Bujo, Nyamiti is also on the bandwagon of gap and fulfilment theory using inculturation methodology and analogy to depict Jesus Christ. With the notion of inculturation, he set out to define African theology as, "The very self-same Catholic doctrine expressed and presented by African mentality and needs,"[154] while he defines inculturation as, "the effort to incarnate the Christian message in African culture."[155]

With these two definitions that serve as a bulwark to his thinking, Nyamiti persuasively shows how the ancestor motif is an ideal ally in the configuration of African Christology. Thus, in his great publication of 1984 dubbed, *Christ As Our Ancestor: Christology from an African Perspective*, he outlines two distinctive elements of ancestorship: ancestorship by progeny and ancestorship that is the consequence of death. And it is in this latter category, acquisition of which is contingent upon ones' "good life according to Africa moral standards that Jesus Christ perfectly fits in."[156] Furthermore, Jesus's ancestorship to us is "qualified by His divine sonship with us."[157] In addition to that Jesus Christ is as well our brother ancestor through the bond of consanguinity. Nyamiti believes that a brother ancestor is "a relative of a person with whom he has a common parent, and of whom he is a mediator to God, the archetype of behaviour and with whom – thanks to his supernatural status acquired through death – he is entitled to have regular sacred communication."[158] "If Christ is the Brother Ancestor (as Nyamiti concedes), then God the Father is also our Ancestor, our Parent ancestor. . . .

---

153. Éla, 14.

154. Charles Nyamiti, *African Theology: Its Nature, Problems and Methods*, Gaba Institute Pastorl Papers 19 (Kampala: Gaba Publications, 1971), 1.

155. Charles Nyamiti, "A Critical Assessment on Some Issues on Today's African Theology," *African Christian Studies* 5, no. 1 (1989): 10.

156. Nyamiti, *Christ as Our Ancestor*, 15.

157. Nyamiti, 16.

158. Nyamiti, 23.

But for Nyamiti, 'the Redeemer shines forth as THE Brother-Ancestor par excellence, of whom the African ancestors are but faint and poor images.'"[159]

It is to be noted that Nyamiti's notion of brother ancestor is also comprehensive extending from the terrestrial to the celestial where the saints in heaven and the dead in purgatory are intrinsic members of Christ's family.

At what point in time did Jesus Christ become our ancestor in Africa? Nyamiti posits, "we may say radically speaking Jesus became our Ancestor through the Incarnation at the moment of His conception in the womb of the Blessed Virgin. But like His Incarnation, His Ancestorship gradually grew and reached full maturity through His death and exaltation."[160] Nyamiti believes that the incarnation, death and exaltation position Jesus Christ at the centre of human history, and has, by so doing, made him a universal figure that defies national, tribal and ethnic boundaries. It is hardly surprising that he argues, "Through Incarnation, death and resurrection, Christ is at the centre of all history and is the accomplishment of the cosmotheandric relationship in the universe."[161] Nyamiti further contends that "Incarnation is the highest fulfilment of personality as understood by the African. For the African, to achieve personality is to become truly human and, in a sense, authentically Black; hence, the incarnate Logos is the Black Man *par excellence*. There is, therefore, no genuine blackness or negritude outside him."[162]

The climax of the incarnation is not, in the assertion of Nyamiti, only defined regarding the death and resurrection of Jesus Christ. Beyond those, and at the heart of it, lies ultimately its crux; that of Jesus's priestly mediation. Only through mediation does Jesus perfect his office as the high priest and thus is the redeemer and mediator of humankind. He has, having done this, become the ancestor of humankind and has successfully fulfilled the essential elements of his mission as ancestor-redeemer-mediator. Nyamiti notes, "all the essential elements of his redeeming Ancestorship were fundamentally present in him already at the moment of his carnal conception. Indeed, at that moment his Ancestorship was mediatory, royal, priestly,

---

159. Timothy Palmer, "Jesus Christ: Our Ancestor?" *TCNN Research Bulletin* 42 (2004): 6.
160. Nyamiti, *Christ as Our Ancestor*, 27.
161. Nyamiti, "African Christologies Today," in *Jesus in African Christianity*, 19.
162. Nyamiti, 20.

Adamite, protological and eschatological."[163] These, Nyamiti holds, "are particular aspects of the Redeemer's Ancestorship and of his Incarnation – especially when this latter is understood in the African holistic and dynamic sense . . . both Christ's Ancestorship and his Incarnation are indissolubly and immediately linked with the mystery of the Trinity, redemption, grace, Eucharist, the Church and parousia."[164] Due to the centrality of the doctrine of the incarnation, Harry Sawyer maintains that, "In the African situation the Incarnation should be so presented as to emphasize that Jesus Christ was the manifestation of God's love for man, God's share in human sufferings, God's victory over death and all the disastrous influences which throng man's everyday experience."[165]

While Nyamiti's conception of Jesus as the incarnate Logos has rightly captured the quintessence of his spiritual being, it is also quite obvious however that by articulating the stance that the incarnate Logos is the Black man par excellence, he is simply attempting to manufacture a Christ on the basis of African human race. It seems to us like that is the only legitimate way Nyamiti is saying that Jesus Christ could relate with and save us, and thus fits perfectly well into the black mentality of the Wanyamwezi and Wasukuma worldviews of Tanzania and Africa at large. Nyamiti wrote: "On account of His humanity Christ's Ancestorship is linked with Adam. This fact renders Christ . . . a member of our race,"[166] and one of us, to conclude through the enigmatic assumption of Adamic natures Nyamiti avers.

Essentially, Nyamiti argues that Jesus assumed humanity in the fashion of an African ancestor so that he could destroy the power of original sin in the African descendants of Adam. The position then qualifies Jesus Christ, as it were, for archetypal African man and he quotes the Cappadocian fathers against Apollinarius to prove his case. While Jesus has the power to remove original sin, it is, however, strictly speaking, only through the decisive efficacy of water baptism that original sin is ultimately removed whereby the

---

163. Charles Nyamiti, *Studies in African Christian Theology*, vol. 2, *Jesus Christ, the Ancestor of Humankind: An Essay on African Christology* (Nairobi: CUEA, 2006), 36.

164. Nyamiti, *Studies in African Christian Theology*, vol. 2, 72.

165. Harry Sawyerr, *Creative Evangelism: Toward a New Christian Encounter with Africa* (London: Lutterworth, 1968), 72.

166. Nyamiti, *Christ as Our Ancestor*, 27.

believing African is passively made to return to their pristine state. Revealing his traditional Roman Catholic position on original sin and water baptism, which is deeply shaped by St Augustine's doctrine of original sin, Nyamiti speaks, "It is through Baptism that original sin is removed in us and we regain our original innocence in Adam."[167]

Having dealt with the efficacy of water baptism in his 1984 publication, Nyamiti, in volume 2 of *Studies in African Christian Theology*, expands further the essential elements of Christ's mission as ancestor-redeemer-mediator to include his ancestral significance. Significantly Christ, in the word of Nyamiti, functions as "Prophet and Pastor."[168] As a prophet, Christ is as well not only a "teacher of all humankind who illumines our understanding by showing us the way to the truth."[169] But also, above all and quintessentially,

> he saves us from religious ignorance brought into the world by the deceit of the devil (Jn 8,44; Rom 1,18ff) . . . through his teaching our Saviour exercised his redemptive function because as Redeemer he was sent to destroy the work of Satan, and to free us from his slavery by bringing to us divine light which is Christ himself (Jn 8,12; see also Ps 119,105), the eschatological Mediator and our Brother-Ancestor.[170]

To this end, Nyamiti arrives at this conclusion, "Since Christ's Ancestorship is indissolubly linked with all his ancestral qualities . . ., then his identification with God's Word must be inseparably and immediately associated with the exercise, communication and revelation of all his ancestral characteristics to us."[171]

Nyamiti's next argument is particularly instructive as it revolves around Christ's pastoral ministry which he examines against the backdrop of his redemptive work as the Messiah. He argues that Christ is king over humankind through which he "'redeems' the human will by inculcating in it the demands of thedivine law in a spirit of obedience as opposed to thedisobedience-the

---

167. Nyamiti, 29.
168. Nyamiti, *Studies in African Christian Theology*, vol. 2, 72.
169. Nyamiti, 73.
170. Nyamiti, 73–4.
171. Nyamiti, 76.

root of all sin."[172] The preceding, in the contention of Nyamiti, is the only valid means through which Christ extends his kingdom to human beings and in this way also, humanity has a share in Christ's kingdom.[173]

What is the ultimate purpose of Christ's pastoral ministry? In his response, Nyamiti notes that "Christ's pastoral ministry was ultimately intended to re-establish the original unity between God and humankind by restoring the love of God and his kingdom in all men and women."[174] Nyamiti indubitably believes that restoration; "God's redemptive and life-giving rule over creation and human history"[175] through Jesus Christ, is intricately "linked with his ancestral characteristics,"[176] so that he, Christ,

> makes us – at the same time – sharers in his ancestral qualities of holiness and divine Descendancy (implying his supernatural kingship to us). By so doing, the Saviour also exercises his salvific mediatory functions; and this redemptive mediatory activity endows him with the basis for his right todemand our perpetual sacred encounter with him as our Saviour and king through ritual offering and prayer.[177]

For Nyamiti, Jesus's prophetic and pastoral functions are "particular dimensions of the Ancestorship and Incarnation of our Saviour."[178] And these functions, as he opines, "are immediately linked with the mysteries of redemption, Trinity, grace, Eucharist, the Church and eschatology."[179] Nyamiti believes that, "The implication is that, on account of their being particular dimensions of the Incarnation and Ancestorship of Jesus, his prophetic and pastoral offices must also be directly linked with those same mysteries."[180]

From the elucidation of Jesus's prophetic and pastoral functions, Nyamiti goes further to propose a correlation in function between the prophetic and

---

172. Nyamiti, 77.
173. Nyamiti, 77.
174. Nyamiti, 77–78.
175. Nyamiti, 78.
176. Nyamiti, 78.
177. Nyamiti, 79–80.
178. Nyamiti, 81.
179. Nyamiti, 81.
180. Nyamiti, 81.

pastoral offices and also the Trinity. So in the first volume of his *Studies in African Christian Theology*, he begins, "Is there an ancestral relationship with God?"[181] While he was not affirmative in responding to his question, he concedes the traditional Christian doctrine of the Godhead, and he uses the Trinitarian motif to formulate his ancestor Christology. But then he quickly asserts, "What we can say before-hand is that if ancestorship also applies to God in his inner life, this can be only in an *analogous* sense: with similarities and (many more) differences. For no human term or category can apply univocally to God and his creatures."[182]

Nyamiti's creative use of traditional African concepts to construct an ancestor Christology is highly commendable. However, his inculturation methodology, which employs analogy of proportionality to formulate Christology that portrays Jesus as being similar to African ancestors, seems to me to have failed to keep a clear distinction between the second person of the Trinity and African ancestors as the discrete judgment of my reader would have authenticated. Furthermore, even Thomas Aquinas the great luminary of the analogy exponent became dissatisfied with this method. In his discussion of univocity and equivocity, Aquinas rejects these concepts because, while univocity entails anthropomorphism, equivocity leads ultimately to agnosticism.[183] His dissatisfaction led him to embrace analogy of proportionality which he also rejected later since in his analogy, God is good and people are good he saw a huge gap between the goodness of God and the goodness of people. For this reason, he writes, "Goodness would mean something completely and totally different when applied to God, on the one hand, and then to people, on the other."[184] In addition to Aquinas's dissatisfaction with analogy, research has shown that the Roman Catholic inculturation methodology employed to formulate ancestor Christology in Africa is not suitable even among Roman Catholics. In a study of inculturation among Roman Catholic Igbos in Nigeria, Okey Jude Uche maintains

---

181. Nyamiti, *Studies in African Christian Theology*, vol. 1, 70.

182. Nyamiti, 70.

183. David K. Clark, *To Know and Love God: Method for Theology* (Wheaton, IL: Crossway, 2010), 389.

184. K. Scott Oliphint, *Reasons (for Faith): Philosophy in the Service of Theology* (Phillipsburg, NJ: P & R, 2006), 98.

that "inculturation has not been working because the discussions have been one-sided and the Igbo traditional religious rituals have not been treated with respect and accorded the dignity they deserve. The inculturation process in the Igbo Church has rather been a means of confrontation, condemnation, and intimidation."[185]

From the foregoing, inculturation as a theological method has further compounded the problem of appropriating Jesus Christ in Africa since, at best, it leads to confrontation, condemnation, and intimidation as Uche's research validates. It is critical we state however that Nyamiti's inculturation ancestor Christology is climaxed with his notion of ancestral Trinity. This he did by delving into five elements that defines the ancestral relationship with the Triune God.

First, Nyamiti rightly argues, strictly speaking that ancestorship in Africa is based on filial relationships. Thus, Africans do not accept anyone for ancestor other than their very blood relations or member of their clan. This family centred African community setting becomes the basis of a mystic relationship Nyamiti employs to illustrate the mutual coexistence of the divine persons in the Godhead. For him, God the "Father, being the parent, would be the Ancestor, and the Son would be his Descendant."[186] This scenario presents an incomplete picture of a family since there can be no family without at the same time having a mother. To make it comprehensive, Nyamiti maintains that the "Father is also . . . the Mother of the Logos in the immanent Trinity,"[187] this then completes the circle of the Trinity.

Second, Nyamiti considers what he calls "superhuman sacred status"[188] ancestor acquires at death through which he relates with his living kin. While death remains the only valid means, an African becomes an ancestor, God's ancestorship is intrinsic-based upon his divinity and holy nature which also characterizes the Son thereby giving rise to the "sacred and mystical relationship of divine Fatherhood and Sonship."[189]

---

185. Uche, "Theological Analysis of *Ikpu-Ala*," 286.
186. Nyamiti, *Studies in African Christian Theology*, vol. 1, 70.
187. Nyamiti, 70.
188. Nyamiti, 70.
189. Nyamiti, 70–71.

Third, was mediation, which for me is difficult to accept since theologically and even analogically the Son cannot be said to be inferior to demand the intercession of the Father, similar to Africa's perceived superiority assigned to the ancestor who mediates for his living kin. He confesses, "There is no mediation in God similar to the one ascribed to African ancestors. But this absence does not annul ancestorship in God."[190]

Fourth, Nyamiti explores the core African ethical system to argue regarding the archetypal African man. For him, as he would have us believe, "Just as the African ancestor is the exemplar or model of his descendants' conduct, so also is the Father the exemplar of his divine Son, who is his perfect image in being and activity."[191]

Nyamiti's fifth and final point, which he dubs as title to regular sacred communication, is contentious as argument surrounding it tends toward the debate of whether African ancestors are worshipped or venerated. While it can be argued that in some contexts, there is to a large extent a very thin line between ancestor worship and veneration in Africa, it must at the very outsetbe admitted that such arguments are beyond the scope of this chapter.

In a bid to demonstrate the right ancestors have to enjoy reverence from their living kin in Africa, Nyamiti reveals that oblation is offered along with ritual prayers as way of not only commemorating the memories of their deceased loved one, but also it is by and large a celebration of their functional lives while they were still here on earth. This love, so demonstrated, is reciprocated by the ancestor who is expected to be a benefactor. Nyamiti pointedly declares, "The ancestral prayers and ritual offerings are thus manifestations of the love, homage and thanksgiving of the descendants of their ancestor. For his part, the ancestor is expected to respond favourably to his descendants' petitions and rituals donations by bestowing them material and spiritual benefits as an expression of his ancestral faithfulness, love and gratitude."[192]

"Is there a similar kind of communication between the Father and the Son of the Trinity?"[193] Nyamiti is blunt. For him, there is the communica-

---

190. Nyamiti, 71.
191. Nyamiti, 71.
192. Nyamiti, 71.
193. Nyamiti, 71.

tion of being through begetting which takes place through the Holy Spirit who is jointly produced by the Father and the Son through spiration and communicate him to each other as an expression of their mutual love.[194] Furthermore, Nyamiti contends,

> By its very nature, perfect love implies that the lover gives himself totally and all that he possesses to his beloved. Consequently, the mutual love of the Father and the Son . . . involves the giving to each other of all that they are or possess and, hence also, the Spirit in as far as he belongs to each of them . . . the fruit and expression of their reciprocal love, and as such, he is also called Gift.[195]

Such gift of the Spirit, a gesture extended by the Father to the Son is motivated by the totality of the goodness of the latter. In this way, Nyamiti maintains, "The Father's pneumatic donation resembles the material and spiritual benefits which an African ancestor is supposed to bestow to his descendants as a grateful reward for their ritual offerings."[196]

Finally, Nyamiti also brings into the discussion the Filioque controversy of the fifth century that divided the Eastern and Western Churches in AD 1054 and gave an African face to it. Even though this controversy, as he asserts, has lingered for centuries, by making an African contribution to the rancour, he prides himself on the messianic task that would invariably bring healing to the rift. He speaks, "The schism can only be healed if we find a common answer to the question about the relationship of the Son to the Holy Spirit and of the Holy Spirit to the Son."[197] What is this common answer which once established would bring the schism to its terminal end? Nyamiti perceptively responded that since both parties engaged in the debate affirm ancestral relationship in the Trinity, it is therefore appropriate if they both view such affirmation as complementary. As he argues, "If the African ancestral kinship and its ceremonies are a replica of the ancestral life in the

---

194. Nyamiti, 71.
195. Nyamiti, 72.
196. Nyamiti, 73.
197. Nyamiti, 89.

Trinity, one is justified to look for analogies between the African ancestral ritual and the one which takes place in God's inner life."[198]

We have been able to establish from our investigation so far, the main ground upon which Ntetem, Bujo and Nyamiti situate their christological discourse. It is an appeal to the African ancestral cult through the method of inculturation to formulate theology. It is obvious to us that among the Bantu of Cameroon, the Bahema of Zaire and the Wanyanwezi of Tanzania, where they each held, an ivory tower ancestor Christology aptly speaks to their situation and the passion with which the enterprise is pursued speaks volume. "However, every image is bound to be partial, and a half-truth,"[199] and this provokes the probing questions: Can the analogy which they employed to demonstrate the mystery of the God-human sufficiently capture the ontological being of the incarnate *Logos*? Has the inculturation methodology helped in the evangelization of the Bantus, the Bahemas and the Wanyanwezis so much so that today when you speak of Jesus Christ as ancestor among them, they pause and think you speak the same language and share the same worldview as them? The answers to these questions are urgent and form the basis for the concluding part of this section of the research.

The Problem with the Ancestorship Emblem

Éla enquires, "Can the Church become the place in black Africa where communion with the ancestors is possible?"[200] He adds, "Is there any place in our life in Jesus Christ for maintaining a relationship between the living and the dead? Or must Africans break their relationship with their ancestors if they enter into a relationship with Christ?"[201] These questions, which have remained indelible in the minds of African theologians and biblical scholars, arose essentially out of the sincere concern that "Africa has been a recipient of many foreign images of Jesus Christ since the arrival of the Western European missionaries."[202]

---

198. Nyamiti, 91–92.
199. Aye-addo, *Akan Christology*, 82.
200. Éla, *My Faith as an African*, 14.
201. Éla, 18.
202. Nahashon W. Ndung'u and Philomena N. Mwaura, eds., *Challenges and Prospects of the Church in Africa: Theological Reflections of the 21st Century* (Nairobi: Paulines

Some of these concerns prompted Ntetem, Bujo and Nyamiti to propose an ancestor category in their Christologies. Unfortunately, as Tersur Aben once laments, "There is actually no title as 'ancestor *par excellence*' in African traditional religions, which we can then assign to Jesus Christ."[203] Also, neither does proto-ancestor nor brother and greatest ancestor exist in traditional African belief since such titles carry with them a sense of Jesus's superiority over African ancestors, which some non-Christian African communities will not accept to have an unknown stranger be superior over their respected ancestors. That aside, the biblical testimony of Jesus Christ is that God became human in the man Jesus of Nazareth and made his dwelling among us (John 1:14). "More precisely, Jesus Christ is believed to be both divine and human,"[204] and the event through which he intentionally reveals his identity to us is non-replicable. The writer of the Epistle to the Hebrews wrote: "But he has appeared once and for all at the culmination of the ages to do away with sin by the sacrifice of himself" (Heb 9:26b). The apostle Paul repeats a similar argument, "But when the set time had fully come, God sent his Son, born of a woman, born under the law, to redeem those under the law, that we might receive adoption to sonship" (Gal 4:4–5). We can rightly conclude on the basis of apostolic authority that the incarnation believed in Christendom to be the invasion of God into time and space is a mystery that analogy cannot adequately and satisfactorily explain. While Thomas F. Torrance confirms the notion of God's invasion of human history, D. M. Baillie validates the mysterious aspect of the incarnation. Thus Torrance says, "by the Incarnation Christian theology means that at a definite point in space and time the Son of God became a man, born at Bethlehem of Mary, a Virgin espoused to a man called Joseph."[205] For Baillie, "There is a sense in which the *mysterium Christi* must always remain a mystery . . . the Incarnation presents us indeed with the supreme paradox."[206]

Publications Africa, 2005), 102.

203. Aben, "Ntetem on the Ancestorship," 34.

204. Maina, *Historical and Social*, 105.

205. Paul D. Molnar, *Incarnation & Resurrection: Toward a Contemporary Understanding* (Grand Rapids, MI: Eerdmans, 2007), 88.

206. D. M. Baillie, *God Was in Christ: An Essay on the Incarnation and Atonement* (London: Faber and Faber, 1977), 106.

In view of biblical data, it becomes necessary to submit with Baillie that "When a New Testament writer tells us that 'there are one God and one Mediator between God and men,' he does not mean that the Mediator belongs to some intermediate type of being, for he goes on at once to describe the Mediator as 'a man, Christ Jesus.' Jesus was not something between God and man: He was God and Man."[207] Were the incarnation to be conceived literally as God being other than man, his comprehensiveness without at the same time having put on humanity would have been cloudy and in that sense deny humanity the knowledge of and access to him. On the contrary, the incarnation in the Gospels is "an attempt to interpret the birth narratives of Jesus in faithful, fresh way for our generation."[208] However, our doctrinal interpretation of Jesus's birth narratives must not only be derived from the Bible but also be faithful to it as its *principium* for Christian tradition. This work, therefore, argues that "Our doctrine must derive from the biblical text, and our understanding of any particular passage of Scripture must arise from the doctrine of the whole."[209]

The desire to faithfully interpret Scripture in keeping with the Christian tradition in the early church councils spurred Athanasius in defence of the divine essence of the *Logos*, to assert that the *Logos* is not a creature but is of one substance with the Father (Ὁμοούσιος τῷ πατρί).[210] "Ὁμοούσιος" which has been translated as "substance" in the English language is a borrowed term from Greek philosophy used by the council to solve the problem of the two natures in Christ, at the time of the debate since later, Nicaea or its term as Lewis Ayres puts it would become a hated terminology. For this reason, it was said, "Homoiousion, as it is called, there should be no mention of it whatever, nor should anyone preach it."[211] Furthermore, Ayres writes,

> Strong ambivalence to Nicaea, or a wish to ignore its terms, has turned to direct opposition . . . that resulted in the emergence

---

207. Baillie, *God Was in Christ*, 80.
208. Daniel M. Doriani, Philip Graham Ryken, and Ricahrd D. Philips, eds., *The Incarnation in the Gospels: Reformed Expository Commentary* (Phillipsburg, NJ: P & R, 2008), vii.
209. Doriani, Ryken and Philips, *Incarnation in the Gospels*, vii.
210. Young, *From Nicaea to Chalcedon*, 72.
211. Lewis Ayres, *Nicaea and Its Legacy: An Approach to Fourth-Century Trinitarian Theology* (Oxford: Oxford University Press, 2009), 138.

of "Homoian" theology . . . over the next two or three decades Homoian theologians come in different varieties but are united in their strong resistance to any theologies that see the commonality of essence between Father and Son.[212]

While it is true that in later time after the Nicene declaration the Homoian party arose and resisted the notion of commonality of essence between Father and Son, we must admit however that the Athanasian party presented the most biblically inclined of all positions in the debate. For this reason, I concede Maina's ardent stance that "the study of the person of Jesus Christ has to be based in the testimony of the Sacred Scriptures and the faith tradition in the Christian history."[213] For him, "Sacred Scripture is the 'soul' of Christology while philosophy and other disciplines are aides at analyzing the Christian message on Jesus Christ."[214] That aside, Athanasius himself tells us as Ayres reports that "the Word is the instrument of the Father's creative activity and the Lord of all creation, not part of it. The Son alone is from the Father . . . of the essence of the Father, that we might believe the Word to be other than the nature of things originate, being alone truly from God."[215] In light of this argument, Athanasius is quoted by Ayres saying, "A number of phrases were suggested at Nicaea to describe the status of the one who was truly from God: 'true power,' as 'exact image of the Father,' as 'in [the Father] without division,' and as 'existing everlastingly with the Father, as the radiance of light.'"[216] There are, for Athanasius as Ayres maintained, no qualities (συμβέβηκοι) in God and thus God's name and essence are not distinct. But, when we speak of God's essence we do no more than say that God is, we do not know what God is.[217] This led Athanasius to assert,

> For though to understand what the essence of God is be impossible, yet if we only understand that God is, and if Scripture indicates Him by means of these titles, we, with the intention of indicating Him and none else, call Him God and Father and

---

212. Ayres, *Nicaea and Its Legacy*, 138.
213. Maina, *Historical and Social*, 105.
214. Maina, 105.
215. Ayres, *Nicaea and Its Legacy*, 141.
216. Ayres, 141.
217. Ayres, 142.

Lord. When then He says, "I am that I am," and "I am the Lord God," or when Scripture says, "God," we understand nothing else by it but the intimation of His incomprehensible essence Itself, and that He is, who is spoken of.[218]

Athanasius's argument here culminates the debate and reveals in no uncertain terms the essence of the incarnation of the Son of God. The incarnate Word, as Athanasius is convinced, is the revelation of the invisible Father of humanity. For the above reason, "The humanity and divinity of Christ constitutes the complete revelation of the mystery of God"[219] and we wonder whether Ntetem, Bujo and Nyamiti predicate ancestorship upon Christ on the basis of Bible revelation to shed light on the mystery of the incarnation, or if they have simply succeeded in fabricating an African myth to complicate and thus explain away the theological meaning of the incarnation? Some Africans do know quite well that ancestor belief is not a mystery but a myth. Even if it is in a sense a mystery, we cannot use one mystery to explicate another. After all, there is a huge gap between mystery and myth as the two are not mutually inclusive. And no Christian who uses myth, which is a fiction, to explain the incarnation, remains a Christian recognizably.[220] Therefore as Maina argues, "I find ancestor Christology as complicating more the mystery of the Incarnation of Christ."[221]

Should Jesus be construed as the ancestor par excellence, proto-ancestor and brother and greatest ancestor as Ntetem, Bujo and Nyamiti have proposed?

Nyamiti, in particular, argues that Jesus assumed humanity in the fashion analogous to an African ancestor so that he could destroy the power of sin in the African descendants of Adam. But he admits using this emblem analogically to explain the mystery of the incarnation. Analogy, as we sincerely believe (see ch. 7) cannot sufficiently capture the whole essence of the Incarnation since it is only "applied to things that have some commonality

---

218. Ayres, 142.
219. Maina, *Historical and Social*, 105.
220. John Stott, *The Authentic Jesus: A Response to Current Skepticism in the Church* (London: Marshal Morgan & Scott, 1985), 10.
221. Maina, *Historical and Social*, 105.

between them,"²²² which in the case of Jesus Christ and African ancestors, the two are mutually exclusive. Another strong case that can be made against the use of analogy for Jesus and African ancestors is the fact that Scriptures depict Jesus Christ as God, the second person of the Godhead. The Jews understood this, yet killed Jesus on the ground that he

> arrogated deity to himself . . . We would, therefore, be acting in our epistemic rights if we grant that Jesus Christ is God unique and different from African ancestors. And if we grant that Jesus Christ is God, we cannot predicate ancestorship on God. African traditional religions never predicate the term ancestor of a deity, even in the Bantu religion, which Ntetem alludes to.²²³

Going by this argument, Jesus Christ is viewed more properly to a degree as an archetypal African man. While this approach may sound intelligible, it is to our mind, however, a going back to the very error the early church attempted to avoid, for this view is more inclined to Apollinarius's theology that "tried to make the incarnation intelligible by assuming an eternal tendency to the human in the *Logos* Himself as the archetypal man."²²⁴ However, it was this very theology of the incarnation that the Cappadocian Fathers sought to strengthen. Had Apollinarius got it right, the fourth-century Eastern theologian and the Archbishop of Constantinople Gregory of Nazianzus could not have insisted that;

> If anyone has put his trust in him as a man without a human mind, he is bereft of mind and quite unworthy of salvation. For that which he has not assumed, he has not healed, but that which is united to his Godhead is also saved. If only half Adam fell, then that which Christ assumes and saves may be half also; but if the whole of his nature fell, it must be united to the whole nature of Him that was begotten, and so be saved as a whole.²²⁵

---

222. Aben, "Ntetem on the Ancestorship," 37.

223. Aben, 37.

224. Louis Berkhof, *The History of Christian Doctrines* (Carlisle, PA: Banner of Truth, 2002), 103.

225. For detailed discussion of Gregory Nazianzus's letters to Cledonius against Apollinarius, see Edward R. Hardy, ed., *Christology of the Later Fathers*, Library of Christian Classics, (Louisville: Westminster John Knox, 1954); Bettenson, *Documents of the Christian*

Gregory of Nazianzus advanced this argument against Apollinarius because he perceived an imminent peril capable of misleading the church of his day in this theological construction.[226] It is essential we conclude that as we do theology in Africa, we should be cautious of how we theologize, lest we become victims of the very thing which the early church was out to correct in the name of interpreting the sacred Scriptures; namely and sincerely speaking, heresy. After all, the incarnation "was certainly not something that could be understood as the supreme form of a theology of the symbol."[227] The incarnate God cannot be brought into connexion with creatures to warrant comparison with the so called living-dead of ancient African societies.

Summary

The African ancestor model is very much akin to Karl Rahner's ontology of symbol that tended to interpret the incarnation as a symbol of God and not God in a real existential sense or his real ontological being. This argument is justifiable since using ancestor analogically for Jesus Christ does not make him consanguineously an African ancestor in real biological and existential terms. Of course, when Rahner saw the incarnation as the symbol and not God, he was vehemently refuted by Karl Barth. For this reason, I concede Karl Barth's refutation of Karl Rahner's ontology of the symbol since the latter held that "The incarnate word is the absolute symbol of God in the world, filed as nothing can be with what is symbolised . . . He is the expressive presence of what – or rather, who – God wished to be, in free grace, to the world."[228] For Karl Barth, the incarnation "was certainly not something that could be understood as the supreme form of a theology of the symbol."[229] God's "becoming cannot be brought into connexion with creation. It cannot

---

Church, 44; Alister E. McGrath, *The Christian Theology Reader*, 3rd ed. (Malden, MA: Blackwell, 2009), 268–270; Philip Schaff and Henry Wace, eds., *A Select Library of Nicene and Post- Nicene Fathers of the Christian Church*, second series, vol. 7 (Grand Rapids, MI: Eerdmans, 1983), 437–445.

226. McGrath, *Christian Theology Reader*, 270.
227. Molnar, *Incarnation & Resurrection*, 2.
228. Karl Rahner, *Foundations of Christian Faith: An Introduction to the Idea of Christianity* (New York: Seabury Press, 1978), 127–130. See also Molnar, *Incarnation & Resurrection*, 53.
229. Molnar, *Incarnation & Resurrection*, 2.

be regarded as one of its evolutionary possibilities . . . God's Word becoming a creature must be regarded as a new creation . . . it is a sovereign divine act, and it is an act of lordship different from creation."[230]

Karl Rahner seemed to have found his inspiration for the theology of ontology of the symbol from two sects: Ebionitism and Docetism that were held to be heretical sects in the early church. Karl Barth provides us with helpful information on this explicitly, "According to the former [Ebonite's position], He [Jesus] is the supreme manifestation of human life . . . while according to the latter (Docetism), He (Jesus) is a perfect symbol of divine presence."[231] Armed with these views, Rahner articulated the stance that the incarnation is nothing more than the absolute symbol of God but not the real God in real ontological being the second person of the Trinity. In the light of Karl Barth's position, African theologians should not, therefore, be apt to interpret the incarnation in terms of the "diminution of the divinity of God but a concealment of it and all for the sake of his mercy toward us."[232]

There is no gain saying, however, that Ntetem, Bujo, and Nyamiti have succeeded in breaking some grounds in formulating Christology from an African context. Indeed, they have made a significant contribution to the study of Christ by employing an analogy to compare Jesus Christ with African ancestors through the inculturation methodology. For this, they deserve some recognition. But they seemed to forget too soon that Aquinas himself who invented the notion of univocity, equivocity and analogy of proportionality argued that God cannot be compared with human beings proportionally. Furthermore, recent research has revealed that the inculturation method used to formulate ancestor Christology in Africa has failed as Uche's work demonstrated. Ntetem, Bujo and Nyamiti also need not forget that "Africans make a distinction between Deity, the divinities, and the ancestors: Deity and the divinities are distinct, out-and-out, of the supersensible world, while the ancestors are of the living persons' kith and kin."[233] The inculturation methodology which has a bearing on the ancestor concept

---

230. Molnar, 2.

231. Karl Barth, *Church Dogmatics*, vol. 1, *The Doctrine of the Word of God* (Edinburgh: T & T Clark, 1999), 403.

232. Molnar, *Incarnation & Resurrection*, 2.

233. Idowu, *African Traditional Religion*, 184.

of Christ drew its inspiration from the gap and fulfilment theory and is not suitable for African theological discourse. It introduces Jesus as the only one who can bring, to a total fulfilment, the religious aspirations of Africans, which they struggle to fulfil through some indigenous religious ways particularly the ancestor model.[234]

This work reasons, however, that if ancestors are only of one's kith and kin, Jesus cannot be absorbed or be incorporated into any African family since he belongs to a different ontological set as divinity. To call Jesus an ancestor, therefore, does not only threaten his deity but is as well a gross violation of his metaphysical nature as the *Logos* incarnate: the Second Person of the Trinity who became fully human without mixture, without division and without confusion as Chalcedon declared. "It is to the one single essence of God, which is not to be tripled by the doctrine of the Trinity (as African theologians posit), but emphatically to be recognized in its unity, that there also belongs what we call today the 'personality' of God."[235] As Barth also emphasizes, "God is a person in a way quite different from that in which we are persons."[236] African theologians must learn to avoid the mistake of the past which tended "to sharpen the distinction between the persons of the Trinity and to go farther than theology has been accustomed to go in the direction of regarding them as distinct personal beings between whom there can be a 'social' relationship."[237]

The relationship that subsists in the Trinity between the Father, Son and Holy Spirit is not a relationship of mode and mortals but an ontological hierarchy of the one God who exists as Father, Son and Holy Spirit. For this reason, this work contends that using an analogy to compare God with mere mortals, with whom he does not share the same body chemistry, is not good enough to fathom the mystery of the incarnation. We must stop "trying a theological revival of the concept of an ancestor in Christian theology."[238] Africans have a better name for Jesus Christ that defines his

---

234. Ezigbo, *Re-Imagining African Christologies*, 27.

235. Baillie, *God was in Christ*, 136.

236. Baillie, 136.

237. Baillie, 137.

238. Liboire Kagabo, "Alexis Kagame: The Trail of an African Theology," in *African Theology in the 21st Century: The Contribution of the Pioneers*, vol. 2, eds. Bénézet Bujo and Juvénal Ilunga Muya (Nairobi: Paulines Publications Africa, 2006), 36.

ontological being and salvific work: he is known in almost all African societies as *Jesu/Yesu*, and it is this name which authenticates his person that this study proposes as acceptable nomenclature for the formulation of relevant contextual and contemporary Christology in the continent. For this reason, this book proposes an African Linguistic Affinity Christology methodology which identifies Jesus as *Yesu* or *Jesu* for twenty-first-century Sub-Saharan Africa rather than the inculturation model, since current trends within the Roman Catholic Church see inculturation as a European manufactured ideology not suited to African Christians to formulate theology at the grassroots. Okey Jude Uche has shown that in a study organized on inculturation, in 1988, and in the proceedings published in 1989, it was highlighted not only that something is wrong with the present state of theology, but also that the Europeans cannot make the "theological diagnosis" because they may not appreciate the depth of what went wrong. They are the ones who inflicted the wound on African theology. In the Nigerian church hierarchy, Uche holds that inculturation does not yet seem to be something urgent. For this reason, the church refused to recognize the fact that inculturation is first and foremost a matter for Africans, and that to bring in Europeans is to return to the mistake of the missionary past. Sadly, Uche laments that even after the Synod on Africa of 1994, on the inculturation issue, the status quo has remained the same.[239]

Had inculturation as a theological method provided a tangible and qualitative forum for meaningful engagement between African primal beliefs and Christian theology, the present state of the church in Africa would have been far better than what it is. Unfortunately, Uche laments, "The Nigerian Church has remained a toothless bulldog of Africa in terms of inculturation and has continued to brook no compromise with the local Igbo cultures."[240] Uche's arguments demand that the proponents of the inculturation model need to look elsewhere for a suitable theological method that will fittingly meet the twenty-first-century Sub-Saharan African theological need; since inculturation as a theological method can only lead to a theological anaemia in the continent, at best.

---

239. Uche, "Theological Analysis of *Ikpu-Ala*."
240. Uche.

CHAPTER 3

Historical and Theological Foundations of Christology: Conversing with the Christologies of Tertullian and Athanasius

Introduction

The New Testament is the primary source of the life, person and work of our Lord and saviour Jesus Christ. John Stott wrote, "Our knowledge of Jesus of Nazareth comes almost entirely from the New Testament."[1] In Paul W. Barnett's view, "The New Testament provides our major sources for any inquiry into Jesus and early Christianity."[2] Tim Dowley notes however that "The main sources about Jesus are the four Gospels."[3] While I agree with Dowley that the four Gospels play a vital role in the church's knowledge of Jesus Christ, it is to be remembered however that the Epistles of the apostle Paul also present a vivid picture of the life, person and work of Jesus Christ.[4]

While we concede the fact that the primary Christian source document for meaningful theological engagement and investigation into the life and person of Jesus Christ is the New Testament, this study also argues that the

---

1. Stott, *Authentic Jesus*, 19.
2. Paul W. Barnett, *Jesus and the Logic of History* (Downers Grove, IL: InterVarsity Press, 2000), 39.
3. Tim Dowley, ed., *Introduction to the History of Christianity* (Minneapolis, MN: Fortress, 2013), 26.
4. Robert A. Krieg, *Story-Shaped Christology: The Role of Narratives in Identifying Jesus Christ* (New York: Paulist Press, 1988), 88.

Hebrew Bible, commonly known as the Old Testament, is a cardinal source document and foundational historical source for the Christ event, since Christian theology acknowledges that the New Testament fulfills the Old Testament. Irving L. Jensen persuasively states,

> Both Old and New Testaments make up the inspired Scriptures. The New Testament was never intended to replace the Old Testament. Instead, the New was given to complement the Old, to complete its story. For example, the Old prophesies the coming of the Redeemer; the New reports the fulfilment of that prophecy in Jesus. The New Testament is the sequel to the Old Testament's origins, heir of its promises. Fruit of its seed, the peak of its mountain.[5]

Jensen further makes a passionate claim that, "the ministry of Christ would be an enigma without the Old Testament."[6] The above claim is valid, for that reason this study contends that both Testaments are critical foundational sources for Christian faith and practice. It is pertinent, I state, therefore, that what the apostles confessed and taught in the New Testament has its bearings and foundation in the Old. In fulfilment of the Old Testament prophecies, the apostles confessed and proclaimed in the New Testament that Jesus the Christ exists (Col 1:17; 1 John 1:1) and that he is Lord (Matt 14: 28a, 30c; Phil 2:10–11). Bernard L. Ramm is right to aver, "To believe in the Christology of these creeds is also to say that one believes in the Christology of the New Testament."[7] Bart D. Ehrman says it plausibly, "The Gospels, their sources, and the oral traditions that lie behind them combine to make a convincing case that Jesus existed."[8] The fact of Jesus's existence, which rests on the testimony of Scripture itself (Acts 1:3), together with the writings of the apostles gave the early church a strong foundation of Christian faith

---

5. Irving L. Jensen, *Jensen's Survey of the Old Testament* (Chicago, IL: Moody, 1978), 15.

6. Jensen, *Jensen's Survey*, 15.

7. Brenard L. Ramm, *An Evangelical Christology: Ecumenic & Historic* (Nashville, TN: Nelson, 1985), 16.

8. Bart D. Ehrman, *Did Jesus Exist?: The Historical Argument for Jesus of Nazareth* (New York: HarperOne, 2013), 70.

since the authority of the apostles, the architects and heralds of the truth, was essential to Christianity's survival in the infant church.[9]

Since this chapter is set to present the historical and theological foundations of Christology, it is essential that ample and sufficient historical and theological sources are examined here with a view to not only substantiating the argument of the chapter but also to state also that citing pertinent sources that deal with the history of Christian theology will further enrich and tighten the chapter. Our basic contention is that Christian theology is an ongoing engagement of the Bible with context. The above standpoint explains why building upon the foundation already laid by the apostles, the early church fathers and apologists, formulated concepts from their sociocultural milieu that became the canon of traditional Christian theology. John Macquarrie affirmed, "From the very beginning, the Church's attempt to express its beliefs concerning Jesus Christ have been coughed in the language and ideas of whatever the prevailing culture happened to be."[10] To put it more plainly, Walter Kasper forthrightly states this conviction that, "the New Testament was delivered to us as a canon, that is, as a permanently normative original witness, by the Church of the early centuries. The interpretation of the Christ event by the early Church was decisive in the selection of the canonical scripture. That interpretation has remained valid for all the historical Churches up till now."[11] Similarly, Roch A. Kereszty posited, "The documents taken into the New Testament canon were those in which the Church recognised an authentic apostolic witness to Christ."[12]

While it seems conclusive that there is avowal agreement, from the theologians and biblical scholars briefly examined above, that the data presented about Jesus Christ in the New Testament is cardinal for theological investigation into the life, person and works of Jesus Christ, J. N. D. Kelly, with whom I concur as I demonstrate above, tends to see a lacuna in strictly limiting the origin of the life, person and works of Jesus Christ to apostolic

---

9. Jaroslav Pelikan, *The Christian Tradition: A History of the Development of Doctrine*, vol. 2, *The Spirit of Eastern Christendom (600-1700)* (London: University of Chicago Press, 1977), 16.

10. John Macquarrie, *Christology Revisited* (London: SCM, 1998), 11.

11. Walter Kasper, *Jesus the Christ*, new ed. (New York: T & T Clark, 2011), xiii.

12. Roch A. Kereszty, *Jesus Christ: Fundamentals of Christology*, rev. and updated 3rd ed. (New York: St Paul, 2011), 22.

witness presented in the New Testament era. For him, there is some precedence beyond the New Testament. Since, as he believes, the New Testament is standing on the pillar of the Old Testament, a better place to track down the origin of reference about Jesus Christ is to be found in God himself. From God, we can take a walk up into the New Testament dispensation, which rather than being the foundation is the climax of God's salvific programme. He argues, "God Himself, all the early theologians acknowledged, was the ultimate author of the revelation, but He had committed it to prophets and inspired lawgivers, above all to the apostles who were eye-witnesses of the incarnate Word, and they had passed it on to the Church."[13] Christopher J. H. Wright and Richard Bauckham each also believe that fundamental to New Testament witness on Jesus Christ is the Old Testament. Wright states his thesis,

> The Old Testament tells its story . . . as a part of that ultimate and universal story that will ultimately embrace the whole of creation, time and humanity within its scope . . . in Jesus, we have the climax of this story . . . this story is also our story . . . now the reality of this story is such that it includes us in its scope, for it points to a universal future that embraces all the nations. It is the story that is taken up in the New Testament.[14]

Viewing the story from his own periscope, Bauckham traces God's dealing with mankind from the perspective of his promise to Abraham in Genesis 12 (see ch. 6) to Jesus's commission of the apostles in Acts 1:8, "where the mission of witness moves out from Jerusalem, initially to Judea and Samaria, finally to the ends of the earth."[15] Justo L. Gonzalez casts a new light on this as he moves a step further with his remarkable statement that "From its very beginning Christianity has existed as the message of the God who 'so

---

13. J. N. D. Kelly, *Early Christian Doctrines*, 5th edition (London: Continuum, 2007), 29–30.

14. Christopher J. H. Wright, *The Mission of God: Unlocking the Bible's grand narrative* (Downers Grove, IL: InterVarsity Press, 2006), 55, 58.

15. Richard Bauckham, *The Bible and Mission: Christian Witness in a Postmodern World* (Carlisle, Cumbria: Paternoster, 2003), 28–29, 66.

loved the world' as to become part of it . . . it [Christianity] is the presence of God in the world received and passed by the apostles."[16]

For the purpose of this chapter, we intend to locate the trajectory of Christian theology and Christology in the apostolic era as a frame of reference to the present African ancestor christological discourse since it is the apostles who are the first human witnesses of the Christ event in Christian history and have left for us the records of their experiences with Jesus Christ. To succeed in this endeavour we employ a historical method which describes, reviews and analyzes past events written in a spirit of critical inquiry for the whole truth.[17]

In the investigation of relevant historical and evangelical theological data on the humanity and deity of Jesus Christ, this work argues that the witness of the apostles who were essentially the primary eye-witnesses of the Christ event is necessary for this research work. Richard Bauckham in his, *Jesus and the Eyewitnesses: The Gospels as Eyewitness Testimony* argues that "The Gospels were written within living memory of the events they recount since as he believes they embody eyewitness testimony . . . to the whole course of Jesus' story."[18] True as Bauckham's claim is, we cannot strictly limit the record of Jesus's life and work to the witness and testimony of the Gospels alone since the apostle Pauline had written his Epistles before the Gospels were written. In any case, it is important, we concur with David S. Dockery and Timothy George, that "The history of Christianity is best understood as a chain of memory."[19] The bold assertions of the apostles and apologists, who wrote and confessed that Jesus is the Christ (Mark 8:27c; Luke 9:20; John 20:31),[20] are an object of faith and salvation that lay the foundation

---

16. Justo L. Gonzalez, *A History of Christian Thought*, vol. 1, *From the Beginnings to the Council of Chalcedon*, rev. ed. (Nashville, TN: Abingdon, 1987), 29.

17. Osuala, *Introduction to Research*, 162.

18. Richard Bauckham, *Jesus and the Eyewitnesses: The Gospels as Eyewitness Testimony* (Grand Rapids, MI: Eerdmans, 2006), 7, 114.

19. David S. Dockery and Timothy George, eds., *The Great Tradition of Christian Thinking: A Student's Guide* (Wheaton, IL: Crossway, 2012), 23.

20. The apologists did not hesitate in their resolved and confession that Jesus is the Christ but held unswervingly to the belief in Jesus as Lord and fashioner of all designs. For more on the apologists' christological confession see, William Edgar and K. Scott Oliphint, eds., *Christian Apologetics Past and Present: A Primary Source Reader, vol. 1 to 1500* (Wheaton, IL: Crossway, 2009), 41.

and authority for orthodox evangelical christological articulation. On his prescription against heretics Tertullian writes, "In the Lord's apostles we possess our authority; for even they did not of themselves choose to introduce anything, but faithfully delivered to the nations (of mankind) the doctrine which they had received from Christ."[21] It is this conviction first articulated by the evangelists, whose writings are part of Christian Scripture and the testimony derived from them, that Scripture cannot be broken (John 10:35) that forms the hub of and fabric of evangelical Christian faith. This faith articulated by the evangelists who wrote the Holy Scriptures is

> the fact that Jesus was known to be alive "by many infallible proofs" (Acts 1:3) [and such faith] suddenly transformed hope into certainty. He had been seen to die by reliable witnesses. He had equally clearly been seen to be alive . . . it is not too much to say that the resurrection of Jesus was an event which filled the minds of the disciples from the first moment when it was reported.[22]

And "the mark of a Christian in the early Church was that he was prepared to confess his faith in the words 'Jesus [Christ] is Lord' (Rom 10:9; 1 Cor 12:3; Phil 2:11)."[23] This confession was to mark one out as being separated from and independent of any association with heretical groups and heterodox sects that existed in the ancient world in which the church was born. One's evidence of belonging to and being united in faith and practice with the body of Christ in the early church was to willingly and publicly declare that Jesus is Lord or our Lord (Rom 5:1; 8:39; Jas 1:1; 1 Pet 1:3). In fact, the desire to be distinct from any anti-christian and heterodox sects the church named itself the apostolic and catholic church since during this time it has acquired universal proportion. Gonzalez makes this point vividly, "To separate itself from the various heretical groups and sects, the ancient Church began calling itself 'Catholic.' This title underscored both its universality

---

21. Alexander Roberts and James Donaldson, eds., *The Ante-Nicene Fathers: Translation of the Writings of the Fathers Down to A.D. 325*, vol. 3, *Latin Christianity: Its Founder, Tertullian* (Grand Rapids, MI: Eerdmans, 1980), 246.

22. I. Howard Marshall, *The Work of Christ* (Devon: Paternoster, 1969), 45.

23. I. Howard Marshall, *The Origin of New Testament Christology* (Downers Grove, IL: InterVarsity Press, 1990), 97.

Historical and Theological Foundations of Christology

and the inclusiveness of the witness on which it stood. It was the Church 'according to the whole.'"[24]

From the point that the church became universal there arose also from within her spiritual threats from Gnostics and Montanists which created a crisis of identity in the Christian faith.[25] It begins to look plausible that the apostle Paul seemed to have sensed an incipient and dangerous invasion into the church by heterodox sects when he wrote in 1 Corinthians 3:10–11, "By the grace God has given me, I laid a foundation as wise builder, and someone else is building on it. But each one should build with care. For no-one can lay any foundation other than the one already laid, which is Jesus Christ." The apostle John, who was passionate on the value of remaining within the confine of apostolic tradition and teaching warned, "see that what you have heard from the beginning remains in you. If it does, you also will remain in the Son and in the Father" (1 John 2:24).

From the apostolic age down through the centuries, Christian theology, mainly Christology, has gone through series of modifications with the aim to adapt to the host cultures. This attempt marked the beginning of modern and postmodern christological motifs most, if not all of which, lay claim to apostolic origin. In Africa, ancestor Christology is one of the dominant postmodern christological models articulated by African theologians. Most of these theologians claim that their ancestor Christology models are grounded in New Testament roots, apostolic tradition, and the early church's teaching on the humanity and deity of Jesus Christ. Their primary argument is that "Christian theology is incarnational."[26] African theology "must, therefore, be informed by the contextual milieu of its target audience in such a way that the Word will become flesh among the people."[27] A befitting nomenclature that they think would embrace African primal traditions, identity, cultures,

---

24. Justo L. Gonzalez, *The Story of Christianity*, vol. 1, *The Early Church to the Dawn of the Reformation* (New York: HarperOne, 2010), 81.

25. N. R. Needham, *2000 Years of Christ's Power*, vol. 1, *Age of the Early Church Fathers*, rev. ed. (London: Grace Publications, 2002), 94.

26. The argument that Christian theology is incarnational theology and for that reason African pre-Christian cultural belief and world view should be brought to bear upon how we theologize in Africa is variously articulated by African theologians and biblical scholars. For detail review of this argument, see Imasogie, *Guidelines for Christian Theology*, 14.

27. Imasogie, *Guidelines for Christian Theology*, 14

and thought forms and thereby allow for continuity between African primal traditions and Christian theology, is to formulate a theology that is derived from the cult of the ancestors as a way of making Christ relevant and acceptable on the African continent. Since the groundbreaking publication of Charles Nyamiti's *Christ as Our Ancestor: Christology from an African Perspective*, in 1984, African Christology has been formulated from the framework of ancestor motif. This trend made most African theologians find the ancestral model a haven to land with their christological parachute. Hence Jesus, as they claim, is an ancestor.

Though the works of theologians are commendable, this study argues that the ancestor model has in some significant ways challenged the Christologies of Athanasius and Tertullian. The considerable challenge illustrates that the ancestor model has the solemn tendency of digressing from apostolic tradition upon which the tap roots Nicene and Chalcedonian Christology derived its inspiration, to formulate the early church's Christology since, from a closer examination of their significant presuppositions (see ch. 6), African theologians and biblical scholars have succeeded in formulating subjective Christologies that are not faithful to the Bible and have by so doing colonized the Christology of the apostles, the fathers, and apologists.

The question, however, is how did the apostles and fathers of the early church, notably Tertullian and Athanasius, understand and were able to employ non-Hebrew and biblical concepts that became the universally accepted models to present Jesus Christ to their contemporaries? What can twenty-first-century African Christian communities, with diverse cultural beliefs and different post-colonial struggles and experiences, learn from the proponents of an ancestor Christology model? Is it possible to recover the exact traditional Christian belief grounded in apostolic and ecclesial teaching on Jesus Christ? The daunting task of having to answer these questions is the work this chapter is poised to achieve.

Jesus in the Life and Thought of the First-Century Church

How the earliest disciples thought about Jesus at the beginning of the church is a crucial question for anyone.[28] Jesus, according to biblical data, was not just an imaginary figure constructed out of the religious yearnings of Jewish visionaries, but a definite and even disconcerting fact of world history, so adduces Macquarrie.[29] The previous reasoning is not just a faith-based assertion but indubitably a fact of history. Jesus Christ, as we know, once lived and walked the streets of Galilee and Palestine in the first century AD. To this end, we can also fall back to secular history which very well attests to the fact of his existence.[30] Jan A. B. Jongeneel makes a passionate appeal to the universal historicity of Jesus Christ beyond Christendom when he maintained, "Our calendars reflect his central importance, as most of the world marks the passing of years in terms of the date of his birth: B.C (before Christ) or B.C.E (before Christian/Common Era)."[31] John Stott concurs, "Jesus is the centre of history. At least a large proportion of the human race continues to divide history into BC and AD by reference to his birth."[32]

The effort to either comprehensively explain away by its detractors or prove by its exponents the fact of the historicity of Jesus Christ is behind the debate that engulfed the theological world of the eighteenth century.

---

28. Michael F. Bird, et al., eds., *How God Became Jesus: The Real Origins of Belief in Jesus' Divine Nature. A Response to Bart Ehrman* (Grand Rapids, MI: Zondervan 2014), 94.

29. Macquarrie, *Christology Revisisted*, 84.

30. The history of Jesus Christ has been captured in many secular works ranging from history to anthropology to philosophy to sociology etc. For works on the secular history of Jesus Christ see Easton, *Survey of Ancient*, 69–70. In this work, Easton traces the history of the Jews, their worldview and religious beliefs including Christianity, which founder is traced back to a Jew named Jesus Christ. In his, *Revolutions in Worldview: Understanding the Flow of Western Thought* (Phillipsburg, NJ: P & R, 2007), 37, 71 and 100, W. Andrew Hoffecker, like Easton also examines the historical terrain of the Jews including their religious beliefs among which is Christianity which founder is Jesus Christ. While the first two works captured Jewish history, Paul Oskar Kristeller, in his *Renaissance Thought* (73) went beyond Jewish history to the life of Jesus and maintained that during the renaissance period in Northern Europe there was a movement known as "The Imitation of Christ," which immensely contributed to a reform of secondary education in the continent.

31. Jan A. B. Jongeneel, *Jesus Christ in World History: His Presence and Representation in Cyclical and Linear Settings* (New York: Lang, 2009), 1.

32. John Stott, *The Incomparable Christ* (Downers Grove, IL: InterVarsity Press, 2004), 15.

A pacesetting work in this category was Herman Samuel Reimarus's, *The Wolfenbuttel Fragments: Concerning the Aims of Jesus and His Disciples* (published in 1778 from his essay "On the Aims of Jesus and His Disciples"). This publication opened the Pandora's Box for the investigation of the life of the historical Jesus. Consequently, William Wrede also lends support to Reimarus's argument, seen in his work, *The Messianic Secret*, in 1901. These publications attracted the whirlwind of the historical Jesus movement storm, for Martin Kähler wrote a counter response to Reimarus in 1892 in his, *The So-Called Historical Jesus and the Historic Biblical Christ*. The first phase of this debate was concluded with work from Albert Schweitzer, *The Quest of the Historical Jesus: A Critical Study of Its Progress from Reimarus to Wrede*. In his effort to becloud the reality of Jesus and also to disparage what he had achieved for his church, Schweitzer maintained in that work that, "he [Jesus] came to us as one unknown."[33] This assertion met its match in Martin Kähler's scathing critique of this school of thought. He states, "The historical Jesus of modern authors conceals from us the living Christ . . . I regard the entire Life-of-Jesus movement as a blind alley."[34]

The debates surrounding the quest for the historical Jesus are beyond the scope of this work. We have reflected it merely to prove the fact that Jesus is at the centre of world history. And it is the apostles' apprehension of Jesus Christ theologically, and historically that informed their writing of the story about him encapsulated in the Holy Scriptures that has become the Magna Carta for evangelical Christian faith and practice.

From the submission of Macquarrie that Jesus was not just an imaginary figure but a real historical person, it is natural then to see the evangelists who interacted with him in person to write "that which was from the beginning, which we have heard, which we have seen with our eyes, which we have looked at and out hands have touched – this we proclaim concerning the Word of life" (1 John 1:1). In fact, not even the unfounded arguments of some of the staunchest proponents of biblical criticism, like David Friedrich Strauss and Heinrich Eberhard Gottlob Paulus, centuries much later can

---

33. Alister E. McGrath, *The Making of Modern German Christology: 1750-1990* (Eugene, OR: Wipf & Stock, 2005), 105.

34. Martin Kähler, *The So-Called Historical Jesus and the Historic Biblical Christ* (Philadelphia: Fortress, 1966), 19.

water down the truth of the gospel whose subject the apostles portrayed as Jesus Christ, the expected Messiah and political liberator of the Jews who expected Christ to restore the kingdom to Israel and thus emancipate them from Roman domination (Acts 1:6).

The error of perceiving Jesus Christ solely from a human point led Strauss to the conclusion that "nothing recorded in the Gospels regarding Jesus' life . . . has any historical basis at all."[35] On this ground, he maintained that the miracles of Jesus and his resurrection were not genuine but, "Developed out of the acceptance of Jesus as the Messiah without any basis in historical fact."[36] Ultimately, he argues that "the resurrection of Jesus rests on the idea of 'subjective vision, which, of course, is a theological euphemism for hallucinations.'"[37] To him, the facts of Jesus's life and works – most especially the resurrection of Jesus Christ – are standing on the sinking sand of fraud.[38] Gottlob's blatant denial of the fact of Jesus's resurrection can only be surpassed by Denis Diderot who declares vehemently, "If the entire population of Paris were to assure him that a dead man had just been raised from the dead, he would not believe it."[39] These arguments sound right but only to one who does not think straight. The above view was why, having the same panoramic view with Strauss, Gottlob, whose telescope could not adequately also view the great vistas of Jesus's life and miracles, vehemently argues that "the disciples attributed supernatural causes to facts which they had not fully understood to Jesus."[40]

Whatever the opinions of biblical critics are, with respect to their insights given into the life and person of Jesus Christ, such insights are not open to us and can never therefore override those earlier given by the apostles who first wrote about Jesus Christ to their own audiences and also pass it to the posterity of Christian audiences the world over. It is quite true as

---

35. Robert B. Strimple, *The Modern Search for the Real Jesus: An Introductory Survey of the Historical Roots of Gospels Criticism* (Phillipsburg, NJ: P & R, 1995), 34.

36. Strimple, *Modern Search*, 34.

37. Strimple, 34.

38. David Friedrich Strauss, *The Life of Jesus, Critically Examined* (New York: Cosimo Classics, 2009), 738.

39. McGrath, *Making of Modern German*, 24.

40. Maurice Goguel, *Jesus and the Origins of Christianity*, vol. 1, *Prolegomena to the Life of Jesus* (New York: Harper Torchbooks, 1960), 45.

Veli-Matti Kärkkäinen alluded, "the New Testament itself contains several complementary interpretations of Jesus Christ."[41] C. I. Joy advances the same opinion, "Among the New Testament authors, there are mosaic views in comprehending and presenting the insights of the life and mission of Jesus of Nazareth."[42] Diversity in perception and presentation is not tantamount to confusion. John F. Walvoord notes sharply, "The fact that there is a different emphasis in the four Gospels does not imply that there is a contradiction. It is rather that four different portraits are given of the same person and, though there is variation, it is not a distorted presentation."[43] Diverse though the apostles' mosaics of Christ are, it should be understood that such diversity in portrayal is not in any way a product of confusion but rather, a result of the individual experience of, and unique encounter with, the risen Lord and the facts that ensued from that encounter were variously articulated. Stott makes this point very lucid as he asserts,"The Gospel writers had a serious purpose, namely to be witnesses. Indeed, the primary purpose of the Bible is to bear witness to Jesus Christ. God has given us in Scripture his testimony to his own Son, although he gave it through human witnesses."[44] The evangelists' belief that Jesus is Lord (Jas 2:1), was crucified and died (1 Cor 1:23; Rom 5:8), resurrected (Acts 1:22), ascended to heaven (Luke 24:51) and is seated at the right of God the Father (Heb 12:2), are unprecedented and has far reaching consequences on African ancestor Christology since its proponents hold the view that our ancestors, dead as they are, could be compared with the risen and ever living, incomparable Lord of history to whom he is creator and Saviour.

Apostolic Proclamation of Christ

After Jesus's death, the disciples were not, as one might have expected, rounded up and arrested, and perhaps executed.[45] Had this happened, that

---

41. Kärkkäinen, *Christology*, 10.

42. C. I. David Joy, *Christology Re-Visited: Profiles and Prospects* (Bangalore: Asian Trading Corporation, 2010), 39.

43. John F. Walvoord, *Jesus Christ Our Lord* (Chicago, IL: Moody, 1969), 123–124.

44. Stott, *Authentic Jesus*, 19–20.

45. N. T. Wright, *Jesus and the Victory of God*, vol. 2, *Christian Origins and the Question of God* (London: SPCK, 1996), 109.

would have constituted an extinction of the good news about Jesus Christ and possible witness of the apostles. But they, frightened and doubtful as they were, lived and had daily fellowship in the upper room in Jerusalem[46] (Acts 1:14–15; John 20:19); devoted themselves to the apostolic teaching (Acts 2:42); and public were witness against the thread coming from the religious circle of the day to the death and resurrection of Jesus Christ in the open arena (Acts 4:20). Quintessential to apostolic proclamation is the resurrection of Jesus Christ. Kereszty had argued, "in light of the resurrection, the Church finally understood the mystery of the crucified and risen One: 'My Lord and my God' Thomas cries out when the risen Jesus shows himself to him."[47] The resurrection of Jesus changed the perspective of the apostles thereby transforming their worldview so much so that timidity was transformed into boldness. The ones who went into hiding in the upper room in Jerusalem for fear of the Roman authorities could now stand against all the odds in the public square to witness to the death and resurrection of their Lord (Acts 2:14; 3:11).

Thus, the timid apostle Peter who denied Christ before a girl during the trial could now openly proclaim in the crowd, "God has raised this Jesus to life, and we are all witnesses of it" (Acts 2:32). Furthermore, he states, "Therefore let all Israel be assured of this: God has made this Jesus, whom you crucified, both Lord and Messiah" (Acts 2:36). It is significant we concede the fact that, at this time, Jesus was no longer viewed strictly among the believers in the early church from a human perspective but as the God-Human. With his divinity firmly established in the early church, the concepts of Jesus's lordship and Jesus the Christ begin at this point not only to take proper shape but has become the acceptable traditional formula for Christian confession and proclamation. Central to this confession and proclamation is the death and resurrection of Jesus which has become the most profound event in human history, and principal means of witnessing the apostles were known for among the heathens in the early church. Rather than seeing the crucifixion as disdain and shameful as the Mosaic Law portrays (Deut 21:21–23 cf. Gal 3:13), the apostles proclaimed it vigorously.

---

46. Stephen Neill, *Jesus through Many Eyes: Introduction to the Theology of the New Testament* (Philadelphia: Fortress, 1976), 15.

47. Kereszty, *Jesus Christ*, 22.

In fact, among the first-century Christians, it seems one was ashamed who failed to point to the historical fact of the death and resurrection of Christ in either his polemics or rhetoric. Hence when making a case against the wise and nobility of the society of his day, apostle Paul points to the crucifixion as the power and wisdom of God as opposed to the philosophers', scholars' and wise man's wisdom (1 Cor 1:20, 24). The Judaic meaning of the cross as the place on which the crucified is understood as having incurred God's curse, became transformed to mean not only the wisdom and power of God but the source of redemption in fulfillment of the Abrahamic covenant of promise (Deut 21:22–23; Gal 3:13–14 cf. Gen 12:2–3).

In light of this, Paul, not looking back to his former credentials as an expert in Jewish law and tradition with all its incentives thereon compared to the "surpassing worth of knowing Christ Jesus my Lord, for whose sake I have lost all things. I consider them garbage, that I may gain Christ" (Phil 3:8), tells the sophisticated of his day "we preach Christ crucified: a stumbling-block to Jews and foolishness to Gentiles, but to those whom God has called, both Jews and Greeks, Christ the power of God and the wisdom of God" (1 Cor 1:23–24). For the early church, God's power in Christ is demonstrated in raising him back to life after death (Acts 2:32) and exalted him to his right hand (Acts 2:33; Phil 2:9), giving him a name that is above every name (Phil 2:9–11) as fulfillment of the Old Testament prophecies (Isa 45:23). Accordingly, this crucified and exalted one is now made both Lord and Christ (Acts 2:36) and mediator of a new covenant (Heb 9:15) through whom as our advocate (1 John 2:1cf. 14:16) we receive forgiveness of sin (John 1:29; Acts 13:38), grace and truth (John 1:17). These together led to justification from "through him everyone who believes is set free from every sin, a justification you were not able to obtain under the law of Moses" (Acts 13:39). Jesus who has become both Lord and Christ and by whom we are justified, made us to grow more than conquerors and victors as opposed to vanquish (Rom 8:37) and engrafted us (Rom 11:17) to be members of God's multiracial community (Eph 2) and nation of priesthood (1 Peter 2:9) to walk in the light as he is in the light (1 John 1:7).

The apostles' assertiveness in their proclamation of their risen Lord – their boldness in witnessing for Christ in the early church – stemmed not only from the obvious fact that they (the apostles) "had seen their master and he was alive for-ever!"⁴⁸ However, that they were earlier on called by the risen Christ to bear witness to the fact of the gospel. Xavier Leon-Dufour argues that to have witnessed the resurrection of Jesus Christ from the dead was not enough to establish one's credentials as an apostle. Witness to the resurrection was to be accompanied by the personal call issued by Jesus to be a herald of the fact of his life and work. He states, "To qualify as a 'witness' of Christ, it was not sufficient to have been an eyewitness of his earthly life . . . but also that they have been summoned by God to explain the religious import of this fact."⁴⁹ While communicating their encounter with the risen Lord, the apostles did so in two principal ways, namely; in writing and through oral communication. The former method results in the written word and the latter in Christian kerygma that has ever since been the chief means of proclaiming Christ. The primary source witness to the humanity, divinity and work of Jesus Christ is thus the New Testament which contains the deeds of the apostles.

The Christian New Testament has been through the centuries an invaluable reservoir and weapon in possession of the church with which she has not only fight and win great christological battles but also disclose the experience of the early Christians in the burgeoning life of the primitive church. Robert L. Wilken states this fact succinctly, "The value of the New Testament witness is not that it states the truth about Christianity, but that it bears witness to the earliest experience of Christianity that we possess."⁵⁰ Christianity's experience in the ancient world was that of rejection and persecution coming both from the religious and secular society of the time.⁵¹ First, the name "Christianity" itself was a hated term among the sophisticated people of the society. Second, Christianity's refusal to acknowledge the local gods and pay homage to them via the emperor cult was considered seditious, thus, giving them the name "atheists."⁵² Third, Christians were believed to be preaching

---

48. Dowley, *Short Introduction*, 35.

49. Xavier Léon-Dufour, *The Gospels and the Jesus of History* (London: Collins, 1974), 170.

50. Robert L. Wilken, *The Myth of Christian Beginnings* (London: SCM, 1979), 171.

51. A. M. Renwick, *The Story of the Church* (London: Inter-Varsity Fellowship, 1966), 52.

52. John McManners, ed., *The Oxford Illustrated History of Christianity* (New York, NY: Oxford University Press, 1990), 41–42.

foolish and unreasonable doctrines such as the incarnation, resurrection and worship of a crucified Jew. They were often blamed for natural disasters such as earthquake, floods, famines, and pestilence. Next to these, Christian religious practices, especially church worship in which brethren hugged and kissed one another with a holy kiss, was deemed as infidelity while the taking of the Holy Communion was viewed as cannibalistic.[53] All this earned Christianity a name, and it was branded "Religio Illicita."[54] As an illegal movement, Christianity was banned in the society and its followers forbidden to make a public profession of its founder's name (Acts 4:17–18). The apostles, however, insisted that it was far preferable to proclaim the name of the risen Lord than to obey cersadotal authorities (Acts 4:20–21). The above assertion was made, first, through verbal proclamation and with time, committed to writing that which had earlier on been preached.

The Issues Inherent in the Apostolic Christology: African Apologists Defending Apostolic Christology

Bernard L. Ramm states the basic principles and foundation of evangelical Christology in the following words; "Evangelical Christology is a continuation of historical Christology. It is the Christology stated in The Apostles' Creed, refined in the Nicaean-Constantinople Creed, elaborated in the Chalcedonian Creed, and finally summed up in the Creed of Athanasius."[55] Orthodox evangelical christological formulation is thus a continuation of the apostolic tradition. As I am persuaded, it is embedded in the apostolic creedal confession that defines Christian truth and has through the centuries linked the ancient church with the contemporary church. What the church confesses today as Christian truth has a connection with the past. The past is the bedrock of contemporary Christian truth-claims. As Gerald Bray asserts, "The Creeds . . . of the early Church remain the unique historical basis for

---

53. Bill R. Austin, *Austin's Topical History of Christianity* (Wheaton, IL: Tyndale House Publishers, 1983), 60–61.

54. Harry R. Boer, *A Short History of the Early Church* (Ibadan: Daystar Press, 2003), 44.

55. Ramm, *Evangelical Christology*, 15.

our present understanding of Christian truth."[56] Evangelical Christology is thus a chain which is bound together by apostolic knots. This string is the apostolic proclamation that Jesus is the Christ (Mark 8:29), the *Logos* who incarnated himself in the man Jesus of Nazareth (John 1:14). It is upon the foundation of the apostolic proclamation which also forms the core of the early church's creedal confession that evangelical Christian Christology rests. This creedal confession is the apostolic teaching that calls upon all people:

> To acknowledge ONE AND THE SAME Son, our Lord Jesus Christ at once complete in divinity and complete in humanity, truly God and truly man, consisting also of a rational soul and body; of one substance (*homoousion*) with the Father as regards his divinity, and at the same time of one substance with us as regards his humanity; like us in all respects, apart from sin; as regards his divinity, begotten of the Father before the ages.[57]

The Christian creedal confession was formulated in answer to the Gnostic, Ebionites, Samosatenes, and Arians question of "who is Jesus in the early Church?"[58] Fundamental to this solution is the teachings of Jesus Christ and those of the apostles, which constituted the particular object of thought for the early church fathers. This lesson was at first a living word, not confined to the New Testament writings, which the church fathers had to interpret in a way that harmonized with the tradition of the church rule of faith (*regula fidei*).[59] Of the church rule of faith Tertullian writes;

> Now, with regard to this rule of faith—that we may from this point acknowledge what it is which we defend—it is, you must know, that which prescribes the belief that there is one only God, and that He is none other than the Creator of the world, who produced all things out of nothing through His own Word, first of all, sent forth; that this Word is called His Son, and,

---

56. Gerald Bray, *Creeds, Councils and Christ: Did the Early Christians Misrepresent Jesus?* (Fearn, Scotland: Mentor, 2009), 10.

57. Gerald O'Collins, *Interpreting Jesus*, Contemporary Christian Insights (New York: Mowbray, 2000), 172.

58. Otto W. Heick, *A History of Christian Thought*, vol. 1, rev. ed. (Philadelphia: Fortress, 1965), 32–33.

59. Heick, *History of Christian Thought*, 32.

under the name of God, was seen "in diverse manners" by the patriarchs, heard at all times in the prophets, at last brought down by the Spirit and power of the Father into the Virgin Mary, was made flesh in her womb, and, being born of her, went forth as Jesus Christ; thenceforth He preached the new law and the new promise of the kingdom of heaven, worked miracles; having been crucified, He rose the third day again; (then) having ascended into heavens, He sat at the right hand of the Father; sent instead of Himself the power of the Holy Ghost to lead such as believe; will come with glory to take the saints to the enjoyment of everlasting life and of the heavenly promises, and to condemn the wicked to everlasting fire, after the resurrection of both these classes shall happen, together with the restoration of their flesh.[60]

Tertullian further argued that this rule of faith that shaped and defined the church confessional and doctrinal statement had, until the coming of heretics, remained unchallenged. With the arrival of heretics, however, the church's foundational doctrinal belief was under serious question. He asserted, "This rule, (of faith), was taught by Christ, and raises amongst ourselves no other questions than those which heretics introduce, and which make men heretics."[61]

The relevance of apostolic creedal formulation, confession, and the early church rule of faith – which was fundamental to apostolic belief and doctrinal formulation – with the affirmation that Jesus Christ is the Lord, did indicate that the apostles and early church fathers were faithful to the Bible. For this reason, they were able to use models derived from the Bible to present Jesus Christ to their contemporaries. Their firm resolve to faithfully remain rooted and attached to the Bible mostly led to their victory over the heretics of the time who were extreme in their view of Jesus Christ. The apostolic and early church's faithfulness to the Bible is immeasurably valuable to the overall thesis of this chapter and the entire study, which argues that for Christian theology to be relevant to the African continent it source

---

60. Roberts and Donaldson, *Ante-Nicene Fathers*, 249.
61. Roberts and Donaldson, 249.

should not only be derived from the Bible, but in addition to being faithful to the Bible and apostolic tradition and the early church rule of faith it should as well imbibe and continue with the theological legacies of Tertullian and Athanasius. Known for their steadfast and authentic theologies, Pope Benedict XVI described Tertullian as the ancient church's great personality and teacher of the faith, while Athanasius he labelled as the genuine protagonist of the Christian tradition and the pillar of the church.[62] In my view, when African theologians take as a point of departure the biblical sources and materials which Tertullian and Athanasius used in the third and fourth centuries to formulate standard and universal orthodox Christian theology, then, unquestionably African theology will have an inseparable connection with the past.

To that end, this study generally argues that African theologians who take the cult of the ancestors as a point of departure to explore Christology in Africa, with a view to making Christ and Christianity relevant to Africa, should not only rethink their sources and methodologies but such models and approaches employed need to equally be faithful to the Bible. Anything less than theology derived from and being committed to the Bible, I argue, is capable of leading Africans away from Jesus Christ. Of course, the tendency is the Arian, Marcian and Praxean error which is typical of most theologies formulated from sources other than the Christian Bible, apostolic tradition, and the early church rule of faith that Tertullian and Athanasius wrestled with and defeated in the early church.

The error this study aptly wishes to point out, so that African theologians can run away from, is the heretics' poor perception and wrong comprehension along with incorrect interpretation of Jesus Christ which led ultimately to the violation of the apostolic tradition and the church's rule of faith, that in turn gave rise to heresies which ignited the christological problem and dictated the christological agenda for future generation of Christians. Richard A. Norris, Jr, so eloquently explicates this view as follows;

> To say that this early picture of Jesus dictated an agenda for later Christology is mere to say that when examined closely and

---

62. Benedict XVI, *Church Fathers: From Clement of Rome to Augustine* (San Francisco: Ignatius Press, 2010), 43, 58.

expounded seriously. It raised a whole series of knotty questions. They, in turn, gave rise to critical and systematic thought about the person of Christ. The beginnings of this process are to be sought in the second century when two distinct sets of Christological issues were raised and debated. The first of these concerned the nature and identity of the heavenly "power" which was said to have become incarnate as, or in, Jesus. The second was created by denials of the reality of Jesus' "flesh," that is, his ordinary human nature.[63]

While Norris fails to unveil the architects that provoked the christological question, Otto W. Heick is willing to save the day. According to him, "The early Church Fathers were forced to express themselves on this question against the Gnostics, Ebionites, Samosatenes, and Arians."[64] Furthermore, he states, "In the positive endeavour to formulate the conception of Christ's relation to the Father and then later to the Holy Spirit, the arguments centred around this question."[65] The question and answers to the christological question did not emerge simultaneously. As William C. Placher posited, "The answers emerged only gradually. Perhaps the most important early debate concerned Gnosticism."[66]

J. L. Nerve captures the central doctrine of the Ebionites as follows, "To them, Jesus was merely a man, they rejected the Virgin Birth, and insisted that the Holy Spirit, who was curiously thought of as a female, had descended upon Jesus for the first time at His baptism. The Messianic work of Christ was looked upon as that of a prophet and a teacher."[67] Additionally, Stephen J. Nicholas notes, "The adherents of what is known as the Ebionites heresy assert that Christ was the Son of Joseph and Mary, and regard him as

---

63. Richard A. Norris, Jr, ed., *The Christological Controversy*, Sources of early Christian thought (Philadelphia: Fortress, 1980), 5–6.

64. Heick, *History of Christian Thought*, 33.

65. Heick, 33.

66. William C. Placher, *Readings in the History of Christian Theology*, vol. 1, *From Its Beginnings to the Eve of the Reformation* (Philadelphia: Westminster, 1988), 11.

67. J. L. Neve, *A History of Christian Thought*, vol. 1, *History of Christian Doctrine* (Philadelphia: Muhlenberg Press, 1946), 51.

no more than man."⁶⁸ In the Gnostics, Needham observes; "When we speak of 'Gnosticism' or a 'Gnostic movement,' we must not think of one single united organization or philosophy. There was avast and astonishing variety of different Gnostic groups: Barbelonites, Cainites, Cerinthians, Encratites, Justinian, Marcionites, Marcosians, Nicolaitans, Ophites, Sethians, Severians and Valentinians, to name a few."⁶⁹ William Cunningham also reflects this view: "Gnosticism, indeed . . . may be properly enough used as a general name for the heretical systems of the first two centuries."⁷⁰ Since of the enormity of materials covered by scholars on the works of the apostolic Fathers with respect to their responses on the heresies propounded by the adherents of these sects, this work has selected two apologists from Africa: Tertullian and Athanasius for brief examination in this section.

While the apostles, says McGrath, "first bore witness to faith in Jesus Christ throughout Judea, and established Churches there, after which they went out into the whole world and proclaimed the same doctrine of the same faith to the nations,"⁷¹ this same faith that was proclaimed by the apostles and inherited by the nations was the apostolic "belief that the world was created by God. But the Creator also entered into full human life in the incarnation. The Word who 'became flesh' was the same Word through whom 'all things came to be' (John 1:1–18)."⁷² The Word became flesh was the norm of evangelical Christian faith confessed as Christianity encroached virgin lands and converts were made. "The many converts who joined the early Church came from a wide variety of backgrounds."⁷³ William Edgar and K. Scott Oliphint describes this scenario thus; "They [converts] were farmers, soldiers, highborn, working people, slaves, fathers and mothers, children and adults."⁷⁴ "This variety and diversity in culture and occupa-

---

68. Stephen J. Nichols, *For Us and for Our Salvation: The Doctrine of Christ in the Early Church* (Wheaton, IL: Crossway, 2007), 21.
69. Needham, *2000 Years of Christ's Power*, 95.
70. William Cunningham, *Historical Theology: A Review of the Principal Doctrinal Discussions in the Christian Church Since the Apostolic Age*, vol. 1 (Carlisle, PA: Banner of Truth, 1994), 122.
71. McGrath, *Christian Theology Reader*, 82
72. Dowley, *Short Introduction*, 78.
73. González, *Story of Christianity*, 69.
74. Edgar and Oliphint, *Christian Apologetics*, 14.

tion/vacation enriched the Church and gave witness to the universality of its message. However, it also resulted in widely differing interpretations of that message."[75] With differing interpretations, three challenges presented themselves, requiring an apologetic response. First, there was persecution from outside the church. Second, there was heresy from within the church, and third, there was the presence of unbelieving Jews.[76] On the African continent, God raised many theologians to rise to the occasion. This work focuses on only two early African apologists, who did much to contribute to orthodox Christian theological discourse. These are Tertullian of Carthage and Athanasius the great and defender of orthodoxy. The work examines the thoughts of the proponents of heterodox doctrinal formulation, what they taught, and how the apologists formulated Christology upon which contemporary African ancestor Christology expressed by African theologians should take a cue and then draws a general conclusion on the entire chapter.

I. Tertullian of Carthage: The Ray of God Foretold in Ancient Times in His Birth Became God and Man United

Tertullian, a third-century Latin thinker, generally known as the father of Latin Christianity is attributed with the saying: "The Ray of God foretold in ancient times descending into a Virgin is in his birth God and Man united."[77] Of him, Edgar and Oliphint have this to say, "When we move into the third century, the Church is no longer primarily on the defensive, but became more confident, even aggressive. The foremost thinker from Carthage was Quintus Septimius Florens Tertullianus, commonly known as Tertullian."[78] Acknowledged as a leading thinker, Tertullian indeed dealt with a lot of critical issues beyond the scope of this work, like others before him; we will focus attention on his unique portrayal of Jesus Christ in his response to heretics of the third century.

Before I examine Tertullian's Trinitarian Christology, it is important we first know the foundation from which he derived his principles for Christian theology. Fundamental to his theology is the notion of the church's rule

---

75. González, *Story of Christianity*, 69.
76. Edgar and Oliphint, *Christian Apologetics*, 14–16.
77. Placher, *Readings in the History*, vol. 1, 45.
78. Edgar and Oliphint, *Christian Apologetics*, 115.

of faith which he took as his point of departure in the formulation of his Christology. Starting from the apostolic tradition, Tertullian wrote, "The apostolic Churches are dispersed throughout the world: not only Rome, 'from which the authority of the apostles is at hand for us (Africans),' but Corinth, Philippi, and Ephesus."[79] On the church rule of faith, Tertullian had expressed faith in God the Creator, who sent the Word in his Son to be the God of the Old Testament, and with the Holy Spirit brought down the Word to be enfleshed in Mary. After his mission and passion, Jesus Christ ascended and sent the Spirit on believers, and will return to raise the dead, to take the saints to glory and condemn the wicked to everlasting fire.[80]

For Tertullian, the Lord Jesus Christ himself taught this and passed it to the apostles who also passed it to posterity of believers but when philosophers entered the church, they came and introduced philosophy and heresies which made them heretics and patriarchs of heresies.[81] Thus, he blamed heresy on philosophy. According to him, like Philosophy, heresy asks questions, and argues about fundamental things.[82] This understanding led him to a famous denunciation of philosophy.[83] In his famous slogan articulated against philosophy he states,

> What has Jerusalem to do with Athens, the Church with Academia, the Christian with the heretic? Our principles come from the Porch of Solomon, who had himself taught that the Lord is to be sought in simplicity of heart. I have no use for a stoic or a platonic or a dialectical Christianity. After Jesus Christ we have no need of speculation, after the Gospel no need of research (cf. Praescr. 7 [NE 166-71]).[84]

This denunciation immediately reveals the nature and content of Tertullian's theology.

---

79. Stuart G. Hall, *Doctrine and Practice in the Early Church: A Companion to a New Eusebius and Creeds, Councils and Controversies*, 2nd ed. (London: SPCK, 2005), 69.

80. Hall, *Doctrine and Practice*, 69.

81. F. A. Cayré, *A Manual of Patrology and History of Theology*, vol. 1, *First and Second Books* (Paris: Desclée, 1936), 246.

82. Hall, *Doctrine and Practice*, 69.

83. Hall, 69.

84. Edgar and Oliphint, *Christian Apologetics*, 117–118.

From right, left, and centre, his theology is christocentric hanging upon one of the Reformers' four alone. For him, Christ alone epitomizes Christian theological thought. Tertullian's theology was formulated in response to two principal heresies propounded by Marcion and Praxeas. As Hall rightly observed, "A most conspicuous case of philosophical influence is the concept of God's nature as material (*corpus*)."[85] God as the material was the starting point for Praxeas's theological formulation. Thus, making a case for the monarchy of God, Praxeas taught that God is single, and so Father, Son and Spirit are "one and the same," but he rejects the "economy" or "dispensation."[86] Hall notes that the term "economy" (Greek *oikonomia*, Latin *dispensation*) sums up Tertullian's idea, which among the Greeks was used originally to refer to household administration or stewardship. With the passage of time, *oikonomia* came to be used in ancient theology to refer to God's dispensations for creating and saving the world: among the Greeks in particular "*oikonomia*" often meant the saving work of Christ in the flesh – what moderns often refer to broadly as "the incarnation."[87] In modern theology "economic trinitarianism" is a doctrine of the Trinity in which God is three in his works, but one in his being: it means that to us he operates in a threefold way, but may in himself be one and simple. It contrasts with "imminent" or "essential" trinitarianism, where the being of God in himself has a threefold quality. That is not what Tertullian meant by *oikonomia*.[88]

According to Hall, Tertullian has two leading models of this "economy": imperial administration, and biological or natural organism. Using the emperor as an example, Tertullian argued that the emperor is a monarch whose sole rule is not impaired when he bestows part of his functions on his son: the "economy" is an administrative arrangement of his own sole rule, which is not thereby disrupted. Another illustration Tertullian employed that revealed his understanding of *oikonomia* is taken from Greek botany and wildlife. Among the Greeks, for example, the word of the arrangement of parts in a plant or animal body are used to show that the parts are constituent of the whole. In the same vein, Tertullian argued that Father, Son and Holy Spirit

---

85. Hall, *Doctrine and Practice*, 70.
86. Hall, 70.
87. Hall, 70.
88. Hall, 70.

are one in the same way that a tree has a stem and fruit but they are not separated from the root.[89] For Tertullian, two other images work similarly: the sun, the ray of light, and the point where the light falls; or the spring, the river from it and the irrigation canal which the river feeds (a familiar picture in Roman North Africa).

In each of the above illustrations Tertullian contends that there is only one tree, one light, one water, determined by the single source, which is the root, the sun or the spring. For him therefore, God and his Word (*sermo*) and his Spirit are three stages of one being.[90] These illustrations reveal the Stoic conception and notion of God who is perceived as material. For this reason, the material makes these organic models for God easier to understand.

To prove his point Tertullian invented the customary Latin terms for God as Trinity (*Trinitas*), a standard Latin parlance for "threeness." Against the monarchical party which insists that God is one simple unity (*simplex unitas*) Tertullian had argued that the threeness of God consists of the Father, the Son and the Spirit, each of whom is a person (*persona*). For Tertullian, the three persons in the Godhead are distinct, but not divided. They have a single substance or being (*substantia*).[91] Of Tertullian's innovative invention and employment of the Latin *persona* and *substantia* to describe the mystery of the Trinity and the incarnation, Pope Benedict XVI commented, "Tertullian takes an enormous step in the development of Trinitarian dogma. He has given us an appropriate way to express this great mystery in Latin by introducing the terms 'one substance' and 'three persons.' In a similar way, he also greatly developed the correct language to express the mystery of Christ, Son of God and true God."[92]

It is no error that Tertullian has tried always to dissociate himself from Greek philosophy and philosophers, but he could not succeed in completely abandoning the use of some Greek philosophical concepts to argue his case. As F. Cayré rightly argues, Tertullian does not hesitate to use philosophers and philosophy when necessary.[93] A good example here is his witty invention

---

89. Hall, 71.
90. Hall, 71.
91. Hall, 72.
92. Benedict XVI, *Church Fathers*, 45.
93. Cayré, *Manual of Patrology*, 246.

of the words *persona* and *substantia* which he used to describe the relationship of the three persons in the Trinity. His, therefore, was the honour of having created the now classical formula: *tres personae, úna subtantia*.[94] According to Hall by using *persona* and *substantia*, Tertullian had used logical or philosophical terminology against Praxeas his opponent, whom he perceived had crucified the Father by denying him the personal distinction as Father. Texts like, "I am the Lord, and there is no other" (Isa 45:5), and "I and the Father are one" (John 10:30) were taken to prove that Father and Son were one person, so that in Christ the Father suffered, or at least "co-suffered" (*compatitur*) as the indivisible or spiritual part of Christ.[95] This was an attack he hurled against his detractors who held a dualistic notion of the Trinity since they argued that Christ is twofold: the Son, flesh, man, Jesus and the Father, Spirit, God, Christ.[96]

While God as material was the starting point for Praxeas's theological formulation, Marcion began by dismantling the foundation of Christianity since he taught that the God proclaimed by the Law and the Prophets is not the Father of our Lord Jesus Christ, the one being revealed, the other unknown; the one again being just, the other being good, (Adv. Haer. 1, 27, 1).[97] Accordingly, Marcion vehemently affirmed God to be an evil-doer and fond of wars, and inconstant also in his judgments and contrary to himself.[98] Making a further argument against the Christian belief in the unity of God, Marcion contended that the Christian verity has distinctly declared this principle, "God is not, if He is not one, 'because we more properly believed that that has no existence which is not as it ought to be . . . That being which is the great Supreme, must need be unique, by having no equal, and so not ceasing to be the great Supreme' (1, 3). Thus the maker of the world is identical with the good God."[99]

---

94. Cayré, 247.

95. Hall, *Doctrine and Practice*, 72.

96. Hall, 73.

97. Johannes Quasten, *Patrology Volume 1: The Beginnings of Patristic Literature from the Apostles Creed to Irenaeus* (Allen, TX: Christian Classics, 1995), 268–289, quoting Marcion's heresy.

98. Quasten, *Patrology Volume 1*, 269.

99. Johannes Quasten, *Patrology Volume 2: The Ante-Nicene Literature after Irenaeus* (Westminster, MD: Christian Classics, 1995), 273.

Apparently, Marcion is a dualist who sees a great chasm between the God proclaimed by the prophets in the Old Testament and the God who became flesh in Jesus of Nazareth in the New Testament. What is more devastating in Marcion's theology, however, is his Christology in which at first he argued that the "Messias foretold under the Old Dispensation had not yet come."[100] Against this error, Tertullian argued that the "Christ who appeared here on earth is no other than the Saviour proclaimed by the prophets, and sent by the Creator."[101] Tertullian's critique of this position seemed to have forced Marcion to rethink his christological formulation who would admit later that the Messiah has come but then taught that Christ was not born through the usual and natural means people are born. To defend this position, he vehemently contended, "If the saviour was born as a child, he would have been placed under the rule of the Creator, which would, in turn, deny the radical newness of the gospel. This is why Marcion affirms that Christ appeared as a fully grown man in the fifteenth year of the reign of Tiberius."[102] By denying the physical birth of Christ, Marcion seemed to have had an epiphanic view of Christ, since he argues that "Christ suddenly appeared in the Synagogue at Capernaum in AD 29 as a grown man."[103] The assertion also denies the fact of Christ being the incarnate Son of God. Hence, he held that Christ was not the creator's Son. To drive home his case, he argues with atenacity that there are two gods, "the Creator God whom he equated with Demiurge and the Redeemer God."[104] These gods, Marcion contends, were identical but neither of them is the father of Christ.

The consequence of Marcion's Christology is that he has succeeded in stripping Christ off of his power to save mankind from sin and death. This will mean that, like other depraved men, Christ himself would need a redeemer to save him from sin and its devastating consequence. His theology has also denied the fact of the resurrection since Marcion seemed to say, "As it is appointed unto men once to die, but after this the judgment" (Heb 9:27), so, Christ – like every other man would die and experience decay. It

---

100. Quasten, *Patrology Volume 2*, 273.
101. Quasten, 273.
102. González, *History of Christian Thought*, 141.
103. Dowley, *Short Introduction*, 50.
104. Heick, *History of Christian Thought*, 76.

is against this background that Tertullian marshalled his defence against the errors propounded by Marcion and Praxeas. It is interesting to note however that most of the doctrines of Marcion and Praxeas could only be deduced from the response of Tertullian since we do not have extant copies of most of their works. Donald MacLeod is more precise; "It is a commonplace that history has been unlinked to heretics. In the case of such men as Praxeas and Pelagius we know virtually nothing of their teaching except what we can glean from the voluminous writings of their opponents (notably Tertullian and Augustine)."[105]

In his response to Marcion's latter Christology, Tertullian writes; "Marcion, in order to deny Christ's flesh, denied his birth also, or else he denied the flesh in order to deny the birth. Obviously, he was afraid that birth and flesh might bear witness to each other, since there is no birth apart from flesh or flesh apart from birth."[106] There are, to be sure, Tertullian continued,

> Other things also quite as foolish [as the birth of Christ], which have reference to the humiliations and sufferings of God. Or else, let them call a crucified God "wisdom." But Marcion will apply the knife to this doctrine also, and even with greater reason. For which is more unworthy of God, which is more likely to raise a blush of shame, that God should be born, or that He should die? that He should bear the flesh or the cross? be circumcised, or be crucified? be cradled, or be confined? be laid in a manger, or in a tomb? . . . Have you, then, cut away all sufferings from Christ, on the ground that, as a mere phantom, He was incapable of experiencing them?[107]

Against Praxeas, Tertullian began by interrogating himself with the disturbing question of why he lingered in launching a full-scale defence against his error.[108] Why should he, as he seems to have entertained regret, delay in countering Praxeas's error that there is, between the Father and the Son,

---

105. Donald MacLeod, *Jesus Is Lord: Christology Yesterday and Today* (Fearn: Christian Focus, 2000), 87.
106. Norris, *Christological Controversy*, 65.
107. Placher, *Readings in the History*, vol. 1, 46.
108. Norris, *Christological Controversy*, 61.

Historical and Theological Foundations of Christology

in the Holy Trinity a distinction? From Praxeas's assertions, Tertullian perceived in that doctrine, the danger of likening the relationship that subsists between the Father and the Son to that of "Sun and its ray or a fountain and the stream which flows from it."[109] These two phenomena, when considered against the mathematical law of division, they do not apply. Yet, Praxeas tends to distinguish the indivisible members of the Godhead. In this division, Praxeas argues that the "Son is the flesh [i.e. the human being – Jesus] while the Father is the Spirit [i.e. God – the Christ]."[110]

The christological formulations from Marcion and Praxeas according to Tertullian contradict the prophecy that a Virgin shall conceive by the power of the Holy Spirit and give birth to a "Son – Emmanuel, which means God with us [Matt 1:23]."[111] While driving home his argument, Tertullian says;

> Now let us put our case less figuratively. It was not feasible for the Son of God to be born of human seed, lest, if he were wholly the son of man, he should not also be the Son of God, and should be in no sense greater than Solomon or than Jonah, as in Ebion's view . . . Therefore, being already the Son of God, of the seed of God the Father [that is, spirit], that he might also be the Son of Man all he needed was to take to him flesh out of human flesh without the action of man's seed: for a man's seed was uncalled-for in one who had the seed of God. And so, as while not yet born of the Virgin it was possible for him to have God for his father, without a human mother, equally, when being born of the Virgin, it was possible for him to have a human mother without a human father.[112]

Obviously, Tertullian has made a good genetic argument here, since genetically; all living things without exception reproduce only but their kinds. It logically follows, therefore, that if Jesus was before birth (by a human mother) conceived by the Holy Spirit, he could not have been after delivery,

---

109. Norris, 61.
110. Norris, 61.
111. Norris, 62.
112. Vincent Zamoyta, *The Theology of Christ: Sources* (Milwaukee, WI: Bruce, 1967), 22.

any less God more than he is any less man in keeping with the law of genetics as Praxeas failed to see.

It is sometimes difficult to have a clear-cut dichotomy between Tertullian's argument against Praxeas and those against Marcion, and because the issues are so complex and dicey, they tend sometime to prove inexhaustible, we can therefore only present a tip of the iceberg.

II. Athanasius of Alexandria: The Word Prepares a Body in the Virgin as a Temple unto Himself

González has observed, "From its very beginnings, Christianity had been involved in theological controversies. In Paul's time, the burning issue was the relationship between Jewish and Gentile converts. Then came the crucial debates over Gnostic speculation. In the third century, when Cyprian was bishop of Carthage, the main point at issue was the restoration of the lapsed."[113]

While the controversies of the first three centuries might be viewed as a prelude to christological debates, it was the fourth-century Trinitarian and christological debates that were particularly turbulent. As Robert Letham notes, "Beneath the surface of the third-century debate were problems tickling like time bombs, destined to explode sooner or later. The chief of these was how to reconcile the unity of God with the status of Jesus Christ within the framework of either the monarchian paradigm or the Logos Christology."[114] This situation is succinctly captured by A. M. Renwick and A. M. Harman who see in the Christian church itself the tendencies towards "Priestcraft, sacramentarianism that hampers the wellbeing and the future of the Church."[115] Following this, the "fourth century was marked by prolonged controversies, chiefly in the Eastern Church, about how Christ, the Son of God, was himself God (the doctrine of the Trinity), and how he was both man and God (the doctrine of the person of Christ or Christology)."[116] As Kelly states,

---

113. González, *Story of Christianity*, 181.

114. Robert Letham, *The Holy Trinity: In Scripture, History, Theology, and Worship* (Phillipsburg, NJ: P & R, 2004), 108.

115. A. M. Renwick and A. M. Harman, *The Story of the Church*, 3rd ed. (Leicester: Inter-Varsity Press, 1999), 52.

116. Dowley, *Short Introduction*, 117.

The theological issue at stake was thus the status of the Word and His relation to the Godhead. Was He fully divine, in the precise sense of the term, and therefore really akin to the Father? Or was He, after all, a creature, superior no doubt to the rest of creation, even by thecourtesy designated divine, but all the same separated by an unbridgeable chasm from the Godhead?[117]

In what seemed like an attempt to answer these difficult questions by rightly interpreting the mystery of the God-man, Bishop Alexander of Alexandria fanned into flames the Trinitarian and christological controversy when in AD 318 or 319 he preached to his presbyters, "The Great Mystery of the Trinity in Unity."[118] According to him, Jesus, "The Son of God, as Son, is co-eternal with the Father, since God can never have been without His Word, His Wisdom, His Power, His Image, and the Father must always have been Father."[119] Furthermore, Alexander asserts, "The Sonship of the Word is a real, Metaphysical one, natural as opposed to adoptive (cf. the LXX wording of Ps. 110, 3: 'Before the dawn I begat thee out of my belly'): which implies, although Alexander does not explicitly say so, that He shares the Father's nature."[120]

The preceding referred context gave rise to the debate between Arius and Bishop Alexander of Alexandria in the fourth century. And Arius, a presbyter of the church district of Baucalis in Alexandria vehemently opposed the sermon and argued that Alexander's sermon has failed to uphold a distinction among the persons in the Godhead. "The phrase that eventually became the Arian motto, 'there was when He was not,' aptly focuses on the point at issue."[121] With this word, Arius began, "The Father alone, he argues, is ingenerated, eternal, without beginning, He alone is true, alone possessing immortality, alone wise, alone good, alone sovereign, alone judge of all without equal."[122]

---

117. Kelly, *Early Christian Doctrines*, 223.

118. Earle E. Cairns, *Christianity Through the Centuries: A History of the Church* (Grand Rapids, MI: Zondervan, 1996), 126.

119. Kelly, *Early Christian Doctrines*, 224–225.

120. Kelly, 224–225.

121. González, *Story of Christianity*, 184.

122. Kelly, *Early Christian Doctrines*, 227.

Furthermore, Christ, Arius contends had not existed as the Father from eternity. For him, Christ was a being, created out of nothing, subordinate to the Father and of the different essence of the Father. Accordingly, he asserted, "the Word (Logos) who assumed flesh in Jesus Christ (John 1:14) was not the true God and that he had an entirely different nature, neither eternal nor omnipotent."[123]

In his startling restatement of Arius's view, Kelly succinctly submits, "Although He is God's Word and Wisdom, He is distinct from that Word and that Wisdom which belong to God's very essence.[124]" Furthermore, Arius contends that because of the virtue of his life and obedience to the Father's will, Jesus could be considered divine and be allowed to participate in some appellations that are strictly God's – divinity for him was not tantamount to deity. Jesus was just the perfect design of God; there was no how, therefore, he could be coequal, coeternal or consubstantial with the Father. Jesus, he therefore concludes was divine but not a deity. A clear taxonomy in Arius's exegetical Christology according to F. Cayré may be reduced to the following points:

a) God is one and not engendered (ἀγέννητος). For this reason, Arius believed that it is impossible for God to communicate his substance since everything existing outside God is created *ex nihilo* by God's will.

b) The Word is an intermediary between God and the world, existing before time, but not eternal; there was a time when the Word was not: ἦν ποτε ὅτε οὐχ ἦν.

c) The Word was therefore created: ἐξ οὐχ ὄντων γέγονε . For Arius, the Word was made: γενητός. In the light of this Arius contended that should it be said he was born, engendered γέννητος, such an expression must be taken as meaning a sonship of adoption.

d) It follows that of his nature the Word is fallible, but his moral righteousness preserved him from any fall. He is inferior to God,

---

123. Bruce L. Shelley, *Church History in Plain Language*, 3rd ed. (Nashville, TN: Nelson, 2008), 100.

124. Kelly, *Early Christian Doctrines*, 228.

but so perfect a creature that no other may be created superior to him.[125]

From Christian tradition, the fourth century was almost entirely dominated with the Arian controversies.[126] To that end, many theologians have developed interest in investigating the issues in that controversy. For this reason Nicholas also summarized Arius's central thought which is worth detailing in this research;

> He [Arius] said that what makes God God is not what Christ is. God and Christ are not of identical essence; Jesus is merely of similar (homoi) essence (ousion). Arius further held his teaching to be true to Scripture. First, he held that God created or made Christ on the basis of Paul's reference to Christ as "the firstborn of all creation" (Col. 1:15). Arius also understood the reference to Christ the "only begotten" in John 3:16 as teaching that Christ came into existence, that he was made, and that he had not existed for all eternity. Arius further relied on Deuteronomy 6:4: "Hear, O Israel: The LORD our God, the LORD is one." Arius rejected the notion of the Trinity, that God is one in essence and three in persons. And he rejected the deity of Christ. To be sure, Arius had a high view, a very high view, of Christ, but his view fell short.[127]

Similarly, Letham also sums up Arius's christological views elaborately;

1. God is solitary, the Father unique. (This shows Arius's concern to maintain the unity of the one God.)
2. The Son had an origin *ex nihilo* (out of nothing). There was a time when he did not exist. He was created, existing by the will of God. Before he was created, he did not exist. (The logic here is that since everything created came into being out of non-existence, and the Word of God is a creature, so the Word of

---

125. Cayré, *Manual of Patrology*, 314.
126. Cayré, 309.
127. Nichols, *For Us and for Our*, 61.

God also came into being out of oblivion. Thus, God was not always Father, for before he created the Son, he was solitary.)
3. God made a person (Word, Spirit, Son) when he wanted to create. In short, he created by an intermediary.
4. The Word had a changeable nature, and he remains good by exercising his free will only so long as he chooses.
5. The ousiai (substances or beings) of the Father, the Son, and the Spirit are divided and differ from one another. The Father is Son's origin and the Son's God. There are two pearls of wisdom, one that existed eternally with God, the other the Son who was brought into existence in this understanding. Thus, there is another Word of God besides the Son, and it is because the Son shares in this that he is called, by grace, Word and Son.[128]

These arguments sound orthodox, because with a critical look, Arius's exegesis is more inclined to literalists approach devoid of any philosophical sentiment than allegorical with its attendant errors. Frances Young pushes this point a little bit further;

> The character of Arius' teaching presupposes not any current philosophical monotheism, but an exegetical debate within Christian circle about the status of the Logos. Arius adopted a literalist interpretation of those texts which attributed progress and human weakness to the Son of God, and found this confirmed by John 14:28: My Father is greater than I. He accepted the traditional view that wisdom in Proverbs 8 is identical with the Logos, and on the basis of v. 22 concluded that the Logos was God's creature.[129]

Literal as Arius's exegesis seems, his desire to preserve monotheism, the unity or oneness of God led him ultimately into a dangerous interpretation of Jesus Christ, and his exegesis did not appeal to Alexander the Bishop whose sound theological eyes quickly saw the error in his doctrine. He, therefore, reaffirmed his position in another sermon in 320 by robustly explaining the true faith, "The Word is not created, He is eternal and He is

---

128. Letham, *Holy Trinity*, 111–112.
129. Young, *From Nicaea to Chalcedon*, 62.

God; He is inferior to the Father only in that He is engendered; He derives His being from the very being of the Father (ἐξ αὐτοῦ τοῦ ὄντος Πατρός)."[130] But Arius kept countering Alexander's position, and in 321 Alexander convened a synod that had Arius condemned, and the latter fled to his schoolmate Eusebius the Bishop of Nicomedia "whom he calls his collucianist."[131]

The controversy became bitter and moved out of the church and spilt over the entire Empire where not only the clerics but even the Emperor whose political ears were opened got to hear about the debate. As Alan Richardson underlines;

> The quarrel rented the Alexandrian Church and assumed such serious proportions that by 324 Emperor Constantine felt it necessary to intervene. He sent *Hosius,* Bishop of Cordova, to attempt to heal the breach. The mission of *Hosius* failed, and the Emperor, doubtless acting on the suggestion of *Hosius,* called an Ecumenical or General Council to meet at Nicaea in the following year (325), with a view to ending the controversy.[132]

When the Emperor began to see the severe implications of the debate, he was determined to put an end to the schism and this informed the calling for the Nicene Council where we meet for the very first time the man – Athanasius, whose sound theological ideas would not only transform the fourth-century Christian church and thus save the day, but also would become the norm for subsequent articulation of orthodox evangelical christological formulation the world over.

Such was the situation in which Athanasius got embroiled in the Nicene controversy. As John Piper's epigram carries, "Athanasius became the flashpoint of controversy" and argues his point aptly.[133] His main thoughts are contained in two principal works: *De incarnatione* and *Contra Gentes* believed to have been "written before the outbreak of the Arian controversy."[134]

---

130. Cayré, *Manual of Patrology,* 328.
131. Cayré, 313.
132. Richardson, *Creeds in the Making,* 52.
133. John Piper, *Contending for Our All: Defending Truth and Treasuring Christ in the Lives of Athanasius, John Owen and J. Gresham Machen* (Leicester: Inter-Varsity Press, 2006), 50.
134. Young, *From Nicaea to Chalcedon,* 68–69.

Bromiley echoes this fact by asserting, "The incarnation of the Word predates the Arian campaign. Hence it does not deal at all with the teaching of Arius."[135]

Francis Young's and William Bromiley's submission that Athanasius's *De incarnatione* and *Contra Gentes* were written before the outbreak of the Arian controversy sounds incredible considering how Athanasius tackled issues in his works that sound like he was responding to the error of Arius as is evident in his arguments. One becomes all the more doubtful as he considers the assertion of David W. Dorries, "Athanasius recognized and encountered the fatal flaws in Arianism more capable than any other defender of Christian truth."[136] Dorries implies that the christological debate that engulfed the fourth century was subsequent to Arianism. Hence, Athanasius wrote to counter that falsehood. While this is no place for controversy, it is critical we focus on what Athanasius presents in his work; whether by coincidence or intention or divine inspiration. Thus, in the *contra gentes* (2–5), he maintained, "Man who originally had *theōria* (vision) of God and all that was good, turned to 'things nearer to himself,' the material rather than the spiritual, he became corrupted by selfish desires and worshipped the creature instead of the Creator. This same theme is taken up in the *De incarnatione* [11–16]."[137] Letham categorized Athanasius's argument into three basic assumptions: "creation, incarnation and deification. Athanasius relates his view of God closely to salvation and deification."[138]

On the aspect of creation, Letham summarizes Athanasius's arguments as follows:

---

135. Geoffrey W. Bromilley, *Historical Theology: An Introduction* (Edinburgh: T & T Clark, 1994), 69.

136. David W. Dorries, *Edward Irving's Incarnational Christology* (Fairfax, VA: Xulon Press, 2002), 159.

137. In the *De incarnatione*, Athanasius points out the foolishness of philosophers who thought were sophisticated but are actually in the sight of the Creator foolish since they adore creation in place of the Creator. He makes his point; "whereas in what precedes we have drawn out—choosing a few points from among many—a sufficient account of the error of the heathen concerning idols, and of the worship of idols, and how they originally came to be invented; how, namely, out of wickedness men devised for themselves the worshipping of idols." For detail on Athanasius's critic of human error, see Athanasius, *On the Incarnation* (Willits, CA: Eastern Orthodox Books, nd), 1; Young, *From Nicaea to Chalcedon*, 70; and Letham, *Holy Trinity*, 128.

138. Letham, *Holy Trinity*, 128.

It is, then, proper for us to begin the treatment of this subject by speaking of the creation of the universe, and of God its artificer, that so it may be duly perceived that the renewal of creation has been the work of self-same Word that made it at the beginning. For it will appear not in consonant for the Father to have wrought its salvation in him by whose means he made it.[139]

Athanasius seems to have applied the principle of "give back to Caesar what is Caesar's, and to God what is God's" (Matt 22:21) since his argument points to the fact that only the Creator has the prerogative to redeem his creation.

What is the purpose of the incarnation? Athanasius argues that because the fall of man results in his depravity, God deliberately took unto himself human flesh and got conceived in the womb of the Virgin by condescending to put on mortality so that he might save us. He asserts, "For being Himself mighty, and Artificer of everything, he prepares the body in the Virgin as a temple unto himself, and makes it his very own as an instrument, in it manifested, and in it dwelling."[140] Philip Schaff and Henry Wace underscored the same view, "None, then, could bestow incorruption, but He Who had made, none restores the likeness of God, save His Own Image, none quicken, but the Life, none teach, but the Word. And He, to pay our debt of death, must also die for us, and rise again as our first-fruits from the grave. Mortal, therefore, His body must be; corruptible, His Body could not be."[141]

The question of the incarnation is settled; it is to restore the "corruptible to incorruption, [for] except the Saviour Himself, that had at the beginning also made all things out of naught: and that none other could create the likeness of God's image for men anew, save the Image of the Father; and that none other could render the mortal immortal, save our Lord Jesus Christ, Who is the Very Life."[142]

By becoming human in the flesh, God settled the problem of sin since the incarnation had dealt a death blow to Satan the author of sin and death

---

139. Letham, 128.

140. Athanasius, *On the Incarnation*, 13.

141. Philip Schaff and Henry Wace, eds., *A Select Library of Nicene and Post-Nicene Fathers of the Christian Church*, second series, vol. 4, *St Athanasius: Select Works and Letters* (New York: Charles Scribner's Sons, 1923), 46. Referred to as *St Athanasius* hereafter.

142. Schaff and Wace, *St Athanasius*, 46–47.

and restores anew all the damage done by the fall, when Christ hung on the cross at Calvary. Schaff and Wace capture the essence of the cross in their startling restatement of Athanasius's polemic, "Why the Cross, of all deaths? (1) He had to bear the curse for us. (2) On it, He held out His hands to unite all, Jews and Gentiles, in Himself. (3) He defeated the 'Prince of the powers of the air' in his own region, clearing the way to heaven for us the everlasting doors."[143]

The last point in Letham's taxonomy is deification which could not have been possible had Christ not die on the cross. There is, therefore, a connection between the finished work on the cross and the restoration and glorification of all creatures. Letham makes a robust restatement of this fact thus,

> For therefore did he assume the body originate and human, that having renewed it as its framer, he might deify it in himself, and thus might introduce us all into the kingdom of heaven after his likeness. For man had not been deified if joined to a creature, or unless the Son was very God; nor had man been brought into the Father's presence, unless he had been his natural and true Word who had put on the body.[144]

The climax of Jesus's achievement is now tied together in the themes of incarnation and deification. For Athanasius, the purpose of the incarnation is not only because God wished to become man for just no course. The embodiment is meant to restore man back to his pristine state who now is joined heir with Christ as he shares in his glory. Athanasius made a fascinating connection between the incarnation and deification when he held, "For he was made a man that we might be made God; and He manifested Himself by a body that we might receive the idea of the unseen Father; and He endured the insolence of men that we might inherit immortality."[145]

The notion of God making himself the man that man might be made God is the peak of the incarnation which culminated in deification. From the foregoing, what is the central thesis of Athanasius regarding the relation of God the Father and the Son in the Trinitarian framework? The answer to the

---

143. Schaff and Wace, 49.
144. Letham, *Holy Trinity*, 130.
145. Athanasius, *On the Incarnation*, 83–84.

above question is provided by Placher who briefly summarizes Athanasius's theology from a letter written by Arius to Bishop Eusebius of Nicomedia. In that letter, Arius complains;

> The bishop greatly wastes and persecutes us, and leaves no stone unturned against us. He has driven us out of the city as atheists, because we do not concur in what he publicly preaches, namely God always, the Son always; as the Father so the Son; the Son co-exists unbegotten with God; He is everlasting; neither by thought nor by any interval does God precede the Son; always God, always Son; he is begotten of the unbegotten; the Son is of God Himself.[146]

Letham captures Athanasius's Trinitarian articulation which he believes was the latter's exposition of Luke 10:22 in the following words,

> The divine essence (being) of the Word is united to his own Father. Whatever is the Father is the Son. Since the Father is not a creature, neither is the Son. The will of the Father and the will of the Son are one since they are indivisible. The Son is an exact seal of the Father. The triad is one and indivisible, without degrees; there is no first, second or third God.[147]

Athanasius's primary concern was soteriology, and he will not be contented with what he has presented if the critical and vitally essential aspect of the incarnation is not pointed out explicitly. So, he dwelled elaborately on the doctrine of the incarnation through a series of rhetorical questions meant to stimulate and provoke the thoughts of his opponents thus;

> How can a man be redeemed if Christ is not God? If Christ had not been, of Himself, the consubstantial image of the Father, if He was God only by borrowing and participation, He could never have formed the likeness of God in anyone, since He Himself would have been no more than a God-like being. For he who possesses nothing that he has not borrowed from another can communicate nothing to others since what he has,

---

146. Placher, *Readings in the History*, vol. 1, 52.
147. Letham, *Holy Trinity*, 134.

instead of being really his, remains the possession of the giver, and the alms he has received serves only to cover his poverty and nakedness.[148]

Athanasius's arguments against Arius are reminiscent of Gregory Nazianzus's arguments against Apollinarius in his letter to Cledonius. For Nazianzus, Apollinarius had succeeded in compromising the saving work of Jesus Christ. Thus in one of his two letters to Cledonius against Apollinarius, he insisted,

> If anyone has put his trust in him as a man without a human mind, he is really bereft of mind, and quite unworthy of salvation. For that which he has not assumed, he has not healed, but that which is united to his Godhead is also saved. If only half Adam fell, then that which Christ assumes and saves may be half also; but if the whole of his nature fell, it must be united to the whole nature of Him that was begotten, and so be saved as a whole.[149]

The fear entertained by Nazianzus is as well the fear and the worry of the other two Cappadocian fathers and Hilary of Poitiers. Louis Berkhof wrote, "The three Cappadocian fathers and Hilary of Poitiers maintained that, if the Logos did not assume human nature in its integrity, He could not be our perfect Redeemer, since the whole sinner had to be renewed; Christ had to assume human nature in its entirety, and not simply the least parts of it."[150]

It is obvious from the argument of the Cappadocian fathers and Hilary that Athanasius was not all alone in perceiving and correcting the errors of the heretics of his day as his exposition revealed. With Athanasius's rich exposition, Letham concluded that he has succeeded in mounting a full scale "rebuttal of all in the Arian camp."[151] Certainly, the Arian camp was

---

148. Cayré, *Manual of Patrology*, 351.

149. For detail discussion of Gregory Nazianzus's letters to Cledonius against Apollinarianius, see Andrew Manwarren, "Apollinarius: Know Your Heretics," Pastor Manwarren's Musings, https://pastorandrewmanwarren.com/2010/03/30/apollinarius-know-your-heretics/; Bettenson, *Documents of the Christian Church*, 44; McGrath, *Christian Theology Reader*, 268–270; Schaff and Wace, *Select Library*, vol. 7, 437–445.

150. Berkhof, *History of Christian Doctrines*, 103.

151. Letham, *Holy Trinity*, 134.

shaken to its foundations by Athanasius's witty employment of the Greek iota "i" in the debate to arrive at the notion of *homoousios* since he believed that the Son is co-equal, co-eternal, and consubstantial with the Father as opposed to Arius's fears that removing the first "i" in *homoiousios* will undermine monotheism – the unity and oneness of God and thus make Jesus of Nazareth co-eternal with God since as Arius believed there was a time when he was not.

John Chrysostom alluded to Arius's fallacy and responded in a fashion that resonated with Athanasius's argument against Arius's party. In his exposition of the Gospel of John 1:1 which is generally known in theological and biblical scholarship as Homily IV, he raised a pertinent question that harks back to Athanasius's opposition of Arius's position that there was when the Son was not. Thus, he asked, "And how again, since He is 'Life,' was there a time ever when He was not?"[152] Chrysostom saw a solemn pitfall in Arius's view that associated Jesus with beginning and temporariness. He, therefore, countered such an error by robustly arguing, "For all must allow, that Life both is always, and is without beginning and without end, if It is indeed Life, as indeed It is. For if there be when It is not, how can It be the Life of others, when It even Itself is not."[153] It is interesting to note that both Athanasius and Chrysostom stuck to *homoousios* as the ideal way Jesus Christ should be comprehended and presented in dogmatic Christian belief. The position of the "i" strategically is the letter that determines the victory of orthodoxy over heterodoxy. It is amazing that an "i" and not any giant Greek philosophical idea defeated the whole theological world of Athanasius's day. Because of the tremendous difference between *homoousios* and *homoiousios*, Arius's eloquent mind alongside Eusebius's erudition had to bow down to Athanasius's witty idea in the use of a small letter. This huge difference is the powerful "i." As Needham asserts, "the difference in meaning was serious. *Homoiousios* meant that the Son was 'of a similar essence' to the Father: not the same, but similar."[154] While the Arian camp was careful not to violate a

---

152. Philip Schaff, ed., *A Select Library of the Nicene and Post-Nicene Fathers of the Christian Church*, first series, vol. 14, *Homilies on the Gospel of St John and the Epistle to the Hebrews* (Grand Rapids, MI: Eerdmans, 1983), 18. Reffered to as *Homilies on the Gospel of Saint John* hereafter.

153. Schaff, *Homilies on the Gospel of Saint John*, 18.

154. Needham, *2000 Years of Christ's Power*, 211–212.

fundamental Old Testament belief in the absolute unity or oneness of the sovereign God by using *homoousios* for Jesus whom he believed had a beginning, Athanasius, on the contrary, used the compound Greek *homoousios* to present the real identity and ontological being of the incarnate *Logos* who became human to argue his case (John 1:14).

At this juncture, we need to dissect the Greek word *Homoousios*. *Homoousios*, "a Greek compound word – *homo* meaning 'same' or 'identical' and *ousios* meaning 'essence' or 'substance' largely determined the direction of the Arius/Athanasius debate of the fourth century."[155] With this word, Athanasius is armed with a sophisticated weapon to argue his case. Thus, in the debate, he contends, "Jesus is of one substance or essence with the Father. He is fully divine."[156] With this position, the council accepted and established the divinity of Jesus Christ and also at the same time issued the famous creed of Nicaea which firmly presents Christ as "being one essence (homos-ousios) with the Father.[157]" A fair detail restatement of the Nicene Creed is reproduced by Allan Richardson thus, "There is One Lord, Jesus Christ . . . very God of very God, begotten not made, consubstantial (*homoousios*) with the Father, by whom all things were made."[158]

Henry Bettenson reproduces the revised Eusebian fashion as follows;

> We believe in one God the Father All-sovereign, maker of all things visible and invisible;

> And in one Lord Jesus Christ, the Son of God, begotten by the Father, only-begotten, that is, of the substance of the Father, God of God, Light of Light, true God of true God, begotten not made, of one substance with the Father, through whom all things were made, things in heaven and things on earth; who for us men and for our salvation came down and was made flesh, and became man, suffered, and rose on the third day, ascended into the heavens, is coming to judge living and dead.

---

155. Nichols, *For Us and for Our*, 61
156. Nichols, 61.
157. Austin, *Austin's Topical History*, 93.
158. Richardson, *Creeds in the Making*, 52.

And in the Holy Spirit.

And those that say "There was when he was not,"

and, "Before he was begotten he was not,"

and that, "He came into being from what-is-not,"

or those who allege, that the son of God is

"Of another substance or essence."

or "created,"

or "changeable,"

or "alterable,"

these the Catholic and Apostolic Church anathematizes.[159]

It is interesting to note that in each of those creedal confessions, the phrase, "These the Catholic Church anathematizes," repeatedly featured and this expression was never taken for granted. The seriousness of this expression in the early church is exemplified in the banishment of Arius and his team which was actually anathematized.

The Nicene verdict was firm and stable; Arius was anathematized and banished with two of his companions to Illyria. Unfortunately, Arius's banishment did not end the christological rift. In the light of this Kelly keenly writes, "The Nicene crisis did not come to an end with the closing of the Council. Arianism proper had, for the moment, been driven underground, but the conflict only served to throw into relief the deep-seated theological divisions in the ranks of its adversaries."[160] Kelly's point here is that at the surface, the Arian/Athanasian controversy seemed to have been healed by coming to an end with the banishment of Arius and his team. On the contrary, however, deep on the inside, it is eating like an un-manifested earthquake or a smouldering log of wood. For this reason, two years later after the Nicene victory the strive was renewed with great and fresh intensity and tenacity when Emperor Constantine who seemed to side with the underground party unjustly received Arius back into favour and in turn

---

159. Bettenson, *Documents of the Christian Church*, 25. Reproduced with permission of Oxford Publishing Limited through PLSClear.

160. Kelly, *Early Christian Doctrines*, 237.

banished Athanasius the champion of orthodoxy who at this time was Bishop of Alexandria to Treves.

The great injustice Athanasius suffered here is just but a tip of the iceberg since this was not the only time in his life justice was denied him. According to tradition, Athanasius suffered five different banishments which along with the teaching of Macedonius, Bishop of Constantinople between 341 and 360 became the flashpoint that primarily led to the Council of Constantinople in 381. In his office as the Bishop Macedonius taught that the Holy Spirit is a minister and a servant on the same plane and level with angels. For him, the Holy Spirit was a creature subordinate to God the Father and Jesus Christ the Son. With this assertion, Macedonus succeeds in stripping off the Holy Spirit of his deity as a member of the Trinity and would be as harmful to accept the conception of the Holy Spirit as the view of Arius were to the notion of Christ at Nicaea.[161]

Meanwhile, Emperor Constantine died and after a while Theodosius I (also known as Theodosius the Great), a Spaniard by birth, and educated in the Nicene faith, ascended to the throne in 379 and became instrumental in completing the triumph of orthodoxy over an error in the Roman Empire. This he achieved by issuing in 380, the celebrated edict that requested all subjects in the empire to confess the Orthodox faith, and threatened non-compliance with punishment, and in that same year entered Constantinople and raised Gregory Nazianzen to the patriarchal chair in place of Demophilus who refused to renounce his heretical convictions and drove the Arians out of all the churches of the capital.

To give coercive measures, the sanction of the law and to restore unity in the church of the whole empire, Emperor Theodosius the Great convened the second Ecumenical Council of the church at Constantinople in May 381 in which 186 bishops attended. In this council, the Arian controversy took its own natural course. The truth regained free to play, and the Nicene spirit was permitted to assert its intrinsic power and gradually achieved victory, first in the Latin church, which held several orthodox synods in Rome, Milan and Gaul; then in Egypt and the East, through the wise and energetic administration of Athanasius and three great Cappadocian bishops.

---

161. Cairns, *Christianity Through the Centuries*, 145.

When one compares the comprehensive picture both Tertullian and Athanasius had and presented of Jesus Christ to their African contemporaries and the world at large, one is puzzled how African theologians today have grossly failed to walk on the theological pedestals of their forebearers in the Christian faith by presenting Jesus Christ with the same amount of vividness Tertullian and Athanasius did. Against Marcion and Praxeas, Tertullian argues that "if he [Jesus Christ] was wholly the son of man, he should not also be the Son of God, and should be in no sense greater than Solomon or than Jonah,"[162] while frequently, "Athanasius says that Christ took a human nature just like ours and pointed to the common practice of Scripture to call human beings 'flesh.'"[163]

Both theologians, Tertullian and Athanasius, acknowledged the fact of Jesus's humanity, but nowhere did any of them by any means fix him within the class of mere mortal ancestors as African theologians are fond of theologizing today in the twenty-first century. This is confirmed by Tertullian's argument that if Jesus were solely a human being without divinity, he would not have been any better than men like Solomon and Jonah. Athanasius crowns it all. For him, "Had the Son been a creature, He could not have affected our union with God, and consequently man would have had to remain mortal. A creature does not possess the power to join itself or other creatures to God."[164]

In addition, the way Athanasius presents his argument shows that if Jesus were a mere mortal in the proportion of our African ancestors, he would have been incapable of securing our salvation since he himself would have needed to be saved by one who is greater than he. He maintains; "It was necessary that our regeneration should be the work of an uncreated being—that is to say, of their Creator, that in His person He, being made man for our sakes, might repair our fallen nature and make us a new creature."[165] In his exposition of the Gospel of Matthew in Homily II, John Chrysostom gave the significance of Jesus's birth to include the fact that "He was born after the

---

162. Zamoyta, *Theology of Christ*, 22.
163. Letham, *Holy Trinity*, 133.
164. Dorries, *Edward Irving's Incarnational*, 162.
165. Dorries, 163.

flesh, that thou mightest be born after the spirit; He was born of a woman, that thou mightest cease to be the son of a woman."[166]

To conclude, we concur with Tertullian and Athanasius that it was essential that our regeneration be secured by one whom himself is God. Whether this work of restoration Jesus Christ obtained for the whole world pointed by Tertullian and Athanasius which is being compared with what African ancestors are believed to achieve for their living kin emerged from a real conviction or, it is the result of some distorted and ideal picture of African ancestors viewed in terms of Greek metaphysical dualism is what the next section addresses.

III. Greek Metaphysics and the African Ancestor Realm

In a traditional African worldview, the spirit double of a man becomes an ancestor who is believed to have survived death and to be living in a spiritual world where he originated.[167] Accordingly, "death does not annihilate life" for "the departed continue to exist in the hereafter."[168] Klaus Nürnberger makes a pertinent submission, "In *Traditionalism* ancestors are deemed 'real' because their existential impact on the living is pervasive and decisive."[169] The belief that Africans die only to return to their abode of origin after this physical life signifies not only that there is both in the one physical man, a corporeal personality and an ethereal entity, which can necessarily be assumed in a non-material world. For most African societies, the ethereal being is divine which has now at death become detached from the physical body but requires the same amount of nurture and protection on its journey to the ancestral world much the same as the physical body demanded nourishment and protection while still alive on earth. This explains why in some African societies during burial ceremonies, which at the same time mark the beginning of the journey to the ancestral world, "food and weapons may be

---

166. Philip Schaff, ed., *A Select Library of Nicene and Post-Nicene Fathers of the Christian Church*, first series, vol. 10, *Saint Chrysostom: Homily on the Gospel of Saint Matthew* (Edinburgh: T & T Clark, 1998), 10. Referred to as *Chrystom: Homily on the Gospel* hereafter.

167. E. Geffory Parrinder, *African Traditional Religion*, 3rd ed. (London: Sheldon, 1974), 58.

168. Richard J. Gehman, *African Traditional Religion in Biblical Perspective* (Wheaton, IL: Oasis International, 2012), 202.

169. Nürnberger, *Living Dead*, 14.

buried with the dead body to sustain and protect the person in the journey between the two worlds or places."[170]

The above point, no doubt, resonates with Plato's metaphysics that "there is a dual world: the world of ideas or Forms and the world of phenomena or things."[171] Like the African belief that man at death returns to his original home, which presupposes the pre-existence of the soul, Plato also maintains that "the human soul pre-existed before its union with the body. It pre-existed . . . in the world of Forms before it came into this world to be imprisoned in the body."[172] Frederick Copleston buttresses this argument further as he notes that for Plato, "the soul existed before its union with the body in a transcendental realm, where it beheld the subsistent intelligible entities or Ideas, which would seem to constitute a plurality of 'detached' essence."[173] If the human soul pre-existed before its union with the body, what is the nature of this soul? For Plato,

> the soul is something divine in man, it is immortal, immaterial or spiritual . . . it formerly existed without a body and will continue to exist after its separation from the body at death. But it will go through a series of re-incarnations until it is able to achieve final liberation or release. Then it will go back to the world of Forms from which it came.[174]

Hardly would any African who reads Plato metaphysics fail to appropriate the trend of his thought; for most Africans, hold onto the belief in the reincarnation and the final abode of the dead. Whether there is scarcely any real dividing line between Platonic metaphysics and African view of the destiny of the souls of the departed and what happens to the souls of the ancestors is yet to be established in this work, and it is to it we now turn.

To begin with, it is pertinent we inquire where is the place of virtue in the world of forms in Platonic metaphysics and ethics especially with respect

---

170. Mbiti, *African Religions and Philosophy*, 155.

171. Heick, *History of Christian Thought*, 25.

172. Joseph Omoregbe, *A Simplified History of Western Philosophy: Ancient and Medieval Philosophy*, vol. 1 (Nigeria: Joja Press, 2005), 42.

173. Frederick Copleston, *A History of Philosophy*, vol. 1, *Greece and Rome* (New York: Doubleday, 1993), 166.

174. Omoregbe, *Simplified History*, 43.

to the destiny of the soul? Like in most Greek philosophy which tends to discard anything phenomenal, the only real world as opposed to the phenomenal cosmos is that of ideas. Greek disdain for corporeality is brought to bear upon Plato's metaphysical argument. Hence he clearly maintained, "The world of phenomena, which is constantly changing, is fundamentally nonexistence; it receives real character only insofar as it partakes of the ideas."[175] For Plato this metaphysical differentiation between the two worlds is also ethical. Only the world of ideas, whose summit is God, is the world of good.[176] Furthermore, Plato believes that since God is good, the essence of all things which he calls the forms or ideas derived from the goodness of good God, who is himself the epitome of goodness. In this light, God created all things according to the model or original forms that exist in the transcendental realm of perfection. Copleston makes this point passionately, "In the Timaeus Plato clearly teaches that God or the 'Demiurge' forms the things of this world according to the model of the Forms. The implication of the foregoing is that the forms or Ideas exist apart, not only from the sensible things that are modeled on them, but also from God, Who takes them as his model."[177] For Plato, as for most Greek philosophers, the human soul which is created to model the perfection of its creator is essentially good; nonetheless, some souls are prone to evil. Thus, human souls have two destinations: one for the morally good and another for the bad souls. Plato argues,

> I am confident in the belief that there truly is such a thing as living again, and that the souls of the dead are in existence, and that the good souls have a better portion than the evil. The soul's self-redemption, when successfully worked out, will result in the final attainment of the "beatific vision" of eternal beauty and goodness. For the bad there will be future punishment.[178]

Obviously, Greek eschatology parallels African traditional religious eschatology. The parallelism between the two is so very close that there is hardly

---

175. Heick, *History of Christian Thought*, 25.
176. Heick, 25.
177. Copleston, *History of Philosophy*, 167.
178. Heick, *History of Christian Thought*, 26.

any room for argument on the basis of dissimilarities. In African traditional religious eschatology, the dead are rewarded for that which they have done while on earth. In fact the first criterion for becoming an ancestor in Africa is predicated on one's good living while on earth. Lois Fuller corroborates, "In most ATRs, not every person who dies becomes an 'ancestor' to be consulted and given offerings. Usually the person must have lived a good life."[179] This good life also determines one's rewards and punishment in the ancestral abode. Paul O. Ajah writes, "The abode of the dead is of two compartments: a good place and a bad place. The good place is reserved for the successful souls who therefore become ancestors but the bad place is occupied by the unsuccessful souls who thereby become evil spirits from whom the living needs to be protected."[180]

Plato also believed that God is incorporeal. It thus follows that the forms or ideas which exist in the world of numina represents his kind of person. Thus, the forms or ideas "cannot be known through sense perception because they are not perceptible by the senses. Particular individual things are mere shadow, reflections or imitations of these 'Forms' which are the ideal things, the real things, the essence of things."[181] This brings us to the heart and zenith of African ancestral belief and the basis upon which this work argues that Greek Metaphysics and the African ancestor realm are two on the same plane.

In traditional African belief, man on earth is imperfect, vulnerable and incapacitated to protect himself from the spirits that permeates his environment but when death makes its way and takes the life of a good man, he at once gets united ontologically with the good ancestors in the ancestral realm. In the ancestral world, the ancestor becomes impregnable capable of "speaking a bilingual language of human beings whom they recently left,"[182] as well as "speak the languages of spirits and of God, to whom they are drawing nearer ontologically."[183] In typical African belief, ancestors are

---

179. Lois Fuller, *A Missionary Handbook on African Traditional Religion* (Plateau State: Africa Christian Textbooks, 2005), 59.

180. Paul O. Ajah, *African Traditional Religion* (Uburu, Nigeria: Truth and Life Publications, 2007), 213–214.

181. Omoregbe, *Simplified History*, 40.

182. John S. Mbiti, *Concepts of God in Africa* (New York: Praeger, 1970), 230.

183. Mbiti, *African Religions and Philosophy*, 82.

very powerful and partake in everything that happens in the family of their living kin. Mbiti captures this argument thus;

> they know and have interest in what is going on in the family . . . they enquire about family affairs, and may even warn of impending danger or rebuke those who have failed to follow their special instruction. They are the guardians of family affairs, traditions, ethics and activities . . . act as invisible police of the family and communities.[184]

For the reason of the ubiquitous powers of ancestors, Africans also believe that an ancestor could be vengeful, vindictive and thus punishes wrongdoers.[185] Conversely, ancestors are as well benevolent since they are held to protect their living kin as well as guarantors of fecundity within the family lineage.[186] It is natural from the foregoing, for the cult of the ancestor to be the centre of attraction in African societies since this is where one derives his security and relevance for healthy and prosperous life on earth. As Yusufu Turaki notes, "The cult of the ancestor plays a significant part in the search for spiritual and mystical powers. Traditional Africans believe that maintaining good relations with the ancestors ensures continuation of the life force and spiritual powers."[187]

In Platonic eschatology like traditional African eschatology, "present life and future life for Plato are regulated by the exercise of moral good, with the apex of this exercise being virtue."[188] For Plato, virtuous souls that return to the world of forms are rewarded for their apparent goodness while still on earth. Souls' destiny, then, in the world of forms which resonates with the African ancestral world is determined by how well one lived in the temporal sphere of human existence. He argues, "It is certain that whoever

---

184. Mbiti, 82.

185. Aylward Shorter, *African Culture and the Christian Faith: An Introduction to Social and Pastoral Anthropology* (Maryknoll: Orbis Books, 1974), 59.

186. Shorter, *African Culture*, 59.

187. Yusufu Turaki, "Techniques of African Pagan Spirituality," in *On Global Wizardry: Techniques of Pagan Spirituality and A Christian Response*, ed. Peter Jones (Escondido, CA: Main Entry Editions, 2010), 121.

188. Dario Composta, *History of Ancient Philosophy* (Bangalore: Theological Publications, 2008), 213.

does good in this life will not suffer evils in the afterlife."[189] Our main thesis here is that the Greek idea of a world that exists outside the biosphere of the material world resonates with the African belief in a world wherein the virtuous ancestors' spirits dwell. Cletus Chukwuemeka Nwaogwugwu aptly states a similar thesis,

> It appears that the best description that could be given the abode of the spirits is to liken them to the Platonic world of ideas where the true reality abides with only images existing in the physical world. Perhaps this is an indication that the ancients in various parts of the world could have been thinking and perceiving things alike. They have always longed for better elucidation of the principles that govern the human life. The nature of man and the many things that accompany his life have continued to ginger a lot of speculations and investigations in all parts of the world.[190]

As we conclude, it is no error to concede Nwaogwugwu's thesis that the ancients seemed to have shared a common worldview with respect to the phenomenon around them or the reality of the world in which they lived. In this regard, African forefathers thought of the world in which their ancestors live in terms of Platonic idealism or world of forms.

IV. Biblical and Theological Models of Christ in the Thoughts of Tertullian and Athanasius and the Contemporary African Projection of Christ as an Ancestor: An *Apologia*

The unity of God and man in Jesus Christ, Wolfhart Pannenberg says, is the concluding and principal theme of Christology.[191] From the very beginning, Christian theology was forced to say both that Jesus is indeed God and, at the same time, indeed the man.[192] "The formula of the true divinity and real

---

189. Composta, *History of Ancient Philosophy*, 213.

190. Cletus Chukwuemeka Nwaogwugwu, *Ancestor Christology: A Christian Evaluation of the Ancestral Cult in the Traditional Religion of the Sub-Saharan Africa* (Bloomington, IN: iUniverse, 2011), 61.

191. Wolfhart Pannenberg, *Jesus – God and Man,* 2nd ed. (Philadelphia: Westminster, 1977), 283.

192. Pannenberg, *Jesus – God and Man,* 283.

humanity of Jesus begins with the fact that one describes one and the same person, the man Jesus of Nazareth . . . he is God, and he is man."[193] Thus, the Nicene declaration was the general acknowledgement of not only the essential and eternal deity of Christ but as well his humanity. For before the close of that controversy the realhumanity of Christ at the same came in again for treatment.[194]

The preceding idea necessitates the conclusion that the touchstone of theological orthodoxy is the person of Christ, and the centrality of Christ in the theologies of Tertullian and Athanasius makes it very critical that we seek to know not only the foundation and place which Christology occupied in their thinking but also the source of their christological models with which they formulated their theologies. This roadmap is inevitable since our approach here is to weigh the contemporary African projection of Jesus Christ as ancestor against the backdrop of Tertullian's and Athanasius's Christologies.

Of course, in those centuries, the christological models and formulations of Tertullian and Athanasius, which derived from the Bible and apostolic tradition, set the pace especially for the first two councils held at Nicaea (AD 325) and Constantinople (AD 381) in which it was concluded that the "Lord Jesus Christ is very God of very God, begotten not made, consubstantial . . . with the Father, by whom all things were made."[195] Granted the central place of Christ in the thinking of these two Africans in the third and fourth centuries, the question of source becomes imperative since we believe that their theologies are not ivory tower permutations but are theologies that emerged from meaningful engagement with biblical references alongside traditions that have been handed down to them from Jesus Christ and the apostles.

Heick sheds light here with his elaborate restatement of this thesis, "The teachings of Jesus and the Apostles constituted the special object of thought for the early Christian Fathers."[196] Jesus's teachings were at first oral living

---

193. Pannenberg, 284.

194. Philip Schaff, *History of the Christian Church*, vol. 3, *Nicene and Post-Nicene Christianity: From Constantine the Great to Gregory the Great A.D. 311-600* (Grand Rapids, MI: Eerdmans, 1984), 706.

195. Boer, *Short History*, 115.

196. Heick, *History of Christian Thought*, 32.

words received by the apostles and passed down to the church. "The Church Fathers had to interpret the Church's writings in a way that harmonized with the tradition of the Church (*regula fidei*)."[197] It follows, therefore, that when Tertullian and Athanasius stood their ground in the third and fourth centuries to formulate and defend Christian doctrines from the errors of the day, they were actually standing upon the pillar of inherited traditions passed unto them by the early church. Tertullian's and Athanasius's response to early heretics was thus faith's response against heterodox teachings in the infant church.

Suffice it then, to conclude without reservation, that Tertullian's and Athanasius's rhetoric and polemics were "faith's answer as to the ultimate significance of those things which the historian can demonstrate . . . that in and through Jesus, God had (decidedly) acted powerfully and climactically to make Himself known, to complete His creation, and to save."[198] Those things which the apostles demonstrated were canonized to become the church's creed and its New Testament. As Barr posits, "Both Creed and New Testament are Apostolic witness-eyewitness."[199] The apostles, Barr further observes,

> Played a key role in the primitive community's recalling of the past, their new lives as a result of, and witness to, Jesus' words and deeds. These were the ones who initially asked, "Who is he?" "What is the meaning of the wonder which has happened to us?" It was they who first found the answers which propelled Christianity into a worldwide religion. And it is in them that the Church's faith, now over nineteen centuries old, has its origin, and so is called the Apostolic Witness.[200]

The primary and fundamental source of Christian theology is the testimony of the apostles whose experiences were initially communicated and passed onto posterity as an oral tradition by the early church. Much later the oral traditions were canonized and reduced to writing as the church's creed and

---

197. Heick, 32.

198. O. Sydney Barr, *From the Apostles' Faith to the Apostles' Creed* (New York: Oxford University Press, 1964), 4–5.

199. Barr, *From the Apostle's faith*, 7.

200. Barr, 7.

New Testament. Since the source of Christian theology is rooted in the experience of those who were there together with Jesus Christ as living eye-witnesses, "it merits serious consideration as an individual authority which should set the norm and dictate the tune for the formulation of Christian theology in world Christianity."[201]

The conclusion has a lot of implications for ancestor Christology and thus leads to some critical questions: When African theologians say Jesus Christ is an ancestor, what exactly do they mean? Is Jesus Christ an ancestor in the same way Turbi is an ancestor to Reuben? Or is Jesus Christ an ancestor in some inexplicable and mystical way that they themselves have not been able to demonstrate? Do African ancestors literally exist in a celestial realm other than the paradise of Christian belief? And what does the Holy Bible say about the position of the dead? Nürnberger was curious to find out. Thus he inquires, "What does the Bible say about the role of the deceased in the lives of the living?"[202] It is true to admit that the lives of predecessors always have an impact on the lives of their successors, even after they have relinquished their positions.[203] But what should be the nature of this effect and the relationship that exists between the living and the dead? The questions which lie at the heart of this research demand that we take a brief but critical examination of biblical and theological teachings on the state of the dead. And it is on the basis of this assertion that this chapter concludes with a brief apologetical analysis of African ancestor Christology.

Apologetics as a strong presentation and defence of faith in Christ was first established in the New Testament (1 Pet 3:15). In the New Testament, apologetics is centred on the events surrounding Jesus's life. These events contained in the Gospels are core apologetics for Jesus much the same way the Acts of the Apostles are apologetics to the church. For after the acts of the earthly Jesus follows the acts of the exalted Jesus. Admittedly, the deeds of Jesus, ordinary and extraordinary, including ultimately his death and resurrection, earned him some credence. That aside, Jesus himself left behind some ordinances to the church which are to be used to remember his passion. The Holy Communion, for instance, is one such ordinance that celebrates

---

201. Barr, 7.
202. Nürnberger, *Living Dead*, 56.
203. Nürnberger, 57.

his memory and work of redemption as an instrument of God's redeeming love. Such an ordinance, however, is not a defining example for Africans to Christianize it as a model for remembering their beloved dead relations. And throughout history, Yahweh has used human instruments to bring about the fulfilment of his salvation plan. Prime examples are Abraham, Isaac, Jacob, Moses, Aaron, David, the prophets, some priestly authorities, sages and so on. Yet nowhere and never did these instruments of Yahweh after they die possess any authority of their own over the living.[204] I am quite aware of arguments from some scholars who consider the possibility that in pre-Yahwist times the Israelite tribes may have venerated their ancestors. But there is virtually no trace left of that, whether in the Scriptures or in archaeological findings.[205] As one investigates the Jewish Scriptures, Old and New Testaments, there are long genealogies. Yet the deceased who stand as pillars and founding ancestors of Israel's tribes were considered to be dead.[206] When an old man died, his bones were gathered to those of his fathers in the family grave, while his life continued in his descendants (Judg 2:10). Parents had a divinely ordained task when alive, but their deaths removed them from the scene.[207] They had the duty of educating their children in the faith of Israel and its historical foundations, but deceased family forebears were not deemed to be in charge of their descendants.[208]

An important ancient Near East metaphor that depicts the situation of the dead is *Sheol*. This word which means the place of the dead had mythological connotations in the ancient Near East, but for Israel, it indicated a lifeless sphere. Once there, one could no longer see the sun, enjoy life, or praise Yahweh (Job 7:7–10; Ps 6:5; Sir 17:27–28). Forebears could do nothing for their offspring, and their offspring could do nothing for them. Death was the end of all relationships.[209] If human beings live in one space and time, with one body, and then they die as is written, "Just as people are destined to die once, and after that to face judgment" (Heb 9:27), should we

---

204. Nürnberger, 58.
205. Nürnberger, 58.
206. Nürnberger, 59.
207. Nürnberger, 59.
208. Nürnberger, 59.
209. Nürnberger, 59.

African Christians then revert to our primal traditional belief in an African ancestral spirit realm after death as opposed to what the Bible teaches? It is not written that "the dead know nothing; they have no further reward, and even their name is forgotten. Their love, their hate and their jealousy have long since vanished; never again will they have a part in anything that happens under the sun"? (Eccl 9:5–6).

If theology is faith seeking understanding, where then is the place of the Bible and apostolic witness and tradition in African ancestor theology? It is the lasting conviction of this work that African theologians by formulating ancestor Christology have succeeded in creating a huge chasm between the theologies of Tertullian and Athanasius upon whose shoulders traditional Christian theology hangs. I sincerely and strongly believe that the belief in the validity and potency of dead African ancestors, either as a way of celebrating and preserving their memories or by way of articulating African identity and cultures or still yet by way of preserving African primal traditions through the methods of inculturation and contextualization, is never the way out to evangelizing Africans.

Amazingly, this African belief about the living-dead has found acceptance in some church denominations to the extent that they have approved ancestor veneration as part of their liturgy and tradition over against the normative teachings of Tertullian and Athanasius in the third and fourth centuries. Well, there is nothing novel about them because even some objects they used in their services speak volumes. Much as we strive to have a voice in the global theological enterprise, we should equally be careful of what we offer to Christendom as an African theological contribution. Unless we go back to the apostolic witness, which is built upon biblical teaching, our Christology will continue to paddle the dried sea without water upon which to sail since our approach to Christian theology is more culturally entrenched than biblical. We should allow Jesus Christ to be the measure of African culture and tradition and not the other way around. In fact, Byang H. Kato had argued that

> Jesus Christ wants to redeem the good values found in African culture for the spreading of the gospel in this great continent. Let us not shut Him out by dismissing the fact of the presence of such values in African culture. Rather let us explore them,

using the searchlight of the gospel, depending completely on Him who says, "I am the Light of the world."[210]

Summary

This chapter examined the historical and theological foundations of orthodox Christology. It traces the root of evangelical christological formulation back to the apostles who in the infant church proclaimed Jesus as the risen Lord. After the death of the apostles, the church fathers and apologists whose period overlapped succeeded and continued in the tradition of the apostles and formulated and consolidated the theological legacy and foundation already laid by the apostles. Their work during this period was predominantly that of articulating doctrines and defending the faith against it assailants and heresies. The African apologists Tertullian and Athanasius, whose theological insights became the norm for Orthodox Christian practice and belief in the ancient church, were reviewed. The chapter argues that the way and manner African theologians are presenting Christ as an ancestor in the twenty-first century does not only contradicts the Christologies of Tertullian and Athanasius in the early church but has as well revealed a break away from the traditional orthodox evangelical Christology these theologians and biblical scholars laboured to establish. This assertion prepares the way for the next chapter of the work.

---

210. Byang H. Kato, *African Cultural Revolution and the Christian Faith* (Jos, Nigeria: Challenge, 1976), 36.

CHAPTER 4

African Ancestor Christological Interpretation and Formulation as Rooted in African Worldview and Traditional Belief: Connecting Christ to Africa's Pre-Christian Category

Introduction

We saw in chapter 3 the eruption of christological heresies in the early church and how the church rose to the occasion and countered the debates that were intense with different positions proposed and debated from Nicaea in AD 325 to Chalcedon in AD 451. The Trinitarian Christology of Tertullian and the incarnational Christology of Athanasius that led to the defeat of heretics like Marcion, Praxeas, and Arius successfully and firmly laid the foundation for what we believe is generally held as an orthodox evangelical christological formulation.

With that orthodox foundation firmly established, Christian Christology, which since Chalcedon has been normative, is now in the twenty-first century considered anachronistic and incompatible with Africa's pre-Christian religious categories, particularly the ancestral model. To that end, African theologians are calling for a return to Africa's pre-Christian, traditional, religious group of ancestors as the point of departure for the reformulation of contemporary African Christology. This chapter argues that African theologians' desire to create a paradigm shift in the formulation of Christian theology in the category of an ancestor is inherently embedded in traditional African belief that tends to view Jesus Christ more from cultural spectacles as opposed to biblical lenses. The theologians have also adopted the genre of contextual theology and culture-oriented theological approach. The chapter will, therefore, examine the underlying African beliefs about a man[1] in African cosmology and cosmogony, the role ancestors are believed to play in African worldview, and how some African theologians formulate a theology of correlation that seeks to compare African ancestors with the departed saints of Christian faith.

Man in African Cosmology

The central thesis of this section is that the African worldview and belief system are the fulcrum around which ancestor christological models have been formulated by African theologians. James W. Sire defines worldview as, "A commitment, a fundamental orientation of the heart, that can be expressed as a story or in a set of presuppositions (assumptions which may be true or entirely false) that we hold (consciously or subconsciously, consistently or inconsistently) about the basic constitution of reality, and that provides the foundation on which we live and move and have our being."[2]

In examining the etymology of worldview, David K. Naugle traces its root back to Immanuel Kant who first used the German term "*Weltanschauung*," insignificantly to mean "*Mundussensibilis*; that is, to refer to a world-intuition in the sense of contemplation of the world given to the sense."[3] In later generations, "*weltanschauung* was adopted by Kant's successors and soon became well ensconced as a celebrated concept in German and European intellectual life."[4] Wilbur O'Donovan, Jr, is more African on the subject. For him, worldview is, "The view which a person has of this world. It is the way he understands and interprets the things which happen to him and to

---

1. It is to be noted that man in this context is used in a generic sense rather than strictly applying it to the male gender.

2. James W. Sire, *The Universe Next Door: A Basic Worldview Catalog* (Downers Grove, IL: InterVarsity Press, 2009), 20.

3. David K. Naugle, *Worldview: The History of a Concept* (Grand Rapids, MI: Eerdmans, 2002), 59.

4. Naugle, *Worldview*, 59.

other people. It is a person's way of understanding life and the world he lives in."⁵ O'Donovan's perception of the concept best fit into the African man's understanding of himself and the physical and spiritual phenomena that surround him.

To the African, man and the natural and supernatural forces together interact and impinge upon each other, and it is this way of viewing reality holistically that defines who an African is. Perhaps, this explains why Turaki defines worldview as, "The embodiment of culture, religion, customs, values and traditions."⁶ These five items Turaki captures fall within the total scope of African life and community setting. Where any of them is lacking, an African feels some level of emptiness and void, as he tends to believe that an essential aspect of his life and environment is missing. Perhaps, E. D. Oji's notion of African worldview quoted by Turaki encapsulates the total thought of the African in his community, religion, customs and social setting comprehensively. According to Orji, African worldview is,

> The basic fundamental core of their reality which manifests in their beliefs, values, response to the physical and spiritual realms. This influences the way they think, observe, and perceive; which ultimately controls the way they dress, build their houses, and maintain their environment. It is the basicprinciple of the life of a particular geographical region that affects perception, motivates life, determines values and truth, generates beliefs, moulds behaviour and excites emotions.⁷

A critical look at this definition reveals the fact that worldview is mostly a matter of human heart and mind which are the seats of human emotion and allegiance. Consequently, it has a "profound and pervasive influence upon African thought and philosophy."⁸ This worldview affects virtually every sphere of human life in Africa; it encompasses both one's existence and self-worth within the entire scheme of God's creation. Naugle says it aptly, "Worldviews spring from the totality of human psychological existence:

---

5. Wilbur O'Donovan, Jr, *Introduction to Biblical Christianity from African Perspective* (Ilorin, Nigeria: Nigeria Evangelical Fellowship, 1992), 3.
6. Turaki, *Unique Christ*, 59.
7. Turaki, 60.
8. Turaki, 60.

intellectually in the cognition of reality, effectively in the appraisal of life, and volitionally in the active performance of the will . . . it refers to a person's interpretation of reality and a basic view of life."[9] Grounded in this fundamental psychological belief, African society becomes lopsided tilted toward the male gender. In what follows, I examine African cosmology and cosmogony from the perspective of African anthropology as shrouded in the African ancestor christological discourse.

In the traditional African worldview, man is the centre of the universe, which he manipulates for his own advantage. John S. Mbiti says it decisively, "Man, who lives on the earth, is the centre of the universe."[10] Elsewhere Mbiti states, "African ontology is basically anthropocentric: man is at the very centre of existence, and African peoples see everything else in its relation to this central position of man . . . it is as if God exists for the sake of man."[11] He goes on to tell us how man manipulates the universe by arguing that man is "like the priest of the universe, linking the universe with God its Creator. A man awakens the universe, he speaks to it, he listens to it, he tries to create a harmony with the universe. It is the man who turns parts of the universe into sacred objects, and who uses other things for sacrifices and offerings."[12] On the whole, Mbiti notes, "It is as if the whole world exists for man's sake. Therefore African peoples look for the usefulness (or otherwise) of the universe to man."[13] We could deduce from the foregoing that African traditional religion is anthropocentric since it revolves around the human person. Uchenna A. Ezeh makes this point explicit,

> In the African universe, man occupies a pride of place. Basically, the African traditional religion is anthropological . . . in the African vision of reality everything appears to have its bearing and significance from the position, meaning, and end of man.

---

9. Naugle, *Worldview*, 88, 260.
10. John S. Mbiti, *Introduction to African Religion* (London: Heinemann, 1981), 33.
11. Mbiti, *African Religions and Philosophy*, 90.
12. Mbiti, *Introduction to African Religion*, 33.
13. Mbiti, 38.

This can be explained by the fact that the African traditional religion is essentially anthropocentric and not theocentric.[14]

The anthropocentricity in the African traditional religious system has its root in African creation myths which see man as "prefigured in creation's first beginning and he is the being around whom everything was organized."[15] The imminent peril here is for Africans to see a man in terms of the eighteenth-century enlightenment philosophy which held that man is the measure of everything and thus consequently displaced God.[16] In light of this, Cletus Chukwuemeka Nwaogwugwu has warned that "One must, however, be very careful in asserting this anthropocentrism because man's life and the world around him have no meaning without God who is always recognized as the sole Creator of the entire universe."[17]

Having briefly examined the centrality of man in the traditional African worldview, it is also critical we highlight in this work the origin of man in traditional African cosmogony and the vital place community occupies in the life and thought of an African person. Emefie Ikenga Metuh has defined cosmogonies as the "Theories about the origin of the universe."[18] Metuh's concept of cosmogony here refers to the "myths which explain the origin

---

14. Uchenna A. Ezeh, *Jesus Christ the Ancestor: An African Contextual Christology in the Light of the Major Dogmatic Christological Definitions of the Church from the Council of Nicaea (325) to Chalcedon (451)* (New York: Lang, 2003), 50–51.

15. Benjamin C. Ray, *African Religions: Symbols, Rituals, and Community* (Upper Saddle River, NJ: Prentice Hall, 1976), 133.

16. A fundamental principle of enlightenment philosophy is a "shift from God-centred thinking to human-centred philosophizing. Hence the Cartesian rationalism effectively inaugurated the 'modern self' or the 'subjective turn,'" (Hoffecker, *Revolutions in Worldview*, 254). Immanuel Kant a leading thinker of enlightenment philosophy defines enlightenment as "man's emergence from his self-imposed immaturity. Immaturity is the inability to use one's understanding without the guidance of another. This immaturity is self-imposed when its cause lies not in lack of understanding but in lack of resolve and courage to use it without guidance from another. *Sapere Aude!* (dare to know) 'Have courage to use your own understanding!'—that is the motto of enlightenment." (Hoffecker, 265–266). Another key ideology of enlightenment is "man's coming of age"(John A. T. Robinson and David L. Edward, *The Honest to God Debate* [London: SCM, 1963], 210). For more on enlightenment ideologies, see Robinson and Edward, *Honest to God*. An important work that comprehensively deals with enlightenment philosophy is Hoffecker, *Revolutions in Worldview*, 240–280.

17. Nwaogwugwu, *Ancestor Christology*, 57.

18. Emefie Ikenga Metuh, *Comparative Studies of African Traditional Religions* (Onitsha, Nigeria: IMICO, 1987), 41.

and organization of the universe from the fewest possible elements or from some first principles."[19] This definition forms the basis upon which Africans view the universe and its origin and the reason why we have also earlier on conceded that man is at the apex of the created universe.

It is necessary we state too that all African societies without exception, believe that this being called a man is a creature. In other words, Africans acknowledged God the supreme being the maker of man. Muzorewa confirmed this when he quoted Mbiti who wrote earlier that "It is generally acknowledged that God is the originator of man, even if the exact methods of creating man may differ according to the myths of different peoples."[20] The difficulty in having a generally accepted African view on the particular method God used to design man is further captured in the argument of Muzorewa who cites John Pobee that "*Homo Africanus* is a multi-headed hydra."[21] Muzorewa himself attests however that "difficult though it may be to describe, Africans have a certain image of humanity that can be articulated."[22]

In his, *God and Man in African Religion: A Case Study of the Igbo of Nigeria*, Metuh identifies four basic components of human nature with which Africans define man in his cosmic relationship with the ontological order. First, Metuh maintains that man is conceived as "soul" with a vivifying principle, a life-force which links man in a vital relationship with the other life-forces in the universe. Second, Metuh holds that in man there is the "destiny soul" conceived as an emanation or spark of the creator, which, together with the creator, assist man in realising his individual destiny. Third, Metuh brought to the fore, "The ancestral guardian Spirit" which is held to incarnate in man and links him with the life-force of his clan, family and other human societies. Fourth in Metuh's taxonomy is the human person himself; whom he calls "the real person," the unique individual who is believed by Africans to have been created by God.[23]

---

19. Metuh, *Comparative Studies*, 41.
20. Muzorewa, *Origins and Development*, 17.
21. Muzorewa, 17.
22. Muzorewa, 17.
23. Metuh, *God and Man in African Religion: A Case Study of the Igbo of Nigeria* (London: G. Chapman, 1981).

Restating Metuh's thesis, Turaki defines man as; "(1) man in community and (2) man in cosmic relationships with forces in the universe."[24] Turaki then concludes,

> African doctrine of man strikes a balance between the social and individual dimensions of man. Man is essentially seen as a member of a community of beings as well as a unique individual person. He is a force in a universe of living forces, a member of the community of men and at the same time, a unique individual endowed with a unique destiny which only he himself can realize . . . man is linked to the universe of forces by an ontological principle from inside man himself.[25]

Mbiti presents a more nuanced view of an individual as construed in traditional African worldview. He writes, "The individual is conscious of himself in terms of 'I am because we are, and since we are, therefore I am.'"[26] This philosophical belief which is generally held by all Africans "tends to define man in terms of the social group to which he belongs. A person is thought of first of all as a constituent of a particular community, for it is the community which defines who he is and who he can become."[27]

What makes an African community the centre around which a human's life revolves and takes its meaning is the inevitable question that this work proposes. Turaki outlines five essential elements which serve as the hinge upon which community life in Africa hangs on. These are (1) life passages: birth, adulthood, death; (2) marriage and family; (3) health and wealth; (4) sickness and death and (5) the ancestors. On these five essential aspects of community life Turaki robustly notes;

> In traditional Africa, the meaning of life in the community is the measure of the purpose of life. The reason for existence is defined in terms of community life. The community makes life; the community gives purpose and meaning to life. Outside of the community, there is no life, no peace, no identity, no

---

24. Turaki, "Christianity and African Traditional Religion," vol. 1, 221.
25. Turaki, 221.
26. Ray, *African Religions*, 132.
27. Ray, 132.

> destiny and no existence, in short, no *salvation*! On account of these and many more, man lives in terms of the community. The community is both the lawgiver and the judge. It takes the custody of life in its hands. It is supreme in all matters of life.[28]

This African primal view is shared by many African and Western anthropologists and historians who examined the interaction between the African man and his community. Thus, William A. Dyrness asserts, "It is safe to say that the whole living, pulsating universe comes to focus on the human community."[29] Harry Sawyer extensively discussed the important elements that holistically tie African community life together in the work of Dyrness. He keenly observes, "The worship of ancestors, the attitude to birth, death, sin, sickness, forgiveness and health converge on the central role of the community."[30]

The assertion that man is the centre of the community is very relevant to our argument here, but it must be stated that in Africa, in himself, the man makes sense only in terms of the community. Dyrness concurs, "The human person plays a central role in all African thinking, but always in the context of the community."[31] It should be stated that in African thought pattern, the community is both a physical and spiritual entity and the African man participates in both. For instance, Dyrness who quoted Okorocha contends, "To live is to participate in the life of the spiritual world. So the person cannot be destroyed, his or her existence is tied to the unity of all that exists."[32] Furthermore, Dyrness posit that the unity is "centred on humanity, in such a way that death cannot destroy it. To destroy humanity would, in effect, mean destroying the whole coherence of being."[33]

We have noted how in both African cosmology and cosmogony, man is held in high esteem. What remains to be said is that the prestigious position man occupies in African thought pattern which demands that he

---

28. Turaki, "Christianity and African Traditional Religion," vol. 1, 240, (emphasis added).

29. William A. Dyrness, *Learning about Theology from the Third World* (Grand Rapids, MI: Zondervan, 1990), 49.

30. Dyrness, *Learning about Theology*, 49.

31. Dyrness, 49.

32. Dyrness, 49.

33. Dyrness, 50.

manipulates the universe for his advantage is mainly responsible for Africa's belief system which often is characterized by the rituals perform and the magic powers exercised. All this is aimed at preserving man's life and his community. Hence when death shows its ugly face, Africans do not believe that it can destroy theman who is a unity in arelationship with other forces around him. At death, therefore, Africans are held to get united with their ancestors in the ancestral realm.

Africans also believed that there is a spirit world which is replete with malevolent powers capable of harming man. Hence they make every effort necessary to preserve life through prayers and rituals in other to secure the protection of the ancestors and the local deities around them. This is not to suggest that Africans think that man is eternal. Africans have a high sense of the temporality of human beings and the transient nature of life itself. It is this premise that Africans believe there is death which takes the deceased to the abode of the ancestors to be united with those that went there before him as the next section demonstrates.

Death in African Cosmology: The Journey to *Ghi Dhen Derrhe* (The Hereafter)

In the traditional African beliefs, it is held that man is made up of two parts: a physical body and an immaterial soul often called the "breath." Nwaogwugwu pushes this point further by maintaining that "Man for the African is not only a bundle of possibilities but also astride of two worlds-the visible and the invisible."[34] While Africans believe that the physical body dies in the visible world, the "breath" does not. In all African traditional societies, it is generally believed that the soul, the bodiless aspect of a human at death goes on a journey to the invisible ancestral world to get united with the spirits of other ancestors and to continue to live for an indefinite period of time.

Scholars who wrote on African Traditional Religion and worldview echo this belief. Kofi Asare Opoku, for instance, observes, "It is generally believed that the dead goes on a journey and that death does not end life. This present life is seen as a preparation for the after-life where the dead continue to

---

34. Nwaogwugwu, *Ancestor Christology*, 59.

live after they have completed this life."³⁵ Citing an example with the Benin (now Edo) people of South Southern Nigeria, Opoku notes, "The Benin people of Nigeria (Binis), . . . believed that God has ordered every human being to make fourteen tours throughout life and that the tours begin at birth and end at death."³⁶ Chinua Achebe elaborated more on this position when he wrote, "A man's life from birth to death was a series of transition rites which brought him nearer and nearer to his ancestors."³⁷

What is at issue here is the notion of time, which in traditional African belief is relative. Or as Mbiti puts it, "African concept of time is silent and indifferent."³⁸ And because the world and the period in which African ancestors continue to exist does not fall within the sphere of physical human existence, Africans tend to interpret it in terms of an indefinite period of time or no time at all. Mbiti carries this argument further, "What has not taken place or what has no likelihood of an immediate occurrence falls

---

35. Kofi Asare Opoku, *West African Traditional Religion* (Lagos, Nigeria: FEP International, 1978), 137.

36. Opoku, *West African*, 137.

37. Chinua Achebe, *Things Fall Apart* (Oxford: Heinemann, 2008), 97.

38. Mbiti, *African Religions*, 21. Mbiti's notion of time in Africa generated scathing criticisms from Byang Henry Kato, Ernest Balintuma Kalibala, Anatoli Tibaryehinda Balyesiima-Byaruhanga-Akiiki and A Lugira. In his PhD dissertation titled, "A Critique of Incipient Universalism in Tropical Africa," (Dallas Theological Seminary, 1974) Kato devoted chapter 3: "African Theology and Incipient Universalism," to the critique of Mbiti's employment of the Swahili words *Sasa* and *Zamani* which denotes the absence of future time in Africa or that African concept of time is different. In this work Kato notes, "Mbiti makes the concept of time the heart of his theology comes out in his Ph.D. Dissertation, later published under the title, 'New Testament Eschatology in an African Background'" (Kato, "Critique of Incipient," 68). This statement prepares the ground for Kato to criticize Mbiti for over generalization since he used the Akamba worldview and notion of time to conclude that it represents all African idea of time. Kato also argued that Mbiti was inconsistent and arbitrary in his argument and presentation of the concept of time. In a similar fashion, Ernest Balintuma Kalibala rejected Mbiti's understanding of time in Africa and argues, "This is absurd, the African theologian who believes that kind of thing is following what Europeans have taught him. He has not been home to find out things for himself. We absolutely believe in the future. We even believe in a future resurrection. This is demonstrated by burial ceremonies and the contact we maintain with the spirits of the dead." (87) For Byaruhanga-Akiiki (from Kampala in Uganda), "The People here believe firmly that there is life after death. For example, the tomb of Buganda going back to 1814, is guarded by the wives of the king buried there. Our people firmly believe in the future. Mbiti's claim of absence of future thought can be limited only to the Akamba people." (89) A. Lugira, another Bugandan contends, "Professor Mbiti is giving his own opinion, it is academic. His basis is Akamba, and that should be limited there. My people, Buganda, do have a future concept of time." (90–92). For detail investigation of these criticisms, see Kato, "Critique of Incipient," 94–95.

into the category of 'No-time.' What is certain to occur, or falls within the rhythm of natural phenomena, is in the category of inevitable or potential time."[39] Accordingly, because the world occupied by African ancestors and the period in which they continue to exist in the hereafter does not fall within the rhythm of natural phenomena, Africans do not categorically assert the longevity of their ancestors in future and past tenses. Mbiti employs two words: "*Sasa*" and "*Zamani*" from the Swahili of South Africa to defend this thesis.

In his characteristicly witty argument, Mbiti rightly postulates,"'*Sasa*' is the verb tense that covers the 'now-period' and has the sense of immediacy, nearness, and 'now-ness'; and is the period of immediate concern for the people, since that is 'where' or 'when' they exist."[40] Mbiti's Swahili "*sasa*" which has the sense of immediacy has its cognate in other African tribes. For example, the Yoruba of Western Nigeria has the word "*sisi*." The Yoruba use this word for the immediate existential now. Modupẹ Oduyọye sheds light, "For Swahili *sasa* 'now,' 'I match the *sisi* in Yorúbá *ni sisiyi* at this *sisi*, at this time, now.'"[41] When therefore the Yoruba employ *sisi* in spoken or written language, they use it in the sense of "now-ness" or "nearness" the same way it is used among the Swahili of South Africa. In Nigeria, it is not only the Yoruba who have a word that gives the sense of now or nearness in time. The Atsam who are often referred as the Chawai of northern-central Nigeria, for instance, use the word "*khábini*" in the sense of urgency or now-ness.

While *sasa* for Mbiti denotes the immediate present, *Zamani* is more complex as its use goes beyond the now to an undefined moment of time that is not necessarily in the future. To him, *Zamani* is "beyond what the English called the past. It is a macro time beyond which nothing can go."[42] Little wonder, Mbiti calls it, "The period of the myth,"[43] and it is indeed a "myth" since it falls outside any obvious time in human history and vocabulary. Mbiti continues, however, saying that "*Zamani* is the graveyard of

---

39. Mbiti, *African Religions*, 16.
40. Mbiti, 20.
41. Modupe Oduyoye, *The Vocabulary of Yoruba Religious Discourse* (Ibadan, Nigeria: Daystar Press, 1972), 51.
42. Mbiti, *African Religions*, 22.
43. Mbiti, 22.

time, the period of termination, the dimension in which everything finds its halting point. It is the final storehouse for all phenomena and events, the ocean of time in which everything becomes absorbed into a reality that is neither after nor before."[44]

Grounded with the ideology the Africans hold that "death does not write 'finish' to life."[45] In fact, among the Atsam people, death to an average Tsam person is a journey to *ghi dhen derrhe* (the ancestral world) in which one continues to live in the indefinite *Zamani* period. Paul O. Ajah stresses this point, "Africans value life, they do not accept its termination or extinction . . . human life continues even after this physical life on earth."[46]

African traditional religions do not only hold onto the belief in the continued existence of the dead but also teaches that the dead continue to have a relationship with their living relatives and loved ones who are left behind. Lois Fuller says it bluntly, "All ATRs believe that people continue to exist after death. Most believe that the dead continue to have a relationship with their relatives who are left behind. Ancestors are linked to the very family, clan and tribe that they were born into."[47] The link ancestors maintain with their living relatives is not a physical one in the sense that one can have a one-on-one conversation with their dead ancestor, no, there is truly no such a thing as physical and material personal communication with the departed ancestors. In fact, Mbiti is right in saying, "Such spirits (of ancestors) have no personal communication with human families."[48]

Obviously, the relationship between the ancestors and their living relatives is more spiritual than physical since Africans believe that after death a person changes his mode of existence and becomes a spirit or ghost that cannot be seen with the naked eye. Even though the dead ancestors are not perceived with the physical senses, Africans do believe that these ancestors exert a lot of influence in the community of the living. J. N. K. Mugambi is right to state, "Physical death was not the end of existence. After death, a

---

44. Mbiti, 22.
45. Idowu, *African Traditional Religion*, 186.
46. Ajah, *African Traditional Religion*, 208.
47. Fuller, *Missionary Handbook*, 58.
48. Mbiti, *African Religions*, 26.

person changed his mode of existence and became a spirit (ghost)."[49] There are many echoes of this view in Sub-Saharan Africa. Robert B. Fisher states the same conviction, "Once the deceased is properly escorted into the abode of the ancestors, he or she joins the revered forbears of the clan. The *mogya* turns into the *saman*, or ghost, which is a *sasa*, spiritual power, which can influence the living for good or bad."[50] It was believed that "the spirits of people who had physically died continued to influence the life of the community, positively or negatively, depending on the conduct of those in the community who were physically alive."[51]

It has been established in this study that death does not terminate life in traditional African belief, rather, death is the gateway to *ghi dhen derrhe* (the ancestral world), the living-dead as Mbiti dubs them and the living-memories in my terms, continue to exist and have social interactions with their living kith and kin even after death. The influence ancestors are believed to exert on the lives of their living relations is seen in Africans' preoccupation with some traditional religious practices. And this also informs the notion that ancestors are involved with the life of the community as the next section attempts to show.

The Perceived Role of an Ancestor

That death does not terminate life in traditional African belief is no news, when one's physical breath ceases in this earthly life at the end, a new transition into the spirit or ancestral world begins. When one dies and enters the spirit world, he has more powers than before. Since he is still a member of his family, clan, or tribe, he can use his new powers to help or punish his people. Okonkwo's Father, Unoka in Chinua Achebe's *Things Fall Apart* alludes to this notion as he tended to blame his ancestors whom he concluded had punished him hence he could not have a good yield in a certain harvesting season. This could be construed to mean that he lived a

---

49. J. N. K. Mugambi, *Christianity and African Culture* (Nairobi, Kenya: Action, 2009), 66.

50. Robert B. Fisher, *West African Religious Traditions: Focus on the Akan of Ghana* (Maryknoll: Orbis Books, 1998), 95.

51. Mugambi, *Christianity and African Culture*, 66.

poor life among his kinsmen at the hands of his ancestors.[52] "The range of an ancestor's authority depends on what his position was while he was still alive, whether his influence extends to just the family, to the whole clan, or even to the whole tribe (like royal ancestors)."[53] The conscious awareness of divine powers associated with African ancestors led to the belief that they are the watchdogs that ensure and secure the community's welfare. In some instances, the ancestors acquire their powers while they were still alive here in the physical world. Fuller corroborates this fact and rightly points out that "Some ancestors were so powerful in their lifetime they even became divinities after they died (like Sango among the Yoruba)."[54]

The type and nature of powers attributed to ancestors are best explicated in the thesis of Samuel Waje Kunhiyop who notes, "Ancestral spirits are omnipresent, affecting the affairs of men and women on a constant basis."[55] Furthermore, Kunhiyop points out,

> Ancestors often reveal themselves to their descendants through dreams and visions in order to provide information, such as warning against a badbehaviour or revealing some medicine. The departed usually appear to the oldest in the family who in turn will communicate the will of the ancestors to the other members of the family. These appearances have a revelatory authority and are binding upon all members of the family . . . It is because of their significance in the lives of the descendants that great care was taken to give old people a befitting burial and subsequent rituals that would follow . . . The memory of ancestors is kept alive through rituals; telling and retelling of his biography to his descendants and above all, seeing that the living follow the teachings and instruction of the ancestor.

---

52. When Okonkwo was still a young man, his father, Unoka who perceived in a certain year the poor performance of his Yam farm decided to consult the Agbala priestess for possible solution. In his confession, Unoka told the priestess that he had failed that particular raining season to offer sacrifices of cock to Ani and the shrine of Ifejioku, the god of yams, but the priestess proved him wrong and chided with him instead for being lazy. For more on Unoka's confession, see Chinua Achebe, *Things Fall Apart*, 13–14.

53. Fuller, *Missionary Handbook*, 58–59.

54. Fuller, 59.

55. Samuel Waje Kunhiyop, *African Christian Ethics* (Bukuru, Nigeria: ACTS, 2008), 19.

Thus one can see that ancestors are continually involved in the lives of their descendants. They see to it that their descendants' welfare is maintained. What the living does or does not do affects them greatly.[56]

Similarly, Okopu who adds to Kunhiyop's menu pointedly declares,

Even in the after-life, the dead are not cut off from the living, for they may reveal themselves in dreams or appear to their living relatives to give instructions, warnings, or information which are normally taken seriously by those who receive them. The dead may also summon living relations to appear before them to explain their misconduct, especially in thecase where the living may have expropriated family property or sold family land in exchange for money, and punish them. Some deaths are explained as punishment in several West African communities.[57]

The duties and activities of ancestors are not just limited to those areas already discussed by Kunhiyop and Okopu. In some African societies, mainly the living-dead determine virtually everything that takes place in the community. This includes but is not limited among others to what constitutes acceptable conducts in the community of living but by and large; ancestors are the custodians of the legacy, tradition, and history of their tribe, family, and clan. Fuller underscores this fact, "The ancestors are the guardians of the group's morals, customs, traditions and history. They are the owners of the land, in which they are also buried. As such they can punish wrongdoers and those who change the customs or reveal the group's secret. They can show their displeasure if the land is sold or used contrary to their wishes."[58]

Other functions ancestors perform as Fuller elaborately deals with include the fact that ancestors also need to have the family, clan, and tribe preserved so that they will not be forgotten. Hence, they use their powers to give children, good crops, health, and protection to their people. This is exemplified by Uchendu's prayer for his nephew Okonkwo at leaving Mbanta toward the end of his exile back to Umufia his biological village when he prayed

---

56. Kunhiyop, *African Christian Ethics*, 19–20.
57. Opoku, *West African*, 137–138.
58. Fuller, *Missionary Handbook*, 62.

to the ancestors on behalf of Okonkwo for, "Health and children."[59] Apart from the blessing of health and children ancestors dispense to their living kins, Fuller maintained that

> Ancestors come back to the family through new children who are born . . . they may possess mediums who give a message; they are thought to visit their families in the form of animals, such as a python, dove or lizard. In some instances, ancestors also show their pleasure or displeasure by omens, miracles, calamities, hauntings and the behaviour of a child in which they are reincarnated.[60]

In his "African Cultural Knowledge," Michael C. Kirwen gives an extensive treatment of the role ancestors are believed to play in the community of the living in Africa which this work summarizes. According to him, ancestors, protects the living, are moral guardians, give people their identity, give blessings, are intermediaries between people and God and other spiritual beings, are community guides, owners of land, owners of livestock, sources of life, set up laws that govern people in different aspects and areas of the community, owners of vital resources, punish offenders, acts as models, warn people of misfortunes, develop customs and values, are custodians of culture, maintain communication with the living whenever there is an event, assist the living when necessary, are care givers, give people wisdom, and pray for the community.[61]

Kirwen captures most of the functions ancestors play in most African communities. It must be stated however that his discussion on the issue is not in any way exhaustive and normative. Richard J. Gehman while considering the role African ancestors perform wrote, "The living-dead play a crucial role in the social unity of the people. The ancestors help to unite the people together and bind them to the traditions of their fathers."[62] Other functions ancestors perform as Gehman endeavours to show are strengthening of a tie, guardians of family solidarity, responsible for every good thing that comes

---

59. Achebe, *Things Fall Apart*, 132.
60. Fuller, *Missionary Handbook*, 62–63.
61. Michael C. Kirwen, *African Cultural Knowledge: Themes and Embedded Beliefs* (Nairobi: MIAS Books, 2005), 17.
62. Gehman, *African Traditional Religion*, 216.

to their descendants, giving of rain, health, protection, are mediators and givers of every conceivable blessing.[63]

Turaki takes the subject further and states, "The ancestors hold a place of pre-eminence in the traditional society. If they are not worshipped, they are at least highly revered."[64] While Mbiti argues that "worship is the wrong word to apply in this situation;" maintaining that "Africans themselves know very well that they are not 'worshipping' the departed members of their family . . . remembering them . . . is not worshipping them,"[65] Harry Sawyer, on the contrary, taking a cue from Idowu's assertion before he feels that when Africans pray and pour libation to their dead ancestors, they indeed worship them. He asserts,

> Dr Idowu says without qualification, that to the Yoruba, "Egungun designates the spirit of the deceased to which worship is offered at the ancestral shrine." We may, therefore, summarise the present discussion so far by saying that Africans do worship their ancestors as they do their divinities. This worship consists of prayers, sacrifices, and divination on communal occasions or prayers and divinations on private occasions.[66]

Masamba ma Mpolo reiterated the same thesis but went a step further to say that "What follows logically from this assertion is that the belief in the ancestors is part of the totality of life, including worship, veneration, prayer, respect, reconciliation and therapy."[67] Philip John Neimark also subscribes to the notion that Africans worship their ancestors in the traditional religious rituals. Thus he devoted a whole chapter to ancestor worship. In chapter 2 which he tags, "Ancestor worship: Working the past to improve the Future," Neimark argues in several places that ancestors are worshipped in Africa. For example, he writes, "The ritual process of ancestor worship can provide

---

63. Gehman, 216–217.
64. Turaki, "Christianity and African Traditional Religion," 34.
65. Mbiti, *African Religions and Philosophy*, 9.
66. John Parratt, ed., *The Practice of Presence: Shorter Writings of Harry Sawyerr* (Grand Rapids, MI: Eerdmans, 1996), 55.
67. Masamba ma Mpolo and Wilhelmina Kalu, eds., *African Pastoral Studies* (Ibadan, Nigeria: Daystar Press, 1985), 103.

us with profound, quantifiable changes in our everyday lives."[68] This same argument is again taken later, where he notes, "Ancestor worship fits perfectly into the Ifa devotee's integrated view of the physical and spiritual world."[69] Similarly, Neimark further contends, "Ancestor worship will provide you with the knowledge that life is a continuum by enabling you to actually communicates with the energy of your departed family members and feel the profound feelings that that engenders,"[70] in the same page, he also states, "Through ancestor worship, Ifa allows you to experience life as a continuum."[71]

The debate about ancestor worship can prove to be a complicated issue in the African traditional religious system. While many agree that ancestors were worshipped, others would argue to the contrary. Whether we concede that ancestors were worshipped or not, one is left with no choice but to argue based on firsthand experience that those who fail to stand on the pedestals of ancestor worship would hardly win the day. The key problem with many scholars who write about African Traditional Religion is that they do not have even an implicit knowledge of the system let alone advocate it. Thus they do not have the epistemic right to argue on the issue objectively since they have never been initiated into it. If however, E. Geoffrey Parrinder will remark that "In South Africa, the ancestor spirits are the most intimate gods of the Bantu and in Zambia, the family divinities are the ghosts of one's grandfathers, grandmothers, father and mother, uncles and aunts, brothers and sisters."[72] And if we concede that these gods and divinities are worshipped in the Bantu and Zambian societies, then certainly ancestor worship cannot be disputed. After all, Herbert Spencer who is quoted by Bolaji asserts, "Ancestor worship is the root of every religion."[73] E. Bolaji Idowu is very blunt on the issue, as he argues that ancestor veneration, which is the term many African scholars prefer, is used by African Christians who

---

68. Philip John Neimark, *The Way of the Orisa: Empowering Your Life Through the Ancient African Religion of Ifa* (New York: HarperSanFrancisco, 1993), 21.
69. Neimark, *Way of the Orisa*, 24.
70. Neimark, 25.
71. Neimark, 25.
72. Parrinder, *African Traditional Religion*, 2nd ed., 57.
73. Idowu, *African Traditional Religion*, 178.

might not like to be associated with the primal beliefs. He writes, "Those who set up the cult of ancestors inside Churches are careful not to use the term 'worship': they choose 'veneration' instead. It is, however, needless to say, that between worship and veneration in religious buildings or precincts, the dividing line is often only a hair's breath, the human mind being what it is."[74] The conclusion is logical to note that ancestors in some African societies are worshipped as the discussion above reveals.

Factors for Change: From African Ancestors to Christ as Ancestor

The notion of ancestors or the living dead is deeply embedded in African religious consciousness. For many Africans, ancestors pervade almost every dimension of their lives.[75] This explains why scholars like Nyamiti, Bujo and Ntetem have felt the urge to sustain the place ancestors occupy in their lives by giving Jesus Christ African pre-Christian religious models. Thus, they have endeavoured to explain Christology in African images. However, the ways in which these theologians have treated the subject of the meaning of Christ in relation to African religious life has been quite heterogeneous. Interestingly enough, each study from the first part of the period treated the doctrine of Christ under the figure of an ancestor,[76] "as a way of 'Africanizing' Jesus,"[77] so that in effect, "Africans become Christians without losing their identity."[78] This passion drove Ntetem, Bujo and Nyamiti into articulating the notion that Jesus Christ is one of the African ancestors. After all, as Ntetem argues, "acceptance of the Christian faith does not involve a complete break with African tradition, for it has its source in God, and thus finds its fulfilment in Christianity."[79] Bujo did not begin with the same

---

74. Idowu, 180.
75. Henry Johannes Mugabe, "Christology in an African Context," *Review and Expositor* 88, no. 4 (1991): 346.
76. Olson, "Contextualised Christology," 259.
77. Donald J. Goergen, "The Quest for the Christ of Africa," *African Christian Studies* 17, no. 1 (2001): 5–51, available online: https://sedosmission.org/old/eng/goergen.htm.
78. Nicholas Mbogu, *Jesus in Post-Missionary Africa: Issues and Questions in African Contextual Christology* (Enugu: san Press, 2012), 423 Seiten, 6.
79. Ntetem, "Initiation, Traditional and Religion," 99.

bold affirmation Ntetem started with, but instead asks subtle questions that eventually led to his conclusion. "Would it not be possible to develop a theology . . . which is capable of integrating African culture, and out of which an African Christian ethic could be constructed? . . . could not the recognition of the place which the ancestors and elders occupy in the life of Africans stimulate theologians to construct something new?"[80]

The carefully articulated questions above find their responses when Bujo notes that "A reading of the gospel shows that the positive elements in African anthropocentrism are thoroughly endorsed in the person of Jesus Christ . . . When Africans narrate the deeds of Christ, they are acting in complete conformity with the biblical and Christian tradition."[81] By biblical and Christian tradition here Bujo means the apostolic teachings of the person and work of Jesus Christ which became the fundamental doctrinal statement of the early church. His next argument is very instructive in this direction, "It is therefore clear that the African concept of Jesus as Proto-Ancestor in no way contradicts the teaching of the New Testament."[82] Masumbuko Mununguri made a similar assertion, "We can, without risk of being contradicted by the biblical tradition, say that Christ is the Proto-Ancestor."[83]

While Mununguri arrives at this conclusion, he at the same time raises an essential epistemic question whose answers lie at the heart of ancestor Christology; "But how does Christ as Proto-Ancestor help us to understand that the God of our Ancestors has come among us?"[84] His response is very incisive and conveys the necessary mentality of African theologians in constructing a theology that harks back to the African pre-Christian cultural category of an ancestor. He opines,

> The African has a great "aspiration" for life. In welcoming Christ as the Messenger of God, he welcomes at the same time the God who sent him (Cf Mk 9:37). But for a long time, he had known that God's life came to him through his Ancestors.

---

80. Bujo, *African Theology*, 72.

81. Bujo, 81.

82. Bujo, 86.

83. Masumbuko Mununguri, *The Closeness of the God of our Ancestors: An African Approach to the Incarnation* (Nairobi, Kenya: Paulines Publications Africa, 1998), 70.

84. Mununguri, *Closeness of the God*, 72.

Then Jesus comes and says to him today that he and the Father are one (Cf Jn 17:22) from the beginning (Jn 1:1). In order to grasp this Good News, the African thinks of Christ and compares him to the Ancestors whom he knows better than Christ. For lack of an adequate language to express the "precedence" of Jesus over the other Ancestors, he calls him "Proto-Ancestor" that is, the "first of all Ancestors."[85]

Mununguri applauds the effort in which African theologians formulate African Christology around the ancestor model, but then raises a question that seeks justification for such an approach. He says, "This is all very good. However, the question arises for the African, Does Christ stand up to a detailed examination of all the qualities of an African ancestor? In other words, can it be said that Christ as Proto-Ancestor is really an Ancestor for the African, seen in his life and in his death?"[86] This question raises the issue of what it takes to qualify for an ancestor in African traditional belief. Moreover, most if not all scholars who write on Jesus's ancestorship and those who direct their investigation into African traditional religious belief attempt at one time or the other a discussion on the criteria of being an ancestor in Africa.

It is true that the belief in the ancestors is widespread but not every African who dies becomes an ancestor. Ajah observes that those who qualify for an ancestor are, "The men who lived a successful and righteous life, died well, and were properly buried and settled according to all the traditional rites. They are the dead who left virile offsprings among the living. They are the dead who still retain a branch on earth. That is, their life has continued on earth through the offsprings they left behind."[87]

Nwagwugwu gives two important Spanish words that vividly delineate the notion of ancestorship in the traditional African belief system, *antepasados* and *ancianos*. While the former is used for "Those who have gone before" or the grandfathers or simply the ancient fathers, the latter is used in reference to "the older ones."[88] The simple fact illustrates through the

---

85. Mununguri, 72.
86. Mununguri, 73.
87. Ajah, *African Traditional Religion*, 224.
88. Nwaogwugwu, *Ancestor Christology*, 75.

usage of these words that there are ancestors among ancestors. It is right to insist that within the ancestral cult there are ancestors whom by virtue of the number of years they spent here on earth before they die as well as the years spent in the ancestral world, are to be given the prior place of senior ancestors. While Nwagwugwu concedes this fact, he however asserts, "In a strict African traditional sense, a lot of things come into play before one qualifies to receive the appellation and homage as an ancestor."[89] The point Nwagwugwu wants for us to grasp is that the death of one's parents or grandparents is not sufficient as he shows to establish one's status as ancestor. Among other things, one becomes an ancestor only when,

> One's death must have been perceived as a good one, which means that the person was not abandoned to a disgraceful end, and neither was the person killed for a grave criminal offence. One must have enjoyed a long life that culminated in in a very ripe age with lots of descendants to whom one must have bequeathed the legacies that were entrusted by the forebears. The person must have played a significant role in the maintenance of peace and welfare of the family and the community. Usually such a person must have been one of the eldest members who fostered the communion between the living and the dead by offering useful pieces of advice when due and necessary. The person must also have enjoyed the respect of all and sundry on whom he or she imparted the blessings of the ancestors and divinities, and for whom sacrifices and prayers must have been offered . . . anyone who does not receive adequate and due funeral rites is incapable of enjoying a comfortable position among the ancestors . . . anyone who dies prematurely must reincarnate to complete the circle of life before that one could qualify to join the ancestors.[90]

It is valid to submit that the named ancestor and how one becomes one is not as easy as the named ancestor itself sounds and is easily pronounced. Randee Ijatuyi-Morphé alludes to this in his carefully crafted words, "Core

---

89. Nwaogwugwu, 75.
90. Nwaogwugwu, 77.

to African religion, cultural understanding, and even shaping and defining other aspects of the traditional social life of Africans, are the meaning and role accorded to the ancestors."[91] For Morhpé, "there are two levels of ancestorship: one as an *entitlement* (by right), the other as an *achievement* (by merit)."[92] Having established these categories, Morphé explicates further what each of these levels stands for. Accordingly, he maintains, "The first conveys a 'primordial' sense: it designates only the originators of a given community (the 'formative' role); while the second has a 'progressional' sense: it refers to future progeny who carry on the agenda of their progenitors for their community . . . how one achieves the state of an ancestor, is indissolubly tie to that person's community origins and moral life."[93]

With all this, could we go ahead to predicate ancestorship upon Jesus Christ in African context still? Nyamiti would not hesitate to say yes even though he is well aware that ancestorship in Africa is based on filial relationships. Thus, Africans do not accept anyone for an ancestor other than their very blood relations or member of their own clan. That aside, the circumstances that surround Jesus's life and death do not in any way qualify him for an African ancestor. It is a known fact that Jesus was killed as a young man, he never begot any children, and his burial was not done by the community of his kinsmen and of course, his death was construed as seditious or the hanging of one who is a rabble-rouser. How then could Jesus qualify for an African ancestor? For Jesus Christ, however, Nyamiti does not see his ancestorship of Africans in terms of filial relationship or biological origin. On the contrary, Jesus Christ relates to us as he argues through and through, "On account of His humanity Christ's Ancestorship is linked with Adam. This fact renders Christ . . . a member of our race,"[94] and one with us to qualify for an African ancestor through the enigmatic assumption of Adamic nature. With this submission, Nyamiti like Ntetem and Bujo raises his case and finds the ancestor model congenial to build an African doctrine of Christ upon.

---

91. Ijatuyi-Morphé, *Africa's Social and Religious Quest*, 22.
92. Ijatuyi-Morphé, 22.
93. Ijatuyi-Morphé, 22.
94. Nyamiti, *Christ as Our Ancestor*, 27.

Connecting the Communion of the Dead Saints in Christian Tradition with Africa's Ancestral Cult

A belief in the continued existence and influence of the departed fathers of the family and tribe is very strong in all of Africa. Not only are the ancestors revered as past heroes, but they are felt to be still present, watching over the household, directly concerned in all the affairs of the family and property, giving abundant harvests and fertility.[95] Among the Bantu of South Africa, the ancestor spirits are not only revered as past heroes, but "are the most intimate gods of that society."[96] In Rhodesia, Parrinder observed that "The family divinities are the ghosts of one's grandfathers, grandmothers, father and mother, uncles and aunts, brothers and sisters."[97] Other African tribes who share this same belief are the Yoruba, Baganda, Ruanda, and Urundi. Thus, the two most powerful and dreaded deities in Yoruba traditional society, *Sango* and *Oduduwa*, were originally believed to be kings while "The Bugandan spirits *kibuka* and *Mukasa* were one time war heroes. So too, the *Ryangombe* spirit among the Ruanda and Urundi peoples, which had a highly organized cult, was probably a historical person."[98] It thus follows therefore that "life from day-to-day – we might legitimately say from moment to moment – has no meaning at all apart from the ancestral presence and power," so admits Dyrness.[99]

The power the ancestors are believed to vent on their living kin and the constant fear of retribution accounts largely for African veneration of their ancestors. Buti Tlhagale notes, "Ancestor veneration or at least the belief and acknowledgment of their intervention in human affairs, continues to be a common practice among Africans."[100] This traditional African concept of ancestor veneration finds its match in the declaration of the fathers of the Second Vatican Council who addressed the saints as Christian ancestors. In

---

95. Geoffrey Parrinder, *West African Religion: A Study of the Beliefs and Practices of Akan, Ewe, Yoruba, Ibo, and Kindred Peoples* (London: Epworth, 1978), 115.
96. Parrinder, *African Traditional Religion*, 57.
97. Parrinder, 57.
98. Metuh, *Comparative Studies*, 145.
99. Dyrness, *Learning about Theology*, 47.
100. Buti Tlhagale, "Saints and Ancestors: A Close Look," in *Inculturation in the South African Context*, ed. Patrick Ryan (Nairobi, Kenya: Paulines Publications Africa, 2000), 27.

Lumen Gentium, no. 51, the fathers state, "This sacred council accepts loyally the venerable faith of our ancestors in the living communion which exists between us and our brothers who are in the glory of heaven or who are yet being purified after their death."[101] Pius Oyeniran Abioye sheds more light, "what has been called the ancestor worship is only a means of communion and communication with those already departed from earth. This is reminiscent of the Christian belief about communion or cult of the saints. "[102]

Besides, the Roman Catholic bishops of Nigeria wrote in their pastoral letter on the occasion of national independence, "The Communion of Saints embraces those African ancestors who have gone to heaven just as much as it does those who have been called the 'holy pagans of the Old Testament.'"[103] The saints in this context as Mugambi endeavour to show refers to, "those whom the Church recognised as 'the faithful.'"[104] In Roman Catholic tradition, the faithful departed believed now to be in the glory of heaven are usually canonized as saints. These same canonized saints which the Roman Catholic Church calls ancestors are in traditional African belief "held to be closer to the Supreme Being and the deities and acts as intermediaries between these divine beings and members of their families."[105] There is a good deal of precedent to support this view. Accordingly, Tlhagale notes,

> The Saints considered here are the Saints as understood by pious Christians during the late Roman and early Middle Ages. The supernatural powers possessed by the Saints were believed to derive from their close communion with God. They intervened on behalf of the living because they were believed to have direct access to God. They also intervened in human affairs because they understand the conditions of the living. After all they themselves lived on earth and had similar experience as the living. They knew human pain and joy. They had similar

---

101. Austin Flannery, ed., *Vatican Council II*, vol. 1, *The Conciliar and Post Conciliar Documents* (New Delhi: Rekha Printers, 2013), 373.

102. Pius Oyeniran Abioye, "Christian Theological Literature on Ancestor Veneration in Africa: An Overview," in *Christology in African Context*, eds. S. O. Abogunrin, J. O. Akao, and Dorcas Olu Akintunde, Biblical Studies Series 2 (Ibadan: NABS, 2003), 279.

103. T. A. Beetham, *Christianity and The New Africa* (London: Praeger, 1967), 75.

104. Mugambi, *Christianity and African Culture*, 67.

105. Metuh, *Comparative Studies*, 149.

desires and aspirations. It is for these reasons that the living were confident that the Saints would be sympathetic and therefore intervene on their behalf as intermediaries. Like the ancestors who took a personal interest in the affairs of their descendants, the Saints were seen as "vassals" of the Lord of heaven who stood in his presence and enjoyed his favour, and so were in a position to act as friends at court.[106]

Apparently, this lengthy quotation reveals that African Traditional Religion provides African theology with a theological framework; that of inculturation within which to construct ancestor Christology vis-à-vis the communion of the dead saints in the Christian tradition. Tlhagale's argument here is most telling because much the same as Africans believing that their ancestors play a vital role in their lives and in the community generally, so also some Christians and church denominations think and teach that the Christian saints are interested in their affairs and thus help them in their daily struggle with the matters of this life. If indeed, as African theologians would have us believe that the dead Christian saints could intervene in the affairs of the living; the same way African ancestors were held in the primal beliefs to be deeply involved with the life of their society, then this end is worth pursuing with every enthusiasm and tenacity.

To further reinforce the concern on the theology of Christian saints and African traditional ancestors, Tlhagale compares the role ancestors play for their living kin in traditional society and the role of the saints in some Christian churches. He wrote, "The living appealed to the ancestors because of family ties. Ancestors were expected to heed the cries of their descendants because they were family. The saints on the other hand were open and receptive to prayers from any Christian who devoted him or herself to them."[107] It is glaring here that this point is reminiscent of the African belief that the ancestors, "punish with sickness or misfortune those who infringe them,"[108] while at the same time they are held to be, "responsible for every

---

106. Tlhagale, "Saints and Ancestors," 28.
107. Tihagale, 28.
108. Parrinder, *West African Religion*, 115.

good thing that comes to us and we must offer gifts and sacrifice to them as thanksgiving"[109]

Earlier on, the question of whether all African men who die become ancestors was raised and the answer was, "death alone is not a sufficient condition for becoming an ancestor entitled to receive worship . . . a person who leaves no descendants cannot become an ancestor spirit."[110] Similarly, Metuh says, "death by itself does not turn one into an ancestor. The deceased must have the requisite qualifications and some processes must be followed before he attains the status of ancestor."[111] Interestingly enough, churches that hold onto the belief that the faithful departed now resting in heaven should be canonized as saints also teach that not everybody becomes a Saint after death. Tlhagale again notes passionately, "Not everybody becomes a Saint after death. Martyrs for example, were declared saints on account of suffering for the faith. Saints were those who performed miracles during their lives on earth and after their death."[112]

There is without doubt a good connect between what Africans believe and teach about their ancestors and what some church traditions believe and teach about the saints. In both views, for instance, there are criteria that one must satisfy in other to become either an ancestor or a saint. Pivotal in both beliefs is one's virtuous life while he was still alive on earth and both the ancestral cult and the tradition of canonizing the saints emphasizes this point time and again as a key criterion for becoming either an ancestor or a saint. On this note, African theologians saw an overwhelmingly good fit to fuse the two beliefs intricately together. For them, "The widely held African belief in ancestors as mediators between God and man, and between man and man, was replaced in the African expression of Christianity by faith in Jesus Christ, by belief in the communion of the saints, and by belief in the power of the Holy Spirit."[113] The aforesaid is the contentions of pro-ancestor-saint relation that demands the church recognizes and appreciates

---

109. Gehman, *African Traditional Religion*, 217.

110. Meyer Fortes and G. Dieterlen, *African Systems of Thought: Studies Presented and Discussed at the Third International African Seminar in Salisbury* (London: Oxford University Press, 1966), 16.

111. Metuh, *Comparative Studies*, 146.

112. Tlhagale, "Saints and Ancestors," 29.

113. Mugambi, *Christianity and African Culture*, 67.

therefore the connection between the two and thus make it an acceptable practice within the Roman Catholic Church. As they believe, "If the Church does not recognize the cult of the ancestors, people will be forced to practise it in secret."[114] There is indeed no mincing of words here to extenuate the intensity with which this assertion is forcefully raised.

Given that African pre-Christian cultural category of ancestor fits perfectly well into Christian tradition, the conclusion is that Africans are not in any way imitating a foreign tradition and raising unfounded assertions when they call for the insertion of the ancestors in the community of church saints. On the contrary, the traditional Roman Catholic practice of venerating saints perfectly dovetails with what is believed here in Africa, even before the advent of Christianity on the continent. As the following argument goes, "Today, when Africans search for their identity, the question is not to imitate a particular saint from the Roman calendar, but to situate the ancestors within the mystery of the Christian faith."[115] To that end, "The communion of the saints thus includes communion with the ancestors."[116]

For some who associate African ancestral communion with the Christian tradition of the communion of the saints, "Christian theology in Africa stands in need of a new approach, a new method, that will not be determined by 'white' or 'European' presuppositions."[117] Consequently, to be accommodated on the continent, Christianity must do violence to itself and break away from the hermeneutical hegemony of Western scholarship.[118] This avowed conclusion is hardly surprising because before now Mbiti, a

---

114. Éla, *My Faith as an African*, 28.
115. Éla, 29.
116. Éla, 30.
117. Parratt, *Reinventing Christianity*, 194.
118. David Adamo expressed some worries on the influence of Western theological enterprise on African scholarship and argues for the decolonization of biblical interpretation in Africa. He defines decolonization as "The analysis of the text that is done from the perspective of African world-view and culture and a reading of the Christian Scripture from a premeditated Africentric perspective." Furthermore, Adamo maintained that the goal of decolonization is to, "Break the hermeneutical hegemony and ideological stranglehold that Eurocentric biblical scholars have long enjoyed." Accordingly, decolonization is a "method, which appraises ancient biblical tradition and African world-view, culture and life experience with a view to correcting the cultural ideological conditioning to which Africans have been subjected. For more on David Adamo's articulation of decolonization, see David T. Adamo, "What Is African Biblical Studies?," in *Decolonization of Biblical Interpretation in Africa*, eds. S. O. Abogunrin (Ibadan, Nigeria: NABIS, 2005), 17.

staunch advocate of Afrocentric biblical hermeneutics, had expressed dissatisfaction with the way African scholars take and use at face value theological concepts and models from the West without an African face to it. In a proverbial tune, he expresses his dismay this way, "You cannot fill your granaries with borrowed grains."[119] This cliché is fraught with a rich message which meaning African theologians aptly appropriated and thus began to articulate a distinctively African theology that is a mixture of Western and African elements.

Cardinal to the effort to meaningfully engage Christian theological discourse in Africa without grains that are completely borrowed from the West as Parrat puts it, is "a new approach, a new method that will not be determined by 'white' or 'European' presuppositions."[120] And it is precisely here that the African cult of venerating the ancestors chimed in with the Roman Catholic veneration of saints and became the epicentre for the formulation of ancestor Christology in light of the communion of the Christian saints that has an African face to it.

Also, there is good ground to laud such efforts of the exponents of ancestor Christologies because of their desire to make Christianity relevant and acceptable in Sub-Saharan Africa but to also offer such a paradigm as an African christological contribution to the universal body of Christ. The problem, however, as Teresa Okure remarks is that "one factor which all the new Christologies have in common is that 'they start and end in the classroom'"![121] Similarly, Cécé Kolié also expresses his frustration at the manner in which African theologians appropriate christological titles from African Traditional Religion.[122] Jesus in Africa could be understood in more explicit and better biblical manner than in the local pre-Christian category of an ancestor. No one will dispute the obvious fact that the Bible remains the key source from which Christian theology can be derived and formulated in any context. Since therefore the communities of African theologians cannot

---

119. Mbiti, *Bible and Theology in African Christianity* (Nairobi: Oxford University Press, 1986), 7.

120. Parratt, *Reinventing Christianity*, 194.

121. Part II: *Challenge and Response in the 1980s and '90s*; taken from Ritchie, "African Theology," 12.

122. Part II: *Challenge and Response in the 1980s and '90s*, 11.

name Christ personally without going to the Bible or Catechism, they do just the opposite and attribute to Christ, the traditional title of an ancestor that they would like to see him given in the communities.[123] This approach, of course, is misleading because Africans know Jesus Christ for who he is and prefer to call him by a name that is familiar to their ears. The name Africans at the grassroots have for Jesus Christ is not only derived from but is as well faithful to the Bible, and that name is *Jesu* or *Yesu*.

Little wonder, considering the proliferation of titles for Jesus Christ in Africa, Jesse Mugambi once argued, "The current rash of Christologies is oppressive." He continued, "The stereotyping—'Jesus as a witchdoctor,' 'Jesus as an ancestor,' etc. is oppressive and reductionist. We need to look at Christianity in Africa in its broadest dimension, not in any reductionistic fashion."[124] Furthermore, Mugambi writes, "The relationship between 'departed' saints and the Christians who are physically alive, is distinct from that between ancestors and their living descendants."[125] For this reason, it is not always right at all to formulate Christology around the notion of the ancestors in relation to the communion of the departed Christian saints for the sake of making Christian theology African.

Summary

Conceivably, it is right and justifiable to concur with Keith Ferdinando that the veneration of ancestors is the focus of religious devotion for many African people.[126] Indeed, African tradition is centrally concerned with human life and wellbeing by whatever means that may be achieved.[127] This explains why in some African societies, the departed loved ones are immortalized so that their memories are not forgotten by their living relations. Some African theologians feel that one way of immortalizing the memories of African ancestors is to formulate a theology that seeks to compare the role ancestors were known to perform in the traditional society with the functional role

---

123. Part II: *Challenge and Response in the 1980s and '90s*, 11.
124. Part II: *Challenge and Response in the 1980s and '90s*, 12.
125. Mugambi, *Christianity and African Culture*, 68.
126. Ferdinando, "Christian Identity," 129.
127. Ferdinando, 129.

of Christ. This of course is a severe and fatal flaw to conclude that the most suitable way Jesus Christ could be welled and adequately understood and accepted in Africa is only through the use of local categories, – ancestor.

For me, Christ even by the analogy of proportionality is far more significant in dimension and incomparable in proportion to our ancestors. For this reason, the chapter argues that the devotion of living Africans to their departed beloved ancestors under the parameter that they would, in turn, guarantee their security and wellbeing in the community cannot, these days, be substantiated and sustained. It is also a known fact that in some African societies, the ancestors are considered as deities and thus object of worship. This is exemplified in the case of *Sango* and *Oduduwa* among the Yoruba of South Western Nigeria, the *Kibuka* and *Mukasa* spirits of the Bugandan people of Uganda and *Ryangombe* spirit among the Ruanda and Urundi peoples of Ruanda. For this very reason, African cosmology and cosmogony are anthropocentric and African peoples see everything else in its relation to this central position of man.

The chapter also contends that the very paradigm of formulating ancestor Christologies stems from the fact that in Africa "death does not write 'finish' to life."[128] Instead, death is just but the beginning of transition to *ghi dhen derrhe* – the realm in which the ancestors live. The cognate of African ancestral domain is the Christian paradise where the souls of the faithful departed continue to exist forever. For this reason, African theologians and biblical scholars find it convenient to construct ancestor Christology vis-à-vis the Christian communion of the saints as a way of christening Christianity on the continent. This sounds natural since in African traditional thought form only "the virtuous" earn the right to be called ancestors and that the African conception of the community includes both the living and the dead of that community, a conception African theologians consider analogous to the Christian doctrine of the communion of the saints.[129]

---

128. Idowu, *African Traditional Religion*, 186.

129. Part II:*Challenge and Response in the 1980s and '90s*; taken from Ritchie, "African Theology."

CHAPTER 5

Theological Sources of African Ancestor Christologies: Exploring Inculturation and Contextualization as Theological Methods

Introduction

Shortly before Jesus's ascension, he commanded, "All authority in heaven and on earth has been given to me. Therefore go and make disciples of all nations . . ." (Matt 28:18–19). The theological imperative for global evangelization is derived from the Great Commission Jesus gave his disciples to go make disciples of nations and "to do so in a way people of all cultures would understand and effectively respond to."[1] Thus, the church in Africa throughout the centuries in her attempt to live out this mandate has employed a variety of missiological approaches ranging from indigenization to Africanization, adaptation to acculturation, interculturation to incarnation, enculturation to contextualization, and inculturation among other methods to make Christianity relevant in the continent. Of these different methodologies, two stand out: contextualization and inculturation.

This chapter argues that besides the biblical mandate given by Jesus Christ to go make disciples of all nations, there are now in Africa some theological sources largely from church magisterium, Vatican II, pronouncements from

---

1. Agatha Radoli, "Preface," in *32 Articles Evaluating Inculturation of Christianity in Africa*, eds. Teresa Okure and Paul van Thiel (Kenya: AMECEA Gaba Publications, 1990), x.

sacerdotal authority, and the Code of Canon Law of 1983, that gave impetus to the current quest for the formulation of ancestor christological discourse employing the approaches of contextualization and inculturation. The chapter, therefore, raises the concern that it is on the basis of these theological sources that the exponents of ancestor Christology drew their inspiration to construct theology around African ancestor Christology with inculturation as a model setting the pace. To succeed in this quest, I employed the historical method to briefly fashion out the historical development of and basic tenets of inculturation vis-à-vis Christian missiological endeavour.

Church and Missions in Global Christianity: The Quest for Contextual Theology

During Jesus's conversation with the Samaritan woman, Christ made a profound declaration, "Salvation is from the Jews" (John 4:22). Thus, Christianity began as a Jewish movement fulfilling Jewish hopes, promises, and expectations.[2] When, however, the Jews to whom salvation came experienced a hardening (Rom 11:25–32) and became unwilling to evangelize the Gentiles, the event of Acts 6 and 7 paved the way for Gentile missions. For example, Tenent notes, "Acts 11:19 begins by recounting how, after the persecution in connection with Stephen, these scattered believers began to share the gospel 'as far as Phoenicia, Cyprus and Antioch, telling the message only to Jews.'"[3] Tenent's second statement is fascinating as it states that, "The next verse records one of the most important missiological moments in the entire New Testament: 'some of them, however, men from Cyprus and Cyrene, went to Antioch and began to speak to Greeks also, telling them the good news about the Lord Jesus'. This is the beginning of a new cultural frontier."[4]

Ever since the gospel first reached Gentile environment, the church of Jesus Christ has continued to grow universally among all cultures at an amazing proportion. The Protestant Reformation can be traced to 31 October 1517, when a relatively unknown Augustinian German Monk named Martin

---

2. Tennent, *Theology in the Context*, 3.
3. Tennent, 3.
4. Tennent, 3.

Luther nailed ninety-five theses of protest against abuses in the church to the door of the Castle Church in Wittenberg.[5] This Latin document was quickly translated into German,[6] and the newly invented printing press helped spread Luther's message of "justification by faith" and "the authority of Scripture alone" through Germany and eventually most of Europe.[7] This movement became known in Christian history as the Protestant Reformation whose counter version is called the Roman Catholic Reformation.

The Protestant Reformation of sixteenth century, led by Luther (1483–1546), along with the Roman Catholic counter Reformation led by Ignatius Loyola (1491–1556), "represents renewal movements that helped to stimulate new vitality among previously Christianized peoples who had become mainly nominal . . . a revitalized European Christianity eventually led to dramatic missionary endeavour"[8] which in turn led to changes in the worldwide distribution of Christianity which became established adequately in Africa toward the end of the nineteenth century and at the beginning of the twentieth century.[9]

Ever since the church became well-founded on the African continent, various methods had been employed to make it feel at home. This conforms to Gerald C. Davis's assertion that "the marks of a new church in a unique situation must relate to the marks of the society where it finds itself. In order to be sensitive to local cultures, the church in a foreign land must abandon

---

5. Tennent, 1.

6. Tennent, 1.

7. William C. Placher, *Readings in the History of Christian Theology*, vol. 2, *From the Reformation to the Present* (Philadelphia: Westminster, 1988), 11–12.

8. Tennent, *Theology in the Context*, 5.

9. Justo L. González had shown how Portuguese exploration of Africa led ultimately to the founding of Western Missionary bodies that eventually brought about the evangelization of the continent. Yusufu Turaki, an African ethicist lends support to González's submission. Thus, he noted the trends that led to the establishment of Western missionary organizations in Toronto, Canada by the middle of the nineteenth century. Driven by the zeal to reach the unreached dark shores of the African continent, those missionary bodies trained missionaries for foreign missions and sent some of them to Africa toward the end of the nineteenth century and at the beginning of the twentieth century. For more on the founding and subsequent sending of Western missionaries to Africa see González, *Story of Christianity*, 473–485; see also Turaki, *Theory and Practice*.

the original culture from whence it was imported and begin to think and act locally".[10] Craig Ott and Harold A. Netland underscore a similar thesis,

> The shift of Christianity's centre of gravity is good news because it means that, as a global reality, the Christian faith is increasing at home in many cultures and will not be imprisoned by any single culture. The good news, in this case, is that since people of colour now represent the majority of Christians in the world, the perception of Christianity as a Western religion can be corrected. Making a case for Christianity on the basis that it is a worldwide global religion can, especially in Africa, erase the stigma of Christianity as a white man's religion.[11]

Ott and Netland used the phrase "people of colour" loosely in a non-restricted and non-derogatory sense to refer to the non-Jews who have embraced Christianity as a world religion and had become the major nucleus and stakeholders of Christianity, other than that used by Latin American liberation theologians.[12] Accordingly, as the argument goes, for the Christian gospel that has now penetrated this group of believers to be truly at home in their societies and cultures, it has to be reinterpreted and reformulated in the language or vocabulary and thought of the form of the host culture. For Ott and Netland, "If Christianity is de-Westernized, Christians in Africa, Asia, and Latin America will be able to defend themselves when accused of being agents of Westernization and puppets in the hands of foreigners whose intention is the destruction of local cultures and religions."[13]

While we concede the fact that this argument is tenable, non-Western theologians, particularly Africans, should not however in their quest to inculturate and contextualize theology be quick to forget that even the Jews

---

10. James N. Amanze, "Globalisation of Theological Education and the Future of the Church in Africa: Some Critical Reflections Towards Edinburgh 2010 and its Aftermath," *Missionalia* 38, no. 2 (2010): 294–306, available online at https://journals.co.za/content/mission/38/2/EJC76141.

11. Ott and Netland, *Globalizing Theology*, 41.

12. The concept "people of color," was strictly employed in the formulation of Liberation theology in Latin America to mean Americans of African descent whose skin pigment is "Black" as opposed to the white racists Americans who marginalized and oppressed African Americans by reason of their skin colour. For more on the notion of "people of color," see James H. Cone, *God of the Oppressed* (Maryknoll, NY: Orbis Books, 2015), 88.

13. Ott and Netland, *Globalizing Theology*, 42.

to whom the revelation of Yahweh first came, were instructed by God to abandon their former beliefs and practices in favour of the laws of Jehovah. The Ten Commandments, for example, were given so that Israel would sever all relationships with foreign gods and cultural practices that are contrary to the established laws and holy requirements of Yahweh and thus stick to him alone (see Exod 20). In fact, God himself did not say minced word with Moses at Mount Sinai when he passionately and unwaveringly declared,

> You yourselves have seen what I did to Egypt, and how I carried you on eagles' wings and brought you to myself. Now if you obey me fully and keep my covenant, then out of all nations you will be my treasured possession. Although the whole earth is mine, you will be for me a kingdom of priests and a holy nation." These are the words you are to speak to the Israelites. (Exod 19:4–6).

When God revealed himself to and gave these commandments to Israel, they were already living and practising their own traditional beliefs and cultural practices, but those beliefs and practices did not stand up to God's righteous standards. The call of Abraham from among his people to, "Go from your country, your people and your father's household to the land I will show you" (Gen 12:1), signifies that God is interested in renewing human minds, traditional beliefs, and cultural practices. For when Abraham left Ur of the Chaldeans, I believe, he equally left his former ways of idolatry and began the new life of cultural and religious transformation. As I understand it, leaving Ur implies abandoning old ways while entering the land of Canaan means new beginnings, since the life and worldview of the Jews in the promised land was going to be shaped and modeled after the perfect laws of Yahweh, who was calling them out of their previous idolatrous lifestyle into being a holy nation and people of God. Klaus Nürnberger makes a pertinent contribution by suggesting that at the foundational beginning of Israelite history the prime ancestor was told to abandon the familiarity and security of his family structures and his homeland and move into the unknown, depending solely on the guidance of Yahweh, his God.[14]

---

14. Nürnberger, *Living dead*, 60.

For Nürnberger, this radical turn from the known to the unknown, from the past to the future, from where the fathers had been to where the descendants were going to be, is echoed again in the exodus, arguably the most important narrative defining Israelite-Jewish religion. Moses is told to forget what had become and explore what was to become. Israel is told to leave a predictable situation behind and embark upon a precarious pilgrimage.[15] Yahweh's demand for Israel to abandon her former situation is a clear case in which he desires for people whom he calls to have a clean break with their past into a transformative experience where he is encountered in a real existential situation as a God who transforms our worldviews. If God is, therefore, really interested in changing people's worldviews and cultural practices, why then should some African theologians of the twenty-first century, in their quest for contextual theology, clamour for a return to African pre-Christian religious and cultural practices that are not faithful to the Bible as the ideal way to make Christianity feel at home in Africa in the name of inculturation and contextualization?

Coming to the New Testament, when Jesus Christ gave the Great Commission to his disciples for the entire world, was he aware of ethnic and cultural diversity among the peoples that the gospel was going to reach them? If the answer is in the affirmative, it is relevant we ask another question. Did Jesus Christ expect that his message would be subsumed under foreign cultures and traditional beliefs and practices or did he expect it to shape and transform people's culture? It is important to be aware of Andrew F. Walls's argument for the plurality of expression in Christian practice. He contends, "Perhaps it is not only that different ages and nations see different things in Scripture – it is that they need to see different things."[16] Walls seems to believe that without plurality in Christian expression, the Christain faith and church will remain a parochial movement. He writes, "The fullness of the Church would only come with the fullness of the national manifestations of different national Churches."[17] The main thrust of his assertion is

---

15. Nürnberger, 60.

16. Andrew F. Walls, "The Gospel as the Prisoner and Liberator of Culture," in *The Missionary Movement in Christian History: Studies in the Transmission of Faith* (Maryknoll: Orbis Books, 1996), 102.

17. Walls, "Gospel as the Prisoner," 102.

that "We all approach Scripture wearing cultural blinkers, with assumptions determined by our time and place."[18]

While Walls is right to argue that the adatability and translability of the Christian message makes it possible for it to be at home in non-Jewish cultures, caution must be taken however on how the plurality of the Christian message is expressed among the various ethnic groups in the world, since Jesus Christ is an essence and not simply an expression. For me, such an expression must conform to the expression of early Christian traditions in apostolic and patristic era. After all, he argues, "In AD 37 most Christians were Jews. Not only was Jerusalem the main Christian centre; Jerusalem Christians laid down the norms and standards for other people."[19] The same Walls asserted that his imaginary long-living scholarly space visitor had "recognised an essential continuity in Christianity: continuity of thought about the final significance of Jesus, continuity of a certain consciousness about history, continuity in the use of Scriptures."[20] For me, Walls articulates his argument here very well since he believes that there should be continuity in Christian belief, doctrinal formulation, and teaching about the final significance of Jesus Christ, Christian history and the use of Christian Scriptures which has been the burning passion and argument of this study that African theologians need to maintain continuity with orthodox and evangelical Christian tradition as we do theology. When African theology conforms to orthodox and evangelical Christian tradition and makes reference to the past as the pillar upon which our own is standing, only then can we boast about making a universal contribution to Christian theology since our approach to theology would have gone beyond just a parochial African primal belief about the ancestors to the universal orthodox and evangelical confession of Jesus the Christ and redeemer of human beings the world over. His argument, however, that "We all approach Scripture wearing cultural blinkers, with assumptions determined by our time and place"[21] seems problematic to me because, as I believe, if care is not taken in the process of transmitting the gospel message, there is high possibility of leading to

---

18. Walls, 102.
19. Walls, 95–96.
20. Walls, 97.
21. Walls, 102.

cultural romanticism. For this reason, it is critical we ask a further question. When the apostle Paul wrote to the church in Rome of being transformed by the renewing of your mind (Rom 12:2), what exactly did he mean? This transformation and renewal, for me, include but are not limited to our minds but also the complete conversion and total transformation of our cultures and worldviews. After all, God himself is a critic of culture as the story of Noah makes clear in Genesis 6:5–6.[22] In the Noahic generation, John M. Frame argues, that the flood was God's judgment on the culture of Noah's day. He sent the flood in judgment, but the flood didn't make everything right. We might reason that because of the fall, all human culture stands equally under God's judgment.[23]

The subject of the relationship between Christ and culture as missions attempt to make the Christian faith relevant in any given context has been variously and thoroughly discussed through the centuries in Christian circles.[24] H. Richard Niebuhr's great *Christ and Culture* has remained a benchmark in this area. From the outset of the book, Neibuhr remarks, "The question of Christianity and civilization is by no means a new one: that Christian perplexity in this area has been perennial, and that the problem has been an enduring one through all the Christian centuries."[25] To that end, he explicitly reveals the central motif of his book as the,

---

22. John M. Frame, "Christianity and Culture," Lectures given at the Pensacola Theological Institute, 23–27 July 2001, 21.

23. Frame, "Christianity and Culture," 21.

24. The word "culture" seems to be a highly slippery and flexible concept since it discussion ranges from culture as the way of life of a particular people group to culture as a postmodern anti-christian ideology formulated to displace or replace Christianity from the minds of its adherents. For more on the subject of culture, see B. J. Van der Walt, *When African and Western Cultures Meet* (Potchefstroom: ICCA, 2006); Kato, *African Cultural Revolution*; Clifford Geertz, *The Interpretation of Cultures: Selected Essays* (New York: Basic Books, 1973); Bob Goudzwaard, *Idols of our Time* (Downers Grove, IL: InterVarsity Press, 1984); Bruce Ellis Benson, *Graven Ideologies: Nietzsche, Derrida & Marion on Modern Idolatry* (Downers Grove, IL: InterVarsity Press, 2002); Francis Nigel Lee, *The Central Significance of Culture* (Nutley, NJ: P & R, 1976); Francis A. Schaeffer, *He Is There and He Is Not Silent* (Wheaton, IL: Tyndale House, 1972); Francis A. Schaeffer, *A Christian Manifesto* (Westchester, IL: Crossway, 1982); Ernest Becker, *Escape from Evil* (New York: Free Press, 1975); and Frame, "Christianity and Culture."

25. H. Richard Niebuhr, *Christ and Culture*, fiftieth anniversary expanded ed. (New York: HarperCollins, 2001), 2.

> Typical Christian answers to the problem of Christ and Culture and so to contribute to the mutual understanding of variant and often conflicting Christian groups. The belief which lies back of this effort, however, is the conviction that Christ, as living Lord is answering the question in the totality of history and life in a fashion which transcends the wisdom of all his interpreters yet, employs their partial insights and their necessary conflicts.[26]

In this seminal work, Niebuhr achieved limelight through an extensive examination of five stances in the interaction between Christ and culture. First, is Niebuhr's Christ against culture, in which he highlights the fact that as believers, Christians are a new people; thus, their loyalty to Christ overrides loyalty to cultures and the community in which they lived. Consequently, Tertullian maintains that "Christians constitute a 'third race,' different from Jews and Gentiles, and called to live a way of life entirely separate from culture."[27] For this reason, he vehemently argues in his famous slogan,

> What has Jerusalem to do with Athens, the Church with Academia, the Christian with the heretic? Our principles come from the Porch of Solomon, who had himself taught that the Lord is to be sought in simplicity of heart. I have no use for a stoic or a platonic or a dialectical Christianity. After Jesus Christ, we have no need of speculation, after the Gospel no need of research.[28]

This marked the genesis of the monastic movement where believers abandoned societies for the ascetic life. Second is Christ of culture, which is more inclined to Gnostic philosophy. This position holds that Christ is not only the fulfilment of all cultural norms and values but the great educator, reformer, philosopher, as well as the one who directs all men in their culture for the attainment of wisdom, moral perfection and peace. In a nutshell, Christ came to entire culture by converting and transforming people from their pre-Christian worldviews and ideologies. Third, is Christ above culture, whose leading exponents are Thomas Aquinas and Clement

---

26. Niebuhr, *Christ and Culture*, 2.
27. D. A. Carson, *Christ and Culture Revisited* (Grand Rapids, MI:Eerdmans, 2008), 13.
28. Edgar and Oliphint, *Christian Apologetics*, 117–118.

of Rome. This school of thought sought to harmonize the first two positions but then argues that Christ is the Son of God, the Father Almighty who created the heavens and earth, and that the Christian life is an engine of cultural change. Therefore, believers must associate with non-believers to bring about change to society. Fourth, is Christ and culture in Paradox, which is a cognate of Christ above culture. This view holds that there is an ongoing battle between God and humankind or human culture which is believed to be sinful, corrupt and sick unto death.

The paradox, as Cone succinctly puts it, is that "Christians are redeemed persons but also sinners."[29] Thus, the advent of Christ was, therefore, to achieve reconciliation and forgiveness for both humankind and human cultures since man belongs to culture and cannot get out of it.[30] Proponents of this school of thought are the apostle Paul, Martin Luther, Søren Kierkegaard and Ernst Troeltsch. Fifth, is Christ the transformer of culture which begins with the concept of conversion. Accordingly, men and women of culture need to be converted and transformed into the image of Christ. Thus, history is defined as God's mighty acts in order to bring about a complete transformation in society. This view is illustrated in Augustine's city of God which provides an insightful interpretation of the development of modern Western society, vis-à-vis the emerging philosophical thought of the time.[31] As the transformer of culture, Christ redirects, reinvigorates, and regenerates all human cultures.

Niebuhr's insights that best explain the interaction between Christ and cultures are, to my mind, pivotal once the evangelization of a given context takes place. Christians should never forget that they are new creation with renewed minds perfected by the finished work of Christ who made the engine of cultural change with a view to interacting with human society only

---

29. Cone, *God of the Oppressed*, 80.
30. Carson, *Christ and Culture*, 23.
31. In his philosophical defense and refutation of the charges brought against Christians by the empire that they were largely responsible for the fall of Rome, St Augustine argues that the fate of Rome lies not in the actions of Christians in the empire but by and large in Roman paganism which bore within itself the seed of its own destruction. Furthermore, Augustine presents a cosmic interpretation of history in terms of Greek dualism as demonstrated in the incessant battle or struggle between good and the forces of evil or light and darkness etc. For more on Augustine's refutation of pagan charges against the church of his day see Augustine, *The City of God* (New York: Modern Library, 2000).

to the effect that such intercourse becomes the sole and necessary means for cultural transformation. When, however, the church fails to make Christ but our cultures the standard for the formulation of Christian theology, the inevitable result would be that of having a multi-hydra Christ, constructed to conform to our cultural patterns as opposed to models derived from the Bible as its *principium* for Christian tradition. Cone cautions rightly that,

> The theologian must be careful not to absolutize linguistic concepts and propositions in relation to Jesus' person because all theological statements are limited by the theologian's cultural standpoint. No theologian can define Jesus Christ's essence once and for all time, for Jesus is not a category but the divine event in history who is not subject to the limitations of human concepts.[32]

It goes without saying therefore that any missions approach that seeks to make the host culture the norm for the formulation of Christian theology stands the risk of what Stephen B. Bevans has aptly identified as the "danger of making theology to fall into a kind of a cultural romanticism and popular religiosity which do not represent the current trends of the host culture."[33]

It is the argument of this study that what is constructed as ancestor Christology today in twenty-first-century, or postmodern Africa, in which the teeming population dwells in cities, in the name of contextualization and inculturation does not in any way represent our current situation since ancestors are not always openly revered. For this reason, this study contends that the ancestral model has fallen into serious disfavour since it is by and large a contextual attempt to promote African cultural beliefs and practices that are not faithful to the Bible. So, couldn't there be a better way of constructing a contextual Christology other than the ancestral theme? After all, how many "percents" of present-day African Christians, particularly the teeming youth still maintain a link with the past? Of course, the figure is negligible, and in some ethnic groups, you hardly can find any youth making reference to primordial beliefs and traditions as those are completely strange to them. Nyamiti had noticed this irrefutable fact that the modern African

---

32. Cone, *God of the Oppressed*, 81.
33. Bevans, *Models of Contextual Theology*, 25–26.

youth of the twenty-first century have abandoned their cultural beliefs and cultural practices. Hence he rightly admits "those contemporary Africans (especially the young) who ignore or reject their traditional cultures; one has to re-educate them first by drawing their attention to the anomalous and inhuman condition in which they are by ignoring and rejecting their own African cultural roots."[34] While Nyamiti interprets the ignorance or rejection of some African pre-Christian cultural heritage by youth as inhuman, he forgot admitting, "African Theology is more than a question of mere dialogue between Christianity and African traditional religion or cultures . . . it essentially involves the effort to purify, rectify and transform or Christianize African traditional religious and cultural values."[35]

In what significant respect can the purification, rectification and transformation of African traditional religious and cultural values be done? Definitely, this cannot be done through contextualization and inculturation since both approaches do not talk about Christianity purifying, rectifying and transforming African traditional religious beliefs and cultural practices but they seek to create room for dialogue between Christianity and the cultural beliefs and practices of ancient African societies. Unfortunately for the champions of inculturation, the method has failed to achieve its desired objectives as Uche's research reveals (see chs. 1 and 2). This work, therefore, argues that the passionate attempt to compare Jesus Christ with African ancestors through the methods of contextualization and inculturation that have their roots from ecclesial declarations of the past do not generally represent contemporary African religious and cultural trends.

Motivation from Pre-Vatican II Ecclesial Declarations

The first modern encyclical issued by a pope was the apostolic letter *Maximum Illud* of Pope Benedict XV, dated 30 November 1919.[36] This encyclical was concerned to strengthen and coordinate the Roman Catholic

---

34. Nyamiti, *Studies in African Christian Theology*, vol. 1, 19.
35. Nyamiti, 6.
36. Aylward Shorter, *Toward a Theology of Inculturation* (Marknoll, NY: Orbis Books, 1988), 179.

missionary effort at a moment of unprecedented expansion.[37] Seven years later, in 1926, Pope Pius XII, who became known as the "Pope of the missions," issued his encyclical letter *Rerum Ecclesiae*.[38] These encyclicals led to a tide that evolved into a flood of contributions that eventually laid the foundation for the Second Vatican Council's emphasis and obsession for global evangelization. For this reason, the word inculturation became dynamic in the ecclesiology of Vatican II, and it resulted in the theology of culture, developed by the council and found principally in *Gaudium et Spes*. Basically, the promulgation of these encyclicals sought to have the church of Christ instituted and established in unreached people groups in such a way that Christianity becomes at home in the host environment. In what follows, we present the thought of Pope Pius XII and Pope John XXIII on the need for the Roman Catholic Church to propagate the faith through inculturation.

I. Pius XII – *Evangelii Praecones* (1951) and *Musicae Sacrae Disciplina* (1955)

An important landmark in the development of the theology of inculturation was the address given by Pope Pius XII to the Pontifical Mission Aid Societies in 1944.[39] In this all-important conference Pope Pius XII passionately declared, "Let not the Gospel, on being introduced into any new land, destroy or extinguish whatever its people possess, that is naturally good, just or beautiful."[40] This rhetoric appears to be the first ever recorded instance in which the Roman Catholic Church officially recognized the plurality of cultures and the inevitable necessity to incarnate the gospel in the thought and categories of the host culture. An epithet from Aylward Shorter vividly paints the picture of this speech thus, "The one Catholic Faith had to be extrinsically adapted in order to render it acceptable to different groups of people. To employ a commercial metaphor, the same product was to be 'packaged' in various ways, in order to sell it successfully in different countries."[41] This was the basic thesis of *evangelii praecones* of 1951, in which

---

37. Shorter, *Toward a Theology*, 179–180.
38. Shorter, 181.
39. Shorter, 183.
40. Okure and van Thiel, *32 Articles Evaluating*, x.
41. Shorter, *Toward a Theology*, 183.

the Pope vehemently argued metaphorically that "The Church, when she calls people to a higher culture and a better way of life under the inspiration of the Christian religion, does not act like one who recklessly cuts down and uproots a thriving forest. No, she grafts a good scion upon the wild stock that it may bear a crop of more delicious fruit."[42]

Definitely, in most cultures of the world there are some good elements that should be employed to make Christianity relevant in a given context. African drums for example have been used as means of contextualization during worship services by women fellowship groups in all congregations of the Evangelical Church Winning All (ECWA) in place of the Western musical instruments. However, such pre-Christian elements to be used should not only be contemporary but also categories that do not seek to be the ultimate norm for the formulation of Christian theology in local contexts or in the church liturgy. The fact of some good elements found existing in human culture before Christianity reaches a people group moved Pope Pius XII to assert, "Human nature, though owing to Adam's fall, is tainted with Original sin, has in itself something that is naturally Christian; and this, if illumined by divine light and nourished by God's grace, can eventually be changed into true and supernatural virtue."[43]

Pope Pius's submission resonates with the apostle Paul's argument in Romans 1:18–32 that men naturally have some knowledge not only of God yet suppress it but also an inner conscious awareness and prompting to want to relate with this God who is the author of their being. Paul's argument reaches its crescendo in Acts 17:24–28 when he asserts that all that God did in creation is that men may know and serve him as has been acknowledged by their poets, "We are his offspring." It is this intrinsic inner knowledge of God in man that is responsible for man's religious quest which often leads to misdirected religion seen in his unhealthy cravings and the worship of creatures in place of the Creator. In its declaration on the relationship of the church to non-Christian religions, *Nostra aetate* (28 October 1965), Vatican II ardently declared,

---

42. Shorter, 184.
43. Okure and van Thiel, *32 Articles Evaluating*, 3.

> Throughout history even to the present day, there is found among different peoples a certain awareness of a hidden power, which lies behind the course of nature and the events of human life. At times there is present even recognition of a supreme being, or still more of a Father. The awareness and recognition of the surpreme being results in a way of life that is imbued with a deep religious sense.[44]

James M. Houston robustly states the ultimate fact of man's misdirected religious quest thus, "For God alone is man's true good, and since man has rejected him it is strange that nothing has been found in all creation to take his place: The stars, the sky, the world, the elements, plants, cabbages, leeks, animals, insects, calves, serpents, fever, disease, war, famine, vice, adultery, incest."[45] Houston further contends, "Since he lost his true good, man is capable of seeing it in any object, even to his own destruction, although it is so different from what God ordained for him."[46]

In the same vein St Athanasius in his great classic, *On the Incarnation*, calls attention to the error of heathen beliefs and practices that are capable of damning human souls. For him, the heathen belief system is the product of man's wickedness, which culminates in man manufacturing his own gods and has by so doing usurped the place of the Creator God. He contends, "we have drawn out – choosing a few points from among many – a sufficient account of the error of the heathen concerning idols, and of the worship of idols, and how they originally came to be invented; how, namely, out of wickedness men devised for themselves the worshipping of idols."[47]

It is against the consequential error of misguided cultural norms and practices that earns man the wrath of God (Rom 1:18–21) that Pope Pius sought to baptize in order to free human culture from its error. Accordingly he maintains,

> After freeing them from error and all contamination she has perfected and completed them by Christian revelation. So

---

44. Flannery, *Vatican Council II*, vol. 1, 653.
45. James M. Houston, ed., *The Mind on Fire: An Anthology of the Writings of Blaise Pascal* (Portland, OR: Multnomah, 1989), 109.
46. Houston, *Mind on Fire*, 109.
47. Athanasius, *On the Incarnation*, 1.

> likewise the Church has graciously made her own the native art and culture which in some countries is so highly developed. She has carefully encouraged them and has brought them to a point of aesthetic perfection that of themselves they probably would never have attained. By no means has she repressed native customs and traditions but has given them a certain religious significance; she has even transformed their feat days and made them serve to commemorate the martyrs and to celebrate mysteries of the faith.[48]

The Pope's desire for cultural transformation would continue unabated. Hence his return to his first encyclical *Summi Pontificatus* of 1939 to rehearse, "Whatever there is in native customs that is not inseparably bound up with superstition and error will always receive kindly consideration and, when possible, will be preserved intact."[49] With this declaration, the Pope made a quick transition to knit together his argument by introducing a lengthy quotation from his 1944 address to the Pontifical Mission Aid Societies thus,

> The herald of the gospel and messenger of Christ is an apostle. His office does not demand that he transplant European civilization and culture, and no other, to foreign soil, there to take root and propagate itself. His task in dealing with these peoples, who sometimes boast a very old and highly developed culture of their own, is to teach and form them so that they are ready to accept willingly and in a practical manner the principles of Christian life and morality; principles, I might add, that fit into any culture, provided it be good and sound, and which give that culture greater force in safeguarding human dignity and in gaining human happiness. Catholic inhabitants of missionary countries, although they are first of all citizens of the kingdom of God and members of his great family, do not for all that cease to be citizens of their earthly fatherland.[50]

---

48. Shorter, *Toward a Theology*, 184–185.
49. Shorter, 185.
50. Okure and van Thiel, *32 Articles Evaluating*, 4.

These words which express Pope Pius XII burning passion for global evangelization with the host culture in view, became the catalyst and hinge upon which the Second Vatican Council would emphasize and build the Roman Catholic doctrine of inculturation. Pope Pius XII will however be restless if this approach does not also encompass church liturgy. To make church worship complete, he brought to the fore the principles of sacred art, especially music, and enjoined the artist whose faith is firm and whose way of life is worthy of a Christian to use such God-given skills to express Christian truth claims as taught in Holy Scriptures. To boost the morale of Christian artists, the Pope notes, "The Church has always held such artists in honour, and will always do so. Her doors lie open to them, for their art and skill give great help to the Church in carrying out her apostolic ministry more fruitfully. She is grateful for all the help that she receives from this quarter."[51]

For the reason that the central role artists play in Christian worship, Pope Pius XII called for the formation of societies for sacred music. For him:

> If a diocese has one of those associations that have been wisely founded for the improvement of sacred music, and that has been so greatly praised by the popes, the bishop will be able, if it seems prudent to him, to make use of this means as well in fulfilling his responsibility in this matter. Thus encouraged, such societies will be eager to promote throughout the whole diocese the knowledge, love and use of sacred music, in accordance with the Church's laws and in full obedience to our directions.[52]

Today music has become one of the essential ingredients that spice up worship in the Roman Catholic Church, and this is done with great flexibility depending on the worshipping community or context.

It is true, to conclude that Pope Pius XII left behind lasting legacies for the Roman Catholic Church most especially, its doctrine of inculturation as promulgated by the Second Vatican Council, which was convened by Pope John XXIII who drew his inspiration from Pope Pius's insights and

---

51. Okure and van Thiel, 8.
52. Okure and van Thiel, 11–12.

thus announced the council on 25 January 1959 and proclaimed it on 25 December 1961.

II. John XXIII – Allocution to African Writers and Artists (1959)

Although the ideas of Pope Pius XII were cardinal for the formulation of Roman Catholic liturgy particularly its principles on sacred art and music, on the African terrain, however, it was his successor Pope John XXIII who gave impetus to the integration of African traditional music in Christian worship. For him, "dogmas or faith-based statements are a culturally conditioned expression of revelation; therefore, a cultural rereading of the history of dogma is indispensable, and an invitation to reformulate dogma in accordance with the dictate of different cultures."[53] In his celebrated and incisive speech to participants in the Second International Congress of Negro Artists and Writers[54] in Rome on 1 April 1959, the Pope remarked,

> Wherever real values of art and thought are capable of enriching the human family, the Church is ready to encourage such work of the spirit. The Church herself, as you well know, is not bound to any culture, not even to the Western culture with which, however, her history is so intimately linked. For its mission proper is of quite a different order that of religious salvation of man. But, the Church, full of youthfulness, ever renewed by the breath of the spirit, remains disposed to recognize, to accept, and even to animate whatever is to the honour of the human mind and heart in any part of the world other than the Mediterranean basin, notwithstanding that here stood the providential cradle of Christianity. We, therefore, follow, with the greatest interest, your efforts in searching for the basis of the cultural fellowship of African inspiration, and we express the wish that it may repose on the right criteria of truth and action.[55]

---

53. Shorter, *Toward a Theology*, 188.
54. Shorter, 186.
55. Okure and van Thiel, *32 Articles Evaluating*, 13.

This statement hints at the notion of adaptation which recognizes and appreciates cultural multiplicity. "Once the cultural diversity of humanity was acknowledged, it could be seen that adaptation was a necessary condition of catholicity. The one Gospel of salvation had to be proclaimed to people of varying cultures and be understood and lived by them."[56] This was why for the very first time in the history of the Roman Catholic Church, a direct allusion and call for the integration of African traditional music and art in Christian liturgy became an issue. Pope John XXIII's defining message did not only dictate the tune and set the pace for the inculturation of African traditional music and art, but, as David L. Smith also opines, his role "set the tenor of the council by declaring that the world needs healing rather than condemnation. He held out an olive branch to all Christian groups, seeking a true ecumenical spirit."[57] It is hardly surprising that James C. Livingston says, "The decision to call the Second Vatican Council is the major contribution of Pope John XXIII (Angelo Giuseppe Roncalli, 1881–1963)."[58]

Similarly, Teresa Okure and Paul van Thiel observe that among John XXIII's writings, is his pontifical letter, *Iucunda Laudatio*, in which he encouraged the inculturation of some traditional African music for use as Christian, sacred music.[59] Similarly, the Pope also gave impetus to intercultural, or cross-cultural or cross-border, approach to missions. Okure and Thiel also note, "In his Encyclical *princeps pastorum* (1959) he encouraged the study of missiology and the promotion and use of indigenous personnel, ordained and lay faithful, and cultural resources in evangelization."[60]

Essential to Pope John XXIII's teachings is that the church being *communio*, its music should aim at not only the unification or fusion of disparate tribal genres into one massive nucleus but that such music to a large extent should reveal in a sense the cohort of fraternal human community devoid of ethnic differences. He speaks loudly,

---

56. Shorter, *Toward a Theology*, 188.

57. David L. Smith, *A Handbook of Contemporary Theology: Tracing Trends & Discerning Directions in Today's Theological Landscape* (Grand Rapids, MI: Baker Books, 2001), 87.

58. James C. Livingston, *Modern Christian Thought*, vol. 2. *The Twentieth Century*, 2nd ed. (Upper Saddle River, NJ: Prentice Hall, 2000), 236.

59. Okure and van Thiel, *32 Articles Evaluating*, 13.

60. Okure and van Thiel, 13.

> The Church's worldwide attention to the human resources of all peoples places her at the service of true world peace. She helps the elite that turns to her guidance, in developing the cultural possibilities of their countries and their race, and in doing so, the Church invites them to collaborate harmoniously and in a spirit of deep understanding, with other current issues from authentic civilizations. Is it not at that price that the conquests of the mind progress, and thus, that the spiritual bonds are tied of a truly fraternal human community?[61]

There can be no gain saying that this rhetoric greatly influenced African theologians in the formulation of ancestor Christology which derives its source from the Second Vatican Council's emphasis on the doctrine of inculturation.

Vatican II and Its Aftermath: A Turning Point in Global Christian Movement – Toward Inculturating Christianity in the Various Cultures of the World

The Second Vatican Council opened on 11 October 1962. Unlike its predecessor of 1869, the non-Western cultures were not exclusively represented by missionary bishops. Of the 2,540 council fathers, a high proportion were native to Latin America, Africa, Asia, and Oceania.[62] While the notion of liturgical inculturation dominated the first plenary session of the council, it was not until more than a decade after the start of the Second Vatican Council, in the forum provided by the Synods of Bishops and the various regional and continental episcopal associations, that the voice of the "Third Church" began to have an impact. For the development of the concept of inculturation, the Synod of 1974 was crucial. Up until that moment, the inadequate notion of adaptation prevailed.[63] Be that as it may, "A major contribution of the Council's new emphasis in its understanding of the

---

61. Okure and van Thiel, 13.
62. Shorter, *Toward a Theology*, 189.
63. Shorter, 189.

Church comes to the fore in the Constitution on the Liturgy (*Sacrosanctum Concilium*), which was the first constitution promulgated at the Council."[64]

We need from the foregoing, therefore, to come to terms with the obvious fact that before Vatican II, a full fletched ecclesiology of the multicultural church had not worked out, but the seed was there.[65] Thus, the church's cultural pluralism is clearly affirmed.[66] Hence Pope John XXIII could say that "the Church does not identify with any particular culture to the exclusion of the rest. The cultures of Europe and the West are not privileged, even the historical cultures of the Mediterranean."[67] The notion of particular churches and their cultural character was to be developed by the Second Vatican Council and by Pope Paul VI's *Evangelii Nuntiandi* of 1975.[68] In what follows, we examine the post-Vatican II Roman Catholic Popes' perspectives on the doctrine of inculturation.

I. Paul VI – *Africae Terrarium* (1967), SECAM, Kampala (1969) and *Evangelii Nuntiandi* (1975)

Shorter points out that "Even before the end of the Second Vatican Council important contributions to the development of a theology of inculturation were associated with the name of Pope Paul VI."[69] While the council was still in session, he visited and addressed the Eastern Rite Bishops in the Church of St Anne, Jerusalem, on 4 January 1964. Later in the same year, during the third session of the council, he visited India for the thirty-eighth International Eucharistic Congress, held in Bombay.[70] This congress, which later metamorphosed into a conference on "Christian Revelation and Non-Christian Religions," helped publicize the advances in salvation theology which were incorporated into the main doctrinal documents of Vatican II.[71]

Pope Paul VI is reputed as the itinerant pope who travelled far and wide and on his worldwide travel; he demonstrated the concern and interest

---

64. Livingston, *Modern Christian Thought*, vol. 2, 240.
65. Shorter, *Toward a Theology*, 187.
66. Shorter, 187.
67. Shorter, 187.
68. Shorter, 187.
69. Shorter, 206.
70. Shorter, 206.
71. Shorter, 206.

of the church in all peoples. His open address in *Evangelii Nuntiandi*, 8 December 1975, speaks volumes, "The preaching of the gospel to the men of our times, full as they are of hope, but harassed by fear and anxiety, must undoubtedly be regarded as a duty which will redound to the benefit, not only of the Christian community, but of the whole human race."[72]

The first pope to visit Africa, in 1969, Pope Paul VI challenged the Africans saying, "by now, you Africans are missionaries to yourselves."[73] While Africans might have reluctantly taken for granted the pope's call for Africanizing Christianity during this meeting, he went back to the root of Western theology to convince them that Western theology stands or falls on the ideas of African church fathers of the past. He wooed them thus, "The Church of the West did not hesitate to make use of the resources of African writers, such as Tertullian, Octavius of Mileto, Origen, Cyprian and Augustine . . . such an exchange of the highest expressions of Christian thought nourishes, without altering the originality of any particular culture."[74]

Before the historic visit to Africa in 1969, Pope Paul VI had, in 1967, issued his *Africae Terrarum* to the people of Africa in which he "appraises the potential resources in African cultural heritage for promoting Christianity in Africa."[75] This patent address was reiterated in his address for the closing of the inaugural meeting of the Symposium of the Episcopal Conferences of Africa and Madagascar (SECAM) in Kampala, Uganda in 1969. In this all-important address, which African bishops cherish and consider as the Magna opus of inculturation theology, Pope Paul VI keenly notes,

> While the faith is one, the expression, the language and mode of manifesting this one faith, may be manifold; hence it may be original, suited to the tongue, the style, the character, the genius, and the culture, of the one who professes this one faith. From this point of view, a certain pluralism is not only legitimate but desirable. An adaptation of the Christian life in the fields of pastoral, ritual, didactic and spiritual activities is not

---

72. Austin Flannery, ed., *Vatican Council II*, vol. 2, *More Post-conciliar Documents* (Northport, NY: Costello), 735.

73. Peter Schineller, *A Handbook on Inculturation* (New York: Paulist Press, 1990), 41.

74. Okure and van Thiel, *32 Articles Evaluating*, 35.

75. Okure and van Thiel, x.

only possible; it is even favoured by the Church . . . And in this sense, you may, and you must have an African Christianity.[76]

This address bolstered and wetted African theologians' appetites and gave them an edge to formulate theology around the pole of inculturation. Since as the quotation indicates Africans and the African church has come of age, are at liberty to have their own version of Christianity, and thereby formulate Christian theology with African cultural heritage in view. The Pope's call for the wedding between Christian belief and African primal religious heritage in evangelization and church liturgy is further encouraged when he explicitly states, "The teaching of Jesus Christ and his redemption are, in fact, the compliment, the renewal, and the bringing to perfection of all that is good in human tradition. And that is why the African, who becomes a Christian, does not disown himself (or herself) but takes up the age-old values of tradition 'in spirit and in truth.'"[77]

Pope Paul VI's worry is the relevance of the gospel and the insertion of the church's teaching in the hearts and minds of Africans. This is made clear when he raises the question of "How can the word of God, the teaching of the Church and the postulated faith be made easily accessible, clear and persuasive to the many and varied peoples of Africa and Madagascar?"[78] His second question is most telling; "Does the Church in Africa retain a certain Christian religious form that was brought in from outside, and which makes it, as it were, a stranger and pilgrim among its peoples?"[79]

Definitely, the answers to these questions would invariably be stated in the fashion that Christian theology and African belief are antithetical and incompatible variables which Africans find too difficult to reconcile. Perhaps, this explains why later on 8 December 1975, the Pope issued his "The Evangelization of Peoples,"[80] and "warned of the dangerous split between gospel and culture and called positively for the evangelization of cultures."[81] He laments, "The rift between the gospel and culture is undoubt-

---

76. Schineller, *Handbook on Inculturation*, 42.
77. Okure and van Thiel, *32 Articles Evaluating*, 19.
78. Okure and van Thiel, 39.
79. Okure and van Thiel, 39.
80. Schineller, *Handbook on Inculturation*, 42.
81. Schineller, 42.

edly an unhappy circumstance of our times just as it has been in other eras. Accordingly, we must devote all our resources and all our efforts to the sedulous evangelization of human culture, or rather of the various human cultures."[82] The pope also remarks, "in the building up of the kingdom it is inevitable that some elements of these human cultures must be introduced."[83] For Pope Paul VI, "What matters is to evangelize man's culture and cultures (not in a purely decorative way, as it were by applying a thin veneer, but in a vital way, depth and right to their roots)."[84]

Pope Paul VI rightly believed that the "process of evangelization is a creative process of insertion, incarnation and inculturation,"[85] and he would go great lengths in encouraging the church in Africa to imbibe the notion of adaptation. His conclusion in this area is captivating, "A burning and much-discussed question arise concerning your evangelizing work, and it is that of the adaptation of the gospel and of the Church to African culture. Must the Church be European, Latin, Oriental . . . or must she be African? This seems a difficult problem, and in practice may be so, indeed."[86] Difficult though this problem seems, Pope Paul VI believed that "Catholicity demands, therefore, a common bond of faith, founded upon the teaching of Christ, professed by the authentic tradition of the Church and guaranteed by its divinely instituted teaching authority, or *magisterium*."[87]

II. John Paul II – The Gospel and African Culture, Inculturating and Africanizing Evangelization (1980), and Inculturating Christianity in Africa (1982)

The Christian faith never exists except as "translated into a culture."[88] This concurs with Pope John Paul II's assertion, "evangelization in general that it is called to bring the power of the Gospel into the very heart of culture and cultures."[89] Robert J. Schreiter holds that "There is now a realization

---

82. Flannery, *Vatican Council II*, vol. 2, 743.
83. Flannery, 743.
84. Schineller, *Handbook on Inculturation*, 42.
85. Schineller, 42.
86. Shorter, *Toward a Theology*, 208.
87. Shorter, 209.
88. Bosch, *Transforming Mission*, 458.
89. Flannery, *Vatican Council II*, vol. 2, 819.

that all theologies have contexts, interests, relationships of power, special concerns – and to pretend that this is not the case is to be blind."⁹⁰ This buttresses Bevan's thesis, "There is no such thing as 'theology;' there is only contextual theology."⁹¹ This is what Pope Paul VI examined above, and Pope John Paul II, now under review, mean with their urge for the evangelization of culture. For Okure and Thiel, "One of the aspects of this evangelization is the inculturation of the Gospel, the *Africanization of the Church*."⁹² The objective of inculturation according to P. S. Raj is "To enable the gospel message to be readily understood, accepted and lived out in the thought-forms of the culture as it is expressed in its vocabulary, art forms and imagery."⁹³ This seems to have addressed David Kyeyune's curiosity when he anxiously asked, "How are the African Churches to embark on this course of moving from 'ideology' to genuine religious experience, from a dichotomized to a more holistic Christianity?"⁹⁴ Kyeyune entertained these worries because he believes that Christianity and African beliefs are diametrically opposed to each other. The panacea as he endeavours to show is to integrate African symbols with Christian categories, or as he puts it, "One way would be to concentrate on the meaning of the terms that are common to African religion and Christianity."⁹⁵ Evangelizing culture thus means here bringing the gospel message into all strata of all humanity, making the different cultures

---

90. Robert J. Schreiter, *Constructing Local Theologies* (Maryknoll, NY: Orbis Books, 2003), 4.

91. Bevans, *Models of Contextual Theology*, 3.

92. Okure and van Thiel, *32 Articles Evaluating*, 40.

93. Inculturation as P. S. Raj explains is the encounter of faith with culture. This encounter is both incarnational and confrontational insofar as the gospel finds a home in the culture such that it is experienced and understood through particular and recognizable cultural clothing with which its people readily identify the incarnational principle at work. This method Raj maintains is often referred to as enculturation. However, Raj argues that the gospel also confronts culture with a truth which challenges its thought forms and worldview and seeks to transform it, and this is the other dimension of inculturation. For more on Raj's discussion of the relationship between gospel and culture, see P. S. Raj, "Inculturation," in *Dictionary of Mission Theology: Evangelical Foundations*, ed. John Corrie (Downers Grove, IL: InterVarsity Press, 2007), 181.

94. David Kyeyune, "The Presence of the Triune God in the Church," in *Inculturating the Church in Africa: Theological and Practical Perspectives*, eds. Patrick Ryan and Cecil McGarry (Nairobi, Kenya: Paulines Publications Africa, 2001), 163.

95. Kyeyune, "Presence of the Triune," 163.

breathe the air of salvation of the gospel.[96] To preach the gospel to all nation, Bernard J. F. Lonergan asserts to preach it to every class in every culture in the manner that accords with the assimilative powers of that class and culture.[97]

This is the ultimate goal that Pope John Paul II set out to achieve for Africa. In his address to the Bishops of Zaire in May 1980, during his pastoral visit to mark the country's centenary celebration of Catholicism, the pope said, "The Church must become all things to all people. There is a long and important process of inculturation ahead of us so that the Gospel may penetrate the very soul of living cultures. By promoting this process, the Church responds to the people's deep aspiration and helps them to come to the sphere of faith."[98] The pope then reminded Africans, "You wish to be at once fully Christians and fully Africans."[99] According to him, "The Holy Spirit asks us to believe, in fact, that the leaven of the Gospel in its authenticity, has the power to bring forth Christians in the different cultures, with the riches of their heritage, purified and transfigured."[100] Taking a cue from Poland, his homeland, which had successfully blended their "ways of thinking and living,"[101] the pope advised Zairean bishops thus, "It should be possible for Christianity to unite with what is deepest in the Zairean soul for an original culture, at the same time African and Christian."[102]

This of course perfectly resonates with Vatican II's *Lumen Gentium*, promulgated on 21 November 1964. No. 13 of the Dogmatic Constitution of the Church provides that "The Church . . . does not take away anything from the temporal welfare of any people. Rather, she fosters and takes to herself, in so far as they are good, the ability, the resources and customs of peoples. In so taking them to herself she purifies, strengthens and elevates them."[103] In keeping with the spirit of Vatican II's *Lumen Gentium* and in light of his previous visit to Africa in 1980, Pope John Paul II addressed nine

---

96. Udeafor, *Inculturation*, 57.

97. Bernard J. F. Lonergan, *Method in Theology* (Toronto: University of Toronto Press, 2007), 328.

98. Udeafor, *Inculturation*, 57.

99. Okure and van Thiel, *32 Articles Evaluating*, 40.

100. Okure and van Thiel, 40.

101. Okure and van Thiel, 41.

102. Okure and van Thiel, 41.

103. Flannery, *Vatican Council II*, vol. 1, 332.

Mozambique bishops, who had gone to Rome for their *ad limina apostolorum* visit on 23 September 1982. Accordingly, he begins,

> I realize how much the African culture helps towards an authentic evangelization and constitutes a providential resistance against the attacks of atheism and of foreign ideologies . . . I wish to reaffirm here the Church's commitment to incarnating herself in the various civilizations and cultures. Your position in the Church, as Africans among Africans, is an example of this concern to naturalize the Church in Africa and amid its own people.[104]

While he seems as it were to speak ex-cathedra, John Paul II however refers to the source of his authority as derived from Vatican II to relate that

> It is, therefore, our task, according to the mind of Vatican II, to seek to translate the Gospel into forms suited to your culture, so as to make it well understood and (even more) well lived by your people, without—clearly—prejudice to that necessary ecclesial unity and evangelical substratum, which must be present and firm in the diversity of peoples and of cultures.[105]

This speech injects like serum, a renewed commitment into the bloodstream of African theologians of both Roman Catholic and evangelical persuasion to seriously pursue the agenda of inculturation and contextualization vigorously. Hence, more than any other methods, the notion of inculturation and contextualization have been dictating the tune and set the pace for the formulation of African theology in recent times.

Since the source derives from church magisterium, inculturation and contextualization as theological methods present a novel but yet intricate means of constructing theology along the grid of cultural context. This feat is not only required but also in a sense a compulsory and necessary theological method for Africa as John Paul II's closing remarks to the Mozambique bishops conveys, "Not alone must you absorb these suitable cultural expressions, but you must evangelize African culture itself, so that little by little one may

---

104. Okure and van Thiel, *32 Articles Evaluating*, 46.
105. Okure and van Thiel, 46.

come to recognize a true African Christian culture."[106] Interestingly enough, Pope John Paul II himself realizes this is not an easy feat, he thus admits, "Without adoubt, this is an immense and challenging work. It calls for men of solid faith, having profound culture, blending the sense of the Gospel with the sense of their own people. But, it is such an important work, that I would even say: it is the necessary condition for the survival of Catholicism in your country, amid the contradictions, so often encountered."[107]

III. Francis Arinze and M. I. Fitzgerald – Pastoral Attention to African Traditional Religion (1988)

Vatican II's *Nostra Aetate* no. 2, of 28 October 1965 in regard to the Roman Catholic Church's relationship to non-Christian religions stipulates, among others,

> The Catholic Church rejects nothing of what is true and holy in these religions . . . the Church, therefore, urges her sons to enter with prudence and charity into discussion and collaboration with members of other religions. Let Christians, while witnessing to their own faith and way of life acknowledge, preserve and encourage the spiritual and moral truths found among non-Christians, also their social life and culture.[108]

The council's toleration to non-Christian religions did open a new chapter in the history of the Roman Catholic Church in which pages of theological investigation were written and tailored toward sociocultural issues. And since Africa seems to be the place confronted with sociocultural and socio-religious matters, it finds *Nostra Aetate*, which permits the accommodation of foreign ideologies and belief systems, an ideal ally with which to partner together in formulating a contextual Christian theology.

The magisterial or sacerdotal letter of the president of the Pontifical Council for Dialogue Between Religions, Francis Cardinal Arinze and his secretary Michael I. Fitzgerald, to the participants at the Symposium of Episcopal Conferences of Africa and Madagascar reveals this lingering

---

106. Okure and van Thiel, 46.
107. Okure and van Thiel, 46.
108. Flannery, *Vatican Council II*, vol. 1, 654.

phenomenon and interest. This letter, which was a sequel to two previous conferences: Grottaferrata, 1975, and Lagos, 1987, gave pastoral attention to traditional religion. The contents of the letter made clear, "This conviction is reinforced by the express wishes of many bishops of Africa and Madagascar."[109] It goes then to formerly assent to such wishes in a four-part reflection discourse as "(i) Reasons for pastoral attention to African Traditional Religion (ATR); (ii) some elements of ATR; (iii) some key doctrinal points, (iv) suggested action by Bishops' conferences."[110]

Before now, Pope Paul VI and Pope John Paul II had each, on separate occasions, given African and Madagascan bishops the authority to come up with guidelines that would allow for the smooth inculturation of African and Madagascan traditional religious categories. Reflection (i) section 10 notes as follows; "His Holiness Pope PAUL VI, in his message to Africa, *Africae Terrarum*, in 1967, and in his SECAM concluding address at Kampala in 1969; and His Holiness Pope John Paul II, in his apostolic journeys in Africa, have given this pastoral effort their authoritative approval and traced the major guidelines to be followed."[111]

These authoritative approvals resonate with Vatican II, *Gaudium et Spes* (Pastoral Constitution on the Church in the Modern World), 7 December 1965. Number 58 on the "Relations between Culture and the Good News of Christ,"[112] affirms,

> The good news of Christ continually renews the life and culture of fallen man; it combats and removes the error and evil which flow from the ever-present attraction of sin. It never ceases to purify and elevate the morality of peoples. It takes the spiritual qualities and endowments of every age and nation, and with supernatural riches it causes them to blossom as it were, from within; it fortifies, completes and restores them in Christ. In this way, the Church carries out its mission, and in that very act it stimulates and advances human and civic culture, as well

---

109. Okure and van Thiel, *32 Articles Evaluating*, 47.
110. Okure and van Thiel, 47.
111. Okure and van Thiel, 49.
112. Flannery, *Vatican Council II*, vol. 1, 846.

as contributing by its activity, including liturgical activity, to man's interior freedom.[113]

Beyond exaggeration, the fundamental principles of inculturation and contextualization as theological methods hinge on this provision. In fact, the council was down to earth on culture and the Christian faith. Thus, it robustly declared, "We must do everything possible to make all persons aware of their right to culture and their duty to develop themselves culturally and to help their fellows."[114] Armed with this sacerdotal authority and upon which they drew their inspiration, Arinze and Fitzgerald formerly instructed African and Madagascan bishops to do theology in light of culture, particularly, African and Madagascan traditional religious and cultural categories.

From that point, Roman Catholic theology became intrinsically embedded in the doctrine of inculturation that does not seek strictly to sever links with one's pre-Christian categories. To that end, you can integrate traditional African beliefs with the Christian faith and carry the two together, which has come to characterize and depict the hard facts of Africa's situation. Of a truth, an average African who claims to be a Christian would in the critical moment instead resort to traditional means for a solution than first going to God, who in most cases offers the last answer. Okey Jude Uche confirmed this assertion when he lamented the Roman Catholic Church in the southern part of Nigeria, saying that "The most disturbing fact about the Catholic Church in Igbo land is that the Church hierarchy seems to be blind to the reality of the life of Christians in Igbo land. They do not believe that most of their followers are Catholics on Sundays and traditionalists during the week."[115]

Contextualization and Inculturation as Contextual Theological Methods

All throughout, this work argues on the one hand that the ground upon which ancestor Christology is formulated among Roman Catholic theologians in Africa rests entirely with Vatican II's teaching on inculturation,

---

113. Flannery, 846–847.
114. Flannery, 848.
115. Uche, "Theological Analysis of Ikpu-Ala," 286.

it is however, our conviction on the other hand that contextualization as theological method gives room for the formulation of ancestor Christology among Protestant/evangelical theologians in Africa as is the case with Gabriel Setiloane's Christology below (see pages 211–212).

The question each of these theological methods seeks to answer is, how we can make the gospel relevant in the contemporary world? This circumstance was an integral feature of Christianity from the very beginning. It should, therefore, come as no surprise that in the Pauline churches, Jews, Greeks, Barbarians, Thracians, Egyptians, and Romans were able to feel at home.[116] The same was true of the post-apostolic church where the faith was inculturated in a variety of liturgies and contexts. This attests to Desmond M. Tutu's theory that "Christianity, to be truly African, must be incarnated in Africa. It must speak in tones that strike a responsive chord in the African breast . . . it must speak out of and to his own context."[117]

Schreiter has posited that while the basic purpose of theological reflection has remained the same – namely, the reflection of Christians upon the gospel in light of their own circumstances – much more attention is now being paid to how those circumstances shape the response to the gospel. This focus is being expressed in terms like "localization," "contextualization," "indigenization," and "inculturation" of theology.[118]

Despite slightly different nuances in meaning, all of these terms point to the need for and responsibility of Christians to make their response to the gospel as concrete and lively as possible,[119] and this is precisely the notion of inculturation and contextualization.[120] Accordingly, Pedro Arrupe defines inculturation as,

---

116. Bosch, *Transforming Mission*, 458.

117. Desmond Tutu, "Black Theology and African Theology—soulmates or Antagonists?," in *A reader in African Christian Theology*, ed. John Parrat (London: SPCK, 2001), 41.

118. Schreiter, *Constructing Local Theologies*, 1.

119. Schreiter, 1.

120. Inculturation is mainly used in Roman Catholic circles, while contextualization is the dominant term among Protestant/evangelical scholars. Both terms have the same meaning-of making the gospel relevant and meaningful to the existing local culture. While Schreiter maintains that localization, indigenization, contextualization and inculturation mean one and the same thing, Bosch on the contrary holds that inculturation differs remarkably from indigenization, adaptation, and accommodation in some very important respects. First, it differs in respect of the agents. In all earlier models it was the western missionaries who either

The incarnation of Christian life and of the Christian message in a particular cultural context, in such a way that this experience not only finds expression through elements proper to the culture in question (this alone would be no more than a superficial adaptation) but becomes a principle that animates, directs and unifies the culture, transforming it and remaking it so as to bring about a new creation.[121]

While Shorter defines inculturation as, "The on-going dialogue between faith and culture or cultures, more fully, it is the creative and dynamic relationship between the Christian message and a culture or cultures,"[122] J. M. Waliggo et al., see inculturation as, "The deliberate, organized and therefore conscious effort of a society, touched by the phenomenon of cultural encounter, to develop a satisfactory and appropriate culture which takes into account the contingent event of the cultural encounter and considers this event as henceforth fundamental to and the foundation of its future history."[123]

---

induced or benevolently supervised the way in which the encounter between the Christian faith and the local cultures was to unfold. The very terms "accommodation," "adaptation," etc. suggested this. The process was one sided, in that the local faith community was not the primary agent. In inculturation, however, the two primary agents are the Holy Spirit and the local community, particularly the laity. Second, the emphasis is truly on the local situation. Inculturation is, however, not only a local event. It also has a regional or micro-contextual and micro-cultural manifestation. Third, inculturation consciously follows the model of incarnation. Fourth, the coordination of gospel and culture should, however, be structured christologically. That is, the missionaries do not just take "Christ" to other people and cultures, but allow the faith the chance to start a history of its own in each people and its experience of Christ. Incultruation suggests a double movement: there is at once inculturation of Christianity and Christianization of culture. The gospel must remain good news while becoming, up to a certain point, a cultural phenomenon, while it takes into account the meaning systems already present in the context. On the other hand, it offers the cultures "the knowledge of the divine mystery," while on the other it helps them to bring forth from their own living tradition original expressions of Christian life, celebration and thought. Fifth, since culture is an all-embracing reality, inculturation is also all-embracing. See Bosch, *Transforming Mission*, 463–465.

121. Pedro Arrupe, "Letter to the Whole Society on Inculturation," in *Other Apostolates Today: Selected Letters and Addresses of Pedro Arrupe*, vol. 3, ed. J. Aixala (St Louis, MO: Institute of Jesuit Sources, 1981), 172. See also Bosch, *Transforming Mission*, 446. In response to Arrrupe's definition of inculturation, Bosch criticized him that such a definition focuses on the new creation on the transformation of the old, on the plant which, having flowered from its seed, is at the same time something fundamentally new when compared with the seed.

122. Shorter, *Toward a Theology*, 11.

123. Waliggo et al., *Inculturation*, 68.

All these definitions hark back to Vatican II *Lumen Gentium*, whose doctrine of inculturation as an ideal theological method discourages the gospel from destroying people's culture once it enters their land. While inculturation seems to focus strictly on the encounter between the gospel and people's culture, contextualization does not narrow itself to culture but seeks to have a broader dimension since it has in view the entire context in which the gospel enters. David J. Hesselgrave and Edward Rommen defends this thesis. According to them, "Contextualization is a new word – a technical neologism . . . it goes well beyond the concept of indigenization . . . it also goes beyond the Roman Catholic notion of accommodation."[124] Bevans believes that contextualization is a necessary catalyst in the formulation of theology. He sheds light on this saying, "The contextualization of theology – the attempt to understand Christian faith in terms of a particular context – is really a theological imperative."[125] Douglas John Hall reached the conclusion, that "Contextualization . . . is the sine qua non of all genuine theological thought, and always has been."[126]

In the context of these definitions, Gabriel Setiloane, a Protestant theologian, argues, "To take the ancestors away from an African is robbing him of his personality."[127] Setiloane also writes that

> we must acknowledge that the dialogue with the primal world occurs not only outwardly . . . but also inwardly when both the institutional structures and individual lives of Christians in the older Churches . . . the primal inheritance is operative here also in varying and largely unknown degree. Past attitude towards African primal religions have been such that it has been exceedingly difficult to acknowledge this inheritance.[128]

---

124. David J. Hesselgrave and Edward Rommen, *Contextualization: Meanings, Methods, and Models* (Grand Rapis, MI: Baker Books, 1989), 32.

125. Bevans, *Models of Contextual Theology*, 3.

126. Douglas John Hall, *Thinking the Faith: Christian Theology in a North American Context* (Minneapolis, MN: Augsburg, 1989), 21.

127. Gabriel Setiloane, "How the Traditional Worldview Persists in the Christianity of the Sotho-Tswana," in *Christianity in Independent Africa*, ed. Edward Fashole-Luke (London: R. Collings, 1978), 406.

128. Setiloane, "How the Traditional," 411.

Setiloane further notes, "But now Africans, especially those in position of leadership seem to be determined to express their faith without denying their origins."[129] His contention is predicated upon the assumption that,

> ... for all Africans, even after many years of Christianity, and standing fully within the Christian Revelation, the spirituality and world-view of their fathers is still very present. We feel, therefore, that all the expressions of the Christian Faith up to now, from whatever area which makes up the Christian Church (Orthodox, Roman Catholic and Protestant) do not speak to us at the depth of our situation, past present and future.[130]

Kwame Bediako further reveals the basic arguments of Protestant contextual theologians thus, "Christological, and like other recent explorations into an Ancestor-Christology in African theology, it is meant to show that Christ, by virtue of his Incarnation, death, resurrection and ascension into the realm of spirit-power, can rightly be designated, in African terms, as Ancestor, indeed Supreme Ancestor."[131] Bediako did not only make a full defense of ancestor Christology but he also expressed its value this way, "One of the values of an Ancestor-Christology is precisely that it helps to clarify the place and significance of 'natural' ancestors."[132] One is tempted to find out – in what important respect does Jesus Christ as ancestor clarify the place and significance of our natural ancestors? This question for me is left unanswered. After all, contextualization as a theological methodology was meant to shed light and not to blur the Scriptures.

This was why, in reference to contextualization, Byang H. Kato wrote, "It is an effort to express the never changing Word of God in ever-changing models for relevance . . . contextualization of the models of express is not only right but necessary."[133] He then defines the term as, "Making concepts or ideas relevant in a given situation."[134] The obvious pitfall here is that most discussion on contextualization tends almost always to focus on the context

---

129. Setiloane, 411.
130. Setiloane, 411.
131. Bediako, *Christianity in Africa*, 217.
132. Bediako, 217.
133. Kato, *Biblical Christianity in Africa*, 23.
134. Kato, 23.

without at the same time recourse to how faithful such a theological method would be to the revealed word of God. The problem shows its ugly face not only in contextualization as a theological method but it seems to us by and large that in almost all the available theological methods attention has been devoted ultimately to context and culture without reference to whether it does injure and infringe upon the authority of Scripture. Of course, a careful look at the definition of these methods reveals the fact that they ignore the notion of faithfulness to God and his word.

As true as the case seems, Hesselgrave and Rommen have charted a course on the discussion that serves as a panacea. In their definition of contextualization, they are apt not to relegate the place of God in making the gospel relevant to a context, who is, after all, the central subject that contextualization seeks to present. To that end, they define contextualization as, "The attempt to communicate the message of the person, works, word, and will of God in a way that is faithful to God's revelation, especially as it is put forth in the teachings of Holy Scripture, and that is meaningful to respondents in their respective cultural and existential contexts."[135]

While the benchmark of contextualization in Hesselgrave's and Rommen's perspective is faithfulness to God's revelation, they were also careful not to give a second or virtually no place to what transpires in the context. Hence they continue that "Contextualization is both verbal and nonverbal and has to do with theologizing, Bible translation, interpretation, and application; incarnational lifestyle; evangelism; Christian instruction; Church planting and growth; Church organization; worship style – indeed with all of those activities involved in carrying out the Great Commission."[136]

The previous definition is comprehensive enough for it leaves out nothing that forms one of the quintessences of evangelism and the insertion of the gospel in a context. Seen from this angle, contextualization goes far beyond inculturation, the main thrust of which is the interaction of gospel and culture. In contextualization, the gospel, God its author (whom the gospel presents), the recipient culture, and the theologian theologizing are all brought to bear upon the task. Hesselgrace and Rommen note, "The

---

135. Hesselgrave and Rommen, *Contextualization*, 200.
136. Hesselgrave and Rommen, 200.

contextualizer's initial task is an interpretative one: to determine not only what the text says but also the meaning of what has been said. It may be useful to think of contextualization as a process with three distinct elements, revelation, interpretation, and application."[137]

As critical or relevant although contextualization and inculturation as theological methods are, care must, however, be exercised not to absolutize and place them on par with dogma. To be overly dogmatic over Christian theological methods is to be myopic and insensitive to authoritative apostolic tradition. After all, there is a grave flaw with some fluid Christian theological methods which tends toward cultural romanticism and, at the time, they are incomplete and obsolete methods that do not represent extant trends found in the host culture. In light of this, Hesselgrave and Rommen note that "Unlike dogmatic biblical theology, all contextualized theologies are incomplete and relative."[138] With this, one wonders whether African theologians who employ African primal traditions to articulate ancestor Christology have forgotten that twenty-first-century Africa, which has been tremendously influenced by postmodernism and globalization, is not exactly the same as nineteenth- and twentieth-century Africa.

The Theological Framework of Vatican II, Church Magisterium and Inculturation and African Ancestor Christology

This section reasons that the theological basis upon which ancestor Christology is formulated in Africa employing inculturation as a theological method is grounded in the debate between Tatian, Tertullian and Clement of Alexandria on the encounter between Christianity and the Graeco-Roman culture of the early Roman Empire, Vatican II – church magisterium and the Canon Law of 1983. While the debate between Tatian, Tertullian and Clement of Alexandria in the early church are beyond the scope of this section, the theological role of Vatican II, church magisterium, and the Code of Canon Law of 1983 which are pivotal Roman Catholic theological

---

137. Hesselgrave and Rommen, 201.
138. Hesselgrave and Rommen, 57.

sources for the construction of African ancestor Christology shall be briefly examined.

To begin with, the English word "church" is probably derived from the Greek word *kuriako ~ (kuriakos)* meaning "belonging to the Lord." Biblically the church belongs to Christ who did not only love her and gave himself up for her (Eph 5:25), but he also gave her powers to forgive sin (John 20:22–23) and authority to make informed decisions (Matt 18:18) and formulate doctrines (2 Tim 3:16). According to Roman Catholic tradition, the authority to teach, (i.e. the magisterium of the church) is exercised in the name and authority of Jesus Christ who said to the apostles, "He who hears you hears me," (Luke 10:16, RSV).

Jesus's statement in this passage establishes the Roman Catholic basis for church magisterium which guides the dogmatic or doctrinal teachings of the universal church. The *New International Webster's Comprehensive Dictionary of the English Language* defines the Roman Catholic concept of magisterium as, "The authority of the Church to teach dogmatically."[139] To that end, we can rightly surmise that the Roman Catholic Church depends solely on the teaching authority of the magisterium. The word magisterium is derived from the Latin *magistra* or, as Maureen Sullivan succinctly puts it, "The word magisterium is taken from a Latin word, *magister*, meaning 'teacher.'"[140] Francis A. Sullivan, notes that the English word that corresponds to the Latin "*magister* is 'master,' not only in the specific sense of 'schoolmaster,' or teacher but in the broad spectrum of senses in which a person can be a 'master': e.g. master of the ship, master of servants or slaves, master of an arts or trade, etc."[141] For Sullivan, the Latin word *magister* has a connotation of authority, coming as it did from the root *magis* (more), as contrasted with the *minister*, from *minus* (less).

Similarly, the word *magisterium* in classical Latin meant the role and authority of one who was a *magister*.[142] Accordingly, Sullivan defines magis-

---

139. *The New International Webster's Comprehensive Dictionary of the English Language*, encyclopedic edition (Naples, FL: Typhoon Media Corporation, 2010), 765.

140. Maureen Sullivan, *101 Questions and Answers on Vatican II* (Mumbai, India: St Pauls, 2004), 105–106.

141. Francis A. Sullivan, *Magisterium: Teaching Authority in the Catholic Church* (New York: Paulist Press, 1983), 24–25.

142. Sullivan, *Magisterium*, 24–25.

terium as "the pastoral teaching office."[143] Thus, *Lumen Gentium* 18 speaks of the infallible magisterium of the Roman Pontiff; in n. 22 it says that the order of bishops is the successor to the college of the apostles in magisterium; in n. 25 speaks of the "authentic" and "supreme" magisterium of the Roman Pontiff.[144]

It is obvious from the foregoing, to deduce that the notion of magisterium as the didactic body of Roman Catholic theology derives from Vatican II's *Lumen Gentium*, of 21 November 1964. Article 25 especially provides,

> The bishops are heralds of the faith, who draw new disciples to Christ; they are authentic teachers, that is, teachers endowed with the authority of Christ, who preach the faith to the people assigned to them, the faith which is destined to inform their thinking and direct their conduct; and under the light of the Holy Spirit they make that faith shine forth, drawing men form the storehouse of revelation new things and old . . . they make it bear fruit, and with watchfulness they ward off whatever errors threatens their flock.[145]

Magisterium as the teaching authority of the church is thus the apex body of the Roman Catholic Church vested with absolute and unchallenged authority. Its composition includes the Pope and Bishops from all over the world who are held to have the power to teach and interpret divine truths without error.[146] For instance, the doctrinal formulations of Vatican Council I (1869–1870) and Vatican Council II (1962–1965) are good examples of church magisterium. Vatican II's first plenary session on liturgical inculturation especially gave impetus to the theology of inculturation which in turn stemmed from Pope Paul VI's stance that the "process of evangelization is a creative process of insertion, incarnation and inculturation."[147] Building upon the foundation already laid by Paul VI, the council's article on *Gaudium et Spes* (Pastoral Constitution on the Church in the Modern

---

143. Sullivan, 24–25.
144. Sullivan, 24–25.
145. Flannery, *Vatican Council II*, vol. 1, 345.
146. Sullivan, *101 Questions*, 129.
147. Schineller, *Handbook on Inculturation*, 42.

World), 7 December 1965, number 58 on the "Relations between Culture and the Good News of Christ,"[148] stresses the notion of inculturation and gives it a magisterium twist.

I. *Aggiornamento*

Aggiornamento, an Italian word for "renewal,"[149] or "a bringing up to date,"[150] is so used to refer to "the renewal of Roman Catholic theology within the post-World War II European situation."[151] The luminary at the forefront of the quest for church renewal was Yves Marie-Joseph Congar whose basic writings dealt with the "structure of the Church, the role of the laity within the Church, and the nature of Church reform and tradition."[152] Congar's writings were a sequel to French revival of Catholicism which he participated. Livingston had maintained that "the renewal of theology and of Church life in France involved both new academic directions and pastoral initiatives. Academically, there was the call for *resourcement,* a call for the return to the historical and biblical sources of faith. The return to the *sources* led to a renaissance in biblical and patristic studies."[153] Consequent upon this renewal a movement known as the Catholic Action and Mission de France arose in France and Belgium which encouraged lay participation. For the very first time in the history of the Roman Catholic Church, laypersons felt not only a sense of belonging and recognition but became active players in the movement. The active role played by the laypersons challenged the Roman Catholic Church to "rethink the role of the laity within a Church structure that was heavily clerical and hierarchal."[154]

The emergence of Mission de France was a clarion call from French Roman Catholics who, before now, were grossly alienated from their faith. While missionary activities were underway, the need for church renewal and reform became quintessential for the aggressive evangelization of France, a development which appealed to Congar who took advantage of the situation

---

148. Flannery, *Vatican Council II*, vol. 1, 846.
149. Karl Rahner, *The Church after the Council* (New York: Herder & Herder, 1966), 19.
150. Sullivan, *101 Questions*, 25, 127.
151. Livingston, *Modern Christian Thought*, vol. 2, 233.
152. Livingston, 234.
153. Livingston, 234.
154. Livingston, 234.

and began to publicize his view of what it means to return to the sources. From the framework of church renewal and reform, Congar wrote several books among which are: *Holiness and Sin within the Church*, and *Why the People of God Should Ceaselessly Reform Itself*. Together these books were combined into a volume, *True and False Reform in the Church*, which took up the clarion call for reforms.[155]

The return or resourcement would provide the foundation for a reform of the church and for the Second Vatican Council since it was the single catalyst upon which Pope John XXIII largely drew his inspiration to convoke Vatican II[156] "which was the decisive religious, intellectual, and political event within the contemporary Roman Catholic Church."[157] Before Vatican II, John XXIII had acquired a copy of Congar's *True and False Reform in the Church* which he meticulously read and fully comprehended its contents. Of John XXIII's interest on Congar's works, Livingston notes, "He relates that he had underlined his own personal copy and had been strongly influenced by its call for Church reform. When he became pope, he convoked Vatican II and insisted that the French theologians associated with the *nouvelle theologie* be invited as experts to the Council."[158]

Aggiornamento, the Roman Catholic theological framework, which seeks to reform the church was the heartbeat of John XXIII who believed that Vatican II was the best forum that could bring the Catholic faith up-to-date and thereby adapt itself to the dynamics of a rapidly changing modern society. It was to mark a new dawn in the Roman Catholic Church where everything was going to be renewed to key in with modernity. The above point was why Vatican II called for the doing of theology in the light of the culture and worldview of a given context vouchsafes this goal. This approach is radically novel. Indeed *aggiornamento* was a new beginning. As Rahner puts it, "The Council marked the decisive beginning of the *aggiornamento*, it established the renewal, it called us to the ever necessary repentance and returned; in other words, it was only the beginning of the beginning."[159]

---

155. Livingston, 234.
156. Livingston, 233, 236.
157. Livingston, 237.
158. Livingston, 236.
159. Rahner, *Church after the Council*, 19–20.

Rahner's beginning of the beginning could only be understood in context for by the end of Vatican II in 1965; the council fathers had made a decisive break with some promulgations of Vatican I that had hitherto directed the course of Catholicism. This is the paradigm shift that gave birth to inculturation theology which proponents formulate Christology from the framework of African ancestrology.

II. *Instrumentum Laboris*

A new dawn in the history of African Catholicism began on 6 January 1989. On this all important day that will remain indelible in the memories of African Roman Catholics, "the solemnity of the Epiphany of the Lord, the Holy Father made the surprise announcement during his Angelus talk to convoke a Special Assembly for Africa of the Synod of Bishops so as to celebrate the communion and collegiality of the African episcopate with Rome and the universal church"[160] and the chosen topic for the Synod was, "The Church in Africa and her evangelizising Mission towards the year 2000: You shall be my witnesses (Acts 1:8)."[161]

The papal announcement was followed immediately with an inauguration of pre-preparatory commission strictly composed of various members of the African episcopate which preliminary work was completed and the commission was expanded in June, 1989 to constitute the Council of the General Secretariat entrusted with the actual preparation of the Special Assembly.[162] The outline produced by the initial pre-preparatory commission is known as *Lineamenta*, while the main document was itself referred to as *Instrumentum Laboris*. In reference to *Instrumentum laboris* the document states, "The *Instrumentum laboris* is by its very nature a document of preparation."[163]

---

160. These are the introductory remarks contained in the *Lineamenta* of Synod of Bishops Special Assembly for Africa which general theme was, "The Church in Africa and Her Evangelizising Mission Towards the Year 2000; You Shall be My Witnesses." The word *Lineamenta* is defined in that document as "Outline." For detailed examination of the content of *Lineamenta*, see Synod of Bishops, Special Assembly for Africa, *Lineamenta* (Vatican City: Libreria Editrice Vaticana, 1990), vii.

161. Synod of Bishops, *Lineamenta*, vii.

162. Synod of Bishops, vii.

163. Synod of Bishops, Special Assembly for Africa, *Instrumentum Laboris: The Church in Africa and her Evangelising Mission towards the year 2000: "You shall be my witnesses" (Acts 1:8)* (Vatican City: Libreria Editrice Vaticana, 1993), 4.

The preparatory document has an introduction with two parts and a recap of the work. *Instrumentum Laboris* states, "The Introduction seeks to locate the Synod for Africa within the dynamism of the synodal process in the Church. Part I is a theological framework which highlights the central concern of the Synod, namely, the theme of evangelization . . . Part II considers . . . sub-themes of proclamation, Inculturation, Dialogue, Justice and Peace, and Means of Social Communication."[164]

The essential content of *Instrumentum Laboris* is evangelization which the document did not only trace back to Jesus Christ but also argues that "Jesus himself, the Good News of God, was the very first and greatest evangelizer,"[165] who was passionate in proclaiming the reign of God. To accomplish his task of evangelism Jesus became man as a demonstration of total surrender to the Father's will. The becoming of God in the man Jesus of Nazareth led ultimately to his sacrificial death on the cross at Calvary. Jesus's death dealt a death blow on death since death did not hold him back in the tomb but he resurrected triumphantly and commissioned a band of followers with the work of evangelization to all people groups and cultures, and the Synod would have to cave a befitting nomenclature that would address this need.

Therefore, the second major theme in *Instrumentum Laboris* explores inculturation and states that "It consists, in fact, of a process by which Christian belief takes flesh in the cultures . . . because the incarnation of the Son of God was concrete and integral, it was a cultural incarnation."[166] In a related document, Synodus Episcoporum – Coetus Specialis Pro Africa: Relatio Ante Disceptationem Relatio Post Disceptationem Nuntius, inculturation has been portrayed as, "Marriage of professed faith and concrete life, harmony between faith and culture."[167] With inculturation now understood in terms of the wedding between Christian theology and African pre-Christian religious heritage, the document proposed four key areas within

---

164. Synod of Bishops, *Instrumentum Laboris*, 3–4.
165. Synod of Bishops, 10–11.
166. Synod of Bishops, 44.
167. Synodus Episcoporum, Coetus Specialis Pro Africa, *Nuntius, Relation Ante Disceptationem Relation Post Disceptationem* (Vatican City: Libreria Editrice Vaticana, 1994), 54.

which inculturation was to be carried out, namely, Bible, liturgy, pastoral work, and theological research.[168]

Now that the Vatican City has identified the African church as vibrant and one that has come of age, it no longer needs to depend on the discrete judgment of the mother church in Rome for missions. Thus Paul VI rightly said at Kampala that "By now, you Africans are missionaries to yourselves."[169] Evangelization of the African continent, the main feature upon which the African Synod of 1994 in Rome anchored revolved around, was in five critical areas: Proclamation of the good news, inculturation, dialogue, justice and peace, and the means of social communication respectively. Of the five, inculturation became the hub which was extensively discussed to tie together the total essence of the Synod. Thus the aspect dealing with "Incarnation of the 'Logos,'" states that "Inculturation or the process through which the Christian faith is 'incarnated' in cultures, is bound by its nature to the proclamation of the Gospel. The foregoing is explained by the fact that inculturation is rooted in the Incarnation of the Word of God (Logos 'Word') . . . the incarnation of the Son of God was an incarnation into a culture."[170]

Following that Synod, inculturation became a fashionable term and theme in the formulation of African ancestor theology. In fact the Synod almost viewed inculturation as being tantamount to redemption. Note the following statement; "Through its relation to the Incarnation, inculturation ought 'to take resolutely the road to Jerusalem' (Lk 9:51) and to be realized in the Paschal Mystery. In effect, even cultures are called to 'surrender their lives for the sake of Christ and the Gospel,' if they wish to be saved (cf. Mk 8:35)."[171]

III. Code of Canon Law

It has been welled established in this work that magisterium remains the sole apex body that enacts laws and formulates doctrines in the Roman Catholic Church. Article can. 749 subsection 1 of the 1983 Code of Canon Law states; "In virtue of his office the Supreme Pontiff is infallible in his teaching

---

168. Synod of Bishops, *Instrumentum Laboris*, 47.
169. Synod of Bishops, 14.
170. Synod of Bishops, *Lineamenta*, 48.
171. Synod of Bishops, 49.

when, as chief Shepherd and Teacher of all Christ's faithful, with the duty of strengthening his brethren in the faith, he proclaims by definitive act a doctrine to be held. . . ."[172] Subsection 2 stipulates, "The College of Bishops also possesses infallibility in its teaching when the Bishops, gathered together in an Ecumenical Council, exercised the magisterium."[173] Indubitably, the magisterium is the supreme council in the Roman Catholic Church vested with absolute powers to enact edicts. These laws enacted by the magisterium are called the Canon Law adopted by the magisterium to regulate and also govern the operations of the Roman Catholic Church.

Before the Second World War, the Roman Catholic Church had operated the 1917 code. Shortly after the war, an impulse was felt within the church to "bring the 1917 code up to date and to adapt it to the changed circumstances of the world."[174] Hence during his announcement of Second Vatican Council, Pope John XXIII hinted that the aftermath of the council would be a revision of the Code. In the same theological thought in 1977 Pope Paul VI also called for the revision of the Code. These calls finally materialized on 25 January 1983[175] when a new Code, which repealed some sections of the 1917 Code, was promulgated and passed into law under Pope John Paul II to reflect the documents and theology of Vatican II which basic goal was global evangelization through the method of inculturation. Thus, the 1983 Code of Canon Law together with the main documents of Vatican II are fundamental promulgations that gave impetus for the emergence of inculturation theology in Africa where the ancestor model is used in relation to Jesus Christ.

---

172. *The Code of Canon Law*, new rev. English ed. (Bangalore, India: Theological Publications, 2004), 174.

173. *Code of Canon Law*, 174.

174. *Code of Canon Law*, ix.

175. *Code of Canon Law*, xi.

African Symbols and Christian Beliefs: Towards Comparing African Pre-Christian Model of Ancestor and Christian Model of Christ

Some African theologians argue that "the notion and reality of Ancestors are omnipresent in African cultures. According to this school of thought, ancestors are a masterpiece in the construction of traditional African religion."[176] Jean-Marc Ela, for example, has painted that Africans are "constantly recalling the presence of the ancestors in the warp and woof of their existence."[177] This explains why in most traditional societies, ancestors are presumed to receive life from God and to transmit it to the living terrestrials.[178] This position which ancestors occupy in traditional belief is now applied to Christ, incarnate Word of the Father.[179] To that end, most christological thinking in the Majority World accepts as axiomatic that reflection on Christ must be done in the light of local realities.[180] The theological ground for this assertion which this work states elsewhere is that the Christian faith never exists except as "translated into a culture."[181] Hence "experience with Christ in one place [culture] must not be made normative elsewhere."[182] This means that the ideal presentation of the picture of Christ as a universal figure should stem from the cultural models obtained in a given culture. Among the many symbols that make up African culture are the ancestors.

Scholars agree that the ancestors are a most powerful symbol of African culture.[183] S. U. Urivwo ardently maintains that, "No approach to any appreciation of indigenous ideas regarding God can take any path but that through the thought area occupied by the ancestors."[184] T. C. Young cor-

---

176. Mununguri, *Closeness of the God*, 71.
177. Éla, *My Faith as an African*, 14.
178. Mununguri, *Closeness of the God*, 71.
179. Mununguri, 71.
180. Dyrness, *Learning about Theology*, 181.
181. Bosch, *Transforming Mission*, 458.
182. Dyrness, *Learning about Theology*, 181.
183. Barth Chidili, *Inculturation as a Symbol of Evangelization: Christian Faith Taking Root in African Soil* (Jos, Nigeria: Mono Expressions, 1997), 107.
184. S. U. Urivwo, "Traditional Religion and Christianity Among the Urhobo," in *The Gods in Retreat*, ed. Emefie Ikenga Metuh (Enugu, Nigeria: Fourth Dimension Publishers, 1986), 27.

roborates this stance thus, "To Africans, living from day to day, has no meaning at all apart from ancestral presence and power."[185] This preoccupation informs the incessant quest for the formulation of Christology in which African theologians compare Jesus Christ with ancestors and thus construct Christology in light of that African pre-Christian model. The desire to make Christian theology rhyme with traditional African categories has been the approach of Kwame Bediako. While reviewing Bediako's *Christianity in Africa: The Renewal of a non-Western Religion*, Valenti Dedji notes that for Bediako, "The essence of the quest for an African Christian theology . . . is to translate faith in Jesus Christ to suit the tongue, style, genius, character and culture of African peoples."[186]

If this venture – of translating faith in Jesus Christ to suit the tongue, style, genius, character, and culture of African peoples – must succeed, African theologians will have to think of an ideal method with which to chart this course. Thus, Christology from below – from the existential historical human figure of Jesus of Nazareth who once lived and walked the Streets of Galilee and Palestine in Israel – would "work out well [for ancestor Christology] instead of starting from 'high' or metaphysical Christology which has been the only way of studying Christology formally."[187] Granted the critical nature of Christology from below in the formulation of ancestor Christology, African theologians employ models from the New Testament to construct Christology. Chidili states, "The Scriptural presentation of Jesus is full of marvellous images and striking titles."[188]

Some images and titles of Jesus derived from the New Testament that Chidili find to resonate with an African description of Jesus are where the apostle Paul describes Jesus Christ in Ephesians 4:14 as "our peace, the One who 'has torn down the barrier wall that separate Jews and Gentiles.'"[189] Furthermore, Chidili opined that the church throughout the centuries has exegetically employed the image of Christ portrayed in Isaiah 9:6 "to refer

---

185. T. C. Young, "The Idea of God in Northern Nyasaland," in *African Ideas of God*, ed. E. Smith (London: Edinburgh House Press, 1950), 38.

186. Dedji, *Reconstruction and Renewal*, 194.

187. Chidili, *Inculturation as a Symbol*, 113.

188. Chidili, 114.

189. Chidili, 114.

to Jesus as 'Wonderful Counselor, Prince of Peace, Father-Forever,' at the Christmas vigil."[190] Citing more Pauline passages, Chidili demonstrates, "The Apostle Paul, talks of 'the love for Christ,' (2 Cor. 5:14), or the love is shown by Christ (Gal. 2:20, Rm 8:35-38), by dying for all as a model of authentic existence (2 Cor. 15). These images shape what the Church thinks of him."[191] By "him," here Chidili has in mind Jesus Christ.

Making reference to what Christendom has held unto throughout its existence, Chidili asserts that Christian thinkers have always been unanimous in their perception and portrayal of the image of Jesus Christ in every dispensation of believers as the perfect God-Man. This for him is the only one and best delineation of the incarnation – the Christian confession that Christ became flesh in the man Jesus of Nazareth and made his dwelling with men. This he believes is exactly what Karl Rahner meant when he wrote, "God definitively appropriated humanity in the incarnation. That is to say, that when God uttered God's Word, the Word became human flesh. By that action, God immersed himself in the 'void' of 'godlessness' and 'sin,' so that from that moment it became possible for humankind wishing to meet God, to meet God through the man Jesus."[192]

While Chidili fails to tell us how exactly through the incarnation Jesus Christ can be happily compared with African ancestors without major difficulties, his argument that "To ignore the man Jesus is tantamount to denying humanity completely," alludes to the notion of ancestors because, as we sincerely believe, his use of Pauline passages which present Christian virtues seems to hark back to African beliefs about the good deeds of the ancestors. The argument that "It is the this cultural experience of a universe intimately related to God that can become the vehicle for African religious believers to open themselves fully to the Christ-symbol"[193] speaks volumes that what he had in mind is presenting Christian symbols from African spectacle. His next sentence is most revealing, "The Incarnation of the Word

---

190. Chidili, 114.
191. Chidili, 114.
192. Chidili, 114.
193. Chidili, 113–114.

of God means . . . the meeting between God and humankind . . . If Jesus Christ is the explication of God, he is the explication of humankind too."[194]

It is therefore only natural, as he seems to conclude, if Jesus Christ is analogically presented to Africans in their religious and cultural categories most especially the ancestor model. But we have earlier on maintained that analogy works only with things or persons that are similar or things that are two of a kind. In the case of Jesus Christ and African ancestors, the difference is not that of degree or more precisely that of numerator and denominator, no the two are diametrically opposed to each other because the Sovereign God and Lord of all creatures who intentionally condescended low to assume human flesh cannot at the same time himself be judged in the fashion of the mortal flesh he assumed. Hence Jesus Christ, whether described metaphorically or analogically, can never be an ancestor in the proportion of African ancestors.

Inculturating Christian Faith through the Ancestor Model: Church Magisterium and Vatican II and the Theological Implications of Inculturating Christian Model through the Ancestor Model

The analogy between the way the ancestor functions in African culture and the role that theology accords to Jesus as the very incarnation of God is obvious. But apart from the theology of the incarnation, Jesus Christ, in his life, suffering and death, serves for the humblest Christian as a model of how to live a life open to God, how to suffer its indignities and to die surrendered to the Father; he functions as the symbol of a perfect human being.[195]

The picture painted of Jesus Christ in Scripture as a perfect human being is what endears most African theologians to him since they also regard their ancestors as the perfect spirit beings now living in the ancestral realm. As Chidili notes, "It is this thought of 'perfect-human-being-ness' that compels both Christians and Africans to regard Jesus and Ancestors respectively as their hero, someone that must be emulated."[196] One way of emulating Jesus

---

194. Chidili, 115.
195. Chidili, 115–116.
196. Chidili, 116.

Christ will not just remain at the abstract level of describing and comparing his virtues with those of African ancestors; such a comparison must as well encompass a name that befits those virtues. Since therefore, as we admitted elsewhere in this work, the communities of African theologians cannot name Christ personally without going to the Bible or Catechism, they do just the opposite and attribute to Christ, the traditional title of an ancestor that they would like to see him given in the communities.[197]

While this may be considered a step in the right direction, caution should, however, be exercised in the way African theologians contribute to the overall global theological discourse. It is true to admit that the New Testament gives spectacular images and striking titles of Jesus which African theologians find irresistible. That notwithstanding, African theologians can still explore other themes that are biblically inclined as opposed to categories derived from African pre-Christian religious heritage. For example Paul's argument in Ephesians 2:14 that Jesus made peace by destroying the barrier, the dividing wall of hostility could be used to formulate a theology that seeks to address the needs of victims of Boko Haram in Internally Displaced Persons (IDPs) camps in Nigeria and Africa at large. To my mind, I have no doubt that presenting Jesus Christ as the prince and medium of peace the same way the prophet Isaiah did in Isaiah 9:6 to aggrieved victims of Islamic fundamentalists would go a long way in healing their wounds and traumatized hearts.

Of course, African theologians are quite aware of this critical aspect of Jesus's ministry of reconciliation, reconstruction, and rehabilitation but often fail to build their theologies around the concept of peace vis-à-vis traumatic experiences. Where it becomes necessary to formulate theology using peace, it has always been linked to the function performed by ancestors instead of Christ who achieved true peace for humanity. Chidili justifies this assertion in his work. Accordingly, he observes, "The quality of peacemaker with which Paul asserts about Jesus is one of the qualities which Africans find in their Ancestors. Because the Ancestors are characterized by peace, love and fraternal concern for their progenies, their children see them as the symbol of peace, love and fraternal concern."[198]

---

197. Part II: *Challenge and Response in the 1980s and '90s*, taken from Ritchie "African Theology," 11.

198. Chidili, *Inculturation as a Symbol*, 116.

With this perception, theologians in Africa are comfortable to inculturate these pre-Christian models into Christian models so that Christianity will reach the nooks and crannies of the continent. A case in point is the Gbaya people of Cameroon who believe that the Sore Tree is a symbol of peace and accept it as such. Chidili keenly notes, "Now the Gbaya Christians speak of Jesus as *Sore-ga-mo-k'ee*, 'Jesus our Sore-cooling-things' because they discover from their Bible that Jesus, by the blood of his cross makes peace and creates a new community and new village just like the Sore Tree."[199] Chidili argues that this actually is the underpinning reason that people will realize when they are naturally exposed to biblical values in their natural life setting; they "traditionalize" the values, and that is the hallmark of inculturation. This dynamism of Jesus's peace-making quality is now fully understood by the Gbaya people just because it is couched in their traditional experience. Now Jesus is known as a peacemaker, but instead of calling him Jesus, they call him *Sore-ga-mo-k'ee*, a name that means peacemaker for them.[200]

This makes a lot of sense to me because, as is argued throughout this work, Africans will be more comfortable to use titles for Jesus Christ that are biblically inclined and the Gbaya people notion of Sore Tree as a symbol of peace vis-à-vis Jesus Christ, the peacemaker is directly taken from the Bible. My concern with the ancestor model is that though more than any ethnic group the Jews understand the idea of ancestors but nowhere in the entire Bible do we have them compare either Abraham or Isaac or Jacob – their ancestors – with Jesus Christ the same way we engage the Bible in Africa. This exactly is the pitfall that this work sees and is seeking to point out to theologians in Africa who think that Africans will be impressed if Jesus Christ is compared with our ancestors and the gospel is proclaimed to people from within the perspective of their culture. Unfortunately, the reverse is the case since most Africans are far more comfortable using only biblical titles for Jesus Christ.[201] Jørn Henrik Olson who cited Cécé Kolié raises the same

---

199. Chidili, 117.

200. Chidili, 117–118.

201. In his dissertation questionnaire which seeks to know which name Akan AICs prefer to use for Jesus Christ, which was eventually published by Pickwick in 2011 as *African Christology: Jesus in Post-Missionary African Christianity*, Clifton R. Clarke gives the following results: Saviour – 1867 (74.6 percent), Messiah – 1551 (62 percent), Lord – 1444 (57.7 percent), Healer – 1382 (55.2 percent), God – 724 (28.9 percent), Conqueror – 334 (13.3

argument, "African peasants call Jesus only by biblical names since they cannot or will not make use of African titles."²⁰² Furthermore, Kolié holds that, "African theologians are actually trying to introduce Christological paradigms, which are unknown to the population at large."²⁰³

Kolié is not alone in articulating this worry for the exaggerated overgeneralizations of an ancestor title for Jesus Christ in Africa, as if all Africans have and do venerate their ancestors. Donald J. Goergen, makes the same observation, "Traditions concerning ancestors vary with different ethnic communities. It is difficult to generalize as varied conceptions exist."²⁰⁴ While Goergen sounds polite, Henry Johannes Mugabe is blunt. For him, "It is dangerous to generalize when one is talking about Africa because it is a continent of hundreds of distinct and different traditional ethnic groups."²⁰⁵

The complex and heterogeneous nature of the African continent will hardly pass for generalization. Among the Samburu people of Northern Kenya for instance, the notion of ancestors do not exist in their traditional worldview let alone have Jesus for an ancestor. Dean Apel notes, "Most African attempts at Christology are based on a sedentary lifestyle and oriented toward a worldview which contains the 'living dead' or 'spirits' or 'chiefs,' none of which exist among the Samburu."²⁰⁶

---

percent), Chief – 76 (3 percent), Brother – 61 (2.4 percent) and Ancestor – 60 (2.4 percent). With these statistics in which the ancestor model was the least preferred title for Jesus, Clarke concludes;

> Given the popularity of this concept as a Christological model for a West African context, the extent to which this analogy was ignored as a Christological title was surprising. The survey indicated that only 60 (2.4%) of Akan AICs opted for this as a title that best described Jesus to them . . . the ancestor model was being rejected . . . I would therefore question John Pobee's notion that Jesus be looked at as the Great and Greatest Ancestor-in Akan *Twi Nana*. The centrality of the Bible within the context of Akan AICs would make it unlikely that such a traditional and non-biblical title be applied to Jesus. This harks back to our argument that Africans are more comfortable when they use biblical titles for Jesus than the ancestor model which is a reductionist ivory tower model being formulated in the classroom by African theologians and biblical scholars.

For a thorough investigation of Clarke's statistics, see Clarke, *African Christology*, 82–93.

202. Olson, "Contextualised Christology," 247.
203. Olson, 247.
204. Goergen, "Quest for the Christ."
205. Mugabe, "Christology in an African Context," 343.
206. Dean Apel, "Towards a Samburu Christology," *Currents in Theology and Mission* 23, no. 5 (1996): 357.

With this blunt and avowal rejection of ancestor title for Jesus Christ at the grassroots, we want to feature the theological implications ancestor Christology holds for African Christianity. First, it is critical we recall from our discussion in this chapter that African theologians and biblical scholars drew their inspiration from church magisterium, pre-and post-Vatican II's sacerdotal promulgation of the doctrine of inculturation as an ideal theological method for global evangelization. Second, it is important we recall too that throughout the centuries, scholars have made an attempt to examine the relationship between Christ and culture but no scholar has magnified culture to the extent that the gospel and culture are seen as parallel. Third, when God called our ancestor Abraham to come out of Ur to the promised land, he never had in mind that the gospel was going to be subsumed to culture. All missiologists, without exception, working on the subject of the gospel and culture are unanimous that the gospel is able to transform culture.

However, the church magisterium or the Vatican II's *Nostra Aetate* no. 2 (28 October 1965) open declaration that the church rejects nothing of non-Christian traditions and cultures opened a new chapter in Roman Catholic beliefs which articulate theology as a theology of faith in culture. Ever since this ecclesial declaration found acceptance in Roman Catholic theological circles, the theology of inculturation became a catalyst that empowered African theologians to formulate Christology from the perspective of African culture. For most ancestor Christology advocates, Vatican II lifted off the mist that hitherto had blurred their thinking and scratched where they were itching. More so that the legislative documents of the Second Vatican Council were authenticated and enacted into law as the Code of the Canon Law of 1983, Roman Catholic theologians and biblical scholars see themselves as the herald of the gospel in the light of culture.

While the primary purposes of inculturation and contextualization have been the reflection of Christianity upon the gospel in the light of people's circumstances, we should not forget quickly what mission really is. According to Charles Van Engen, mission is,

> The people of God intentionally crossing barriers from Church to nonchurch, faith to nonfaith, to proclaim by word and deed the coming of the kingdom of God in Jesus Christ; this task is achieved by means of the Church's participation in God's

mission of reconciling people to God, to themselves, to each other, and the world, and gathering them into the Church through repentance and faith in Jesus Christ by the work of the Holy Spirit with a view to the transformation of the world as a sign of the coming of the kingdom in Jesus Christ.[207]

Engen's understanding of mission should challenge the proponents of ancestor Christology to rethink their methodology and stances about Jesus's ancestorship. If indeed mission is overcoming the barriers of non-faith to faith, non-church to church, reconciling people to God, to themselves, to each other, and the world, this presupposes the emergence of a radical culture that seeks to unify every other culture under one supreme culture and we think this is exactly where the notion of transformation comes in, insofar as we concede the fact that there is such a thing as a Christian worldview. If the notion of African ancestors stemmed from our pre-Christian traditional religious heritage, by mission, the church in Africa is called into a new culture that comes with the conversion that goes with new status as children of God. Paul addresses this directly as he tells us, "Therefore, if anyone is in Christ, the new creation has come: The old has gone, the new is here!" (2 Cor 5:17).

Summary

It seems to me that the proclamation and insertion of the good news are inconceivable in Africa without contextualization and inculturation, which shows that mission is the gospel being entirely African and genuinely Christian. The theological basis for these methods derives right from the debate between Tatian, Tertullian and Clement of Alexandria on the encounter between Christian faith and the Graeco-Roman/Hellenistic traditions in the one hand and pre- and post-Vatican II church magisterium which called for the renewal and bringing up-to-date the teaching of the Roman Catholic Church in the light of the perspective of people's culture on the other hand.

On the African continent, the Bishops' Synod on Africa and the Synod on Consecrated Life in 1994 both highlighted and emphasized the importance

---

207. Charles E. van Engen, *Mission on the Way: Issues in Mission Theology* (Grand Rapids, MI: Baker Books, 1996), 26–27.

of inculturation and inter-religious dialogue.[208] Consequently, the aftermath of this Synod empowered African Bishops to call for the inculturation of African pre-Christian heritage. Ndung'u and Mwaura point out, "The constant call by the Church authority to inculturate the gospel message has sparked off many theological reflections. Each cultural context has come up with its own understanding of who Jesus Christ is to them in the given cultural, religious and political realities . . . so that Jesus is at the service of the local people."[209]

This work contends that theologians who employ new methodologies from African worldview and primal traditions to formulate Christian theology can produce Christologies in ways that present Jesus as a multi hydra figure since there are no theological norms to establish a universal identity of Jesus Christ in Christendom.

---

208. Nahashon W. Ndung'u and Philomena N. Mwaura had maintained that the Synod fathers are quite aware that the way forward in any theological reflection must carry with it the attitude of pluralistic and inclusive elements. Each cultural context will manifest a different face of Jesus Christ. Africa has been a recipient of many foreign images of Jesus Christ since the arrival of the Western European missionaries. These argument are raised in Ndung'u and Mwaura, eds., *Challenges and Prospects*, 102.

209. Ndung'u and Mwaura, 103.

CHAPTER 6

Theological and Biblical Interpretations of African Ancestor Christologies: Exploring African Linguistic Affinity Christology

Introduction

While chapter 5 discussed the theological sources of ancestor Christology, this chapter explores the theological and biblical interpretations of ancestorship and messiahship from the perspectives of the Old Testament and African traditional beliefs. This will be done through a comparative approach. To this end, the chapter compares and contrasts the messianic concepts in the Old Testament to the ideas of ancestors in African traditional worldview.

To this end, a survey of the central presuppositions of African ancestor Christologies will be done along with a brief restatement of the significance of ancestors in African cosmology with a view to highlighting the theological and biblical differences between African and Jewish ancestors.

Presuppositions of the Ancestorship of Christ

In his seminal work, *Re-Imagining African Christologies: Conversing with the Interpretations and Appropriations of Jesus in Contemporary African Christianity*, Victor I. Ezigbo unearths four fundamental presuppositions that shape christological discourse in Africa: gap and fulfillment presupposition, destructionist presupposition, reconstructionist presupposition, and solution presupposition.[1] Each of these presuppositions generates Christology from a particular bent. While the theologians that use the gap and fulfillment presupposition (Luke Mbefor, Mercy Oduyoye, E. Bolaji Idowu to mention but a few) contend that "Jesus does not need to destroy all the core values and beliefs of the indigenous religions,"[2] the destructionists "dismiss the idea that there are major valid areas of convergence between the gospel of Jesus Christ and the religious traditions."[3]

Staunch destructionists who vehemently raised voices for a clean break between Christian theology and African beliefs; Byang H. Kato, Yusufu Turaki and Tokunboh Adeyemo, argued that African traditional beliefs are the products of human initiatives aimed to satiate his religious quest. To that end, African traditional beliefs cannot measure up to God's salvific requirements for the redemption of humanity. This argument is taken further by Karl Grebe and Wilfred Fon who ardently noted that "Religion is man's effort to reach out to God in accordance with the desire God has put into his heart (Acts 17:27), ATR [African Traditional Religion] is one expression of this desire. Like all other non-biblical religions it is built around some truths yet totally incapable of leading man to God."[4]

The third position, reconstruction, is a synthetic attempt to reconcile the first two opposing positions. The basic objective of the reconstructionists is to present Jesus Christ as the one who does reconstruct African traditional beliefs and values. Thus, Jesus they maintain is "One who reconstructs the indigenous religions by challenging, satisfying, transforming, and rebuilding it."[5] Justin Ukpong and the Kenyan theologian J. N. K. Mugambi are leading luminaries of this view. For them, Nigerian and African traditional categories can contribute positively to the appropriation of the Christian teachings and beliefs in Africa.

The last view, solution presupposition, represents folk yearnings and aspirations embedded in songs, prayers, and life experiences of Christians with

---

1. Ezigbo, *Re-Imagining African Christologies*, 27.
2. Ezigbo, 27.
3. Ezigbo, 37.
4. Karl Grebe and Wilfred Fon, *African Traditional Religion and Christian Counseling* (Wheaton, IL: Oasis, 2006), 35–36.
5. Ezigbo, *Re-Imagining African Christologies*, 43.

no formal theological education. This stance is closely akin to liberationists' ideology since Jesus is not only perceived essentially as the "Superman" who proffers quick solutions to every one of their needs but above all, he is the enabler who never gets tired of the petitions of the masses. Jesus to them is, as Gustaf Aulén puts it, "Christus Victor."[6]

These four presuppositions represent a perennial problem of the relationship between Christianity and culture that has lingered for centuries in Christian circles, and many scholars have wrestled tirelessly in one way or the other to resolve this canker. In his *Theology and Identity: The Impact of Culture on Christian Thought in the Second Century and in Modern Africa*, Bediako examines the cultural tension that engulfed and threatened the second-century church. Similar to current theological discourse in Africa, Tatian and Tertullian stood opposed to each other in their perspectives of the Christian relationship to Hellenistic and Graeco-Roman cultures, while Justin and Clement of Alexandria gave a symbiotic approach to the issue.[7] Of Clement of Alexandria, Bediako writes, "If there are in Clement's writings the combinations of Greek philosophical ideas with Christian Doctrines, it is because Clement is able, through his Christian understanding, to see affinities between the various positions which he seeks to harmonise."[8]

Even though Ezigbo admitted that some of these presuppositions overlap and impinge upon each other, this work concerns itself with the first presupposition, gap and fulfillment, which seems to fall within the ambit of inculturation theology since its proponents "contend that Jesus does not need to abolish the preparatory work of the ancestors but fulfills them."[9]

---

6. In his investigation of the history of the three main theories of atonement through the centuries, Gustaf Aulén argues that the total package behind the mystery of the incarnation of the Son of God is that God the Father had in Christ redeemed fallen humanity from the slavery of Satan the enemy of mankind. For more on Aulén's argument, see his, *Christus Victor: An Historical Study of the Three Main Types of the Idea of Atonement* (New York: Collier Books, 1986).

7. Bediako's *Theology and Identity: The Impact of Culture upon Christian Thought in the Second Century and in Modern Africa* is a ground-breaking publication in the discussion of the relationship between Christian belief and African tradition. See Kwame Bediako, *Theology and Identity: The Impact of Culture upon Christian Thought in the Second Century and in Modern Africa* (Oxford: Regnum, 1999).

8. Bediako, *Theology and Identity*, 175.

9. Ezigbo, *Re-Imagining African Christologies*, 34.

What are the basic assumptions of the ancestor Christology? In a paper titled, "Christ as Our Ancestor," Wellington O. Wotogbe-Weneka, a professor of Religious Studies writes, "If Christ and what he stands for is preached to Africans, drawing analogies from the African notion of the ancestors, it would make more sense to them, and eventually make Christ and his message more acceptable to the people than it had been hitherto."[10] This bold assertion gives a clue as to the significant assumptions African theologians and biblical scholars hold onto for predicting the ancestorship of Jesus Christ.

Though Wotogbe-Weneka fails to explain precisely what he meant by "What Christ stands for,"[11] one is forced to draw an inference from the argument of Charles Nyamiti, who once stated that one aspect of Christ's ancestorship to Africans includes "His being our Model of behaviour."[12] From Nyamiti's view, Jesus's virtuous life, which endears him to Africans, makes him our model and the archetypical African man. His main assumption for predicating the ancestorship of Jesus Christ can be gleaned from his definition of African Christology which he contends that it is "a discourse on Christ in accordance with the mentality and needs of the people in the black continent."[13]

What is the undefined mentality and needs of Africans that Nyamiti seeks to unravel? While that has not been elaborated in his notion of Christ, elsewhere he hints at the African worldview and traditional belief and culture. He writes, "There is African (non-Christian) Christology. At first, this appellation seems contradictory, but it refers to an important reality, for it designates what one might call 'the discourse on the hidden Christ in African traditional religions and cultures.'"[14]

It could be discerned from the foregoing that the desire to replicate Christ in African traditional thought form and cultural categories is the underlying

---

10. Wellington O. Wotogbe Weneka, "Christ as Our Ancestor," in *Christology in African Context*, eds. S. O. Abogunrin, J. O. Akao, and Dorcas Olu Akintunde, Biblical Studies Series no. 2 (Ibadan: NABS, 2003), 290.

11. Weneka, "Christ as Our Ancestor," 290.

12. Nyamiti, *Christ as Our Ancestor*, 30.

13. Nyamiti, "Contemporary African Christologies: Assessment and Practical Suggestions," in *Paths of African Theology*, ed. Rosino Gibelini (Maryknoll, NY: Orbis Books, 1994), 63.

14. Nyamiti, "Contemporary African Christologies," 63.

reason many African ancestor Christology theologians construct ancestor Christologies. This for me constitutes one of the significant weaknesses of ancestor Christology since it is an old model centred on the traditional African worldview. Nyamiti has undermined the strength of ancestor Christology when he admits that this Christology is non-Christian which can be understood to mean also non-biblical discourse about Jesus Christ since its source is neither the Christian Bible, nor Christian theology, nor apostolic tradition but the African reality and mentality. But in what significant ways has this model served to illuminate or magnify an accurate understanding of Jesus Christ to Africans? It is critical we probe further. Since its inception in African theological and academic circles which at the same time made it famous in the 1980s, what crucial role has the ancestor model helped in the evangelization of Africans?

These critical questions should stimulate and provoke the thought of not only African Christians but also believers the world over in the direction of this subject. Whether or not they conjure up a mental picture in the path this work charts, we must admit that it is not meant to articulate an answer to all the questions raised. However, in addition to the voices of Weneka and Nyamiti, an attempt will be made to probe further the underlying assumptions of ancestor Christology advocates vis-à-vis the first question.

Ezigbo has delved extensively into the central assertions of African theologians on the ancestorship of Jesus Christ, and this section leans heavily on his ideas. In a fresh discussion of the subject, Ezigbo has observed that fundamental to the extrapolation of the ancestorship upon Jesus Christ lies in traditional African epistemology. Thus, the foundation upon which most African theologians associate Jesus with the ancestors hinges on the understanding that "The cult of the ancestors proffers the best 'theological meeting-point' for Christianity and African indigenous religions."[15] This resonates with Abbé Marc Ntetem's conclusion that, "acceptance of the Christian faith does not involve a complete break with African tradition, for it has its source in God, and thus finds its fulfilment in Christianity."[16]

---

15. Ezigbo, *Re-Imagining African Christologies*, 71.
16. Ntetem, "Initiation, Traditional and Christian," 99.

How God is the source of African traditional beliefs, to the extent that Africa's primal beliefs find fulfilment in Christianity, as Ntetem will have us believe, is not very clear to me, and this does not only leave the door open to unanswered questions but makes his argument porous. Beyond the notion of understanding also comes the display of worldview and allegiance by which religious piety is demonstrated and domesticated. His next statement is explicit on this, "The 'ancestral cult' is the heart of the African tradition and culture . . . 'ancestors stand as the middle point between the visible and invisible worlds.'"[17] Uchenna A. Ezeh describes the invisible world as, "The . . . home of the ancestors."[18]

The notion in a traditional worldview that the ancestors are spirit beings, who can be perceived by the physical senses or be experienced in an existential situation, accounts mainly for the belief that they occupy an invisible realm. This view poses a serious challenge to the notion that Africans can and do actually have a real physical encounter with their departed ancestors. I wish to argue here that whatever mental picture or image an African can conjure up in their mind in terms of relating with the ancestors physically, it is at best a conceptual but not in any way truly a person to person, eyebrow to eyebrow contact between two or more individual persons. This assertion is buttressed by Diane B. Stinton's research findings in an oral interview with Kenyans in 2004. In that oral interview, Stinton's respondents had argued that Jesus can only be appropriated as ancestor conceptually but not experientially since Christ is not an ancestor in the usual sense one's biological father or grandfather can be an ancestor to them.[19] This claim suggests that ancestors exist only in the imagination of those twenty-first-century Africans who deliberately chose to be enslaved to this archaic religious and cultural ideology.

Returning to the issue of the ancestral realm, a conundrum that has remained unexplained but yet forms one of the critical assumptions for predicating the ancestorship upon Jesus Christ by the proponents of African ancestor Christology is the realm African ancestors are believed to occupy. Is it possible for African Christians, by maintaining affinity with the ancestors,

---

17. Ezigbo, *Re-Imagining African Christologies*, 71.
18. Ezeh, *Jesus Christ the Ancestor*, 38.
19. Stinton, *Jesus of Africa*, 157.

to have direct access to the kingdom of God? While that has not been made manifest, Ntetem insinuates that acknowledging Christ as ancestor leads automatically to the kingdom of God. He claims, "Once Jesus Christ's sovereignty is acknowledged as the supreme ancestor over *muntu*, a new affinity is established in which *muntu* is engrafted and assured of a place in the coming kingdom."[20]

An obvious pitfall with Ntetem's submission, which also characterizes the arguments of ancestor Christology advocates, is the tendency to construe salvation in Jesus Christ via the ancestral cult without which redemption seems to be invalid since as the assertions seem to go, God and ancestors are partners in the atoning work of Christ. Perhaps this explains Bénézet Bujo's view that "When Africans honour the ancestors they are at least implicitly, also honouring God."[21] This statement leaves no room for doubt that it is the assumption of ancestor Christology exponents that when African Christians honour God, they are at least by the same token equally lavishing honour on the ancestors.

While these are very good assumptions, one, however, finds consolation in the definition of the term since it implies that one can only use it analogically to compare Jesus Christ with the African ancestors. But does the significance of African ancestors really warrant this comparison? This is the daunting task of the next section to which we now turn.

The Significance of Ancestors in African Cosmology

The significant role ancestors are believed to play in African cosmology has been examined in chapter 4. This section will briefly build upon the issues raised therein.

Klaus Nürnberger asks a fundamental question about ancestors in African traditional worldview, "Are spirits and ancestors nothing but psychological phenomena located in our minds, or do they have an independent reality of their own out there?"[22] In answer, he points out that in "traditionalism

---

20. Ntetem, "Initiation, Traditional and Christian," 100.
21. Bujo, *African theology*, 23.
22. Nürnberger, *Living Dead*, 14.

ancestors are deemed to be 'real' because their existential impact on the living is pervasive and decisive."[23] Furthermore, Nürnberger maintains that the reality of African ancestors is not located in their vitality, however, but in their authority that also depends on power. So ancestors are ascribed greater power than they had when they were still physically alive. As bearers of authority ancestors depend on being remembered, honoured and obeyed by their offspring.[24] For this reason, the religious practices associated with the ancestors are without question the most prominent aspect of African religions in the sub-Sahara and the very heart of the African worldview.[25] For many people, the ancestors provide for their communities and also are benevolent guardians and protectors of people. Some African Christians feel that even God is unable to do anything without the assistance of ancestors, as they are mediators giving people power to pray to God.[26] In some ancient African communities, Nürnberger argues that ancestors define collective and individual identity, underpin the hierarchical system, have legitimate positions, and uphold communal traditions. They make their will known, and express their displeasure in the form of drought, barrenness or other mishaps in the lives of their descendants.[27]

The central function of ancestors in the traditional African worldview has been affirmed in the *Instrumentum Laboris* (see ch. 5) of the Synod for Africa, "In Africa there is still a widespread conviction that life and death, the living and the dead, even the as-yet-unborn, are mutually dependent."[28] "The network of beliefs constitutes the bedrock of the African worldview. . . . The fact that the ancestors hold a key position in African traditional religion makes this all the more important."[29]

Significantly, ancestors are powerful intermediaries between man and man, and man and God. They are believed to attend weddings and also give

---

23. Nürnberger, 14.
24. Nürnberger, 14.
25. Allan H. Anderson, *African Reformation: African Initiated Christianity in the 20th Century* (Asmara, Eritrea: African World Press, 2001), 202.
26. Anderson, *African Reformation*, 202.
27. Nürnberger, *Livind Dead*, 29.
28. Nwaogwugwu, *Ancestor Christology*, 84.
29. Nwaogwugwu, 84.

their blessings to the newly married couple.[30] In some traditional societies, burnt offerings are made to the ancestors who in return give good luck to the one who made the sacrifice.[31] In other societies, ancestors are still part of their human families; they know and have interest in what is going on in the family. They are the guardians of the family affairs, traditions, ethics, and activities. At the same time they warn of impending danger or rebuke those who failed to follow their special instructions.[32]

In addition ancestors are perceived as custodians of the law and customs of the tribe who can punish with sickness or misfortune.[33] In other words, ancestors are ever at hand to harm or help[34] since they have authority to punish and also restore well-being and order.[35] This conscious awareness of the presence of ancestral spirits is due in part to the fact that tribal people are only too keenly aware of the great difference between a man and a divinity, for they know how defenseless they are before the hazards of life and how it is necessary to depend on superior powers to help them. With this strong sense of continuing communion with the living-dead, and the honour and service given to them, Africans place great significance on their ancestors.[36]

Richard J. Gehman presents an elaborate discussion on the significant place ancestors occupy in African cosmology. Of African ancestors and other spirits, he has this to say, "Their main responsibility is the welfare of the whole tribe, concerned with rain, the crime of incest and the appointment of a new chief. A hierarchy prevails among the various 'tribal spirits' with *Dzivaguru* being the closest to God who passes all requests to the Supreme Being . . . they are associated with natural phenomena like thunder, lightning, the Sun and moon."[37] This explains why in most African tribal societies,

---

30. Mbiti, *Introduction to African Religion*, 63, 103–104.
31. Mia Brandel-Syrier, *Black Woman in Search of God* (London: Lutterworth, 1962), 131–132.
32. Mibiti, *African Religions and Philosophy*, 82–83.
33. Parrinder, *West African Religion*, 115.
34. Geoffrey Parrinder, *African Traditional Religion* (London: Sheldon Press, 1962), 59.
35. Fortes and Dieterlen, *African Systems of Thought*, 18–20.
36. Harold Turner, *Living Tribal Religions* (London: Ward Lock Educational, 1971), 16.
37. Gehman, *African Traditional Religion*, 201–202.

ancestors are held to be alive, they are present, they are respected, they offer guidance, and they are to be consulted always.[38]

The discussion on the significant position ancestors occupy in traditional belief will be incomplete if mention is not made of the assumed powers they have to reincarnate themselves. This is because over the years, Africans have held a belief that a new born child into a family whose physical features like the shape of the nose, the size of the head and hair, open teeth, eye blink, voice and behaviour which resembles that of a deceased member of the family are indication that the deceased ancestor has been born back into the family. Mbiti expounds that,

> It is possible for something of the features, characteristics and personality of such a spirit (the living dead) to be noticed in a newly born child. Then people would say that "so and so" has come back, has returned, or has been reborn. The child may then be given the name of that deceased person, or people may make sacrifices and offerings to express joy and gratitude.[39]

This belief is transmitted from one generation to another through persons, networks and structures. To this end, life in Africa is a circle of death and rebirth. As Mbiti posits children born into the families with these features are named after the deceased person or are given names that show the deceased has come back to the family.[40] Among the Chawai of northern-central Nigeria in West Africa reincarnate children are given the following names *Ayhie'Ngna* (S/he has come back), *N'bah-dakut* (father has come back), and *Nkha-dakut* (mother has come back) or the name of the deceased person may be given to the newly born child directly. Similarly, among the Igbo *Nnamdi* is the name given to a child believed to have reincarnated.[41]

In "Reincarnation: Re-Appraising the Belief of Yoruba Muslims within the Context of Islamic Orthodoxy," Shaykh Luqman Jimoh pointed out that among the Yoruba the belief in reincarnation is commonplace. Thus reincarnate children are named as *Babatunde* (father has come back) and

---

38. Ajah, *African Traditional Religion*, 224.
39. Mbiti, *Introduction to African Religion*, 119.
40. Mbiti, 119.
41. Chidili, *Inculturation as a Symbol*, 109.

Iyabo (mother has come back). In most cases, as Jimoh argues, oracles are consulted to determine who is it that has come back so that the newborn child is named appropriately. He writes, "Indeed it is a common thing among the Yoruba to consult the oracle when a child is born into the family with the view to knowing which of the ancestors, who they also regard as the living dead, has come back."[42]

It has been established that the religious practices associated with the ancestors are without question the most prominent aspect of African traditional beliefs and worldviews. Ancestors are the custodians and protectors of the society while the society itself shapes one's identity and personhood since life takes its meaning within the community in interaction with other members of the community. For this reason, Africans believe that life revolves around the community outside of which life is meaningless. Besides this, ancestors are held to be the channel through which Africans can have access to the supreme being. The notion that access to the supreme being is via the ancestors is the subject we examine below.

Ancestors as the Channel of Interacting with the Supreme Being

It is axiomatic that one thing that characterized human existence in every society of the world, sophisticated or primitive, technologically advanced or backward, is good health or the quest for a good life. In Africa, one way for achieving good health, prosperity, and general security replete with qualitative living is through the ancestral cult where libations are poured, and sacrifices are made to secure the protection of the ancestors who are held to intercede for their descendants before the supreme being. This section argues that the quest for a good life that often leads to religious cravings as seen in the way people are changing from one church or prayer house to the other in the search for meaning to life, healing, and protection is due to our belief that the world is replete with malevolent forces. For this reason, ancestors are sought to help protect their descendants from demonic spirits and Satan.

---

42. Shaykh Luqman Jimoh, "Reincarnation: Re-Appraising the Belief of Yoruba Muslims within the Context of Islamic Orthodoxy1," *Ilorin Journal of Religious Studies* 2, no. 1 (2012): 81–96.

I. African Traditional Notions about the Potency of Divinities and Spirit Beings

The spiritual world of African peoples is very densely populated with spiritual beings, spirits and the living-dead. Their insight into spiritual realities, whether absolute or apparent, is extremely sharp. To understand their religious ethos and the philosophical perception it is essential to consider their concepts of the spiritual world in addition to their idea of God.[43]

These spirit beings, with whom a peaceful and harmonious relationship must be maintained at all times, are believed to affect the daily life of the community positively or negatively, depending on whether or not the members of the community managed to observe that obligation.[44] The details of the beliefs in spirits vary from community to community. For example, among some peoples in West Africa, there are pantheons of divinities and large numbers of spirits. Within the category of spirits, in general, are included those that were once human (ancestral spirits) and those that were never human.[45]

The ancestors in particular, once they are provoked, are held to inflict pain and disease upon the descendants who disobeyed their instructions. In some other cases, it may not necessarily be a disease but defeat they imposed on their victims. According to African interpretation, such a situation invariably begs the attention of religious personages. Therefore to deal with the situation, people revert to religious practices to find out which of the ancestors has been offended in order to placate him.

Where it has been diagnosed and established that ancestors have no hand in the malady, the misfortune is attributed to non-ancestral spirit beings. Mugambi notes that a spirit might enter the life of an individual, causing them to behave in an extraordinary or unusual manner. When such behaviour is observed, the victim is taken for diagnosis in which exorcism is done, and the victim is freed.[46] On the other hand, Mugambi notes that the diviner might attribute the spirit-possession to the failure on the part of the patient or their relatives to maintain a harmonious relationship between

---

43. Mibiti, *African Religions and Philosophy*, 74.
44. Mugambi, *Christianity and African Culture*, 64.
45. Mugambi, 64.
46. Mugambi, 64.

the living and the dead. To restore health, the damaged relationships would have to be restored.⁴⁷

Among communities in which belief in spirit possession was strong, there was an established cult of spirit-mediumship which specializes in the removal of and communication with the spirits. Such a cult has been reported, for example among the Banyore, Segeju, Lugbara, Sukum, Alur, and Ankole.⁴⁸

Generally, in traditional African beliefs, the notion of the potency of divinities and spirit beings accounts for why people were normally consumed with unnecessary fear since they are believed to be potentially harmful to the life of the community unless the members kept them happy and at peace. Although God was believed to be invisible, there was a distinction between him and other spirit beings which were held to cause untold hardship and misfortune in human societies.⁴⁹

II. Ancestor as Powerful Intercessors

We have highlighted the fact that in the traditional African belief system ancestors belong to the category of spirit beings that do not only inhabit the world but are deeply involved with the life of the family or community of the living. Or as Mbiti puts it, "They know and have interest in what is going on in the family."⁵⁰ This interest is demonstrated when a family or community is plagued into serious calamity which often defies human remedy, and the ancestors are invoked to intercede and proffer solution to the calamity. Nwaogwugwu underscores this fact as he maintains that, "One of the factors that characterize them [ancestors] is their power of intercession. They are regarded as indispensable intercessors for their families and their communities. Apart from their daily prayers for the welfare of their people, the ancestors are always consulted before any major event in the family or society to seek and obtain their permission."⁵¹

Where, however, the ancestors themselves are deemed incapable directly of offering valid succour to their living relations or the community, they,

---

47. Mugambi, 64.
48. Mugambi, 64.
49. Mugambi, 64.
50. Mibiti, *African Religions and Philosophy*, 82.
51. Nwaogwugwu, *Ancestor Christology*, 91.

in turn, consult the supreme being on behalf of their family or community for a solution. As Ezeh reports, "The ancestors are generally believed to be the mediators between the living and the Supreme Being."[52] Nwaogwugwu restates the same thinking, "From their experience of life and their closeness to the Supreme Being the ancestors are able to interact with both aspects of life, presenting the human problems to the divinities and offering their help and response to the human needs."[53] For Nürnberger, ancestors are "believed to act as the 'go-between.'"[54]

Gehman describes the intermediary role of ancestors in a fascinating fashion, according to him, "Not only are many problems blamed on the living-dead, but thevarious blessings of life are also attributed to them. The living may implore, beg, request or ask their ancestors for assistance. Every blessing is thought to come from them."[55] Gehman notes further that "Being closer in time to the living, the living-dead can best understand man's need; being closer to God, they have 'full access to the channels of communicating with God directly.' Even as the living approach the chief through the sub-chief and as a daughter approaches her father through her mother, so the living approach God through the living-dead."[56]

Mbiti raised an important argument as to why most African traditionalists would prefer to go to the supreme being or the local deities through the ancestor rather than approaching him in person. He writes, "People feel themselves to be very small in the sight of God. In approaching him, they sometimes need the help of someone else. Just as in social life it is often the custom to approach someone of a high status through someone else. For that reason, some African peoples make use of helpers in approaching God."[57] Aside from the fact that some African people often feel unworthy to approach the supreme being directly, there is as well the notion of insecurity since they feel that approaching God in person might endanger their lives. This does not only explain one of the strongest reasons why some Africans

---

52. Ezeh, *Jesus Christ the Ancestor*, 91.
53. Nwaogwugwu, *Ancestor Christology*, 92.
54. Nürnberger, *Living Dead*, 33.
55. Gehman, *African Traditional Religion*, 205.
56. Gehman, 206.
57. Mbiti, *Introduction to African Religion*, 62.

often prefer to approach the ancestors to plead their case before God, but also why the ancestors themselves and the notion of ancestry mediation cannot depart from them. Mbiti keenly reports,

> The notion of intermediaries also helps people to feel protected from the greatness of God which might otherwise crush the individual. People fear to come alone too close to God. By using intermediaries, they feel that someone speaks on their behalf, taking their message to God. The dead are used as intermediaries because it is felt that they speak both the language of the invisible world and the language of human beings.[58]

With this belief, when Christianity came to Africa, and some Africans were converted to the Christian faith and perceived that Jesus Christ had been portrayed by the evangelist who wrote the New Testament as the mediator between God and man, they swiftly found a convenient ground to juxtapose the perceived intermediary role of the ancestors of their African past with Jesus Christ the Mediator who established a new covenant (see 1 Tim 2:5–6; Heb 7:25) and this informs the theology of Jesus Christ, the ancestor.

Rich though this analogy is, it serves only to explain the considerable gulf African Traditional Religion has created between man and his Creator. Traditional African belief has failed to give a satisfactory explication of man's religious quest and his need for redemption. This system, which African theologians are busy singing its praise and overtly using it to formulate a comparative Christology, has no explanation for heaven and hell; it has not presented any hope for a life with God in paradise. Grebe and Fon concurred that in African Traditional Religion, "There is no hope of life with God in paradise."[59]

The lack of hope for afuture life with God and fellow human beings led ultimately to a big void that needed to be filled. It follows therefore that when the gospel message came to African soil and Africans appropriated it, Christianity became the means for filling the emptiness created by the African traditional belief system and African theologians would have to look for Christian models and African pre-Christian categories that dovetail to

---

58. Mbiti, 63.
59. Grebe and Fon, *African Traditional Religion*, 21.

formulate theology. Grebe and Fon buttressed this argument thus, "When the message of the Gospel came to Africa proclaiming Christ as the Mediator to God and the way to paradise, it provided the answer to a deeply felt need within the heart of the traditional African."[60]

From the foregoing argument, this work wishes to state explicitly that the basis for predicating the ancestorship of Jesus Christ in Africa is the seeming similarities that exist as it were between traditional African belief and Christian theology. This assertion would be taken further in the section that follows below.

III. Ancestors as a Way of Understanding the Acts and Powers of Jesus Christ

In Africa, we cannot adequately dispute the glaring fact that there are many valid convergence points between African pre-Christian categories and Christian models. The cult of the ancestors provides the best example. In Africa, the living members of the extended family have a direct link to the ancestors through one of their members who function as the family priest and mediates for the entire family.[61]

One way of mediation is a sacrifice that the family priest performs.[62] At that time he does not only ask the ancestors to overlook the offences committed by their descendants but is powerful enough to watch over their living kin and the community, ancestors are also invoked through the petition to protect the living from demons and Satan. When this happens, Africans assert that their ancestors have given them peace and tranquillity, security and prosperity which have been established in the family and the community at large through the assumed intervention of the living-dead.

Conversely, where the family or community blatantly fails to pacify the ancestors, it is assumed that they become vengeful and harmful and can even cause the death of their descendants. Allan Anderson notes that ancestors are believed to bring harm to those who ignore or neglect their instructions given through dreams or diviners. Their sanctions have a fearful control over

---

60. Grebe and Fon, 22.
61. Grebe and Fon, 12.
62. Grebe and Fon, 13.

people's lives.[63] Shorter observes that ancestors are thought to be revengeful and vindictive on occasion, but they have a right to be in order to punish man's sins, especially those of impiety.[64]

Geoffrey Parrinder made an immense contribution to the discourse on ancestors in Africa. For him, "No approach to any appreciation of indigenous ideas regarding God can take any path but that through the thought-area occupied by the ancestors."[65] Among the Bantu of South Africa for instance, Parrinder points out that the ancestor spirits are the most intimate gods of that society.[66] Thus, ancestors are ever present to watch over the family, its health and fertility, ever at hand to harm or to help, men try to coerce and placate their ancestors by means of sacrifices. But the ancestors are unpredictable. It is their power to injure and their sudden attacks on routine well-being, the ever-present watchful dead and their power to smite or bless the living.[67]

Emefie Ikenga Metuh describes the role of ancestors in the following words, "The ancestors are . . . symbols of peace, unity and prosperity in the family . . . protectors of the traditional laws and customs . . . and the welfare of their families."[68] Apparently, unlimited power ascribed to the ancestors are expressed in the beliefs that they protect their descendants from demonic spirits and satanic powers that warrant African theologians and biblical scholars to articulate a theology of power encounter in which the acts of ancestors become the necessary medium for understanding the deeds and powers of Jesus Christ.

There is a good deal of precedent to support this assertion. As Nwaogwugwu has shown, "The religious experience of the Africans has been associated with power and authority which made the gospel presentation of Christ as a man who exercised the tremendous power to appeal very much to them."[69] In a similar fashion, Ezigbo argues that in "contemporary African

---

63. Anderson, *African Reformation*, 203.
64. Shorter, *African Culture*, 59.
65. Parrinder, *African Traditional Religion*, 3rd ed., 57.
66. Parrinder, 58.
67. Parrinder, 57–59.
68. Metuh, *God and Man*, 96.
69. Nwaogwugwu, *Ancestor Christology*, 391.

Christianity, the belief in demons, evil spirits and Satan, particularly at the grassroots level, shapes the ways many Christians relate to and perceive the person and work of Jesus Christ . . . many Christians talk about the power of Jesus Christ to defeat and destroy the works of the evil spirits, demons and Satan in their prayers, preaching, songs, and books."[70]

There are many echoes of prayers offered, sermons delivered, songs composed, and books written in Africa from the perspective of Christus Victor to support Ezigbo's position. A good example is Madam Christina Afua Kuma's *Jesus of the Deep Forest* cited by Clifton R. Clarke. In her characteristic African tune, Madam Afua prays, "*Yesu Kristo* you rose from the dead to give us life. Your blood gives us power and heals us . . . Jesus, you are solid as a rock! Jesus, you are the Elephant Hunter, Fearless One! You have killed the evil spirit, and cut off its head!"[71] This quotation reveals that in Africa when oral christological prayers invoke the name *Yesu Kristo*, the petitioner expresses a broad sense of personal encounter with Jesus Christ in the light of their conscious awareness of the presence of and constant battle with the evil spirits of their African past which they now subject to the authority of Jesus Christ. This experience seems to prepare a solid ground which allows the African a smooth transition from their African past to the present in which one engages Christology using the pre-Christian cultural category of an ancestor as the leitmotif for the formulation of Christian theology. Ezigbo persuasively shows how the motif of spirit power fits perfectly well with ancestor Christology. He elucidates,

> Given that many Christians locate some of their discussions on the person of Jesus Christ and the manifestation of his power in their lives within the context of the spirit beings they consider to be evil and wicked, any Christological model seeking to be relevant to them needs to engage with the Christians' beliefs in the existence and activities of the malevolent spirit beings.[72]

Obviously, the heritage of African tradition situates us within a very definite horizon of truth. This truth is that our pre-Christian religious heritage

---

70. Ezigbo, *Re-Imagining African Christologies*, 215.
71. Clarke, *African Christology*, 144–145.
72. Ezigbo, *Re-Imagining African Christologies*, 215.

finds its parallel in Christian theology. To assert otherwise is to deny Jesus's declaration that "The Spirit of the Lord is on me, because he has anointed me to proclaim good news to the poor. He has sent me to proclaim freedom for the prisoners and recovery of sight for the blind, to set the oppressed free, to proclaim the year of the Lord's favour." (Luke 4:18–19; see also Isa 61:1–2). Ultimately, Luke's report of the activities of Jesus Christ in Acts is reminiscent of the African situation. He narrates, "How God anointed Jesus of Nazareth with the Holy Spirit and power, and how he went around doing good and healing all who were under the power of the devil, because God was with him" (Acts 10:38). The Christian Holy Bible contains the story of the work and powers of Jesus Christ over evil spirits. For this reason, it becomes somewhat natural for African theologians to formulate theology in the light of Africans' preoccupation with the spirit world taking a cue from Jesus's exorcism.

The Cult of the Ancestors as a Theological Meeting Point for Christianity and African Indigenous Religions

Over the years, biblical scholars and theologians alike have been making concerted efforts to preach the gospel of Christ in Africa in such a way that the gospel message can be understood better in the context of the African sociocultural background.[73] This quest was motivated in part by the desire to strip African Christian theology of its western trappings. As Mbiti once lamented, "You cannot fill your granaries with borrowed grains."[74]

Since all grains contain chaff, Mbiti believes that for Christian theology to be authentically African and authentically Christian, the Western chaff must be replaced by African chaff. Like the emerging chick from the broken eggshell, so is African theology. For it to become genuinely and authentically African, it needs to "break the hermeneutical hegemony and ideological stranglehold that Eurocentric biblical scholars have long enjoyed."[75]

---

73. Weneka, "Christ as Our Ancestor," 289.
74. Mbiti, *Bible and Theology*, 7.
75. Adamo, "What Is African Biblical Studies?," 17.

From this call, African theologians drew their inspiration for the expression and representation of Christian concepts in the light of African socio-religious ideas in which the ancestral cult provides the best bridge that links African tradition and Christian theology.

I. The Cult of Ancestors as the Heart of African Primal Tradition and Culture

It was Parrinder who postulated, "No approach to any appreciation of indigenous ideas regarding God can take any path but that through the thought-area occupied by the ancestors."[76] Ezeh stresses that the ancestral cult is the heart of the African tradition and culture.[77] It is to be understood therefore that among the many symbols that make up African culture are the ancestors[78] who are held to be the most powerful symbol in African culture[79] since their presence is felt in the daily life of the traditional African community.[80]

Donald J. Goergen, has written that the traditions venerating ancestors in Africa are strong and widespread, even if not universal. More attention has been given to ancestor as a way of "Africanizing" Jesus than to almost any other metaphor.[81] Thus, E. J. Pénoukou, a francophone theologian from Togo, articulates a nomenclature for Jesus as "l'ancêtre Joto" (a concept of the Ewe-Mina tribe of Togo), namely an ancestor who is the source of life, the ancestor who generates and regenerates life.[82] This same motif is taken further by François Kabasélé Lumbala who began by acknowledging that "Christ came to give 'life' and to give it in abundance."[83] He then makes a good transition to connect Christ with the ancestors. Thus, he notes, "As the Ancestors watch over the life of their descendants and continuously strengthen it, so does Christ continuously nourish the life of believers."[84]

---

76. Parrinder, *African Traditional Religion*, 57.
77. Ezeh, *Jesus Christ the Ancestor*, 285.
78. Chidili, *Inculturation as a Symbol*, 107.
79. Chidili, 107.
80. Ezeh, *Jesus Christ the Ancestor*, 285.
81. Goergen, "Quest for the Christ," 1.
82. Goergen, 13.
83. François Kabasélé, "Christ as Ancestor and Elder Brother," in *Faces of Jesus in Africa*, ed. Robert J. Schreiter (Maryknoll: Orbis Books, 2005), 120.
84. Kabasélé, "Christ as Ancestor and Elder Brother," 120.

Given that the ancestral cult is the heart of African traditional religion and culture, the answer to the question surrounding the identity of Jesus Christ in Africa has been acutely promulgated in the twenty-first century along the lines of Africa's socio-religious, sociopolitical and sociocultural backgrounds. Emmanuel Martey raises the same concern and writes, "The question. 'Who is Jesus Christ for us today?' confronts the African just like everyone else, and therefore the question, 'What do African say Jesus Christ is?' is a legitimate one."[85] He then continued, "Every Christological inquirer sets out on the track of this Jesus with the inquirer's own questions and concerns in mind. For the African, these concerns and questions must be informed and shaped at the same time by Africa's socio-political and economic realities."[86]

The sociopolitical and socio-economic factors that precipitated and served as the platform for the framing of African theology have been briefly examined in chapter 2. The primary concern this section raises is how the socio-religious and sociocultural factors define, dictate and shape the formulation and interpretation of the person and work of Jesus Christ in Africa. While the vast majority of African theologians seem to have no issues with the idea and identity of God, to a more significant measure they do have with respect to the identity of their Saviour.

Most African theologians would argue that God the Father is the one supreme being with whom nothing can be compared. This explains why no African even by way of analogy has ever made an attempt verbally or in writing to equate God with any of his creatures. Christologically, Jesus is fully human (as well as fully God). God the Father, unlike God the Son, does not have a human nature. These African Christian theologians concede, yet they employed an analogy to compare Christ with the ancestors whom he created (John 1:3) under the premise that as an ancestor, Christ is still part of the human family.[87] Accordingly, he does not live in a far distant heaven without relating to us. Never for a moment does he forget this world which

---

85. Emmanuel Martey, *African Theology: Inculturation and Liberation* (Eugene, OR: Wipf & Stock, 2009), 84.

86. Martey, *African Theology*, 84.

87. Martey, 85.

gave him his being.[88] This conclusion reveals the myopic view of African theologians concerning Jesus Christ, since Martey demonstrates that it is the world that gave Jesus his person as opposed to Jesus giving the world its being as its creator (John 1:3).

Martey seems to situate his argument within the framework of transcendental and immanent theologies. However, when African theologians contend that Jesus is not far from us and relates with us to the extent that he is being compared to the ancestors, do they mean ancestors are transcendent and immanent the same way God is? It is true, to admit that Jesus relates to his creatures but he is never part of the created system. So, in what ways can he be an ancestor? It is equally valid as Martey concedes that a significant dimension in the role played by the ancestors is how they were assumed to transmit and safeguard life[89] but what sort of life and how true is this belief? Can the cult of the ancestors, which at the same time is the heart of African tradition and culture, be a sufficient metaphor with which to formulate a theology that compares Christ with African ancestors?

For some African theologians, the answer is invariably yes, and it hinges on the theological presupposition that God assumed flesh in the man Jesus of Nazareth. Thus, the incarnation should be the paradigm for the formulation of contextual theologies on the continent. The manifestation of the Son of God which becomes the catalyst for ancestor Christology is examined below.

II. Incarnation as Impetus to Ancestor Christology

A typical thesis found in the assertions of most ancestor Christology advocates is that God became man in Jesus Christ through the incarnation and dwelled among men. Similarly, Christian theology by the same token should be incarnated in the traditional beliefs and in the cultures of African tribal groups. An excerpt from *Instrumentum Laboris* speaks very loudly, "Wherever the Word is proclaimed by the Church there it must take flesh in and for the culture . . . the missionary task of the Church in Africa at the dawn of the third millennium is to make possible in an adapted way the event of two thousand years ago, the incarnation of the Word of God."[90] What this

---

88. Martey, 85.
89. Martey, 86.
90. Synod of Bishops, *Instrumentum Laboris*, 56.

statement means is that the incarnation – that is, the theological doctrine that teaches the coming of God in the man Jesus of Nazareth – should provide a theological base for deepening the Christian faith in Africa through the use of pre-Christian cultural and traditional categories. Nwaogwugwu elaborates, "In African Christian thought, incarnation has come to be ordinarily associated with deepening the knowledge and person of Christ in the culture of the tropical Africans. Inculturation is therefore at the service of the incarnation."[91]

A helpful example of the value of inculturation in constructing local theology in the light of people's culture is that highlighted in Synodus Episcoporum – Coetus Specialis Pro Africa: Relatio Ante Disceptationem Relatio Post Disceptationem Nuntius, which views inculturation as the "Marriage of professed faith and concrete life, harmony between faith and culture."[92]

Most African theologians firmly believe that the incarnation illuminates and shapes the theological meaning of inculturation without which it remains a blur. Teresa Okure makes this point explicit; "Our understanding of the mystery of the Incarnation should serve as the solid foundation for understanding inculturation."[93] She then concludes that "inculturation has to do with the incarnational union between Christ and the peoples of a given culture."[94] Restating the same thesis Peter Schineller, argues that the most directly theological word to express the meaning of inculturation is an incarnation.[95] Quoting Pedro Arrupe, he demonstrates that the incarnation of the Son is the primary motivation and perfect pattern for inculturation. Just like him, and because he did so, the church will become incarnate as vitally and intimately as it can in every culture, being enriched with its values and offerings in the unique redemption of Christ.[96]

---

91. Nwaogwugwu, *Ancestor Christology*, 147.
92. Synodus Episcoporum, *Nuntius*, 54.
93. Teresa Okure, "Inculturation: Biblical/theological bases," in *32 Articles evaluating Inculturation of Christianity in Africa*, eds. Teresa Okure and Paul van Thiel (Eldoret, Kenya: AMECEA Gaba Publications, 1990), 55.
94. Okure, "Inculturation," 55.
95. Schineller, *Handbook on Inculturation*, 20.
96. Schineller, 20.

Considering that the incarnation is but a theological concept that seeks to explicate the Christ event – the coming, birth, growth, daily life and struggle, teaching, healing, resting, celebrating, suffering, dying, and rising of Jesus Christ[97] – Schineller seeks to show how the incarnation can be inculturated to make Jesus Christ the subject of the Nigerian kerygmatic proclamation and emancipation from evil spirits. He asks; "Should Jesus Christ not be preached as the one who liberates or saves from the power of evil, which in Nigeria is often felt to be the power of evil spirits?"[98]

Schineller did not wait for some other person to provide an answer to the question he raised but went ahead himself to posit that since Jesus Christ has triumphed over Satan, and Christians now share in that victory, we could as well conclude along with the apostle Paul in Romans 8 that nothing – no evil spirit, no wicked forces – can separate us from the love of God in Christ Jesus.[99]

While at first glance he seems not to be in a rush in correlating the functional role of Christ with the functional role of the ancestors, Schineller reveals that the incarnation is the medium through which ancestor Christology could be formulated in Africa. He writes,

> In a society characterized by strong ties and respect for ancestors, should we not emphasize with Saint Paul that Jesus Christ was the first to rise from the dead and hence can be considered our proto-ancestor? Giving Jesus the title ancestor fits in very well with African understanding. It means that he is for us an elder in the community, an intercessor or mediator between God and humanity, one who guards and protects the human community.[100]

Schineller would not shy away to predicate ancestor of Christ because he draws inspiration for doing so from Pope John Paul II who, in his 1980 visit to Africa, challenged African Bishops to develop a theological method that makes sense of the mystery of Christ. The Pope exhorts, "There is no

---

97. Schineller, 20.
98. Schineller, 87.
99. Schineller, 87.
100. Schineller, 87.

question of adulterating the word of God or of emptying the cross of its power (cf. I Cor 1:17) but rather of bringing Christ into the very centre of African life and of lifting up all African life to Christ. Thus not only is Christianity relevant to Africa but Christ, in the members of his body, is himself African."[101]

A Tsam (Chawai) proverb says, "*Tsen yhisomben, amma bhá yhigyekgnwo mi bha*," meaning a child knows how to run but does not know where to hide. Where, however, the child is taught how to run and where to hide, he would find the game of hiding and seek a pleasant adventure. Perhaps, this proverb is quite true of Pope John Paul II's encouragement to African theologians who before now had probably entertained doubt in formulating ancestor Christology. Having now been told authoritatively that Christ is himself an African, they find their underpinnings to formulate ancestor Christology with the concept of incarnation as the yardstick.

Ancestors in the Jewish Worldview: An Overview of the Adamic Covenant of Redemption and the Abrahamic Covenant of Promise

The historical background of Jewish ancestors otherwise known as the patriarchs appears in Genesis chapters 12–50. John Bright posits that their stories form the first chapter in the great theological history of Israel's origins captured in the first six books of the Bible.[102] These books tell us that centuries before Israel took possession of Canaan her ancestors had come from faraway Mesopotamia and as semi-nomads had roamed through the land, supported by the promises of their God that it would one day belong to their posterity.[103] It is therefore not uncommon and out of place to conclude with Brown that Abraham, Jacob, and Isaac were commonly explained as the eponymous ancestors of the Jews whose nomadic religion was described as animism or polydaemonism.[104] G. W. Anderson expresses

---

101. Schineller, 88.
102. John Bright, *A History of Israel*, 4th ed. (Louisville, KY: Westminster John Knox, 2000), 67.
103. Bright, *History of Israel*, 67.
104. Bright, 68–69.

a similar idea when he writes, "The picture of the patriarchs which Genesis gives us is of semi-nomads moving from one part of the Fertile Crescent to another, and sometimes even venturing as far as Egypt in search of food and pasture. 'A wandering Aramaean was my father'"[105] as the Jews would always remind themselves.

To these Mesopotamian nomads and animists, God revealed himself and made an everlasting covenant of promise to Abraham (Gen 12, 15, 17) and reiterated it to Isaac (Gen 26) and to Jacob whose name was to be changed to Israel (Gen 32:28). The promise given by God to Abraham would culminate in the birth of the Messiah in fulfilment of God's prophecy of a coming Redeemer during the judgment of Adam and Eve, his wife, and the Serpent in Genesis 3:15.

I. Adam: The Crown of God's Creation and the Mysterious Figure in the Garden

This work does not concern itself with the various scientific and evolutionary theories on the origin of humanity. Preferably, its aim is to explore the theological meaning of human creation and the fall as presented by the narrators of divine revelation.

Genesis 1:1 opens with a sublime declaration that in the beginning, God created the heaven and earth. In verses 26 and 27 of this same text the Creator God says, "'Let us make mankind in our image, in our likeness, so that they may rule over the fish in the sea and the birds in the sky, over the livestock and all the wild animals, and over all the creatures that move along the ground.' So God created manking in his own image, in the image of God he created him; male and female he created them." (Gen 1:27–27). Millard J. Erickson notes that the biblical picture of humanity's origin is that an all-wise, all-powerful, and good God created the human race to love and serve him and to enjoy a relationship with him.[106] Erickson further notes that Genesis gives two accounts of God's creation of humans – verses 26 and 27

---

105. G. W. Anderson, *The History and Religion of Israel* (London: Oxford University Press, 1966), 19–20.

106. Millard J. Erickson, *Christian Theology*, 2nd ed (Grand Rapids, MI: Baker Academic, 1998), 498.

of chapter 1 record God's decision to make man in his image and likeness, and God implemented his decision by creating humankind.[107]

The theological meaning of image and likeness in the context of humankind's creation is intensely debated in theological circles. For example, Wayne Grudem notes that theologians have spent much time attempting to specify one characteristic of man, or a few, in which the image of God is primarily seen in man but then concluded that the image and likeness of God in man is to be located in the Hebrew usage. For him, both the Hebrew word for "image" (*tselem*) and the Hebrew word for "likeness" (*demût*) refer to something that is *similar* but not identical to the thing it represents or is an "image" of. The word *image* can also be used for something that *represents* something else.[108] John M. Frame also maintains that theologians have longed puzzled over what exactly the image of God in man consists of but then made a convincing point that image and likeness "are more or less synonymous, using the Hebrew terms *tselem* and *demuth*" as common parlance for "ancient statues or pictures, intended to represent someone, often a god or a king."[109]

Michael Jenkins concurs with Frame that image and likeness are parallel and refer to the same thing, not, of course, to a physical appearance but what we might call an analogical correspondence between God and humanity.[110] Michael F. Bird shares Frame's view too. Citing an ancient Egyptian dynasty, he opined that the Egyptian Pharaoh was held to be an incarnation of the sun god Ra. Thus, during the Ptolemaic period, a king was referred to as a "living image of Zeus, son of the Son."[111] According to Bird, rather than interpreting the image of God in man as an ontological statement, if we

---

107. Erickson, *Christian Theology*, 498.

108. Wayne Grudem, *Systematic Theology: An Introduction to Biblical Doctrine* (Leicester: Inter-Varsity Press, 2007), 442–443.

109. John M. Frame, *Systematic Theology: An Introduction to Christian Belief* (Phillipsburg, NJ: P & R, 2013), 78

110. Michael Jenkins, *Invitation to Theology* (Downers Grove, IL: InterVarsity Press, 2001), 169–170.

111. Michael F. Bird, *Evangelical Theology: A Biblical and Systematic Introduction* (Grand Rapids, MI: Zondervan, 2013), 660.

take into account the ancient Near Eastern context, Genesis 1:26–27 may be saying no more than humanity is royal in God's eyes.[112] He also notes,

> Whereas the image was restricted to an elite few monarchs in oriental thought, the privilege of bearing God's image is democratized so that all humanity shares in it. Humanity is thus royal and is made in order to rule over creation as God's vice-regent. The main functions of this royal reign in Genesis 1:26–28 include having dominion over the earth. Consequently, humanity is the cosmic media for expressing God's sovereignty and presence in the world.[113]

H. L. Willmington however referred to the image and likeness of God in man as; the trinity of man, God's consciousness and that sense of morality in man and that image and likeness are a reference to the incarnation of Christ.[114] A current discussion of the subject of *Imago Dei* has been presented by Ryan S. Peterson. In his *The Imago Dei as Human Identity: A Theological Interpretation*, Peterson argues, "The Imago Dei is humanity's identity, and this identity is basic to all human existence. God created humanity to establish an earthly image of God in the world. Humanity is thereby bound to God and God's purposes for creation."[115] David J. A. Clines writes, "One essential meaning of the statement that man was created in the Image of God is plain: it is that man is in some way and in some degree like God."[116] Elsewhere, Clines gives profound insights, "Humanity is God's invisible corporeal representative of the invisible, bodiless God."[117] This same idea is taken further by Ian McFarland. He asserts, "An image conveys knowledge

---

112. Bird, *Evangelical Theology*, 660.

113. Bird, 660.

114. H. L. Willmington, *Willmington's Guide to the Bible* (Carol Stream, IL: Tyndale House, 1984), 670.

115. Ryan S. Peterson, *The Imago Dei as Human Identity: A Theological Interpretation* (Winona Lake, IN: Eisenbrauns, 2016), 1.

116. David J. A. Clines, "The Image of God in Man," *Tyndale Bulletin* 19 (1968), 53–105.

117. Clines, "Image of God," 101.

of the thing imaged. The Imago Dei does not deliver knowledge about humanity; rather, it delivers knowledge of God."[118]

These differing positions indicate there is in mankind the image and likeness of God. Willmington supports this notion as he declares that at any rate, that is, despite the presence of opposing views there seems to be an image of God in all men.[119] And it is this image and likeness of God in mankind that makes them unique and quite distinct from all other creatures that God has created in heaven and on earth.

The unique image and likeness of God in man which also defines his peculiarity was marred when in the Garden of Eden mankind deliberately succumbed to the deception of the Serpent and fell into sin as Genesis 3 reveals. The nature and personality of the Serpent are much debated, and this work is not going that direction. Interestingly enough, the Bible does not present an explicit account of how the Serpent also called Satan and dxragon, fell (Rev 12:9). We only find some hints from two Old Testament passages. From biblical data, however, he was one of the creatures of God (Job 1:6; 2:1) who had fallen on account of his beauty and obsession for power. Ezekiel tells us that Satan was a model "of perfection, full of wisdom and perfect in beauty," "your heart became proud on account of your beauty," "and I expelled you, guardian cherub" (Ezek 28:12, 17, 16). When the narrative opened in the book of Isaiah, the narrator presents Satan as already fallen on account of his consuming passion for power; "'I will ascend to the heavens; I will raise my throne above the stars of God; I will sit enthroned on the mount of assembly . . . I will ascend above the tops of the clouds; I will make myself like the Most High.' But you were brought down to the realm of the dead, to the depths of the pit" (Isa 14:13–15).

The devastating effect of the fall of Satan, Adam, and Eve led to the ruin of God's good creation recorded in Genesis 1 and 2. From the Genesis account of a good creation, the fallen world in which we live rests on the foundations of a creation that was good.[120] We are, however, left with inex-

---

118. Ian McFarland, *The Divine Image: Envisioning the Invisible God* (Minneapolis, MN: Fortress, 2005), 11.

119. Willmington, *Willmington's Guide*, 670.

120. Herman Bavinck, *Reformed Dogmatics: Abridged in One Volume*, ed. John Bolt (Grand Rapids, MI: Baker Academic, 2011), 340.

plicable questions about the origin of sin and evil and its entry into God's good creation through the human desire for autonomy from God.[121] Herman Bavinck argues that, "To know good and evil is to determine good and evil, right and wrong, by oneself, and refuse to submit to any external law."[122]

The narrative in Genesis 3, therefore, tells us sin has entered the world through the crafty agency of Satan's lie. Bavinck also notes that the Serpent's speaking has often been mistakenly considered as an allegory for lust, sexual desire, or errant reason.[123] Whatever theories scholars propound with respect to the entrance of evil and sin into the world, we are left without conjecture about, "The entrance of a spiritual superterrestrial power whose nature remains unknown to us. Genesis 3 simply sticks to the obvious facts; it describes but does not explain."[124] Paul Enns describes the inexplicable entry of evil into the world thus, "It must forever remain a riddle as to where sin came from; it is one of the mysteries of life."[125] For Gerald Bray, "The existence of evil in a world made and governed by a good God is the paradox known to theologians as 'theodicy.' And it has never been satisfactorily explained or resolved."[126] Mysterious though sin is, we know from Isaiah 14:13–15, Ezekiel 28: 12, 16, 17 and also Revelation 12:7–17 that it did not start on earth but in heaven with Satan trying to usurp God's throne. In the case of humankind, the temptation by Satan resulted in the fall.[127] Enns is also convinced, "The solicitation to sin came to Eve through the Serpent."[128] According to Enns, the fact that the Serpent could tempt Eve suggests that evil was present.[129]

The lie concocted by the Serpent blatantly opposed the glory of God and sought to disrupt man's fellowship with God and man's rule over God's creation. Satan, through the Serpent, raised doubt about God's word (Gen

---

121. Bavinck, *Reformed Dogmatics*, 340.
122. Bavinck, 341.
123. Bavinck, 341.
124. Bavinck, 341.
125. Enns, *Moody Handbook*, 41.
126. Gerald Bray, *God Is Love: A Biblical and Systematic Theology* (Wheaton, IL: Crossway, 2012), 353.
127. Bavinck, *Reformed Dogmatics*, 341.
128. Enns, *Moody Handbook*, 41.
129. Enns, 41.

3:1); he lied by saying that man would not die, expressing it in strongest terms, "You surely will not die!" (Gen 3:4, NASB) Eve submitted to the temptation, sinning in the manner typical to the human race: through the lust of the flesh, lust of the eyes, and the boastful pride of life (1 John 2:16).[130]

The devastating effect of the fall of Adam and Eve reveals itself in mankind's attempt to manufacture his own religion and be his personal saviour when the man and Eve, his wife, having been deluded by the Serpent sewed fig leaf aprons for themselves as means of covering their nakedness (Gen 3:7) and sin from God. But God moved and salvaged the situation with a promise of the "seed" of the woman who would "crush the Serpent" (Gen 3:15). Since then, the apostle Paul reports that the entire creation which the author of Genesis states that it is good has been frustrated and is groaning as unto a birth pang waiting eagerly for our adoption as sons, the redemption of our bodies (Rom 8:20–23).

From what has been presented so far, it is evident that the notion of redemption was a consequence of the fall of mankind which culminated with the call of Abraham, the founding father of Jewish ancestors and the birth of Israel as a nation under Moses and the subsequent establishment of Israel's theocratic rule (Exod 19:4–6).

II. The Origin of Ancestors in Jewish Religious Context

It was to wandering Mesopotamian nomads and animists that God first revealed himself and made an everlasting covenant of promise which would culminate in the birth of the messiah. First to Abram Yahweh appeared and instructed, "Go from your country, your people and your father's household to the land I will show you" (Gen 12:1). This call came with a promise, "I will make you into a great nation, and I will bless you; I will make your name great, and you will be a blessing. I will bless those who bless you, and whoever curses you I will curse; and all peoples on earth will be blessed through you" (Gen 12:2–3). Later the Lord God appeared again to Abram and declared, "To your offspring, I will give this land," and Abram built an altar to the Lord (Gen 12:7).

The Abrahamic promise was confirmed by a covenant which was sealed with the slaughter of a ram and affirmed and ratified through the sign of

---

130. Enns, 41.

circumcision (Gen 15, 17). Ronald Youngblood maintains that the sign of the Abrahamic covenant was circumcision (17:11). From this time forward the rite of circumcision would become, for every Israelite, a token of God's solemn promise to bless his people numerically.[131] Enns had presented three main features of the Abrahamic covenant as follows: "[1], the promise of land (Gen 12:1), [2] the promise of descendants (Gen 12:2) and [3] the promise of blessing and redemption (Gen 12: 3)."[132] The blessing would be the fact that Abraham's descendants will become a great nation and that from them the Saviour would come.[133]

It should be understood in the context that "when God makes a covenant with Abraham (Gen 15:18–21), it is not really a compact but a pledge. God's promise obliges him to fulfil it, and he passes between the pieces of the sacrificial animal. Elsewhere he swears by himself (Gen 22:16), by his life (Deut 32:40), by his "soul" (*nephesh*; Amos 6:8; Jer 51:14) to show to people "the unchanging character of his purpose" (Heb 6:17, RSV).[134]

Given this background, this work wishes to propose with Jamie A. Grant and Alistair I. Wilson that when God calls Abraham, he establishes a special relationship with him as he promises him a new land, many descendants and great blessing (Gen 12:1–3, 7).[135] This particular administration of God's commitment to effect redemption appropriately may be designated, says O. Palmer Robertson, "the covenant of promise." God sovereignly confirms the promises of the covenant to Abraham.[136]

In his dealings with Abraham, God elaborately and repeatedly appeared time and again to reaffirm his promise to him. Since God the covenant maker deems it fit to bless Abraham with numerous descendants (Gen 12:2), "in the course of time God would also announce to Isaac that the descendants of Abraham, and therefore of Isaac also, would be exceedingly numerous (Gen

---

131. Ronald Youngblood, *The Heart of the Old Testament* (Grand Rapids, MI: Baker Books, 1997), 46.

132. Enns, *Moody Handbook*, 52.

133. Tim Chester, *From Creation to New Creation: Understanding the Bible Story* (Carlisle, Cumbria: Paternoster, 2003), 21.

134. Bavinck, *Reformed Dogmatics*, 395.

135. Jamie A. Grant and Alistair I. Wilson, eds, *The God of Covenant: Biblical, Theological and Contemporary Perspectives* (Leicester: Apollos, 2005), 26.

136. Robertson, *Christ of the Covenants*, 128.

17:19), because Abraham obeyed my voice (Gen 26:5)."[137] Enns believes that the "unconditional and eternal nature of the Abrahamic covenant is seen in that the covenant is reaffirmed to Isaac (Gen 21:12; 26:3–4) and is further confirmed to Jacob (Gen 28:14–15)."[138]

The promise of blessing and redemption (Gen 12:3) God made to Abraham demands a future fulfilment. This calls for the making of another covenant, not really and necessary to repeal the previous one but to expand further and elaborate its stipulations. Thus God raised Moses in Egypt to not only deliver his people out of Egypt but to also reaffirm his commitment to blessing and redeeming the nations through the Abrahamic covenant. Particular though the Abrahamic promise is since it began with an individual (Abraham) and one nation (Israel), it is universal in outlook. While Bray interprets God's salvation drama as the scandal of particularity since "God revealed himself to particular individuals in a single nation,"[139] Christopher J. H. Wright rightly argues that the particularity of Israel's election has in its content "the plurality of the Bible's vision for all nations and cultures, and sees the fullness of the gospel brought into ever more visible glory through the two-way task of cross-cultural mission."[140] Wright is right to assert that the particularity of God's election of Abraham and Israel points to plurality since God's salvation plan, Richard Bauckham contends, has always been in two directions of movement: the centripetal and the centrifugal ("centripetal" refers to movement in towards a centre, "centrifugal" to movement out from a centre).[141]

Back to cross-cultural mission, a perfect example is found with Old Testament proselytes like Zipporah the Midianite who married Moses (Exod 2:21–22), Rahab the prostitute (Josh 2; 6:17), Ruth the Moabite who married Boaz (Ruth 4) and even some unidentifiable Egyptians who believed and worshipped the God of the Jews that became part of the liberated persons during the exodus from Egypt to Canaan.

---

137. Youngblood, *Heart of the Old Testament*, 45–46.
138. Enns, *Moody Handbook*, 52.
139. Bray, *God Is Love*, 38–40.
140. Wright, *Mission of God*, 46.
141. Bauckham, *Bible and Mission*, 72.

Israel's exodus out of Egypt is crucial since it serves to consummate the Abrahamic covenant of blessing and redemption insofar as the exodus becomes an essential part of the redemptive history of God. For Israel, the going out of Egypt marks the abandonment of old ways while the coming into Canaan signifies new ways with Yahweh as the sovereign God and redeemer of Israel his chosen people. Wright robustly and succinctly notes that "redemption is biblically defined in the first instance by the exodus," which "models for us the contours of what God himself means by redemption and the rest of the Bible clearly takes it as paradigmatic."[142]

But redemption in the context of the exodus only makes sense within the Sinaitic, or Mosaic covenant which serves as a crucial phase in God's fulfilling his earlier covenant of blessing and redemption to Abraham and the subsequent establishment of Judaism which became the sole monotheistic religion of the Hebrews. Youngblood keenly notes, "Of the many agreements between God and man described in the Old Testament, none is so significant or has such far-reaching implications as the Sinaitic or Mosaic covenant . . . the story of that covenant lies at the heart of the Old Testament."[143] As the Abrahamic covenant, the Mosaic covenant (Exod 19:1–6) is also unconditional and carries with it the centrifugal movement since it begins by establishing the Hebraic religion of Judaism firmly with Yahweh as the only God of the Hebrews as opposed to the heathen with a plurality of gods and goddesses. From the lips of Moses, as also contained in the Decalogue to the oracles of the prophets, Yahweh warns Israel again and again to have no other gods but him (Exod 20; Josh 24:14–22; Isa 10; Jer 2; Ezek 14; Hos 4–6; Amos 9). In fact, Yahweh contends with Israel that not even their ancestors with whom he made a covenant were to be compared with him. The nation of Israel became the first beneficiary of Yahweh's redeeming love which then moves outward to the nations of the world as Isaiah would show later (Isa 49:6).

Judaism is the foundation of Israel as a nation under one God who made himself known and made a promise to their ancestors, Abraham, Isaac and Jacob. From these three founding ancestors, the society of Israel was to take

---

142. Wright, *Mission of God*, 275.
143. Youngblood, *Heart of the Old Testament*, 47.

shape and define her worldview in terms of Yahweh's covenant relationship with their progenitors. But this covenant was meant to move beyond the borders of Israel to the world at large. Thus, God promised Abraham, "I will make you into a great nation, and I will bless you; I will make your name great, and you will be a blessing. I will bless those who bless you, and whoever curses you I will curse; and all peoples on earth will be blessed through you" (Gen 12:2–3). Youngblood has summarized God's universal election of humankind from the Abrahamic covenant framework thus,

> The election of the Hebrew people is not merely so particularistic as it may seem at first glance. Even in God's great promise to Abraham as recorded in Genesis 12:1–3 and 22:18 is found the assurance that in him and his descendants all the families of the earth would be blessed, an assurance later given to Isaac (26:4) and Jacob (28:14) as well. After the Day of Pentecost Peter reminded his own countrymen of the ancient promise (Acts 3:25), and Paul applied it to Gentile Christians in his own day (Gal 3:8). We can see, then, that the ultimate worldwide intention of God's election of Abraham is evident from the outset.[144]

Abraham's and Israel's election demonstrate that God is interested in redeeming fallen mankind from Satan and sin back to himself. To bring this to fruition, a wandering Mesopotamian individual nomad and animist, Abraham, and one nation, Israel, became his contact point to penetrate the entire universe through a centrifugal movement that would result in the birth of the Messiah. Hebraic religion is therefore understood in terms of Yahweh making a covenant with their ancestor, and this defines and shapes their worldview and belief system.

---

144. Youngblood, 29.

The Relationship between the Role of Jewish Ancestors and the Role of African Ancestors

I. Jewish Ancestorship and African Linguistic Affinity Christology

This section explores the theological import of the election of Abraham, Isaac and Jacob. It argues that the theological foundation for the understanding of the role of ancestors has been laid in the Abrahamic covenant of promise. The Jews, to whom, Yahweh made a covenant to their patriarchs understood Abraham as a prime ancestor but nowhere do we find in Judaism or in the Hebrew Scriptures the Jews addressing him as an ancestor par excellence. This means the Jews never lifted Abraham, Isaac and Jacob or any other ancestor above his humanity by assigning a divine status to them. Conversely, the Jews never diminished Yahweh's divinity to that of their ancestors, Abraham, Isaac, and Jacob by calling him, ancestor. For this reason, this section contends that African theologians need to maintain continuity with Yahweh's covenant of redemption and promise made to the Jews. A way of being faithful to Yahweh's covenant and the Bible is to formulate a theology which meaning has a direct connection with Jewish and the early church's tradition.

In the Hebrew Bible, Yahweh's promise to Abraham gave birth to the notion of redemption and the word Yeshua has been used to make sense of that covenant which carries with it a feature fulfilment. Thus, the Old Testament Yeshua has been transliterated into the New Testament Greek as Ἰησοῦς. The simple logic of this argument is that the Old Testament's teachings were given and received in a Palestinian milieu and would have to be translated into a Greek milieu. Thus, the concept of Yeshua in a predominantly Jewish milieu became Ἰησοῦς in a Greek milieu. Furthermore, Yeshua is also transliterated into Arabic as *Issah* so that the theological meaning of Yeshua as redeemer is retained. In order to faithfully preserve the theological meaning of Yeshua, Ἰησοῦς, and *Issah*, African Christians also transliterated Yeshua, Ἰησοῦς, and *Issah* into their languages *Yesu* or *Jesu*. Because most African Christians prefer to retain the transliterated and theological meaning of Jesus by calling him *Yesu/Jesu*, this section proposes African Linguistic Affinity Christology. By "African Linguistic Affinity Christology," I mean a unique Christology designed for African Christianity that does not only explore a universal christological title for Jesus Christ that resonates with the Abrahamic covenant of redemption in which Jesus is identified as the Christ who redeems human beings from the power of Satan and sin, but also vividly brings out the theological meaning of Jesus the anointed one. Thus, this Christology has continuity and affinity with God's promise to the Jewish patriarchs. The basic premise of this Christology is that when the gospel moved from the Hebrew to the Greek context, the Greeks did not invent a new name for Jesus that did not have a biblical or Hebrew concept. Rather, they simply gave the Hebrew Yeshua a Greek linguistic transliteration Ἰησοῦς. This also applies to the Arabic *Issah* and the English Jesus which are the transliterated version of the Hebrew Yeshua. It is critical we note that in all these usages, "Y" has consistently featured at the beginning of each transliterated name. For instance, the Hebrew Yeshua begins with "Y," the Greek Ἰησοῦς also begins with "Y" since the Greek "I" is highly flexible and stand for both "Y" and "i." The Arabic *Issah* starts with "Y" since in an actual sense; the word is "*Yessah* or *Yesuha*" (see page 253). This can also apply to the German name for Jesus – *Yohannah*. According to the rule of linguistics, you don't create a symbol that will distort the meaning of the thing you are describing. For this reason, the overwhelming majority of African Christians in their linguistic contexts prefer to use African Linguistic Affinity christological concept that did not move away from the Hebrew and Greek origins by giving Jesus a strange name that would distort his mission of redemption but decided to use a name that has biblical linguistic affinity with Christian history and tradition just as the Greeks, Arabs, English and Germans have done. My research in this important topic (see ch. 7) has shown that the Kikuyu/Bantu (Kenya) ,Moro (South Sudan), Zanaki (Tanzania), Krio (Sierra Leon), Manjago (Gambia), Igbo (Nigeria) and others used transliteration to make sense of the Christ event. This was done not by inventing a different name for Christ, but instead, they chose linguistic affinity concept to make the understanding of Christ as my method captures. With this manner, the question is, would African Christians now have the same theological concept of Christ with the Hebrews, Greeks, Arabs, and Germans? My answer will be yes since the method connects us with what others else where had transliterated and formulated Christology.

I have tried to describe what I mean by African Linguistic Affinity Christology as a prelude to the discussion of the circumstances that led to the Abrahamic covenant and emergence of the Hebrew concept of Yeshua. The section, therefore, argues that Adam and Eve have sinned with a sense of right and wrong, good and bad, but not in the manner they should have.[145] Consequently, the world around them looked different; they recognized their nakedness, and their minds became defiled hindering fellowship with God.[146]

The fallen condition of Adam and Eve necessitated both judgment and redemption. In Genesis 3:15, God moved to resolve the problem; in his judgment, he announced the enmity that would characterize the relationship between Satan and mankind. Theologically, this is termed the *protoevangelium* – the first-ever announcement of the gospel in Scriptures with the promise of global redemption for the fallen children of Adam and Eve. As Enns highligts, "Although Adam and Eve sinned, incurring death, God moved to resolve man's dilemma by pointing to a future saviour who would eliminate death, restore believing man to fellowship with God, and consummate history with Messiah's reign on earth to restore all that Adam had lost."[147]

Human restoration and redemption was the reason for God making himself known to the Mesopotamian pagan nomads Abraham, Isaac, and Jacob and later to Moses, David, and the future generations of Hebrew prophets who predicted the birth of a coming redeemer. With the Abrahamic covenant fully established, both Abraham and Sarah his wife will have to experience a radical transformation through the change of names and circumcision. Thus, Abram which initially meant "Exalted Father" became Abraham "Father of Many nations" while Sarai became Sarah "Mother of nations." The final seal for this transaction was the circumcision which Abraham and his household underwent (Gen 17).

While the circumcision of Abraham underscores God's determination to redeem fallen mankind back to himself, the linchpin of God's love for humanity is tie together holistically in the Sinaitic or Mosaic covenant. Here Yahweh tells Israel, "You yourselves have seen what I did to Egypt, and how I carried you on eagles' wings and brought you to myself. Now if

---

145. Enns, *Moody Handbook*, 41.
146. Enns, 41.
147. Enns, 41.

you obey me fully and keep my covenant, then out of all nations you will be my treasured possession . . . you will be for me a kingdom of priests and a holy nation" (Exod 19:4–6).

Yahweh's instructions to Israel give us hints to information about his virtues; his holiness and he would also want those to whom he reveals himself to be holy (Lev 19:2). Thus, the Ten Commandments come immediately in the next chapter to be the springboard that would not only perfect Yahweh's choice of Israel but would separate and make Israel unique from the surrounding nations. So, he warns, "I am the Lord your God, who brought you out of Egypt, out of the land of slavery. You shall have no other gods before me" (Exod 20:1–3).

With the Sinaitic covenant and the Ten Commandments, God has not only firmly and invariably instituted a new religion, Judaism, in Israel with its comprehensive and rigorous monotheistic doctrine but has as well established and positioned Israel as his chosen nation under theocratic governance. Israel thus became a nation with Yahweh as her supreme God. During the monarchy, God reiterated his covenant with Abraham through David and announced, "I will make your name great, like the names of the greatest men of the earth . . . the Lord himself will establish a house for you . . . Your house and your kingdom shall endure forever before me; your throne shall be established forever" (2 Sam 7:9, 11, 16). In later generations, Isaiah predicted, "The Virgin will conceive and give birth to a Son, and will call him Immanuel" (Isa 7:14). Elsewhere Isaiah reiterates his prophecy for the coming child and describes his reign in terms reminiscent of the Davidic and Messianic reigns since the child shall be "called Wonderful Counselor, Mighty God, Everlasting Father, Prince of Peace," whose government and peace will last forever (Isa 9:6–7).

Toward the end of the Old Testament period, the prophet Micah predicted that Bethlehem Ephrathah would bring forth a ruler over Israel "whose origins are from of old, from ancient times" (Mic 5:2). As we enter the New Testament era, the apostle Paul reports, "But when the time had fully come, God sent his Son, born of a woman, born under the law, to redeem those under the law, that we might receive adoption to sonship" (Gal 4:4–5). The Son the apostle Paul has in mind here, is Jesus the Christ, the Son of the living God as the apostle Peter confesses (Matt 16:16; Mark 8:29). Peter's notion of Jesus the Christ points to the Messiah and the messianic reign to further confirm the Abrahamic and Sinaitic covenants since fundamentally Israel's election denotes the fact that Yahweh is resolutely determined to redeem a covenant people for his own possession and kingdom reign. Peter concretizes these covenants when he alludes to Exodus 19:6 and Hosea 1:9, 10 in 1 Peter 2:9–10 to argue that the saints are intrinsic beneficiaries of that covenant insofar as they belong to the redeemed people of God.

When we examine the genealogy of Jesus Christ according to the apostle Matthew's record, it starts from King David to the patriarch Abraham and terminates with Joseph, the husband of Mary who gave birth to Jesus Christ (Matt 1:1–17). Matthew's genealogy data prepares him for the birth narrative of the child whom he names "Jesus Christ" (Matt 1:18; 2:1; 3:13; 4:1), whose birth both the righteous and devout Simeon and the prophetess Anna, the daughter of Penuel, had identified as the fulfillment of the promise which is to further serve as salvation and a light for revelation to the Gentiles and for glory to your people Israel (Luke 2:25–32). Similarly, Mark calls the child Jesus (Mark 1:1, 9, 14, 21), Luke names him Jesus (Luke 2:21; Acts 1:1), John identifies him as Jesus (John 1:29), and the authors of the epistles too called him Jesus or Christ Jesus (Rom 5:15; Eph 1:1; Heb 2:9, 3:3).

So, the Son of God, the God-human has come to fulfil all prophecies concerning him, but he did not occur in the fashion of theophany but in the form proper to human body chemistry and condition, however, without sin, as Athanasius argues, "For being Himself mighty, and Artificer of everything, he prepares the body in the Virgin as a temple unto himself, and makes it his very own as an instrument, in it manifested, and in it dwelling."[148]

Given that the writers of the synoptic and the fourth gospel – and all the authors of the epistles who trace their history back to Abraham, Isaac, and Jacob and therefore wrote holy Scriptures in the light of that covenant and identified the child of Jewish prophecies and fulfillments as Jesus of Nazareth – have never for any reason compared Jesus to any of their ancestors, but present him as the Lamb who takes away the sins of the world (John 1:29) and died for our sins (1 Cor 15:3) to redeem those under law (Gal 4:4) so that we fix our eyes on him (Heb 12:2), the work argues in the first place

---

148. Athanasius, *On the Incarnation*, 13.

that to call Jesus Christ as ancestor in Africa is to undermine his deity since in the Bible the idea of ancestors is not elevated to the status of divinity. In the second place, the work argues that to be faithful to the Bible, African theologians should not, in the name of inculturation and contextualization, deviate from the biblical titles given to Jesus Christ by the evangelist which carry with them a sense of soteriology and redemption. After all, most Africans prefer to call Jesus by biblical names in fulfilment of the Abrahamic covenant that promises them redemption and also recovers its theological import as the Christ.[149] A biblical name Africans at the grassroots are comfortable to use for Jesus is *Yesu* or *Jesu* since what they have in mind when they use *Yesu/Jesu* is the Jewish concept of Yeshua and the Greek concept of Ἰησοῦς replete with theological and messianic meaning. Granted the pivotal and central role the Abrahamic and Mosaic covenants play in fulfilling God's redemptive scheme announced in the judgment of Adam and Eve and the Serpent in Genesis 3:15, the work contends that a suitable Christology to be formulated in Africa should be that which is tailored toward fulfilling the aspirations and longings of both Jewish, Greek, and African ancestors who look forward to the coming of their redeemer *Yesu* or *Jesu Kiristo*.

II. African Ancestorship Is Rooted in General Revelation

As was shown in chapter 2, Ntetem, Bujo and Nyamiti gave African "ancestors a Christological definition by exploring ways that can be incorporated or rehabilitated into African Christianity."[150] I wish to assert on the contrary that "Jesus the Messiah is neither an ancestor nor 'one of them.' He did not originate from within human nature. He is its Creator. He is also not 'similar' to the ancestors, for He does not derive His similitude from them. But He can be represented 'symbolically,' so long as the meaning derived therefrom retains its Biblical basis."[151] David Gibson and Daniel Strange argue, "Identifying God's revelation with creaturely history and nature led inexorably to the paganization of the Medieval Church."[152] For them,

---

149. Clarke, *African Christology*, 82–93. See also Olson, "Contextualised Christology," 247.

150. Turaki, "Christianity and African Traditional Religion," 95.

151. Turaki, *Unique Christ*, 138.

152. David Gibson and Daniel Strange, eds., *Engaging with Barth: Contemporary Evangelical Critiques* (Nottingham: Apollos, 2008), 349.

"Creatures are not only distinguished from the Creator; the ontological status of the former is rendered questionable."[153]

To unveil the biblical basis for ancestorship, I have first to travel way back to the Abrahamic covenant. Herbert M. Carson notes that the Abrahamic covenant was rooted in the electing grace of God, who took the initiative in calling Abraham and pledges himself to him.[154] This call also came with the promise of blessing to him and through his seed to the nations of the earth. The seal of this covenant is the rite of circumcision which Abraham accepted and performed to fulfil and satisfy the demand of the covenant. But the Abrahamic covenant makes sense only with the Sinaitic covenant in Exodus 19:4 since the redemption in Egypt is its basis which also harks back to the covenant with Abraham. Carson maintains that the Sinaitic dispensation of the covenant really embraces the period from Moses to Christ.[155]

Both the Abrahamic and the Sinaitic covenants look forward to a future fulfilment. Thus, the prophecy in Jeremiah 31:31 when taken in context does not only cast a new light on God's covenant with Abraham but further makes a whole lot of sense in this connection. In that prophecy, the prophet predicts that the Lord was going to make a new covenant with the house of Israel and the house of Judah. In the birth narrative of Luke, the evangelist alludes to this prophecy and interprets the birth of Jesus Christ as the outcome of the promises of God to their ancestors (Luke 1:72).

Theologically, both African and Jewish ancestors "fall under creation theology based upon general revelation."[156] To that end and at best, African ancestors may be compared with Hebrew ancestors in that they share the same body chemistry as creatures but not with Jesus Christ who revealed himself to the Hebrew ancestors and made covenants of redemption with them through which African ancestors who accept this promise become heirs and beneficiaries of the grace of God. In fact, Turaki rightly argues that all human ancestors are still under the general fall of the entire human

---

153. Gibson and Strange, *Engaging with Barth*, 350.

154. Herbert M. Carson, "The Covenant of Grace," in *Basic Christian Doctrines: Contemporary Evangelical Thought*, ed. Carl F. H. Henry (Grand Rapids, MI: Baker Books, 1979), 119.

155. Carson, "Covenant of Grace," 120.

156. Turaki, *Unique Christ*, 95.

race. For this reason, they themselves stand in need of God's redemption as offered in Jesus Christ.[157] Furthermore, he notes ardently that whatever role ancestors had in traditional society it is transformed and made obsolete by God's revelation in Jesus Christ. Jesus Christ came to transform the role and functions of the ancestors. Jesus Christ stands on the other side of revelation and of Redemption Theology.[158] In addition to all this Turaki posits that aside from the reverence given to the ancestors, the Old Testament nowhere contains any record which shows that the Hebrews ever worshipped their ancestors. Worship was directed to Yahweh and Yahweh alone. They were never called "intermediaries" and "mediators"[159] to warrant the comparison that has come to characterize African ancestor Christology formulated by theologians of our day. After all, in the Jewish religious context, the ancestors were never mediators, the role of mediation was strictly the function of the Aaronic priesthood but not that of Abraham, Isaac, or Jacob or anyone like Moses or David. Nürnberger is right to assert that "in ancient Israelite family spirituality . . . ancestor veneration played no role. The little figurines that were found in excavations depicted family gods, not ancestors."[160] Nürnberger had pertinently argued strongly,

> It is significant that in the Old Testament only the three prime ancestors of Israel, Abraham, Isaac and Jacob, played a religious role. They were three because three tribal traditions were combined into one story. They were remembered because they were taken to be the "pioneers" with whom Yahweh had entered into a binding relationship. Their memories were historical monuments of the promises of Yahweh to Israel, but they did not function as mediators or religious authorities.[161]

While the ones to whom Yahweh first revealed himself and his programme of salvation to mankind were never ascribed the role of mediators between Yahweh and the Israelites, Nürnberger laments how, "In Africa, in contrast,

---

157. Turaki, 95.
158. Turaki, 95.
159. Turaki, 95–96.
160. Nürnberger, *Living Dead*, 58.
161. Nürnberger, 59.

the ancestors are spiritual authorities, whether as mediators between humans and the Supreme Being or in their own right."[162] This for me, of course, is a gross distortion of the biblical concept of an ancestor and African theologians who use African primal beliefs to formulate ancestor Christology need to go back to the Bible to rediscover the theological meaning of ancestorship in order for them to develop a sound theology.

III. Both Jewish and African Ancestors Anticipated the Fulfillment of the Adamic Redemptive Covenant and the Abrahamic Covenant of Promise

Given the fact that both African and Hebrew ancestors alike fall under creation theology, the consequential effect of the fall of Adam and Eve has become also their lot insofar as they share in the Adamic nature, and thus have too inherited sin which spread to the whole human race because everyone without exception has sinned (Rom 5:12). It follows therefore that the biblical portrayal of the human situation and predicament after the fall due to God's indictment on mankind takes its toll on all human beings without exception since Jews and Gentiles alike are under sin (Rom 3:9) and prisoners to the law (Rom 7:23) which is fanned into flames by the power of sin the slave driver (Rom 7:14).

Since therefore the judgment of God fell on all, the whole creation has been groaning right up to the present (Rom 8:22) looking forward eagerly for our adoption as sons, the redemption of our bodies (Rom 8:23), we wish to state that the human predicament necessitates the coming of the Messiah through whom all creatures would be redeemed in fulfillment of the Adamic covenant of redemption and the Abrahamic covenant of promise which would be mediated to all the families of the earth (Gen 12:3). Walter C. Kaiser, Jr, is right to assert, "The *protoevangelium* is a presentation of the entire history of humanity in a miniature declaration. Relief will come from the same God who created all things."[163] Herein lies for us the fundamental notion of the Messiah which Christology has come to represent.

---

162. Nürnberger, 59.

163. Walter C. Kaiser, Jr, *The Messiah in the Old Testament* (Grand Rapids, MI: Zondervan, 1995), 41.

Christology stands and falls upon the messianic role mediated by Jesus Christ on the cross at Calvary. Interestingly enough, it is the functional christological role of Christ that forms the hub and core of African ancestor Christology where African theologians employ comparative analysis to relate the role of African ancestors to that of Jesus the Christ. This is good, but we need to remember that Christology stems from the Jewish notion of the anointed one which itself is rooted in "God's covenant promise and prophecy to the Jewish ancestors – the patriarchs. The expectation of the patriarchs and indeed the nation of Israel was that of looking forward to the coming Anointed One. This much expectation of the coming Messiah was Christological."[164] Based upon the conviction that Yahweh had promised their forefathers the coming of the Messiah, the early church explored the content and meaning of Jesus's messiahship and became at the same time the first herald of God's blessed hope to humanity. Donald Juel passionately pushes the point further, "Convinced that Jesus was the promised Messiah, Christians undertook the task of reflecting on the gospel of his death and resurrection in light of the Scriptures."[165]

From the foregoing presentation, I wish to conclude with Turaki who states, "Giving names to Jesus because of what people assume him not to qualify as Christology. Describing Jesus in the eyes of Africans or in their conceptions does not qualify for Christology. We can take and have wonderful research findings, but that does not qualify for Christology. Except if Christology loses its biblical and prophetic meaning."[166] If however Christology retains its biblical and prophetic meaning, then definitely, Jesus Christ can never for that matter for the sake of analogy and comparison be an ancestor in the same proportion ancestors are understood in Africa since in a typical monotheistic Jewish setting, the Jews have never once even likened Abraham the father of the patriarchs to Christ. Instead, Abraham who received the covenant promise in furtherance of the Adamic covenant looked with eager expectations to the coming of the fulfiller of the promise

---

164. Yusufu Turaki, "Christianity and African Traditional Religion: A Systematic Examination of the Interactions of Religion," vol. 2 (unpublished manuscript), 67.

165. Donald Juel, *Messianic Exegesis: Christological Interpretation of the Old Testament in Early Christianity* (Philadelphia: Fortress, 1992), 60.

166. Turaki, "Christianity and African Traditional Religion," 66–67.

inaugurated with Adam's fall. Turaki made an important argument that "It is certain that the Holy Scriptures set Jesus the Messiah apart. For this reason, He cannot be domesticated to join the ancestors."[167]

Any theology that fails to accord appropriately the central redemptive and reconciling work of the cross of Christ may not in practise be able to present and proclaim Jesus the Messiah as the Saviour and the mediator of a new covenant the world over. A weak theology of salvation cannot make a good theology of mission, and it cannot fulfil the primary mission and message of its Lord – Jesus Christ. So it is with a theology of salvation without the cross of Christ. Christology without the cross is mere religion.[168]

Summary

Some African theologians have formulated ancestor Christology along three central presuppositions: gap and fulfillment presupposition, reconstructionist presupposition, and solution presupposition. Though these presuppositions provide a valid basis for comparative analysis between the mediatory role African ancestors play in the traditional religious beliefs and practices of Africans and the mediatory and redemptive function of Jesus Christ in Christianity, we wish to state that the Jews to whom Yahweh revealed himself and called Abraham, Isaac, and Jacob to be patriarchs never deified their ancestors or assign divine status to them. For this reason, therefore, the chapter and entire study argue that an apparent danger of the ancestor model is the tendency of leading to idolatry and syncretism since the theological meaning of Jesus the Christ seems to be distorted through a model that divinizes African ancestors. I wish also to point out that if Jesus Christ is fully man and fully God, then any metaphor that emphasizes one over the other runs the risk of either Docetism or Dynamic Monarchianism which are theological errors the early church decisively dealt with. Thus, describing Jesus as an ancestor, even in the case of an ancestor par excellence does not by definition express his divinity and humanity, which are vital christological concepts connected to the Abrahamic covenant.

---

167. Turaki, *Unique Christ*, 140.
168. Turaki, 201–202.

CHAPTER 7

Towards *Yesu/Jesu* Christology: Conversing with Ancestor Christology and Some Christological Models in the New Testament

Introduction

This chapter explores *Yesu/Jesu* African Linguistic Affinity Christology. In chapters 1 (see pages 10–11) and 6 (see page 328) I argued that *Yesu/Jesu* Christology is that Christology formulated in Africa that explores a universally accepted name for Jesus in the continent that seeks to be faithful to the Bible and also aligns with Yahweh's promises and covenants made to the Jewish patriarchs, Abraham, Isaac, Jacob, and Moses, in the Old Testament that have been fulfilled in the New Testament (see Gen 12:2–3; Isa 7:14; Matt 1:21–23). This Christology vividly brings out the theological meaning of Jesus the Christ and also maintains affinity and continuity with Old Testament prophecies, covenants, and fulfilment. My argument here is that when the gospel moved out from the Hebrew context to Greek and Arab contexts, the recipient contexts did not invent or change the main content of the Hebrew Yeshua. Instead, they merely gave Yeshua a Greek and Arab linguistic transliteration Ἰησοῦς and *Issah* so that the theological meaning of Yeshua is retained. For this reason, I feel that preserving the transliterated Yeshua, Ἰησοῦς and *Issah* which in Africa is *Yesu/Jesu* is most appropriate since theologically *Yesu/Jesu* means Jesus the Christ, the promised Messiah of Old Testament prophecies and fulfillment (Isa 7:14; 9:6–7; Mic 5:2; Matt

1:21–23). This Christology for me which has continuity with Old Testament covenants made to Jewish ancestors is most appropriate for the African context since it bridges the lacuna created by the ancestor Christology formulated from African primal beliefs.

In addition to *Yesu/Jesu* and African Linguistic Affinity Christology, this chapter also investigates the development of christological models in the New Testament vis-à-vis African ancestor christological models. It argues that to understand the meaning of the christological concepts used by the apostles in the early church we have to set them in context and see them in context. S. W. Sykes and J. P. Clayton keenly point out that without context, there is no understanding.[1] Thus to understand the phenomenon of Jesus and how and why it was essential for the evangelists in the early church to describe his person and work using acceptable categories, we need first to relate them to a frame of reference. In Christian theological discourse, the church's principal and primary frame of reference for valid christological models is the messianic prophecies and promises made in the Old Testament and fulfilled through the birth, death, and resurrection of Jesus in the New Testament, which qualified him to be the Christ. For out of the resurrection – faith came the assertion that "God has made both Lord and Christ this Jesus whom you crucified (cf. Acts 2:36)."[2]

Jesus's death and resurrection consummated his vocation depicted in some of the confessional titles given to him by the early church and those our Lord Jesus applied to himself. David Friedrich Strauss, for example, had shown plausibly that the common appellation Jesus gives himself in the gospel is, the Son of Man, ὁ υἱὸς τον ἀνθρώπου.[3] C. F. D. Moule expresses the same thought. For him, the earliest use of the title Son of Man for Jesus is applied by Jesus himself, to his vocation and the vocation of those who responded to him.[4] Moule's view comes close to I. Howard Marshall's position since he argued that the attribution of divine sonship to Jesus was first

---

1. S. W. Sykes and J. P. Clayton, eds, *Christ, Faith and History: Cambridge Studies in Christology* (Cambridge: Cambridge University Press, 1978), 83.
2. Sykes and Clayton, *Christ, Faith and History*, 88.
3. Strauss, *Life of Jesus*, 281.
4. C. F. D. Moule, *The Origin of Christology* (Cambridge: Cambridge University Press, 1984), 23.

made by the early church which does not only regard the resurrection and exaltation of Jesus as the act in which God adopted him as his son, but it was shown that the early church regarded the resurrection as the vindication of a status which Jesus had already claimed for himself.[5] This makes William Barclay's point tenuous that New Testament titles given to Jesus are affirmations and confessions of the early church's faith in Jesus and summaries of what it believed our Lord Jesus to be.[6]

In the primal traditions of Africa, ancestors are given titles that stand for what Africans believed about them and what they are believed to have achieved for their living kith and kin and the community of the living. Thus, it is not uncommon in some African societies to describe an ancestor in terms that resonate with titles given to Jesus in the Bible. With the advent of Christianity in Africa, some African theologians argue on the ground of compatibility of titles and functions that Jesus Christ should be described in terms reminiscent to the activities of African ancestors in the ancestral cult. While I applaud the efforts of these erudite theologians for engaging African primal traditions to formulate Christian theology aimed at vividly portraying the soteriological work of Jesus Christ; this chapter (and the entire study) argues, however, that the theological implications and disadvantages of framing Jesus Christ as an ancestor in African Christianity far outweigh the advantages of such usages, since the predication of ancestorship to Jesus is not based on biblical prophecies and predictions but built around human analogy and metaphysics that are not in concord with African grassroots linguistic name for Jesus Christ, as research has shown.

Background and Theological Significance of New Testament Christological Models

In Africa, names are important as they give us clues about people, places and things. They do not only tell us whether a particular place is to be considered as sacred or ordinary, but they also determine how such a place is

---

5. I. Howard Marshall, "The Development of Christology in the Early Church," *Tyndale Bulletin* 18 (1967): 79.

6. William Barclay, *Jesus as They Saw Him: New Testament Interpretations of Jesus* (London: SCM, 1962), 9.

to be treated. As to persons, African names tell us the kind of power(s) and authority the bearer of the name or title is vested with. Thus, African names have great significance and often summarize what the person has done and of what they are. Among the Chawai people of north-central Nigeria, for instance, the names *Bawa, Roro, Rudeh* and in recent times *Demigie* signify mortality while *Ghiminack* (Female) and *Bhárinyen* (Male) are names given to a gourmand or a glutton. A workaholic or a hard-working person is named *Bháchiya*. *Gamzin* is the name given to a place where footpaths meet. For this reason, a child born at this place is usually given that name to reflect where they were born. In most cases, these names were not given to the bearer at the time they were born but is rather given as a title to a person by virtue of their deeds or character in a real-life situations. This same phenomenon existed in biblical times and in human history generally. Thus the impact of Alexander on the world is summed up in his title Alexander the Great; the relationship of William to England is summed up in his title William the Conqueror.[7] William Barclay is keen to show how titles in which the character of each is summed up do actually reflect such portrayal. A case in point is Queen Elizabeth I of England who is known in history as Gloriana,[8] the name in which the splendour of the Elizabethan age is summed up.[9] Similarly, Francis of Asisi is the Troubadour of Christ, a name which is a witness to his joy in Christ. Judas Maccabaeus by his very name is Hammer of the Enemies of Israel, as Edward the first was the Hammer of the Scots.

The function of John in history is summed up in his title John the Baptist; the politics and character of Simon are contained in his title the Zealot.[10] All this is especially true of Jesus since the name Jesus defines his work of redemption, and Christ is used to depict his mediatorial function. For this reason, this chapter argues that some of the titles given to Jesus

---

7. Barclay, *Jesus as They Saw*, 9.

8. Queen Elizabeth I of England was so called because of her refusal to marry and share her political and monarchical powers. The slogan Gloriana depicted the lengthy period of her forty-five-year reign as the Queen of England as well as the golden age for British culture, whilst having a certain mystical air that suggests an earlier place of glory, in legend and myth. For more on Gloriana, see "Why Was Queen Elizabeth I Called Gloriana?" *Answers*, accessed 13 November 2017, http://www.answers.com/Q/Why_was_Queen_Elizabeth_I_called_Gloriana.

9. Barclay, *Jesus as They Saw*, 9.

10. Barclay, 9.

Christ by the evangelists in the early church even though they were earlier on foreshadowed in Old Testament prophecies and promises were not his initial titles at his birth but were later given to reflect his deeds, character and achievement while alive and after he resurrected from the dead as fulfillment of the Old Testament prophecies and promises. Jerome H. Neyrey, has affirmed, "Traditional New Testament Christologies have focused on the titles ascribed to Jesus, his office, and position."[11]

With the widespread consensus that New Testament christological titles of Jesus Christ depicts his person and vocation, this chapter is poised to investigate the etymology of some titles given to Jesus and what they signify as is the case with Jesus's messianic title to which I now turn.

I. Christ the Promised Messiah

"For what I received I passed on to you as of first importance: that Christ died for our sins according to Scriptures, that he was buried, that he was raised on the third day according to the Scriptures, and that he appeared to Cephas [Peter], and then to the twelve" (1 Cor 15:3–5). This creedal summary, though brief, presupposes a history of reflection on the "basic facts" of salvation; it is not a naïve report of events. Christ died "for our sins," it reports.[12] This same theme of Israel's redemption, which is fundamental to her religious belief and creedal formulation, is taken further by Martin Hengel. He writes, "The early Christian formulations of belief go on to repeat in numerous variations the claim that 'the Messiah (Christ) died for us' or 'for our sins.'"[13] Furthermore, Hengel understands the passion of Jesus as the fulfilment of Old Testament prophecies. He notes, "The shameful death of the Messiah-designate was an unheard-of scandal which from the beginning compelled the primitive community to interpret this horror in terms of the need for it if the Old Testament promise of salvation were to be fulfilled."[14] Fundamental then to New Testament creedal formulation and confession, is the belief that Jesus is the Christ; Israel's promised Messiah the long-awaited redeemer and liberator from oppression. With this understanding, *Yesu/*

---

11. Neyrey, *Christ Is Community*, 29.
12. Neyrey, 6.
13. Martin Hengel, *The Son of God: The Origin of Christology and the History of Jewish Hellenistic Religion* (Eugene, OR: Wipf & Stock, 2007), 61.
14. Hengel, *Son of God*, 61.

Jesu Christology places Jesus Christ in the perspective that the writers of the Old and New Testaments presented him as the promised Messiah and redeemer of mankind. For this reason, *Yesu/Jesu* Christology uncovers the theological meaning and places Jesus Christ as the redeemer of Africans in keeping with God's covenants to Adam, Abraham, Isaac, Jacob and Moses the Jewish patriarchs that find fulfilment in the New Testament. *Yesu/Jesu* Christology is not just a novel employment of nomenclature or category to depict a historical figure. Rather, it has as its main goal, the passion and eschatological work of Jesus Christ.

What, therefore, was arguably the most basic and universal christological belief in the early church was the claim that Jesus is Israel's Messiah.[15] And this is exactly the undergirding assertion of this study. That Jesus – Israel's promised Messiah is *Yesu/Jesu* who engrafts Africans and redeemed us when he died on the cross at Calvary for our sins as the eschatological deliverer. This claim that has its root in the Old Testament prophecies and promises and which is essential for grasping both the matrix of Jesus's life and what the New Testament witnesses have to say about him is what this study articulates and explicates.[16] As William Horbury suggested, "The Old Testament forms the backbone of any study of messianism in the second-Temple period."[17] Ferdinand Hahn concurs, "The concept of the Messiah, of all the expectations of a saviour-figure, has the oldest and most meaningful history. It is deeply rooted in the Old Testament and thus far is to be regarded as genuinely Biblical."[18] In the Pentateuch alone Walter C. Kaiser, Jr, argues that there are six direct messianic predictions.[19]

The wealth of Old Testament messianic themes are built around the poles of Israel's kingly and sacral ceremonies in which the monarch (1 Sam 9:16; 10:1; 16:13; 24:6; 2 Sam 2:4; 1 Kgs 1:39; 19:16) or the chief priest

---

15. Michael F. Bird, *Jesus Is the Christ: The Messianic Testimony of the Gospels* (Downers Grove, IL: InterVarsity Press, 2012), 1.

16. Gerald O'Collins, *Christology: A Biblical, Historical, and Systematic Study of Jesus*, 2nd ed. (Oxford: Oxford University Press, 2009), 21.

17. William Horbury, *Jewish Messianism and the Cult of Christ* (London: SCM, 1998), 5.

18. Ferdinand Hahn, *The Titles of Jesus in Christology: Their History in Early Christianity* (London: Lutterworth Press, 1969), 136.

19. Kaiser, Jr, *Messiah in the Old Testament*, 36.

or the prophet (Exod 28:41; 29; Lev 4:3; 6:22; 8:30; 1 Kings 19:16 and Lam 4:20) were "formally anointed with oil when they were inaugurated into their offices and functions. Their anointing was the point at which God publicly appointed them, and by his, Spirit empowered them for their work."[20] F. F. Bruce has provided us with some helpful insights into the etymology of Israel's messianic concept. For him, the designation "messiah" represents a Hebrew (or Aramaic) verbal adjective meaning "anointed."[21] Peter Lewis corroborates Bruce's stance. Thus he wrote, "The term Messiah means 'anointed.' It is, in its origin, a Hebrew word, and its Greek equivalent is *Christos*, hence our word 'Christ.'"[22]

From the foregoing, the notion of the messiah as found in the Bible is to be located in the Jewish religious setting, and the messianic motif runs throughout the Christian Bible. Hahn had asserted that "the prophetic promises of a messiah are grounded in the Israelite theory of the kingship. From the beginning, the anointing of the king . . . played a decisive part."[23] Thus, beginning with the king of Israel, and especially with the royal dynasty founded by King David upon whom the historic "messianic hope" is most closely related, Israel longed for the revelation of one who would provide the Davidic ideals since the hope is bound up with the promise of perpetual sovereignty made to David's house in Nathan's oracle preserved in prose in 2 Samuel 7:8–16 and quoted in poetical form in Psalms 89:19–37; 132:11–18.[24] Juel is correct corroborating that the promise to David of a dynasty, as recorded in 2 Samuel and Psalm 89, is of enormous importance for those interested in tracing the development of royal ideology in ancient Israel.[25]

Yahweh's promise of a dynasty to King David became the defining measure and hope for Israel's kingship. When, however, from the days of the Assyrian menace onward, the fortunes of David's house began to wane, the contrast between the high hopes of the dynastic oracle and the existing

---

20. Peter Lewis, *The Glory of Christ* (Carlise, Cumbria: Paternoster, 2004), 152.
21. F. F. Bruce, *New Testament History* (New York: Doubleday, 1980), 122.
22. Lewis, *Glory of Christ*, 152.
23. Hahn, *Titles of Jesus*, 136.
24. Bruce, *New Testament History*, 122.
25. Juel, *Messianic Exegesis*, 61.

state of affairs became more and more painfully obvious. But it was in these depressing circumstances that prophets began to speak most confidently of a coming day in which David's fallen house would be rebuilt and its vanished glories restored and surpassed in a second and greater David.[26] The second and greater David is encapsulated in Israel's prophecies as the "anointed one." The Lord's anointed, however, as the sacred writings of Israel unfolded hints began to appear that someone would come, in connection with the promised kingdom of God, who would be more than one of Israel's many kings – greater even than Israel's model king, David – and who would function as more besides: Yahweh's King and Priest and Servant.[27]

Without a doubt the image of the suffering servant, and relevant texts from Isaiah, have been central to recent descriptions of New Testament Christology.[28] Juel has shown persuasively and precisely that "the teaching concerning Messianic suffering and death is bound up in the mind of Jesus with His sense of vocation. . . . The teaching is based on a unique combination of the idea of the suffering servant of Isaiah Liii with that of the Son of man."[29] The notion of the suffering servant and son of man became pivotal to Israel's eschatological hope when from history, the realization of the Davidic dynasty seemed impossible. This view finds support in Oscar Cullmann's idea that God promised David in 2 Samuel 7:12–16 a kingdom that would last forever but history denied the realization of this prophecy in brutal way.[30]

However, the Jewish eschatological hope held fast all the more energetically to this unfulfilled expectation so that "the anointed one of Yahweh," the "Messiah" gradually became an eschatological figure.[31] Thus, Jewish worldview and religious belief became shrouded in an eschatological hope looking forward to the coming of a King who would be Israel's deliverer. Juel makes a pertinent contribution here. For him, "The Messiah is, to be sure, one of the eschatological deliverer in Jewish tradition. . . . The noun, with the definite article, refers to a royal figure, usually called the King-Messiah

---

26. Bruce, *New Testament History*, 122.
27. Lewis, *Glory of Christ*, 152.
28. Juel, *Messianic Exegesis*, 119.
29. Juel, 119–120.
30. Oscar Cullmann, *The Christology of the New Testament* (London: SCM, 1983), 114.
31. Cullmann, *Christology of the New Testament*, 114.

or Messiah-King fashioned in Isaiah 11, Gen 49:8-12; Num 24:17; and Jer 33:14-26."[32] While N. T. Wright argues that on the one hand that the coming King-Messiah would do two main things: he would build or restore the temple and he would fight the decisive battle against the enemy,[33] Craig A. Evans on the other hand points to the activities of Jesus in his response to the disciples of John in Matthew 11:2–6 as echoing the activities of the Messiah, which the Old Testament features in Psalm 146:8 and Isaiah 26:19; 35:5–6 and 61:1.[34] For Juel, "The Messiah can play any of a variety of roles appropriate to a King, but he is a king."[35] N. T. Wright's perception of the coming king and deliverer resonates with Richard N. Longenecker's view in which the Jews believed the coming "Messiah would be a political and nationalistic ruler – even a military leader. And to this idea was wedded the title 'Son of David.'"[36]

While N. T. Wright's picture of the coming King seems to be that of a celebrity and warrior, John Gray however observes that such a king is a servant of God, the vassal of his divine suzerain, of whose will he is the executive.[37] Christopher J. H. Wright adds that the notion of servant underwent transition from Israel as God's servant to individual figures like Cyrus and then ultimately to one who would have a mission to Israel (Isa 49:5), and to the world (Isa 49:6), the mission of compassionate restoration.[38]

Accordingly, the servant is then both a human figure and someone much more than a merely human descendant of King David. Craig Evans has affirmed that in addition to the promised of a future male descendant to King David in 2 Samuel 7:8–16, the promise of a filial relationship with God is

---

32. Neyrey, *Christ Is Community*, 10.

33. N. T. Wright, *The Challenge of Jesus: Rediscovering Who Jesus Was and Is* (Downers Grove, IL: IVP Academic, 1999), 76.

34. Craig A. Evans, *Holman Quick Guide to the Dead Sea Scrolls* (Nashville, TN: B & H, 2010), 333.

35. Neyrey, *Christ Is Community*, 11.

36. Richard N. Longenecker, *The Christology of Early Jewish Christianity* (Vancouver: Regent College Publishing, 2001), 66.

37. John Gray, *The Biblical Doctrine of the Reign of God* (Edinburgh: T & T Clark, 1979), 275.

38. Christopher J. H. Wright, *Knowing Jesus through the Old Testament* (Carlisle, Cumbria: Langham Preaching Resources, 2014), 132–136.

also given in two psalms. Psalm 2:2, 7 and Psalm 89:20, 26.[39] While in the first Psalm, the figure who is called both "anointed" and "Son" received God's approval that he is a Son, the second Psalm has King David calling the same figure "my father," "my God, the rock of my salvation" (RSV). This has all the more confirmed here that the figure in question is more than any of the sons and potential heirs to David's throne but one whose reign has no end. On this note, Craig Evans further elaborates that the oracle of Isaiah adds significantly to the Psalm passages above since the oracles points to the birth of a son whose name will be called "Wonderful Counselor," "Mighty God," "Eternal Father," "Prince of Peace." The son, the oracle of Isaiah, says his "dominion will be vast," and its prosperity will never end. He will reign on the throne of David and over his kingdom, to establish and sustain it with justice and righteousness from now on and forever (see Isa 9:6–7).[40]

I have shown so far in this chapter that the messianic concept is derived from Jewish dynasty, worldview and religious belief. I have also been able to demonstrate that the messiah is an eschatological figure and one who would be more than one of Israel's many kings – greater even than Israel's model king, David – and one who would function as Yahweh's king and priest and servant. I have pointed out too, that such a figure would be someone much greater than a merely human descendant of King David. He is by and large the *ebed* Yahweh described in Isaiah's four servant songs as God's suffering servant (Isa 42:1–4; 49:1–6; 50:4–9; 52:13–53:12) in fulfillment of God's covenant of redemption to Adam and Eve (Gen 3:15), the Abrahamic covenant of promise (Gen 12:1–3) and the Sinaitic promise to Moses (Exod 19:4–6). Hahn was curious to find out the connection between Jesus's titles and the Jewish concept of the messiah-king. To that end, he asks, "How did it come about that the title and the concept of the kingly Messiah were applied to Jesus?"[41] In response, he asserts, "The decisive factor is '*interpretatio christiana*' of the Judaic messianic idea."[42]

For Hahn, the early church's perception and interpretation of Jesus and his vocation accounts largely for connecting Jesus with the Christ. Hahn

---

39. Evans, *Holman Quick Guide*, 309.
40. Evans, 309.
41. Hahn, *Titles of Jesus*, 148.
42. Hahn, 149.

finds justification for his view in the New Testament. Accordingly, he maintains that it is clear there has been the broadening of the Christianized messianic idea, thus, making possible an application to the work of Jesus as a whole.[43] According to him, this first took place in the sphere of the early Hellenistic church which assimilated to messianism the tradition of the earthly Jesus as the new Moses and the eschatological prophet. In this way, as he is convinced, "Christos" could in particular be brought into connection with the miraculous work of Jesus also. Hahn's conclusion is that the early church's association of Jesus with the new Moses and the eschatological figure led ultimately to a use of "Christos" and "Son of God" in a similar sense.[44]

While Hahn is right to argue that early Hellenistic assimilation to messianism underscores the connection between the Jewish concept of messiah and Jesus, I wish to add also that Isaiah's servant song discussed above is not only a key biblical text that lucidly connects Jesus and Old Testament messianism but it also finds ultimate fulfillment in John's gospel. In John 4:34 for instance, John depicts a picture of a servant when he reported Jesus saying, "My food is to do the will of him who sent me, and to accomplish his work." (RSV). Similarly in 6:38 John also reported Jesus saying, "For I have come down from heaven, not to do my own will, but to do the will of him who sent me;" (RSV). Barclay argues that the greatest essential of a good servant is obedience. In Jesus the title Servant of God finds its perfect and unsurpassable application. To call Jesus the servant of God is to say that in him the history and destiny of the nation of Israel found its completion and its consummation.[45]

To make sense of Isaiah's oracle of the birth of a son who will rule on the throne of David his father and John's depiction of Jesus as obedient servant, we turn now to the New Testament and especially the apostle Matthew's genealogical table to establish the credentials of the son Isaiah had in mind.

In the opening verse of his gospel, the apostle Matthew gives the following account: "This is the genealogy of Jesus Christ, the Son of David, the Son of Abraham" (Matt 1:1). Wright had pointed out that the apostle Matthew's "Opening verse sums up the whole story: Jesus, who is the Messiah, was the

---

43. Hahn, 192–193.
44. Hahn, 192–193.
45. Barclay, *Jesus as They Saw*, 162.

son of David and the son of Abraham. These two names then become the key markers for the three main sections of his history: from Abraham to David; from David to the Babylonian exile; from the exile to Jesus himself."[46] In his gospel, Matthew has successfully revealed Jesus's Jewish background and argued that he is the son Isaiah had in mind and is thus a real human being who descended from Abraham.

The genealogical datum no doubt harks back to Genesis 12 in fulfilment of God's promise to bless all the nations through Abraham. This explains why Matthew identified Jesus as the Christ, the Messiah of mankind. Wright suggests that when Matthew announces Jesus as the Messiah, the son of Abraham, it means not only that he belongs to that particular people, but that he belongs to people whose very reason for existence was to bring blessing to the rest of humanity. For Wright, Jesus Christ is a particular man, a Jew, but with universal significance.[47]

Furthermore, Wright has shown vividly that at several points in the most Jewish of all four gospels, Matthew shows his interest in the universal significance of Jesus for foreign nations beyond the boundaries of Israel. This he did by developing and demonstrating through his gospel, that Jesus was the expected Messiah of the royal line of David with the right claim to the title king of the Jews as Pilate's question asserted and Jesus's response in the judgment narrative (Matt 27:11).[48] For Wright, the apostle Matthew has lucidly traced Jesus's descent through the royal line of kings descended from David that ruled over Judah (Matt 1:6–11). At the end of his genealogical account, Wright argues that the apostle Matthew, in verse 17, gives a concise summary of Jesus's profile as follows: "Thus there were fourteen generations in all from Abraham to David, fourteen from David to the exile to Babylon, and fourteen from the exile to the Messiah."[49]

While the apostle Matthew was concerned to prove the pedigree of Jesus Christ, the apostle Mark's starting point is, "the good news about Jesus the

---

46. Wright, *Knowing Jesus*, 6.
47. Wright, 6.
48. Wright, 8.
49. Wright, 9.

Messiah" (Mark 1:1).[50] By presenting Jesus as the Christ, Israel's messiah, I. Howard Marshall argues that Mark is concerned primarily with Jesus and his significance as the author of good news.[51] It becomes all the more plausibly obvious that Jesus is the Messiah and bringer of glad tidings when we consider the baptism narrative in which the heavens were opened, the Holy Spirit descended upon him, so that he is endowed with the spirit. Marshall rightly makes a good connection between the baptism narrative and Isaiah's oracle concerning the messiah. Accordingly, he notes that the messiah in Isaiah 11:1–4 is endowed with the Holy Spirit as an implicit indication that he had been equipped to baptize people with the Spirit. The heavenly voice after the baptism, Marshall, believes is none other than the clear voice of God which says, "You are my son, whom I love; with you, I am well pleased." (Mark 1:1).[52] Furthermore, Marshall suggests that the heavenly voice had identified Jesus: (1) with the Son of God addressed in Psalm 2 who is the Messiah, and (2) with the servant of God in whom God delights (Isa 42:1); this latter figure is a future deliverer and is to be understood as the Messiah.[53]

Of Jesus in Acts-Luke, Stanley E. Porter writes, "A consistent and fundamental development of Jesus as the anointed prophet stands at the heart of Luke's depiction of Jesus as Messiah."[54] In the birth narrative in Luke, for instance, Stanley points out that John is depicted as a forerunner of the messiah in a perfect depiction of the messiah and a sign of John's prophetic status as a forerunner of the messiah. For this reason, the birth narrative reveals Elizabeth's pregnancy precedes Mary's (Luke 1:13, 31); John is described in terms of an Old Testament prophet in the wilderness (1:5); he is to be filled with God's Spirit (1:15); he utters the message of a prophet to repent (1:16–17); he is said to be one who goes before the Lord (1:17); he is described as being in the Spirit and power of the prophet Elijah, seen to be the Messiah's forerunner, possibly citing the prophet Malachi (3:24 LXX)

---

50. I. Howard Marshall, "Jesus as Messiah in Mark and Matthew," in *The Messiah in the Old and New Testaments*, ed. Stanley E. Porter (Grand Rapids, MI: Eerdmans, 2007), 118.

51. Marshall, "Jesus as Messiah," 118.

52. Marshall, 120.

53. Marshall, 120.

54. Stanley E. Porter, "The Messiah in Luke and Acts: Forgiveness for the Captives," in *The Messiah in the Old and New Testaments*, ed. Stanley E. Porter (Grand Rapids, MI: Eerdmans, 2007), 145.

(1:17); and Zachariah labels him a prophet of God destined to go before the Lord to prepare the way (Luke 1:17).[55] The birth narrative might seem apparent that Jesus's messianic credentials have been established. For Stanley however, it was Peter's defining response to Jesus's question that he is the Christ of God (Luke 9:20) and the two post-resurrection episodes which are tied to the prophetic character of Jesus's ministry that Jesus's messiahship is to be found. First, he argued that the risen Jesus travels along the road to Emmaus with two men and talked with them and opened their horizons to the facts surrendering his mission. Second, in the post-resurrection meal with a large group in Jerusalem, Jesus opens his listeners' minds and says, "it is written [γέγραπται] that the Christ should suffer and on the third day rise from the dead" (Luke 24:46, RSV).[56]

Stanley concludes his argument by pointing to Peter's homily in Acts 2:14–36 as the final attestation of Jesus's messiahship. By citing Joel 2:28–32 (LXX 3:1–5) in Acts 2:17–21; Ps 16:8–11 in Acts 2:25–28; and Ps 110:1 in Acts 2:34–35 on the basis of establishing Jesus as the prophesied crucified and resurrected one, Peter then speaks of him as the Messiah.[57] In Acts 2:30–31, Peter says that because David was a prophet, he could look forward to the resurrection of the Messiah. In Acts 2:36, after the crowd is pierced to the heart by what they have heard, Peter tells them to repent and be baptized in the name of the Christ.[58]

For Stanley, Peter's sermon alluded to the Old Testament prophecies about the coming Messiah which now finds fulfilment in the ministry of Jesus Christ. And Peter would affirm his stance in his sermon in Acts 3:18 to the onlookers after healing the beggar in the place called Solomon's colonnade where he attributed Jesus's crucifixion to Jewish ignorance but the perfect fulfilment of Old Testament prophecies that the Christ would suffer.

While the synoptic gospels took their departure in constructing the life and ministry of Jesus the Messiah from his personal ancestral background, the fourth evangelist or the apostle John starts off from Jesus's ontological being. That is, from the metaphysical Christ, the wonderful counselor and

---

55. Porter, "Messiah in Luke," 147–148.
56. Porter, 155.
57. Porter, 160.
58. Porter, 160.

prince of peace whose reign has no end (Isa 9:6–7). For this reason, without apology, he writes,

> In the beginning was the Word, and the Word was with God, and the Word was God. He was with God in the beginning. Through him all things were made; without him nothing was made that has been made. In him was life, and that life was the light of all mankind . . . The Word became flesh and made his dwelling among us. We have seen his glory, the glory of the one and only Son, who came from the Father, full of grace and truth. (John 1:1–4, 14).

This majestic statement by the the apostle John in his prologue echoes the opening words of Genesis 1:1, which lay down a blueprint while John 1:1 gives the commentary. It is interesting to note that John's subject in his commentary is the incarnate Word of God. Beyond the synoptic gospels and Luke-Acts, John traces Christ back to Genesis and tells us that he is the self-existent God who created everything from the beginning.[59] This same creator, John argues, has made his dwelling among men. The startling declaration, that Christ is the incarnate Logos and creator, by John is illuminating, transforming, and unparalleled. John also tells us that Christ is the long-awaited Messiah, this he made clear in his Gospel, the Epistles and Revelation (John 1:11–12; 3:16; 20:31; 1 John 5:11–12; Rev 22:12–16).

John's unique portrayal of Christ as the incarnate Logos, which gives a vivid picture of who Christ is, is his comprehensive summary and presentation of Christ as the long-awaited Messiah prophesied and promised to the Jewish ancestors. As Tom Thatcher writes, "Any discussion of John's messianic beliefs is essentially a discussion of John's view of Jesus."[60] This explains why Thatcher argues that in the "first chapter of the fourth Gospel" and 1-2-3 John, applies a veritable catalogue of messianic titles to Jesus to make the identity of the protagonist immediately clear. Jesus is Joseph's son (1:45), but Joseph's son also happens to be the "Son of God" (3:16; 1 John 5:12), as well as "the Word" (1:1, 14), "the life" (1:4; 14:6; 1 John 1:1),

---

59. Stephen S. Kim, "The Literary and Theological Significance of the Johannine Prologue," *Bibliotheca Sacra* 166 (2009): 421–435.

60. Tom Thatcher, "Remembering Jesus: John's Negative Christology," in *The Messiah in the Old and New Testaments*, ed. Stanley E. Porter (Grand Rapids, MI: Eerdmans, 2007), 165.

"the light of all mankind" (1:4), "Christ" (χριστός) (1:41; 4:25), "the only begotten" (μονογενής) in the bosom of the Father (3:16), "the Lamb of God, who takes away the sin of the world" (1:29), "the Messiah" (μεσσίας) (1:41; 4:25–26), "the one Moses wrote about in the Law, and whom the prophets also wrote" (1:45), "the King of Israel" (1:49), and, finally, Jesus's self-designation, "the Son of Man" (1:51).[61]

Explicit though are the predictions of the coming messiah and *ebed Yahweh* in Jewish Scriptures, the Jews of John's day seemed to have objected the notion of a crucified messiah. Thus, when after the triumphant entry into Jerusalem Jesus asked the Father to glorify his name through the Son, and the Father's voice was heard, Jesus told the crowd that the voice was for their good and not his but then reported that "And I, when I am lifted up from the earth, will draw all people to myself" (12:32), John reports that the crowd responded, "We have heard from the Law that the Messiah will remain forever, so how can you say, 'The Son of Man must be lifted up'? Who is this 'Son of Man'?" (12:34). James F. McGrath is convinced, "It was the use of 'Son of Man' not only in reference to Jesus' apocalyptic parousia but also to his suffering, which was felt to be objectionable."[62] Nevertheless, John found a smooth and immeasurably pleasant way to appeal to Jewish tradition in order to present the death of the Son of Man on the cross as not only scriptural but also a victory over the forces of evil, which is therefore not incompatible with the claim that he is the Messiah.[63] As James D. G. Dunn endeavours to show, John's conviction that Jesus is the Messiah accounts for his use of "the Christ (1:20; 3:28; 7:26, 41; 10:24) and even preserves the Hebrew (or Aramaic) form 'Messias' (1:41; 4:25)."[64] Dunn believes that John's avowal aim in writing his corpus is to demonstrate that "Jesus is the Christ, the Son of God (20:31). And in 11:27 Martha becomes the model for full Christian confession – I believe that you are the Christ, the Son of God' (cf. the Baptist – 3:28)."[65]

---

61. Thatcher, "Remembering Jesus," 165.
62. James F. McGrath, *John's Apologetic Christology: Legitimation and Development in Johannine Christology* (Cambridge: Cambridge University Press, 2004), 213.
63. McGrath, *John's Apologetic Christology*, 213.
64. James D. G. Dunn, *Unity and Diversity in the New Testament: An Inquiry into the Character of Earliest Christianity* (London: SCM, 1984), 41.
65. Dunn, *Unity and Diversity*, 41.

I have shown above that the fulcrum of John's messianic Christology is the incarnation. For the apostle Paul, it is the crucifixion and resurrection. Thus he writes, "we preach Christ crucified: a stumbling block to Jews and foolishness to Gentiles, but to those whom God has called, both Jews and Greeks, Christ the power of God and the wisdom of God" (1 Cor 1:23–24). James D. G. Dunn had shed light by providing rich insight into Paul's meaning of stumbling block in a Jewish context. According to him, the image portrayed in Jewish thought is not simply of someone grieved at or hostile to a particular teaching, but it denotes an obstacle over which someone might actually trip (not simply disapprove of). For this reason, the Jews in Corinth considered it an offence to have been invited actually to believe in and commit themselves to the crucified Christ.[66] In his exegetical analysis of 1 Corinthians 1:23–24, Gordon D. Fee argues that in the phrase "'Christ crucified is the wisdom of God' Paul does not actually called the crucified one 'the wisdom of God.' What he says, rather, is that the proclamation of the crucified one is God's power and God's wisdom – over against all human efforts to discover God."[67]

While the crucifixion is central in Paul's thought, he is quick to also point to the one who was crucified as the Son of God – Jesus (1 Thess 1:10; Gal 4:4; 2 Cor 1:19) and Christ of God (1 Cor 3:23). Thus, the crucifixion and the Son of God are two important elements in his understanding of Jesus's messiahship. Gordon Fee points to this when he rightly stresses, "Paul's designation of Jesus as Son of God gives way immediately to an emphasis on the nature of the Son's messianic destiny: humiliation by way of crucifixion."[68] For Paul, as Fee demonstrates, Jesus the crucified and humiliated eternal Son of God becomes ultimately the exalted Messiah and Lord who is seated at the right hand of the Father.[69] Jesus's glorious exaltation and session in Fee's argument evolves first into a reminder of the Colossians' place in God's history (1:12–14) and then (1:15–20) into a poetic exaltation of Christ as a

---

66. James D. G. Dunn, *The Theology of Paul the Apostle* (Edinburgh: T & T Clark, 2008), 197–198.
67. Gordon D. Fee, *Pauline Christology: An Exegetical-Theological Study* (Grand Rapids, MI: Baker Academic, 2007), 104.
68. Fee, Pauline Christology, 100.
69. Fee, 290.

way of confronting the Colossians with who they are in light of who Christ is.[70] Dunn had shown persuasively how the crucifixion motif is the leitmotif of Paul's messianic Christology since he does not attempt an explanation for his avowal assertion that Christ crucified is the Messiah. He writes, "He (Paul) makes no attempt to prove that Jesus really is 'the Christ' despite his suffering and death. The belief in Jesus as the Christ has become so firmly established in his mind and message that he simply takes it for granted."[71] S. A. Cummins arrives at almost the same conclusion but goes a step further to say, "Paul's understanding of Jesus as Messiah lies at the very heart of his theology, ecclesiology, and eschatology: the Messiah and his faithful followers are agents of the divine life that embraces redemption, reconciliation, and a glorious new creation."[72] For Paul, as Cummins is convinced, God's righteousness has been fully manifest in the atoning death and resurrection of Jesus Christ, so that notwithstanding the sin of humanity (Jew and Gentiles alike), God can declare even now that all those who believe in this God so revealed in this Messiah Jesus are thereby constituted as his covenant faithful people (Romans 1–4).[73]

Paul drives home his argument in Romans 5–8 where he unfolded the amazing outcome and eschatological outworking of God's righteousness in Jesus. He argues that the complete restoration of humanity and creation has, in principle, been accomplished and that those conformed to Christ and the Holy Spirit (who live in the "Spirit" of the Messiah Rom 8:9) are a new creation (2 Cor 5:17) and are even now participants in the messianic age.[74] This, for Paul is the full scale of justification since the believing sinner is saved and justified by grace through faith (Eph 2:8), as,

> we have peace with God through our Lord Jesus Christ, through whom we have gained access by faith into this grace in which we now stand. And we boast in the hope of the glory of God. Not

---

70. Fee, 293–294.

71. Dunn, *Unity and Diversity*, 43.

72. S. A. Cummins, "Divine Life and Corporate Christology: God, Messiah Jesus, and the Covenant Community in Paul," in *The Messiah in the Old and New Testaments*, ed. Stanley E. Porter (Grand Rapids, MI: Eerdmans, 2007), 190.

73. Cummins, "Divine Life," 205.

74. Cummins, 205–206.

only so, but we also glory in our sufferings, because we know that suffering produces perseverance; perseverance character; and character, hope. And hope does not put us to shame, because God's love has been poured into our hearts through the Holy Spirit, who has been given to us (Rom 5:1–5).

With this blessed assurance Cummins eloquently states that Paul unreservedly writes, "Those who are in Messiah Jesus are excluded from God's condemnation because they have been set free from the Torah as taken over by sin and are instead the beneficiaries of the Torah's fulfillment in Jesus and the Spirit, who together effect covenant life (Rom 8:1–2)."[75] Of Paul, Cummins makes the following summary, "Jewish messianic expectations envisage an eschatological redeemer/ruler who would deliver the nation from foreign subjugation and bring about the new age. It was in order to ensure the realization of just such a vision that a zealous Paul opposed the wayward first followers of the crucified messianic pretender Jesus."[76] Interestingly enough, in the course of this opposition, Paul dramatically and transformatively experienced a divine disclosure, as a result of which he realized that this Jesus was indeed the now risen and exalted Messiah, Son of God, and, even more astonishingly, Lord. It was, then, in this way that Israel's God had himself acted to fulfill the Abrahamic covenant and rescued, restored, and in principles re-created Israel and all the nations.[77]

We come now to Hebrews' and the general epistles' messianic perspectives which form the linchpin of this chapter since they are believed to have been written strictly to Jewish audiences or congregations. A point of departure for the study of the messiah in Hebrews and the general epistles is the acknowledgment that the term "messiah" became the central christological concept. At least that holds true historically, and therein lies the rub, "Christ" or χριστός, the Greek term for the Messiah, became the central way of designating the church's understanding of Jesus.[78] This designation

---

75. Cummins, 206.
76. Cummins, 209.
77. Cummins, 209.
78. Cynthia Long Westfall, "Messianic Themes of Temple, Enthronement, and Victory in Hebrews and the General Epistles," in *The Messiah in the Old and New Testaments*, ed. Stanley E. Porter (Grand Rapids, MI: Eerdmans, 2007), 210.

is crucial and has thus buttresses N. T. Wright's thesis that "From its very earliest days, the community of Jesus' followers regarded him as Messiah."[79] Thus, when Christ is used in Hebrews and the general epistles, it is used in the sense this work has already established. That is, the anointed one and God's eschatological divinely appointed and anointed agent whose saving acts would restore or free Israel from oppression and inaugurate the day of the Lord.[80]

The messianic obsession of the above mentioned writers could be gleaned from the devotion given to the term itself. For example, χριστός occurs thirteen times in the book of Hebrews, two in James (1:1; 2:1), twenty-two in 1 Peter, six in Jude, and six in 1 John and every occurrence of Christ is linked with a messianic scenario.[81] For this reason the writer of Hebrews gives an extensive treatment of the fact of believers being members in God's house and partakers in Christ's heritage if we hold fast to that which we profess (3:6, 14). This heritage is that God has promised his faithful ones an eternal rest when Christ the Messiah is revealed and enthroned over all principalities (ch. 4) in fulfillment of the Abrahamic covenant (6:13–15).

In an illuminating exposition of Jesus's enthronement passages, Westfall notes that passages that evoke the enthronement scenario depict Christ as seated at the right hand of God after accomplishing the priestly function of sacrifice (10:12), as the Son over God's house (3:6), unchanging (13:8), and the means to obedience (13:21).[82] This same theme is also taken by James and Jude. While James presents his enthronement scenario in a manner in which the poor believer in the messianic age is raised up in status, given a crown of life, and declared to be an heir of the kingdom, while the humble believer will be exalted by God (Jas 1:5, 9, 12; 4:10). God gives birth to created believers by the word of truth so that they become a kind of first fruits of what has been created (1:18), Jude begins with an apparent doxology: in verse 4, he addresses the Messiah as "Jesus Christ our only Sovereign and Lord," in verse 24, his doxology is made explicit, "To him who is able to keep you from stumbling and to present you before his glorious presence without

---

79. Wright, *Jesus and the Victory*, vol. 2, 486.
80. Westfall, "Messianic Themes," 211.
81. Westfall, 217–227.
82. Westfall, 218.

fault and with great joy – to the only God our Saviour be glory, majesty, power and authority, through Jesus Christ our Lord, before all ages, now and forevermore!"[83] Westfall argues that these patterns alone demonstrate a concern with Jesus's Lordship, evoking enthronement scenario. Jesus is a preexistent source or agent who contributes to God's enthronement.[84]

In the Petrine and Johnnine epistles, the messianic concept is obviously an overriding theme. Thus, in 1 Peter 1:2, Peter argues that believers have been chosen and destined by God the Father and sanctified by the Spirit to be obedient to Jesus Christ and to be sprinkled by his blood, and grace and peace are invoked for them. John however is more apologetic in his approach since he raises the question of denial and asserts, "Who is the liar?" For him, "It is whoever denies that Jesus is the Christ" (1 John 2:22). Here according to John, to not confess that Jesus is the Christ does not only amount to denial but is a sure sign that the evil one is at work. Whereas to confess Jesus is the Christ places the confessor in the same plane with the Messiah since he shares in the Messiah's anointing (2:27).

I conclude this section with the argument of Westfall that:

> The author of Hebrews and the general epistles not only enlarged the scope of what was considered prophetic in the Hebrew Bible, but they were possibly inspired by the variety of messianic expectations and made unique associations with the work of Christ in unexpected ways. Hebrews provided the most detailed and arguably the most original messianic Christology in the New Testament.[85]

II. Christ the Mediator

The Scriptures continually warns us that although God is good and loving, he could be against us on account of sin. He tells us that sin in man has made man hostile to God and God is wrathful toward man.[86] The gulf that sin has created between man and God his creator can only be reconciled through the work of mediation. In the Garden of Eden God set the pace

---

83. Westfall, 226.
84. Westfall, 226.
85. Westfall, 229.
86. Lewis, *Glory of Christ*, 216.

through the animal he sacrificed and clothed Adam and Eve with its skin (Gen 3:21). God's action at Eden of sacrificing an animal to remedy man's fallen situation becomes the defining model for a future and more perfect mediation. Ever since the Edenic example, man has learned to work out ways through which he could have true and lasting peace with God his creator.

Unfortunately, man could not sufficiently proffer a lasting solution to his alienation and predicament since the means employed to remedy the situation has been through animal sacrifice, the blood of which is very temporal and inadequate to permanently take away sins (Heb 10:4). Thus, the notion of mediation becomes deeply entrenched in Christian thought and interwoven into Christian language, especially the language of liturgy and devotion.[87] Barclay points out that the word "mediator" features four times in the New Testament, one in the Pastoral Epistles (1 Tim 2:5) and three in the book of Hebrews (Heb 6; 9:5; 12:24) and each usage is linked to Jesus Christ as the mediator. According to Barclay, mediator is taken from the Greek *mesitēs*, meaning "in the middle." Quoting Westcott, he defines *mesitēs* as "One who standing between the contracting parties shall bring them into fellowship."[88] For Hillard, as Barclay endeavoured to show, a *mesitēsis*, "Anyone who formed the channel of communication between two others."[89]

In current usage, Lewis defines a *mesitēs* or mediator as, "A middle-man, one who stands between two parties, representing the intentions of both and protecting the interests of both."[90] For this reason, the mediator, Lewis argues, must be equally related to the persons between whom he comes. God's eternal Son and equal became man in order that in two-natures, human and divine, he might be all that we needed for our help and all that God required for his vindication.[91]

To this end, God himself became the mediator when he prepares the body in the Virgin as a temple unto himself, and makes it his very own as an instrument, in it manifested and in it dwelling so that he might quicken them from death by the assumption of his body and by the grace of the

---

87. Barclay, *Jesus as They Saw*, 334.
88. Barclay, 334.
89. Barclay, 334.
90. Lewis, *Glory of Christ*, 216.
91. Lewis, 216.

resurrection, banishing death from them like straw from the fire.[92] John Calvin expresses his insight this way, "It deeply concerned us, that he who was to be our Mediator should be very God and very man."[93] St Augustine also wrote, "And hence that true Mediator, in so far as, by assuming the form of a servant, He became the Mediator between God and men, the man Christ."[94]

Barclay has done a good service by helping us to trace the etymology and first usage of *mesitēs* back to Job and Moses in the Old Testament. *Mesitēs* was used by Job in his predicament to complain that there is no one to bring him and God together so that he may plead his innocence (9:33). In association with Moses, *mesitēs* is used in one of the apocryphal or inter-testamental books, *the Assumption of Moses* to depict Moses as saying to Joshua that God designed and "devised me, and he prepared me before the foundation of the world, that I should be the mediator of his covenant."[95] The same book speaks of the commandments, in which Moses was the mediator to us (1:14; 3:12). In the light of the foregoing, Barclay makes the following conclusion, "It was through Moses that God gave the covenant and the Law to Israel. Moses is therefore the mediator between God and his people."[96]

While I concede Barclay's stance, it is also important I stress the fact that the Jews in ancient times had believed that God is unapproachably transcendent. This belief led to a dichotomist view of religion whereby a gulf was created between humanity and divinity with the result that the Jews believed their petition could only reach God through an angelic mediation. Lewis alluded to this as he states, "The theologically significant point is that God cannot be approached at our pleasure, but only when he offers himself for fellowship. From the beginning God taught Israel the real nature of the distance between himself and fallen man. The distance was infinite not only in terms of power, but in terms of purity also."[97] With the belief in angelic

---

92. Athanasius, *On the Incarnation*, 13.
93. John Calvin, *Institutes of the Christian Religion*, trans. Henry Beveridge (Grand Rapids, MI: Eerdmans, 1989), 400.
94. Augustine, *City of God*, 325.
95. Barclay, *Jesus as They Saw*, 335.
96. Barclay, 334.
97. Lewis, *Glory of Christ*, 217.

mediation between man and Yahweh, the Jews placed angel Michael in the capacity of a mediator. Thus, "sometimes in Jewish thought Michael was called the *mesitēs*, the mediator between God and man."[98]

Also, Barclay had shown robustly how *mesitēs* later got currency in pagan religious circle and was popularized in Zoroastrianism which teaches the existence of two great powers: "Oromazes, the power of light, and Areimanius, the power of the dark; and between the two there stands Mithras, who was called the mediator."[99] With all this, Barclay contends that it is in Greek life and thought that the idea of mediation is most deeply rooted. It was the Greek aim to settle all disputes by mediation so that they would never reach the law-courts.[100]

Before now, I have shown that in the Old Testament Moses was the mediator between God and his chosen people the Jews. What was however not established, and to which I now turn, is the particular mediatory function Moses performed. The principal place to begin an investigation into the mediatory role of Moses is the book of Exodus. In chapter 3 God appeared to and assigned him the task of going back to Egypt and asking Pharaoh to let the Hebrews go and worship him. From this point until his death in the wilderness Moses has served as mediator between the Jews and Pharaoh on the one hand and between Yahweh and his chosen people the Jews on the other hand. The Sinaitic scenario in the giving of the Law (Exod 19) is the linchpin that provides a defining example and consummates his role as mediator. First, there is the process of ritual purification which included the solemn washing of garments and abstention from normal sexual relations for over three days (19:10–15).[101]

Second, God's manner of approach dramatically sealed the lesson. In the midst of the thunder and the lightning and the smoke, the strange darkness and the stranger fires, while the mountains trembled and an unearthly trumpet sound grew louder and louder, Yahweh spoke from the midst of his angelic hosts (19:16–25 [see Deut 33:2; Ps 68:17; Gal 3:19; Heb 2:3]).[102]

---

98. Barclay, *Jesus as They Saw*, 335.
99. Barclay, 335.
100. Barclay, 335.
101. Lewis, *Glory of Christ*, 217.
102. Lewis, 217.

Third, the outcome of God's awesome presence and mighty display of majesty and power overwhelmed the people who stayed at distance and cried out and said to Moses, "Speak to us yourself and we will listen. But do not have God speak to us or we will die" (20:19). Lewis understood the Jews' request for Moses and not God to speak to them as the cry for a mediator born out of a sense of holiness and sin, distance and ill-desert. The result was that Moses did indeed become the intermediary between God and the people, the mediator of the old covenant (Exod 24:4–8; 33:7–11; cf. Gal 3:19; Heb 3:2–5). As such he is found pleading with God for the people (Exod 32:31–2) and speaking to the people on behalf of God (Num 12:6–8).[103]

Besides Moses, other clear examples of mediation in the Old Testament included the priest (see heading III below) who represented men to God and God to men (Deut 10:8), the prophet whose duty was to stand in the counsel of the Lord to hear and deliver his word (Jer 23:18, 22) and in a unique way the king, who in his office represented the kingly rule of God and who frequently pleaded for the people before God (2 Sam 24:17; 1 Chron 21:16; 2 Chron 6:21, 42; 14:11; 20:5–12; Isa 37:14–20).[104]

All the mediators I have discussed above were mediators only in their office and delegated functions, not in their persons. For this reason, Old Testament prophecies took a radical dimension and began to point to a future mediator who would fulfill the Adamic covenant of redemption (Gen 3:15), the Abrahamic covenant of promise (Gen 12:1–3) and the Sinaitic covenant (Exod 19:4–6), thereby provide the Davidic ideals (2 Sam 7:8–16 cf. Ps 89:19–37; 132:11–18). Thus, the psalmist presents an impending battle between the messianic king and the kings of the nations (Ps 2) and envisaged the passion that would characterize the mission of the anointed one (Ps 22) before his exaltation (Ps 110).

The Cardinal passages that vividly depict the birth of the mediator employed real imageries rather than abstract images to predict his birth. In the book of Isaiah, the prophet predicts the birth of a child whose name shall be called Immanuel (7:14) and described the child Immanuel in terms reminiscent to the Davidic king (9:6–7). Though great, Immanuel shall be

---

103. Lewis, 217.
104. Lewis, 218.

a servant of the Lord (40–53), a covenant to the people and a light to the nations (42:6), endowed with power and righteousness to proclaim liberty to the captives (61 cf. Luke 4:18), and give sight to the sightless (42:7). Toward the close of the Old Testament era, Micah comprehensively recaps all prophesies concerning the child and described him as one who will be ruler over Israel, whose origins are from of old, from ancient times (Mic 5:2).

As messianic predictions came to a close at the closing of the Old Testament, a new dawn opened with a transition from prediction to fulfilment in the New Testament. Thus, a voice whose owner claimed to had come as a forerunner in the order of Elijah to prepare the way for the coming of the Lord was heard (Mark 1:1–3; Matt 3:1–3; Luke 3:3–6; John 1:23). In John 1:29, John the Baptist, the forerunner, identified Jesus as the Lamb who takes away the sins of the world, the Messiah (1:41), the one Moses wrote about in the Law, and about whom the prophets also wrote – Jesus of Nazareth (1:45). Thus, "In Jesus, every Old Testament mediatory concept or figure comes to a head. He is supremely and in himself Prophet, Priest and King; he is Sacrifice and Offerer; he is Servant and Son; for there is one God, and there is one Mediator between God and men, the man Christ Jesus, who gave himself as a ransom for all"[105] (1 Tim 2:5–6).

As Charles Hodge argues, "Only Jesus Christ has the personal qualifications which the Scriptures clearly teach are necessary for the mediator between God and man."[106] Lewis is right to state, "The new thing as compared with all previous conceptions is that the function of the *mesitēs* [mediator] is related exclusively to Christ . . . Christ's work brought out by the Greek word *mesitēs* are those of attorney and negotiator."[107]

Barclay has outlined three essential functions a *mesitēs* must serve: (1) The *mesitēs* must be able perfectly to represent both parties in the dispute. He must fully understand and sympathize with both. Otherwise, his decision is bound to be prejudiced, one-sided, unjust and inequitable. Jesus is, therefore, the only possible mediator between man and God because he is perfectly God and man. (2) The first duty of the mediator is to establish

---

105. Lewis, 219.

106. Charles Hodge, *Systematic Theology*, abridged ed., ed. Edward N. Gross (Phillipsburg, NJ: P & R, 1992), 364.

107. Lewis, *Glory of Christ*, 219.

communication between the two parties who are in dispute. In the case of Jesus, the problem was not to create connection between God and man, for God never needed to be reconciled to man, the problem was to establish connection between man and God. (3) However, the task of the mediator goes beyond merely setting communication, he has to prove between the two conflicting parties a new relationship in which suspicion has turned to trust, enmity to friendship, and hatred to love. It was the essential task of the mediator to establish, not merely a legal relationship, but a personal relationship in which love is the bond.[108]

The ultimate and best description of Jesus as promised mediator is conspicuously stated in the work of the evangelists who were either eye-witnesses of the Christ event or have inherited the tradition from the apostles as their successors. From apostolic flank, therefore, Jesus as mediator has entered once and for all into the holy of holies to offer priestly sacrifices on behalf of sinners. I turn now to this aspect of Jesus's work of mediation.

III. Christ the High Priest

This section is not concerned to discuss the detailed history of the priesthood in the ancient Near East during Old Testament times, but to show that Jesus Christ is the high priest who epitomizes the Old Testament models of priesthood. W. E. Vine notes that "the Jewish priestly office was established by the Lord in the days of Moses."[109] Barclay has shown why it was essential for the priesthood to emerge since in Old Testament thought it is always dangerous to approach God. To enter into the nearer presence of God is to die, or at least to be in danger of death (Exod 33:20; Deut 5:24; Judg 6:22–23; 13:22). This belief left its mark on the ritual of the Day of Atonement in which only the high priest entered into the holy of holies on behalf of the people.[110] Vine has defined a Priest as, "an authorized minister of adeity who officiates at the altar and in other cultic rites. He performs sacrifices, ritualistic and mediatorial duties; he represents the people before God."[111]

---

108. Barclay, *Jesus as They Saw*, 338.
109. W. E. Vine, *Vine's Complete Expository Dictionary of Old and New Testament Words with Topical Index* (Nashville, TN: Nelson, 2000), 188.
110. Barclay, *Jesus as They Saw*, 348.
111. Vine, *Vine's Complete Expository Dictionary*, 188.

According to Wayne Grudem, the priest exists to offer sacrifices, prayers, and praises to God on behalf of the people. In doing so, they sanctify the people or make them acceptable to come into God's presence, albeit in a limited way.[112] The limited nature of priestly mediation in the Old Testament called for a paradigm shift from something very temporal to a permanent and everlasting redemptive intercession. For this reason, God displaced the Old Testament system of animal sacrifices through Moses by sending his son Jesus Christ as perfect high priest to offer himself once and for all as a fulfilment of God's covenant of redemption made to Adam and God's covenant of promise made to Abraham. John M. Frame has affirmed that through Moses, God displaced his grace through animal sacrifices; through Jesus, he displayed it in his own Son, the Lamb of God. In that sense, Jesus is the great high priest of God.[113]

The transition of priestly function from the Old Testament animal sacrifice which was a type of the dispensation of Moses to New Testament personal sacrifice of Christ has been vividly described in the Epistle to the Hebrews. Robert Duncan Culvert argues that the author of Hebrews explains what a true priest of God is as he portrays Christ's present work in that capacity.[114] For the work of priestly mediation to be perfect and permanent, it was necessary that the mediator should himself be superior to animals and more perfect even than Melchizedek and Aaron who provided an example of the priesthood. The true and perfect mediator must himself be God and man. This assertion perfectly resonates with John Calvin's epigram that "It deeply concerned us, that he who was to be our Mediator should be very God and very Man."[115]

Calvin's notion of very God and very man hints something of the need to have a perfect person who would satisfy God's righteous requirement to stand in the gap in order to make peace between man and God and this makes Jesus the perfect priest since he is at one and the same time perfectly divine and perfectly human; he can bring together man and God because he

---

112. Grudem, *Systematic Theology*, 624.

113. Frame, *Systematic Theology*, 896.

114. Robert Duncan Culver, *Systematic Theology: Biblical and Historical* (Fearn: Christian Focus, 2006), 630.

115. Calvin, *Institutes*, 400.

is man and God. And the writer to the Hebrews drew his inspiration from the Melchizedekian narrative in Genesis which has also been quoted in the book of Psalms as a perfect example to present his idea of the mediatorial work of Jesus Christ the high priest of New Covenant (see Gen 14:17–20). Verses 17 and 18 of the passage read, "After Abram returned from defeating Kedorlaomer and the kings allied with him, the king of Sodom came out to meet him in the valley of Shaveh (that is, the King's Valley). Then Melchizedek king of Salem brought out bread and wine. He was priest of God Most High." To this text, the psalmist alludes, "The Lord has sworn, and he will not change his mind: 'You are a priest forever, in the order of Melchizedek'" (Psalm 110:4).

Genesis 14:17–18 and Psalm 110:4 provide a level ground for the writer to the Hebrews to interpret the Christ event. Oscar Cullmann suggests that "The seventh chapter is the centre of the Epistle to the Hebrews. It uses scriptural proof (Gen. 14 and Ps. 110) to describe Jesus as the true High Priest."[116] Thus, in reference to Melchizedek, the writer to the Hebrews (7:1–17) recaps the event that brought Abraham and Melchizedek together but then added that "Melchizedek means 'king of righteousness' . . . 'King of peace.' Without father or mother, without genealogy, without beginning of days or end of life, resembling the Son of God, he remains a priest forever" (7:2–3). By comparing Jesus with Melchizedek, the author of Hebrews is explicit in his conclusion. For him, Jesus's priesthood is not only a righteous and royal one in the order, which the Melchizedekian priesthood represents, but it also is by far more superior since it has no affinity to human descent and temporality, which the Aaronic priesthood is known for. In this same chapter, the author of Hebrews transforms the Old Testament concept of sacrifice whereby the high priest having been chosen from among his people would first offered up asacrifice for himself before he was made worthy to offer up sacrifices on a daily basis on behalf of his subject. This he did by arguing that unlike the old Levitical system Christ offered up himself (v. 27). In 9:24, 25, and 28, the writer shows a great contrast between the priestly work of Christ and those of other priests.

---

116. Cullmann, *Christology of the New Testament*, 89.

First, the sanctuary in which Jesus entered is not man-made. Second, Christ does not need to go in again and again in a repetitious manner. Third, the blood which Jesus offered, unlike those of animals which characterized the sacrifice of other priests, is Jesus's own blood. Fourth, Jesus sacrificed himself once (cf. 10:1–18) to take away the sins of many. As Barclay argues, "The writer of Hebrew combines two great truths. He sees quite clearly the once-for-allness of the sacrifice of Jesus Christ, and he sees equally clear that the life and death of Jesus Christ are actions in time which show what the heart of God forever is to men."[117] Carl F. H. Henry has also made a profound argument,

> The analogies and contrasts between the Aaronic priesthood and Christ's priesthood are clear. He, as sinless, needed not to off up sacrifice first for Himself as the other priests did; His blood could take away sin, whereas the blood of bulls and goats could not; His work was final while theirs must be repeated. Christ is both priest and victim, both punisher and punished, and herein lies the most profound mystery of Christianity touching the doctrines of the Trinity, incarnation and atonement.[118]

Henry's perspective on Jesus's atonement is critical and it reveals the core concept of our redemption since the Old Testament priestly ritual of the annual sin-offering on the Day of Atonement focused first upon the slaying of the victim in the court of the temple and the subsequent presentation of the blood in the innermost room of the sanctuary were seen to correspond to the death of Christ on the cross which completes the circle of the work of the Trinity, the incarnation and atonement.[119]

The crux of the argument of the writer to the Hebrews is revealed in chapter 8. In this chapter, which ties firmly together with the entire salvation history of God, the author harks back to the various covenants God made with mankind in human history especially with Adam, Abraham, and Moses

---

117. Barclay, *Jesus as They Saw*, 356.

118. Carl F. H. Henry, ed., *Basic Christian Doctrines: Contemporary Evangelical Thought* (Grand Rapids, MI: Baker Books, 1979), 149.

119. Culver, *Systematic Theology*, 631.

and interprets Jesus as the high priest of a New Covenant in the order of Melchizedek. As the high priest after the order of Melchizedek, our Lord Jesus Christ has replaced the obsolete law or covenant which was founded on the Levitical priesthood. This accomplishment merits first mention because it encompasses all the other priestly duties now being carried out by Christ as high priest.[120]

In connection with all Jewish predictions of the coming Messiah who serves as mediator and high priest, the writer to the Hebrews finds what Oscar described as "fulfilled – priesthood of Jesus already foreshadowed in the Old Testament in the puzzling figure of Melchizedek in Genesis 14."[121] To conclude this section, I concede Oscar's idea that the writers of the Bible – especially the writer to the Hebrews – seek justification in the Old Testament for the idea that the priesthood of the Old Covenant is not the last word, but must be replaced by a final priesthood of the New Covenant. He sees this new priesthood as realized in Jesus Christ, who is the priest in an absolute and ultimate sense, the fulfilment of all priesthood and all covenants God has made with Adam, Abraham, and Moses.[122] It is on this ground that this work argues that the biblical models of Jesus as mediator and priest differs remarkably from African primal notion and work of mediation our ancestors are believed to have performed as the next section argues.

Relationship between African Pre-Christian Models and New Testament Christological Models: Biblical Mediation and African Primal Traditions

The notion of mediation is deeply entrenched in Christian theology and African primal beliefs in such a way that the two belief systems are viewed by African theologians as emanating from the same source with practically the same purposes and meaning. For this reason, the mediatory work and priestly function of Jesus Christ seen in laying his life, through which he atoned for the sins of humankind, on the cross at Calvary is compared with the mediatory role African ancestors are believed to have played in

---

120. Culvert, 635.
121. Cullmann, *Christology of the New Testament*, 90.
122. Cullmann, 90.

the ancestral cult. This section argues that it is true that African cultural patterns and forms may resonate with Christian styles or models in their physical outlook but their theological meanings are diametrically different.

I have shown above that the Jews in the Old Testament believed that God could not be approached directly by man (Exod 33:20). Thus, angels were needed to mediate between man and God. With the call of Moses, he became the mediator between Yahweh and the Jews (Exod 20:19). Later on, God instructed him to commission Aaron and Levi and their sons to serve in the capacity of Priests and Levites with a view to mediate between God and man (Exod 28; Lev 8). With the office of the priest now established in Jewish religious belief, the priest represented man to God and God to man (Deut 10:8). With the passage of time, there was a shift in focus from a human mediator to a messianic and eschatological figure who would provide a perfect and final mediation with his own body in fulfillment of predictions of the prophets (Ps 2; 22; Isa 7:14; 9:6–7; 49:6; Mic 5:2). These prophecies were fulfilled in the New Testament to the birth of Jesus Christ as the synoptic gospels carry (Matt 1; Mark 1; Luke 2).

While the synoptic gospels recorded the birth narrative of Jesus the Mediator, the apostles John and Paul, however, point to the Messianic and mediatory work of Jesus Christ. For John, Christ is the Lamb who takes away the sins of the world (John 1:29, 36). For Paul, however, Christ is the one Mediator between God and man (1 Tim 2:5).

All the descriptions above say something about the work Jesus Christ has come to accomplish as Mediator, but it was the writer to the Hebrews who, more than any New Testament author, describes the mediatory work of Jesus Christ vividly. Beginning with the Old Testament pattern in which Melchizedek was a type (Gen 14), he showed how inadequate and imperfect the Aaronic and Old Testament priestly mediation is by contrasting Jesus's work of conciliation and self-sacrifice in which he offered up himself and entered the holy of holiness by means of his own blood thereby fulfilled the Old Testament priestly mediation and became the mediator of a new covenant (Heb 7, 8, 9 and 10).

From what has been said so far, I have demonstrated that Jesus Christ the Messiah and high priest is a mediator of a new covenant. Whether this same work of mediation carried out by Jesus Christ in the Bible is the same as those African ancestors are purported to perform in the primal traditions of Africa is what I am now poised to establish.

In the primal traditions of Africa, ancestors are believed to have survived death and to be living in a spiritual world, but still taking a lively interest in the affairs of their families.[123] According to John S. Mbiti, the living-dead occupy the ontological position between the spirits and men, and between God and man. They in effect speak a bilingual language of human beings whom they recently left through physical death and, of the spirits to whom they are now joined, or of God to whom they are now nearer than when they were in the physical life.[124] Because of this unique position, the living-dead constitute the largest group of intermediaries in African societies.[125] Cletus Chukwuemeka Nwagwugwu has shown robustly how one of the factors that characterize the ancestors is their power of intercession. For him, ancestral intercession is believed to revolve around the daily prayers offered by the ancestors for the welfare of their living kith and kin. Apart from the daily prayers, ancestors are consulted before any major event in the family or society to seek and obtain their permission. Ancestors are also believed to present human problems to the divinities and offering their help and response to the human needs.[126]

For the above stated reason, Masumbuko Mununguri points out, "The Ancestors play the important role of intercessors and arbitrators between the African and his God. That is to ask, to praise, to thank, to call on for help . . . God is the final and most effective recourse."[127] In E. Bolaji Idowu's view, ancestors are mediators in the sense that they abide with their folk on earth invisibly, to aid or hinder them, to promote prosperity or cause adversity. The ancestors are factors of cohesion in African society. To some extent, they are intermediaries between Deity and divinities and their own children.[128] Citing an instance of the critical role ancestors are believed to perform in mediation John Mbiti states, "The Atsam (Chawai) make sacrifices to God, but

---

123. Parrinder, *African Traditional Religion*, 3rd ed., 58.
124. Mbiti, *African Religions and Philosophy*, 69.
125. Mbiti, 69.
126. Nwaogwugwu, *Ancestor Christology*, 91–94.
127. Mununguri, *Closeness of the God*, 11.
128. Idowu, *African Traditonal Religion*, 184–185.

generally through the living-dead who act as intermediaries."[129] Elsewhere Mbiti also notes, "Among the Chawai, it is the heads of the families who sacrifice and pray to God through their living-dead and the Kurama consider the living-dead to be the 'voice' of men in the other world."[130]

From the brief examination of mediation in the traditional religious beliefs and worldview of Africa, this work argues that unlike the biblical mediation which entails the taking of the life of the bulls and goats on the Day of Atonement so that a sinner may be cleansed and made holy and acceptable to God (Lev 16), mediation in the primal traditions of Africa has one overriding motive, it is concerned chiefly with the physical welfare and security of members of community of the living without any reference to the salvation of human souls and eternity. It is obvious that in the traditional religious practices of African societies the best an ancestor was known to offer was to pray daily for the welfare of their living kith and kin as well as to present human problems to the divinities and also to offer their help and response to physical human needs. Among the Chawai people whom Mbiti cite, it was the family head that made the sacrifice and prayed to God through the ancestors.

The implication of the preceding point means primarily that, in Tsam primal beliefs mediation was basically the function of the living family head via the ancestors; since no Tsam (Chawai) ancestor has ever offered up himself and died in the course of mediation for the Chawai people and Tsam community, the same way Jesus Christ offered up himself to take away the sins of many people thereby becoming the high priest and mediator of a new and perfect covenant (Heb 8).

Generally therefore, while no African ancestor has ever offered his blood for his people and community in order to secure eternity for them, Jesus Christ the ultimate sacrifice went into the holy of holies with his personal blood, died and took away the sins of many people (Heb 9:28) and he has saved completely those who come to God through him, because he always lives to intercede for them (Heb 7:25) and he is coming back a second time

---

129. Mibiti, *Concepts of God*, 182.
130. Mibiti, 231.

to take with him those who believe in him to live forever in eternal bliss in heaven (John 14:1–4; Rev 21).

If Jesus is ever living, why should African theologians compare and perceive the living the same with the dead? After all, the angel at the Tomb asked the women, "Why do you look for the living among the dead? (Luke 24:5). So, why should Africans look for a solution to their problem from the dead instead of the ever-loving Lord of glory who is the Lord of lords and the King of kings? Our ancestors are dead and their own personal memories, powers and authorities are obsolete since existentially they are no more in the realm of physicality where memory is active. But Jesus who once died is forever alive and even before his death, he announced that he was not only going to lay down his life voluntarily in order to save those who put their trust in him, but also that he will rise the third day after death again (Matt 16:21; Mark 8:31). Jesus died to free and save people from the bondage of sin and its consequences.

Our ancestors became victims of death and died as powerless and helpless victims of the power of death that subdued them. This is not exactly how Jesus died. Jesus died to render Satan and sin powerless. His death is the death of power and authority. His death gave him power and authority over all powers and principalities. This is not the same with the death of our ancestors. Our deceased ancestors after death have no power and authority over anyone. Klaus Nürnberger is absolutely right when he asserted that "As far as the authority of the deceased is concerned, therefore, the messages of the Old Testament and the New Testament leave no room for doubt: nothing, absolutely nothing, should ever assume authority over God's people, or be given space to stand between God and his people."[131] Similarly, Nürnberger also strongly contends that:

> When God had made himself accessible in Christ, nothing could stand between Christ and his disciples. God is present in Christ; Christ is present in his Spirit. No further mediation is needed. You can turn to God himself, the ultimate cosmic authority, every minute of your life, anywhere in the universe,

---

131. Nürnberger, *Living Dead*, 62.

with any problem you may encounter in any dimension of life. This is typical of the biblical faith.[132]

Perhaps, it is also valid if as Africans we remind ourselves that life in Africa is oriented toward the community and that it is the community that determines the status and authority of the ancestors. Because human life is life in community, ancestral authority is authority in community. Ancestors have no authority as solitary individuals but only as mediators of the life force of the evolving clan. There is no relation with the ancestors that is not, by definition, a communal relationship. As the often-cited adage goes: A person is a person through persons (Sotho: *motho ke motho ka batho*). This is also true for the ancestors.[133]

If Nürnberger's submission is correct, which we know of course it is, could Jesus Christ who has no filial relationship with any African community qualify for an ancestor to any African? One peril with the ancestor model that African theologians have failed to come to terms with when Jesus is portrayed as an ancestor, is that ordinary African folk at the grassroots tend quickly to view Jesus as being equal with one of their helpless deceased parents whom death mercilessly killed and yet is called a mediator. Nürnberger succinctly writes, "If one calls Christ an 'ancestor' in an African environment, for instance, Christ will be understood by the ordinary folk as a deceased father (or mother)."[134]

When one therefore compares biblical mediation with African mediation, the two systems are similar only in form or symbol but are diametrically different in theological meaning and content. Yusufu Turaki has keenly and wittingly shown that in biblical perspective, a mediator is one who stands between God and man in order to reconcile them. To that end, a mediator acts as an intermediary agent in bringing, affecting, or communicating between God and man. By this reasoning, the primary task of a mediator is reconciliation.[135]

Furthermore, Turaki argues, "The task of reconciliation involves personal sacrifice on the part of the mediator. And without this personal sacrifice,

---

132. Nürnberger, 62.
133. Nürnberger, 72.
134. Nürnberger, 100.
135. Turaki, *Unique Christ*, 117.

there is no reconciliation and no mediatorial function."¹³⁶ When, therefore, Jesus Christ offered up himself on the cross of Calvary, he became the final and perfect mediator between God and man. Thus, theologically, the meaning of mediation became entrenched and rooted in the redemptive work of *Yesu/Jesu Kiristo* on the cross at Calvary. For this reason Turaki writes,

> Christ's atoning work on the cross is the basis of God's willingness to make peace with rebellious humanity and to restore fellowship with man and also to restore His fallen creation. At the cross of Calvary, God's wrath and judgment on man were atoned for by Christ's sacrificial death, thus reconciling man to God. The cross of Christ is the foundation of salvation and redemption, repentance and forgiveness, peace, love, grace, justice and reconciliation.[137]

It is important as I conclude this section to stress the fact that the complete package of redemption that Jesus Christ has offered on the cross at Calvary includes the totality of mankind with of course African ancestors since they too looked forward in eager expectation for the coming of the messiah whose sacrificial death achieved reconciliation for all. For this reason, theologically, African ancestors cannot be mediators to warrant comparison in the same proportion that Jesus Christ is the mediator.

It is a historical and theological fact that Jesus suffered outside the city gate to make the people holy through his own blood in order to attain the ultimate goal of a messianic mediator between God and man (Heb 13:12). That is what Christology is all about: the promise, death, and resurrection of Jesus for human redemption. So, in Christian theology, Jesus died to redeem mankind from sin and its consequences. This is not exactly what African ancestors do for their living relations and community.

In our understanding, Christology is not rooted in role and functions of ancestors or in humanity. Because Jesus Christ does what ancestors did or they have similar role and functions does not qualify as Christology. Giving names to Jesus because of what people assume him to be does not qualify for

---

136. Turaki, 117.
137. Turaki, 168.

Christology. Describing Jesus in the eyes of Africans or in their conceptions does not qualify for Christology.[138]

Theologically, we must see beyond the symbolic body and cross of Christ to grasp its true spiritual meaning that brought ultimate redemption and salvation to mankind.[139] When we remove the theological meaning of Christology, we are left with symbols which of course are subject to and warrant comparison. But even so, Jesus and African ancestors are not two of a kind and their difference is not one of degree. The theological difference between Jesus and our ancestors is as big and wide as that between a Creator and creature. For this reason, African ancestors who stand theologically within general revelation cannot be placed in the same position with the almighty God who holds the universe in his hands.

God and the African Ancestors: The Theological Significance of the Being and Otherness of God

In this section, I shall argue that God is beyond time, wholly other and incomparable with great chasm between him and human beings yet he willfully made himself known to mankind. In the light of this, "Christian theology commonly confesses that God is simultaneously hidden and revealed."[140] God revealed himself when he became man in an original and unique event in the incarnation to rescue humanity from the fetters of individual and collective sin.

The coming of God in human flesh is the final revelation of God to humanity. The coming has been prepared by God himself to welcome the mystery for which the promise had been made to Abraham, to Isaac, and to Jacob, the ancestors of Israel and to all those who, in history have been integrated into the great family of believers.[141] Our African ancestors, without being fully conscious of it, were being prepared by God in the time of darkness, so that he could integrate them also into the great mystery of the

---

138. Turaki, "Christianity and African Traditional Religion," vol. 2, 66.
139. Turaki, 67.
140. Victor I. Ezigbo, *Introducing Christian Theologies*, vol. 1, *Voices from Global Christian Communities* (Eugene, OR: Cascade, 2013), 33.
141. Mununguri, *Closeness of the God*, 9.

incarnation of his Word. Their spiritual life, wholly centered on faith in God as goodness and as Creator, was fulfilled in this mysterious meeting between God and humanity.[142]

The theological implication of this statement is that God as goodness and Creator is quantitatively and qualitatively other. And this is important because it lays the foundation for the unique biblical understanding of our finite, historical life as creatures that depend utterly upon his sovereign power and love.[143]

I. God Is Transcendent

John S. Mbiti had confessed that the transcendence of God is a difficult attribute to grasp.[144] Masumbuko gives the definition of transcendence from *Le petitdictionnaire de théologie Catholique* as, "A term which does not refer to a single determined domain of beings and cannot therefore be said of a single category, but necessarily refers to every real or thinking being; for instance: being, unity, truth, goodness, etc."[145] In its philosophical usage, Colin E. Gunton uses transcendence in its plural form and defines it as, "Those notions which we may suppose to embody 'the necessary notes of being.'"[146]

From a theological flank, Gilkey had posited that transcendence is not obvious. However, it connotes that God "is not 'part of' the ordinary world; He is 'beyond,' 'before,' and 'above' the world as its supreme Ruler and Lord; what characterizes the world in weakness, death, and dissolution does not characterize him."[147] Citing sources from Pseudo-Dionysius, Ezigbo describes the transcendent God as, "Indeed the inscrutable One (God) is out of the reach of every rational process. Nor can any words come up to the inexpressible Good, this One, this Source of all unity, this supra-existent Being. Mind beyond mind, word beyond speech."[148] The aforesaid explains why in the

---

142. Mununguri, 9.
143. Langdon Gilkey, *Maker of Heaven and Earth: The Christian Doctrine of Creation in the Light of Modern Knowledge* (Lanham, MD: University Press of America, 1985), 5, 22.
144. Mibiti, *Concepts of God*, 12.
145. Mununguri, *Closeness of the God*, 17.
146. Colin E. Gunton, *The One, the Three and the Many: God, Creation and the Culture of Modernity*, Bampton Lectures, 1992 (Cambridge: Cambridge University Press, 2004), 136.
147. Gilkey, *Maker of Heaven*, 85.
148. Ezibgo, *Introducing Christian Theologies*, 33.

primal traditions of Africa the transcendence of God is expressed differently. For example, the Akan praise him as, "He who is there now as from ancient time." That is, He who endures forever. The Tonga refers to him as "The Ancient of Days." The Ngombe, who live in the forest address him as, "The Everlasting One of the forest." The Mende call God "The High-up One."[149]

The various ways of describing God in Africa have seriously undermined and have also failed to bring up the real and deeper theological meaning of transcendence since God could be construed to mean any object that is more up there than other things and merely older than his creatures. Thus, Gilkey argues that a traveler on a well-piloted spaceship is more certain of finding God in heaven than is an earthbound churchman.[150] For this reason he proposes that transcendence should be viewed in two perspectives: a literal and divine sense. For him, the idea of divine transcendence involves three major concepts, two of which have to do with "ontology," or the problem of being and existence, and the third has to do with "epistemology," or the problem of the knowledge of God. Gilkey believed that the God who is not ontologically transcendent and unconditioned is simply not a God who can save his creatures.[151]

In a bid to demonstrate what he meant by divine transcendence, Gilkey shows that God transcends other beings in the mode of his existence. As traditional theology has put it: God "exists" in a different way than do other things; he is differently, he possesses a different mode or kind of being. While other things have existence, God is existence, for his essence involves his existence.[152]

Theologically, God is the source of all and different from his finite and dependent creatures. He is self-sufficient in his being, *a se* (self-derived) rather than *ab alio* (derived from elsewhere), unconditioned. He does not receive his being from any force outside of himself. As Gilkey puts it, "No other factors have united in a happy harmony to produce and maintain him. Since he is the source of existence, and not its recipient, he is not at all dependent upon other things to bring him into being; and correspondingly

---

149. Mibiti, *Concepts of God*, 12–13.
150. Gilkey, *Maker of Heaven*, 85.
151. Gilkey, 86.
152. Gilkey, 86.

he is not at all dependent upon outside things to maintain him in being."[153] If, then, he is in this sense "uncreated" by anything beyond himself because he is the Creator of all else, his existence must be derived from himself alone.[154]

It follows from the discussion above that God's being is in some sense eternal and not transient in the proportion of mortal human beings. Gilkey argues that this does not mean that time is negated in God and the passage of years. Rather, as the creator of time, as the preserver and ruler of history, and above all as he who enters time for man's salvation, the Christian God can never be put out of touch with time. The eternity of God, therefore, means that God transcends the temporal passage of creaturely existence, as his self-sufficiency transcends the dependent contingency of our existence.[155] To this end, Christian thought has always maintained that God is the eternal creator of time, related to temporality but transcendent to its passage.

The transcendence of God beyond the finite is thus a significant and an in-depth theological aspect of the biblical understanding of God and of his relation to his creatures. In that understanding God comes into a real world that he has created and rules, that is not himself but on the contrary is estranged from himself, a world that he judges and then redeems.[156] For the Psalmist, God is from everlasting to everlasting (Ps 90:2). For this reason, this work argues that God cannot be really "like" an elder statesman with a white beard and a kindly face or the African archetypical man as African theologians and biblical scholars portrays him in their contextualization and inculturation methodologies. For that methodological conception even analogically pictures him as an ordinary being existing as do other African ancestors and so different from them only in that he is bigger, older, and more "up there" but not qualitatively different from them in mode of being since they too live everlastingly to mediate for their kith and kin the same way Jesus Christ lives to intercede for those who put their trust in him (Heb 7:25).[157]

---

153. Gilkey, 87.
154. Gilkey, 87.
155. Gilkey, 88.
156. Gilkey, 96.
157. Gilkey, 92.

II. God Is Immanent

Gilkey has invited us to concede the fact that immanence and transcendence are polar concepts and, like reason and faith, cannot do without each other. Accordingly, there can be no absolute immanence which contains no semblance of transcendence.[158] *Le petit dictionaire de théologie Catholique* defines immanence as, "Something which does not go beyond a certain limit."[159] Thus the philosophies of immanence, properly speaking, are materialism, monism, and pantheism, insofar as they limit the being to what is finite or what can be an object of experience.[160] A timely illustration which vividly paints a picture of what immanence means in traditional African beliefs is the Lugbara conception of God. Among the Lugbara, God is considered to be "bad" and "dangerous." Thus, people think of him anthropomorphically, believing that as *adro* he comes into direct contact with his creatures on earth, and lives temporarily in the rivers, large trees, thickets, and mountains.[161] The Turu have a similar concept of God's immanence. For them, God is immanent in the bush, and he manifests himself in the form of the lion, hyena, python, lightning, storms, pools of water, and high wind.[162] The Bamileké also believe that God is never absent. Linguistically, they say God is *sie sie*. This phrase has been interpreted among the Bamileké as meaning God is present.[163]

The various mosaic African theologians employ to depict the immanence of God reveals that he is definitely part of their daily concerns. An essential aspect through which Africans portray the immanence of God is shown through the names which affirm his antecedence and primacy in every place. For example, among the Chawai, God is said to be, "*Yie chi yhin or kut*," that is, the overall master of the universe; "*Nosheazinwut na gbwom-gbwom-gbwom*," that is, the one who is forever with us.

---

158. Gilkey, 108.

159. *Le petit dictionaire de théologie Catholique* quoted in Mununguri, *Closeness of the God*, 26.

160. Mununguri, 26.

161. Mibiti, *Concepts of God*, 16.

162. Mibiti, 16.

163. Mununguri, *Closeness of the God*, 26.

Here these descriptive terms or words reveal something of God's general revelation. Simply put, before the advent of Christianity to Africa, Africans had an implicit revelatory knowledge of God in the primal traditions of their ancestors. It is this knowledge that enabled them to describe God linguistically in terms reminiscent of Christian theological terminologies. For when we speak of God in Christian theology, we use such words as, "Reality, existence, essence, being, power, ground, eternity – words derived from and clarified by philosophical analysis, and by the metaphysical quest for ultimate reality the same way Africans describe God in their languages as the ultimate Reality or Being."[164]

For the above reason, this chapter, and the entire work, argues that when we discuss God's transcendence and immanence – his revelatory self-disclosure, his purposive freedom and intentionality, and his dynamic, living relations to history and the world – we find ourselves inevitably using terms and symbols (anthropomorphically) from human personal and historical life to make sense of his being.[165] But we must, however, be conscious of the vast chasm between this inscrutable God – the ultimate reality or being who is out of the reach of every rational process. It is my conviction that the gap and fulfillment presupposition – represented by the contextualization and inculturation methodologies employed by African ancestor Christology theologians to portray who Jesus Christ is and what he did – cannot adequately make sense of the mysterious God since such a method does not reflect Africa's linguistic perception of Jesus Christ in the continent. For this reason, this study calls for African Linguistic Affinity methodology which identifies Jesus as *Yesu/Jesu* instead of using African narrative, analogy and metaphysics which recognises Jesus as an ancestor since Africans prefer to call Jesus by his biblical names.

III. God, the First and Second Commandments and Ancestor Worship

The Ten Commandments or the Decalogue have been of inestimable importance for the development of history and contemporary religious and

---

164. Gilkey, *Maker of Heaven*, 115.
165. Gilkey, 115–116.

cultural life.¹⁶⁶ According to Martin Buber; the Ten Commandments are not part of an impersonal codex governing an association of men. They were uttered by an I and addressed to a Thou. They begin with the every one of them and I address the Thou in person.¹⁶⁷

Thus, the Lord declared to Israel, "I am the Lord your God" (Exod 20:2a). Lehman Strauss argues that in this statement Yahweh declares his "eternality and self-existence in the divine name, 'I am Jehovah.'"¹⁶⁸ G. Campbell Morgan has noted that Jehovah is a combination of three Hebrew words that mean "I am He that will be, I am He that is, I am He that was."¹⁶⁹ Morgan has offered an essential analysis of the name Jehovah in the following words;

> The very name brings man into the presence of the Supreme, the Eternal, the Self-existent God, Who is because He is—a great and perpetual mystery to the finite mind of man, and for the most part beyond all human analysis. If the mind reaches out to the limitless stretches of future generations, God says, "I am He that will be." If a man thinks of the present moment, with all its marvellous manifestations of life and order and mystery and revelation, God says, "I am He that is." If the mind is carried as far back as possible into infinite spaces of the past, God says, "I am He that was."¹⁷⁰

The theological significance of the Hebrew meaning of Jehovah is glaring. It reveals in no uncertain terms that Yahweh is the Omnipresent, Omniscient and Omnipotent God who is neither constrained by time and space nor limited by the laws of nature. For this reason, the finite mind of man finds it very difficult to dissect the mystery of this God who revealed himself to mankind in the man Jesus of Nazareth.

---

166. Alan F. Johnson, ed., *God Speaks to an X-Rated Society* (Chicago: Moody, 1973), 8.

167. Nahum N. Glatzer, "*What Are We to Do about the Ten Commandments?*" in *On the Bible: Eighteen Studies by Martin Buber*, ed. Nahum N. Glatzer (New York: Syracuse University Press, 2000), 118.

168. Lehman Strauss, *The Eleven Commandments* (Neptune, NJ Loizeaux Brothers, 1975), 24.

169. G. Campbell Morgan, *The Ten Commandments* (Chicago: The Bible Institute Colportage Association, 1901), 16.

170. Morgan, *Ten Commandments*, 16–17.

Since without his self-disclosure to man God is incomprehensible, the Ten Commandments serve as a pointer to his person and what his ethical standards are. For this reason, he speaks through the Commandments and gives it as law or constitution to the emerging state of Israel to guide her in the conduct of her affairs while as an independent state in the land of promise. Peter C. Graigie wrote that the Ten Commandments are recorded twice in the Old Testament: they appear first in the description of the formation of Sinai covenant (Exod 20:2–17) and are repeated in the description of the renewal of the covenant on the plain of Moab (Deut 5:6–21).[171]

The Commandments which are described as having been written on two tablets – one belonging to Israel and the other to God – so that both parties to the covenant had a copy of the legislation were initially part of a constitution and served as state law of the emerging nation of Israel. The fundamental principle upon which the constitution was established was love. God had chosen his people and freed them from slavery only because he loved them. In turn, he had one fundamental requirement of them – that they loved him with the totality of their being (Deut 6:5).[172] Love for Yahweh is, therefore, the underlying basis for the first two commandments through which Israel is to express her love for God by abandoning all other gods and clinging to him.

In the first commandment, we come face to face with the object of worship, "You shall have no other gods before me" (Exod 20:3; Deut 5:7). To have no other gods besides Yahweh means that he would have no any object worshipped by human beings for the rivalry. He alone is to be worshipped in spirit and in truth. Thus, "God calls men into his presence, to immediate worship."[173] Morgan describes what worship is and what it is not, "They worship, not when they listen to preaching, not when they are attentive to the form and fashion of music, not when they are thinking of a table upon which the emblems are spread; but when they pass through the preaching,

---

171. Peter C. Graigie, "The Ten Commandments," in *Evangelical Dictionary of Theology*, ed. Walter A. Elwell (Grand Rapids, MI: Baker Academic, 2001), 1171.

172. Graigie, "Ten Commandments," 1171.

173. Morgan, *Ten Commandments*, 35.

and when they pass beyond the emblems, and when they are face to face with God."[174]

The foregoing explains why Thomas Watson points out that the sum of this commandment is that we sanctify God in our hearts, and give him a precedence over all created beings.[175] These created beings are many, and sometimes we bow down to them consciously, subconsciously and even unconsciously. Johnson had taken this assertion further by pointing out that probably few of us have ever bowed down physically before graven images of wood or stone, but have all had our idols, whether they were persons, occupations, pleasures, or possessions.[176] Craigie sheds light and defines idol as, "persons, or even things, that would disrupt the primacy of the relationship with God."[177] J. Vernon McGee sees idolatry as "Anything that takes first place in your heart. Anything that you give yourself to, especially in abandonment, becomes your 'god.'"[178]

One prominent idol of our age, which Bruce Ellis Benson points out, is contemporary ideologies. He keenly notes, "Ideologies and Idolatry are synonymous since when held dogmatically, idols are often held even more so since they are our creations."[179] It is precisely for this reason – that human beings can manufacture their own gods and serve them that the first commandment addresses itself against idolatry. As Strauss argues, "Since man must have a god and have not the true God, he invents a god to suit himself."[180] Morgan shows the imminent peril that occurs when man invents a god and worships it. He wrote, "Whenever a man stops short of that face-to-face worship of the Eternal God, he is working ruin to his own character because he is breaking the commandment of God."[181]

We can deduce from the foregoing that God's intention in giving the first commandment is to prevent mankind from false religious beliefs and

---

174. Morgan, 35.
175. Thomas Watson, *The Ten Commandments* (London: Banner of Truth, 1962), 37.
176. Johnson, *God Speaks*, 19.
177. Graigie, "Ten Commandments," 1172.
178. J. Vernon McGee, *Love Liberation & The Law: The Ten Commandments* (Nashville, TN: Nelson, 1995), 17.
179. Benson, *Graven Ideologies*, 24.
180. Strauss, *Eleven Commandments*, 27.
181. Morgan, *Ten Commandments*, 35.

practices that replace the worship of the true God and thus shifts people's allegiance away from God. Thus, the first commandment, "Prohibits idol-worship, image-worship, and magic-worship – and to this end it is necessary to recognize him as he is, and not in the shape with which people would like to endow him."[182] Johnson makes a profound declaration that to worship God as the only true God commits us to him in full trust and in obedience that recognizes him as the final authority for life. Such worship fixes the ultimate standards and destiny of those who acknowledge him.[183]

Graigie has shown plausibly that the possibility of worshipping gods other than the Lord has been eliminated in the first commandment. The second commandment prohibits the Israelites from making images of the Lord. To make an image of God in the shape or form of anything in the world is to reduce the Creator to something less than his creation, and to worship such an image would be false. The temptation for Israel to worship God in the form of an image must have been enormous, for images and idols occurred in all religions of the ancient Near East.[184] For this reason, God warned Israel of the danger of substituting him for some other local deities or human images they would meet and be tempted to worship in Canaan. Of course, the bronze snake Moses made in Numbers 21:4–9 to provide a remedy for the victims of the snake bite which became an object of worship in a later generation of Jews provides a good illustration and indeed reveals man's predilection for idolatry and distorted concept of God (see 2 Kings 18:4).

As Strauss stressed, man's worship of God is not correct until he has the right concept of God. What God does forbid in the second commandment is any attempt on the part of man to represent God by any natural means like the bronze snake image or the image of any man who before death attained personality cult. This is prohibited simply because God is a Spirit and he must be worshipped in spirit and in truth.[185] Johnson has confirmed that tremendous implications for personality development are in this

---

182. Glatzer, "What Are We to Do," 108.
183. Johnson, *God Speaks*, 20.
184. Graigie, "Ten Commandments," 1172.
185. Strauss, *Eleven Commandments*, 38, 42.

commandment. In addition to the graven images of stone and wood are graven images of the personality.[186]

Against the background of idol worship, God warned Israel to not only desist from practising it but to be careful not to transmit same to posterity. Morgan shows how a distorted worship of God could form a chain system to be inherited by one's children for several generations. He writes, "The prohibition is that their idea of worship will be transmitted to their children, and their children's idea of worship will be transmitted to their children so that the wrong that men do themselves when they misrepresent God is a wrong which they are doing to their children likewise."[187] Morgan shows further the devastating consequences of transmitting to one's posterity the wrong belief system and its worship herein,

> It is a solemn thing thus to pass on to children a wrong conception of God; it is the most awful thing a man can do. When a man puts something, as the object of his worship, in the place of God, he passes on the same practice to his offspring. What a terrible heritage he is thus handing down to the child![188]

While the first commandment deals strictly with the whom of Christian worship, the second commandment describes the how of that worship. Together, the first and second commandments tell us that Yahweh alone is worthy of worship in spirit and in truth. Strauss summarizes the teaching of the first two commandments of the Bible in the following terms, "The teaching of the first commandment is that there is only one true God to be worshipped. The teaching of the second is that God is a Spirit, and therefore he can be worshipped in spirit and in truth only. The first forbids false gods. The second forbids false worship of the true God."[189] Thus, God is not to be likened to an image or the likeness of anything in heaven, on earth or the earth beneath.

> All ideas, portraitures, shapes, images of God, whether by effigies or pictures, are here forbidden. It is unlawful to worship

---

186. Johnson, *God Speaks*, 28.
187. Morgan, *Ten Commandments*, 33.
188. Morgan, 34.
189. Strauss, *Eleven Commandments*, 37.

God by an image; for it is against the homily of the Church, which runs thus: "The images of God, our Saviour, the Virgin Mary, are of all others the most dangerous; therefore the greatest care ought to be had that they stand not in temples and churches."[190]

You need no man-made image to assist you in your worship and understanding of the person and work of Jesus Christ.[191] To worship God in the form of a wood image (or any perceived personality) is to break the commandment. God is transcendent and infinite, and always greater than any words a creature can use of him. The second commandment thus guards the ultimate greatness and mystery of God.[192]

With the clear established norm for Christian worship which prohibits the likening of God to an image, personality, graven images, and effigies and at the same time bowing down to them, this chapter argues that the practise of ancestor worship in African Traditional Religion falls within the prohibitions of the first two commandments described in the Bible. I arrived at this point because this work has already established the fact that in the primal tradition of Africa, ancestors are worshipped (see ch. 4).

E. Bolaji Idowu and Harry Sawyer vehemently argue that when Africans pray and pour libation to their dead ancestors, they certainly worship them. Among the Yoruba for instance, Idowu wrote, "Egungun designates the spirit of the deceased to which worship is offered at the *ancestral shrine*. We may therefore summarise the present discussion so far by saying that Africans do worship their ancestors as they do their divinities. The worship consists of prayers, sacrifices, and divination on communal occasions or prayers and divinations on private occasions."[193]

Masamba ma Mpolo also affirms that "The belief in the ancestors is part of the totality of life, including worship, veneration, prayer, respect, reconciliation and therapy."[194] Philip John Neimark, more than Idowu, Sawyer and Mpolo had articulated the notion of ancestor worship in African

---

190. Watson, *Ten Commandments*, 44–45.
191. Strauss, *Eleven Commandments*, 48.
192. Graigie, "Ten Commandments," 1172.
193. Parratt, *Practice of Presence*, 55 (emphasis added).
194. Mpolo and Kalu, *African Pastoral Studies*, 103.

traditional belief. In his, *The Way of the Orisa: Empowering Your Life Through the Ancient African Religion of Ifa*, Neimark argues in many pages that ancestors are worshipped in Africa.[195] Herbert Spencer as quoted by Idowu sums up the debate by saying that ancestor worship is the root of every religion.[196]

With the various submissions of erudite scholars and founding fathers like Idowu, Mpolo, Sawyer, Neimark, and Spencer, it is obvious that ancestors are worshipped in Africa and this work argues that it is out of the desire to preserve their memories that African theologians and biblical scholars find it convenient to switch from ancestor worship to ancestor Christology by giving ancestors a radical definition in Christian theology. For this reason, they identify Jesus Christ as an ancestor. This of course is against the prohibition of likening God to an image, effigy and personality in the first two commandments given by God. Since such images, effigies and personalities are not only analogically compared with God but are also worshipped in the non-Christian religions the world over, this work wishes to call attention to the danger of idolatry in the name of ancestor Christology by imaging Jesus Christ the second person of the Trinity as an ancestor.

The theological implication for the existing formulation is that the Godhead has become an ancestor since according to the teaching of *perichoresis*, the three divine persons are all bound up with each other, so that one is not one without the other.[197] To this end, the study proposes an African Linguistic Affinity approach to the study of Jesus Christ instead of the unsuitable contextualization and inculturation methodologies that use analogy and metaphysics to give Jesus the image of an ancestor. Since Africans are more inclined to call Jesus by his biblical names, I offer an African Linguistic Affinity methodology to the study of Christ. Thus, the study proposes *Yesu/Jesu* Christology as an option to ancestor Christology.

---

195. In chapter 2 of the work cited above, Phillip John Neimark deals extensively with the subject of ancestor worship in Africa arguing that one finds fulfillment in life only through the worship they offer to the departed relations. For Neimark, the ritual process of ancestor worship can provide us with profound, quantifiable changes in our everyday lives. For detail discussion on ancestor worship, see Neimark, *Way of the Orisa*; Mpolo and Kalu, *African Pastoral Studies*; and Parratt, *Practice of Presence*.

196. Idowu, *African Traditional Religion*, 178.

197. Gunton, *The One, the Three*, 153.

God and Theological Language – Anthropomorphism

John S. Feinberg rightly notes that various motifs and metaphors used in Christian theology to describe God speak not only of the different roles he plays and of how he acts in our world but also of the relationships he enters into with his creations.[198] To describe God's relationships with his creatures, the Jews who wrote the Old Testament employed human characteristics and expression to make sense of God's acts in human history. A generally accepted theological language used in theological discourse to make sense of God's dealings with humankind is anthropomorphism. According to Dewey M. Beegle, anthropomorphism is derived from the Greek *anthrōpos* (man) and *morphē* (form) – a figure of speech that describes God as having human form (Exod 15:3; Num 12:8), with feet (Gen 3:8; Exod 24:10), hands (Exod 24:11; Josh 4:24), mouth (Num 12:8; Isa 40:5), and heart (Hos 11:8), but in a wider sense the term also includes human attributes and emotions (Gen 2:2; 6:6; Exod 20:5; Hos 11:8).[199]

Anthropomorphic expression was relevant in the context of the Old Testament because the Jews, to whom the revelation to God first came, needed to ascertain beyond doubt the magnitude of love God had for them. Beegle had opined that anthropomorphic concepts were

> absolutely necessary if the God of Israel was to remain a God of the individual Israelite as well as of the people as a whole. . . . For the average worshipper . . . it is very essential that his god be a divinity who can sympathize with his human feelings and emotions, a being whom he can love and fear alternately, and to whom he can transfer the holiest emotions connected with memories of father and mother and friend.[200]

For this reason, the Jews made use of anthropomorphic expression to describe God. A common parlance used in Christian theological discourse to describe and compare God with a phenomenon is through the use of metaphor and analogy.

---

198. John S. Feinberg, ed., *No One Like Him: The Doctrine of God* (Wheaton, IL: Crossway, 2006), 55.

199. Dewey M. Beegle, "Anthropomorphism," in *Evangelical Dictionary of Theology*, ed. Walter A. Elwell (Grand Rapids, MI: Baker Academic, 2001), 67.

200. Beegle, "Anthropomorphism," 67.

Metaphor

In Scripture, particularly the Old Testament, a wide assortment of images picture God's relationship to his creatures. An initial category of scriptural images is taken from family life and interpersonal relationships. It includes the image of God as a father (Exod 4:22), mother (Deut 32:18), husband (Hos 3:1–3) and friend (Jer 3:4; 2 Chr 20:7; Isa 41:8; Jas 2:23). The second category of images depicts God in terms of work, crafts, professions, and vocations. One of the best known and loved metaphors is God as shepherd. In Ezekiel 34:31 he is shepherd to his people Israel.[201]

The Old Testament use of metaphor continues in the New Testament. For example, the christological affirmations of the New Testament are metaphors since Jesus was not literally a door, a vine, light, or a loaf of bread. Moreover, the multiplicity of images points to their metaphoricity.[202] Putting the images into a single sentence makes the point: Jesus is the Word of God, wisdom of God, Son of God, Lamb of God, light of the world, great high priest, and so forth. He was all of this. That is, it is not that one of these is literally true and the rest "only" metaphors. Rather, all are metaphors. Metaphors can, of course, be true, but their truth is not literal.[203] Nürnberger is correct to contend that once we take the meaning of metaphorical wording literally, they become not only contradictory but idolatrous.[204] Elsewhere he asserts, "Metaphors may not be reified (= treated as if they were real entities out there) and given out as 'eternal truths.' Deductions from such assumed truths can easily hover off into the otherworldly sphere of speculation."[205] For this reason, Borg and Wright suggested that the essential meaning of the metaphor is "to see as." Thus, to say "Jesus is the true vine" is to see him as the true vine, and to say "Jesus is the Son of God" is to see him as the Son of God. The point is not to believe that Jesus is literally the real vine or Son of God as if these were facts about him. But to see him as the true vine

---

201. Feinberg, *No One Like Him*, 57.
202. Marcus J. Borg and N. T. Wright, *The Meaning of Jesus: Two Visions* (New York: HarperOne, 2007), 150.
203. Borg and Wright, *Meaning of Jesus*, 150.
204. Nürnberger, *Living Dead*, 100.
205. Nürnberger, 107.

implies taking him very seriously as the one upon whom we, as the branches, depend for life, and as one whose life flows through us.[206]

Borg and Wright further shed light that christological metaphors are confessional. That is, they are a confession of faith, not statements of real fact to be taken literally. The christological metaphors and the more conceptual language of the Nicene Creed make a cumulative claim about the significance of Jesus. Taken together, and put very compactly, they claim that Jesus is the decisive relation of God.[207] For them, the recognition that this is metaphorical language is crucial. When we literalize metaphors, we get nonsense. We also lose the metaphors, with their rich resonances of meaning.[208]

Analogy

The first philosopher who did much to popularize the notion of transcendentalism was Thomas Aquinas who himself was influenced by the Arabic philosopher Avicenna. Avicenna attempted to apply the notion of the primacy of being to God by "asserting that God was existence itself, without existence."[209] Having drawn inspiration from Avicenna his paragon, Aquinas begins to apply his interest to an understanding of God and of his world. With being as primary, how should we think about God?[210] In answer to this question, Aquinas propounded that God is one, the only one as it happens, in whom essence and existence are identical. That is, in God, essence and existence cannot be separated or in any substantial way distinct.[211]

While Aquinas wrestled with the notion of being and concluded that God is the ultimate being, Meister Eckhart his successor at the University of Paris disagrees with his predecessor's metaphysical ideas. In discussing being, Eckhart wants to maintain that there is being above which God himself is.[212] It is in the context of discussions of being as a transcendental notion that modern and contemporary philosophers have begun to wonder if it is proper

---

206. Borg and Wright, *Meaning of Jesus*, 150.
207. Borg and Wright, 155.
208. Borg and Wright, 152–153.
209. Oliphint, *Reasons (for Faith)*, 49.
210. Oliphint, 49.
211. Oliphint, 50.
212. Oliphint, 53.

and accurate to speak of God in terms of "being."[213] For John Calvin, it is more than accurate to attribute being to God. He wrote, "From the power of God we are naturally led to consider his eternity, since that from which all other things derive their origin must necessarily be self-existent and eternal."[214] Oliphint also quoted him saying, "(Jehovah) implies that being, or really to be, is in the strict sense applicable to God alone; for although unbelievers may attempt to tear his glory to piece, he continues perfectly and unchanged."[215]

It was in response to this dilemma that Aquinas set out the notion of analogy and has since then become the pacesetting and distinguished Christian effort in Christian thought to workout properly, a theological understanding of the "how of creation by analogy from our common experience."[216] This explains why David K. Clark wrote, "By a nearly inviolable tradition, any discussion of how language refers to God must begin with St Thomas Aquinas and his idea of analogical predication. This is the classical treatment of religious language."[217]

For Aquinas, the question of religious language arises from the intersection of two realities: the words we use and words outside their native habitat.[218] In the words we use and those outside their native habitat, Aquinas shared two boundaries that evangelical commitment layout for us. He wanted to hold to the infinity of God and to the meaningfulness of human language regarding God.[219] For this reason, he used the theory of analogy or analogical predication to describe how the infinite Creator God relates with finite created beings in the universe. In his famous trilemma, Aquinas offered three options: univocity, equivocity, and analogy each of which describes the semantic relationship between the meaning of a specific word in one context and its significance in another.[220]

---

213. Oliphint, 52.
214. Calvin, *Institutes*, 56.
215. Oliphint, *Reasons (for Faith)*, 56.
216. Gilkey, *Maker of Heaven*, 70.
217. Clark, *To Know and Love God*, 386.
218. Clark, 386.
219. Clark, 388.
220. Clark, 389.

In univocal predication, what is attributed to one thing is identical when attributed to another.[221] Thus, univocally speaking in Nigeria, for example, people could say Kola is bitter, and at the same time, they might say John is bitter. Here, bitterness would be an identical property, relating as it does both to Kola and to John.

In equivocal predication, what is attributed to one thing is in no way similar or identical to the same attribution given to another thing. For instance, when we speak equivocally and say Kola is bitter, and John is bitter, bitterness would mean something entirely different when applied to Kola, on the one hand, and then to John since John's bitterness will not have the literalness proportionally Kola has. These illustrations allow for what is true attribution and what is otherwise.

Illuminating as this illustration is, Aquinas would have rejected it because in both univocity and equivocity the predicates of bitterness attributed to Kola and John could not be ascribed either univocally or equivocally to them since essentially Kola and John do not share the same nature. Thus, their bitterness is not proportionally the same. Furthermore, Aquinas rejected the two concepts because while univocity entails anthropomorphism, equivocity leads ultimately to agnosticism.[222] The rejection of univocity and equivocity led Aquinas to analogical predication or "analogy of proper proportionality."[223]

Even though he admitted that there are limits to how words can function analogically and the phrase "proper proportionality" expresses that limitation, nonetheless, Aquinas went ahead to apply the concept of good to argue that goodness could be attributed to God and to people analogically but not in the same proportion since God is truly infinite and distinct from human beings. For this reason, he concluded that "Analogy, at least in this instance, requires a qualitative distinction between two (or more) predicates. That is, there is one term used in two senses, yet the two senses are somehow related."[224]

Going by the definition of analogy offered by Aquinas and his conclusion that analogy requires a qualitative distinction between two or more

---

221. Oliphint, *Reasons (for Faith)*, 98.
222. Clark, *To Know and Love*, 389.
223. Clark, 390.
224. Oliphint, *Reasons (for Faith)*, 98–99.

predicates and that one term can be used in two senses which are somewhat related, I find problematic the methodology that applies analogy to depict the person and work of Jesus Christ in Africa; since Jesus and African ancestors are not only diametrically different humanly speaking but also based on the principles of analogical proportionality they do not proportionally share the same status and body elements.

There is, therefore, a huge gap between Jesus the creator and African ancestors, his creatures. We should also note who an ancestor is in the African context? Frankly speaking, an ancestor is one who belongs by biology and blood tie to a family. So, how humanly speaking could Jesus Christ be an ancestor to any African proportionally his great-grandfather is? African theologians and biblical scholars should not be apt to forget that even Aquinas who propounded the theory of univocity and equivocity himself became dissatisfied with his proposal and rejected it. Sticking to the concept of analogy of proportionality, Aquinas was not also contented with his methodology since he could say God is good and people are good but goodness would mean something completely and totally different when applied to God, on the one hand, and then to people, on the other.[225]

African theologians would save us from the error of ancestor christological methodology if only they remember that "there are limits to how words can function analogically, and the phrase 'proper proportionality' expresses that limitation. It means that God and created beings have properties in proportion to their modes of being, that is, in proportion to being infinite and finite respectively."[226] Clark writes,

> God's nature is infinite, eternal, omniscient, and morally pure. My nature is finite and temporal, ignorant and weak due to limitation and sin, and polluted by moral failure. God and I are simply not comparable. God and I are not on the same scale ontologically, epistemologically, morally, or in any other way. God is qualitatively different from me. God is eternal and

---

225. Oliphint, 98.
226. Clark, *To Know and Love*, 390.

incorporeal. His being is infinite, Wholly other or transcendent. The difference between us is not measurable, but infinite.[227]

Regarding theological language used to compare human beings and God, Clark had shown from the assertions of Aristotle and Cicero how deficient the use of metaphor could be to make sense of God. Quoting Aristotle he writes, "Metaphor takes the name of one object and gives it to another object."[228] For Cicero as Clark endeavoured to show, "Metaphor is an inferior type of comparison."[229] Ultimately with respect to metaphoric language, Clark argues, "A metaphor is a linguistic odd couple. It places two unrelated words next to each other, and by allowing them to interact, it creates new meaning."[230] For this reason, Clark argues, "If all theology is metaphor and all metaphor is irreducible to literal speech, then theology does not assert anything about God."[231]

From the foregoing, I concur with Tersur Aben who said, "I do not think that we can support an analogous predication of ancestor to Jesus Christ either on the basis of Scriptural attestation to Jesus Christ or African traditional religions since analogies are applied to things that have some sort of commonality between them."[232] For me, comparing Jesus Christ with African ancestors as formulated by Ntetem, Bujo and Nyamiti is a clear case of compromise and deviation from biblical Christianity. Consequently, these theologians find it comfortable and convenient to add to the Bible traditions that Tertullian and Athanasius waged war against in the early church. Terry L. Johnson is right to assert, "The case can be made that every corruption of biblical Christianity begins by compromising the principle of sufficiency. Every deviation from the Christianity established by Christ and the apostles begins by adding to the Bible or taking away from it. Every deviation is the Bible plus or minus something."[233] It is precisely because of the fear of the

---

227. Clark, 387.
228. Clark, 403.
229. Clark, 403.
230. Clark, 404.
231. Clark, 405.
232. Aben, "Ntetem on the Ancestorship," 37.
233. Terry L. Johnson, *The Case for Traditional Protestantism: The Solas of the Reformation* (Edinburgh: Banner of Truth, 2004), 38.

tendency to deviate from biblical Christianity that this work proposes an African Linguistic Affinity Christology methodology which uses African linguistic names for Jesus Christ as *Yesu* or *Jesu*, as an eschatological deliverer of Africans in accordance to God's promise to redeem fallen human beings from the power of Satan and sin.

As I am convinced, this methodology would help Africans to differentiate Christianity which is a religion with a living originator from any other world religion which founder is death. The quantitative difference between African Traditional Religion and Christianity is Christ and the qualitative difference between Christ and African ancestors is the empty tomb. The empty tomb is the everlasting testimony that the one who once occupied it is risen and he lives to intercede for those who draw nearer to him. For this reason, the one who defied death and resurrected triumphantly cannot proportionally be compared with the one who subsumed to nature and is occupying his grave until the day of Christ.

African Ancestors and Biblical Eschatology: Christ and Time and the State of the Dead

The psalmist made a profound declaration: "Lord, you have been our dwelling place throughout all generations. Before the mountains were born or you brought forth the earth and the world, from everlasting to everlasting you are God" (Ps 90:1–2). The apostle Peter also says, "But do not forget this one thing, dear friend: With the Lord a day is like a thousand years, and a thousand years are like a day" (2 Peter 3:8). Commenting on this scriptural verse, Oscar Cullmann has opined that "the purpose is not to assert the timelessness of God, but rather the endless character of the time of God . . . only to him does eternity belongs. He is the Lord over the ages."[234] Quoting Rudolf Bultmann, John P. Cock writes, "God is the enigmatic power beyond time, yet master of the temporal; beyond existence, yet at work in it."[235]

---

234. Oscar Cullmann, *Christ and Time: The Primitive Christian Conception of Time and History* (Philadelphia: Westminster, 1950), 69–70.

235. John P. Cock, *The Transparent Event: Post-Modern Christ Images* (Greensboro, NC: Transcribe Books, 2001), 37.

From the argument raised by the psalmist as also commented by Cullmann along with Bultmann's assertion that God is the enigmatic power beyond time, it is obvious that all point to the transcendence and otherness of the Creator God. His being and nature is quite different from that of human nature and being. For this reason, God who is wholly other and creator is master of the universe and all his creatures. Thus, he defies human understanding for no human and theological language can adequately make sense of this enigmatic figure.

The above point explains why Manunguri argues that God is transcendent, that is, he escapes the understanding of man who can only fall down in admiration and reverential awe before a God who is outside all reality.[236] In his definition of transcendence Gilkey had argued that "God is not 'part of' the ordinary world; he is 'beyond,' 'before,' and 'above' the world as its supreme Ruler and Lord; what characterizes the world in weakness, death, and dissolution does not characterize him."[237] The argument makes a lot of sense to me and it does shed light on the fact that God is distinct from his creatures. "He alone is Lord, he alone is the source of all life . . . he alone is '*a se non ab alio*' . . . outside God there is only that which has been created, outside him who is '*a se*,' there is only that which is '*ab alio*;' thus outside the one who is entirely independent, there is only dependent being, the creature."[238] From what has been said so far, this study argues that insofar as African ancestors are creatures, they fall within the purview of creaturely existence with an imminent and terminal end unlike God who is prior to time and rules over time. It is precisely for this reason that this section concerns itself with apologetics.

Apologia contained in the New Testament centres on the events surrounding Jesus's life. These events included in the Gospels are core apologetics for Jesus much the same way the Acts of the apostles were apologetics to the church. For after the acts of the earthly Jesus follows the acts of the exalted Jesus. Admittedly, the deeds of Jesus, ordinary and extraordinary including ultimately his death and resurrection, earned him some credence. We all know, and rightly so, when God in Christ climaxes history and ushers

---

236. Manunguri, *Closeness of the God*, 10.
237. Gilkey, *Maker of Heaven*, 85.
238. Gilkey, 91.

in the new heaven and new earth (Rev 21:1), there can't be any independent realm for African ancestors. If human beings live in one space and time, with one body, and then they die as it is written; "people are destined to die once, and after that to face judgment" (Heb 9:27), should we then revert to a primordial animistic belief in an African ancestral spirit realm after death as opposed to what the Bible teaches? It is not written that "the dead know nothing; they have no further reward, and even their name is forgotten. Their love, their hate and their jealousy have long since vanished; never again will they have a part in anything that happens under the Sun" (Ecc 9:5–6)?

If theology is faith seeking understanding, where then is our biblical theology? Belief in the validity and potency of dead African ancestors as way of doing Christology in Africa and Christianizing African primal traditions is not sufficient to make a complete sense of the Christ event; nor to reflect the Christologies of the Old and New Testaments that are based upon promise and fulfilment, since African ancestor Christology configuration is based on African pre-Christian categories that do not seek continuity with Old Testament prophecies and covenants (Gen 3:15; Isa 7:14; Mic 5:2; Matt 2:5–6).

Amazingly, the African belief about the living-dead and the potency of their spirits has found acceptance in some church denominations to the extent that they approve ancestral veneration. While this proposal has some merits, there are significant problems as well. Significantly, the proposal addresses itself to the spirit of the dead which the Holy Bible does not only forbid Christians to venerate or consult (Lev 20:6) but imposes a death sentence on those who consult them (Lev 20:27). For this reason, this study argues that the African ancestor Christology methodology is problematic since its formulation does not align with biblical prophecies and fulfilment. Thus, it explains that much as we strive to have a voice in global theological scholarship, we should equally be careful of what we offer.

Unless we go back to the basis of biblical tradition, our Christology will continue to paddle the air without water upon which to sail. For Christ to be relevant and well accepted in Africa, this work proposes African Linguistic Affinity Christology methodology which makes Jesus Christ more at home in any African society than the ancestor Christology methodology. To that end, my methodology introduces that Jesus should be called *Yesu/Jesu* since such a method retains the main christological content contained in the Bible and also brings out the real and in-depth theological meaning of Jesus the Christ that has continuity with the Old Testament prophecies and covenants made to the Jewish patriarchs – Abraham, Isaac, Jacob and Moses – that have been fulfilled in the New Testament.

Given that the term *Yesu/Jesu* is widely known and used in Africa, this work argues that it provides a useful context to explore christological ideas in African Christianity. Since no work, as far as this researcher knows, has been done so far on Jesus as *Yesu/Jesu* in the Sub-Saharan Africa, the researcher, therefore, proposes this methodology as his significant contribution to scholarship and hope that the twenty-first-century African theologian and biblical scholar would be more comfortable to use the already accepted nomenclature which is at home in almost all African people groups.

Exploring The Theological Implications of Ancestor Christology in the Light of Contemporary Voices on the Identity of Jesus Christ

In the last three decades, quite a significant number of Protestant and Roman Catholic African theologians have referred to Jesus Christ as our ancestor, and their ideas are being circulated mostly in theological fora. The prolific nature of literature on African ancestor Christology is most likely to convince a first reader that the ancestorship of Christ has been firmly established in Sub-Saharan Africa and that the average African Christian perceives Christ as an ancestor. This, however, is not the case; at the grassroots level and even within African theological academia, there are theologians and biblical scholars from both Protestant and Roman Catholic circles who see a serious pitfall in this juxtaposition. Consequently, Sawyer rejects the notion that Christ is an ancestor. For him, Christ differs from the ancestors because he now lives.[239] For John Baur, the main weakness of African ancestor Christology is that Christ is not an ancestor in the usual sense that Africans understand an ancestor, and if he is a brother-ancestor he is not the source of life.[240] In

---

239. Palmer, "Jesus Christ," 7.

240. John Baur, *2000 years of Christianity in Africa: An African Church History*, 2nd ed. (Nairobi, Kenya: Paulines Publications Africa, 1994), 305.

the same theological thought, Andrew F. Walls argues that the significance of ancestors in Africa has greatly reduced because of the impact of Christianity. To him, the term "ancestor" in the first place is ambiguous and carries a strong problem for the appreciation of Christ in Africa. He writes,

> The impact of Christianity on the relationship between the God component and the ancestor component in African maps of the transcendent has been more ambiguous. Generally speaking, the explicit significance attributed to the ancestors has diminished as the God component expands, especially in religious systems that in the pre-Christian period were ancestor dominated.[241]

Apparently, the permutation of Christ as ancestor under the pretext of constructing a contextual, and inculturation, Christology is inadequate to unravel the mystery of the incarnation of the Son of God insofar as such models do not only lack but are not in the actual sense the same christological concepts derived from the New Testament. In this connection, Victor I. Ezigbo makes a keen observation,

> The challenge for an African theologian who constructs a contextual Christology is not to confine what he or she says about Jesus Christ to the biblical representations of him. It is instead to construct a Christology that truly represents the meaning and significance of Jesus Christ as well as thoroughly situating it within the context which inspires his or her Christology. The problem that is facing the majority of African Christians today . . . is not Western theological hegemony. It is also not the problem of how to explain Christianity as a foreign religion to the indigenous peoples of Africa using a local category. It is an error to assume that the peoples of Africa cannot truly experience Jesus Christ unless he is described witha local metaphor, for example, as an ancestor.[242]

---

241. Andrew F. Walls, *The Cross-Cultural Process in Christian History: Studies in the Transmission and Appropriation of Faith* (Maryknoll, NY: Orbis Books, 2002), 126.

242. Ezigbo, *Re-Imagining African Christologies*, 304–305.

Noticeably, the ancestor christological model is not appropriate for Africans to know and experience Jesus Christ in the continent since it does not illuminate and show continuity with the Adamic covenant of redemption and the Abrahamic covenant of promise, which were fulfilled in the New Testament in Matthew 1:21–25 when Christ was born and crucified for our redemption as the apostle Paul argues in Galatians 4:4–5. For this reason, this work contends that the ancestor model lacks the messianic and mediatorial role of Christ presented in the Bible as the incarnate Logos and high priest who through the crucifixion, death and resurrection became the wisdom of God and now able to intercede for the brethren.

The methodology, therefore, poses a severe problem to the understanding of Christ in Africa. On this ground, many Africans reject the notion that Christ is an ancestor. The fact of this submission is substantiated in a research Tennent conducted on whether Jesus Christ is perceived as an ancestor. His statistics are revealing; the percentage of those who reject the notion of Christ's ancestorship ranges between 44 percent and 63 percent.[243] Similarly, Timothy Palmer on the issue asked a class of eighty students from fifteen States and forty-two Nigerian tribes in April 2004 at the Theological College of Northern Nigeria (TCNN), Bukuru to submit a two-page essay on the appropriateness of speaking of Christ as an ancestor in their own culture. The results were overwhelming as 99.9 percent of the students, according to their grassroots findings, reject in totality the idea that Christ is their lineage ancestor.[244]

Cletus Chukwuemeka Nwaogwugwu also seeks to know, "If Jesus Christ is presented as an ancestor, does it solve the entire problem of deepening the Christian faith in Africa?"[245] He responded, "The task of deepening the Christian faith in the Sub-Saharan Africa does not depend on the presentation of Jesus Christ as an ancestor."[246]

Equally, Samuel Waje Kunhiyop further probes the pervasive quest for reversion to African primal beliefs, being substantially the blending together

---

243. Tennent, *Theology in the Context*, 127.
244. Palmer, "Jesus Christ," 4–17.
245. Nwaogwugwu, *Ancestor Christology*, 533–535.
246. Nwaogwugwu, 533–535.

of two antithetical variables under the umbrella of inculturation or contextualization methodologies. For him,

> Because Christ fulfilled all laws, including those related to our ancestors, the rituals associated with the veneration of our ancestors are now null and void. Christ has assumed all the functions our ancestors fulfilled in traditional beliefs. He is the only mediator between God and humanity (1 Timothy 2:5), and he is able to sympathize with us and intercede on our behalf in all areas of life.[247]

Kärkkäinen thinks along this line when he rightly observes that "A potential liability of the ancestral and similar metaphors of Christ in African theologies is the Arian tendency," After all, he maintained, "Ancestors are not gods, even though they are highly regarded."[248]

In order to test and prove the validity of the submission of these erudite theologians on the universal upright rejection of Jesus's ancestorship in Africa (vis-à-vis Timothy C. Tennent's and Timothy Palmer's research findings on the appropriateness of calling Jesus as an ancestor in Africa) during a course I taught in a 2016 summer school at the Jos ECWA Theological Seminary (hereafter referred to as JETS), I asked a Masters class that comprises of students from nine African countries and one Canadian Korean to submit a three page essay on the appropriate African model for Jesus with which to formulate Christology in the continent.

To buttress and further confirm the validity of my findings from the JETS's essays, I again gave a two page essay to another group of international students comprising of both Masters and undergraduate students at the ECWA Theological Seminary, Kagoro, in the first semester of 2016 between August and December, on what name Jesus is called among their people group, which they would prefer in their theological formulation. It was shown that 99.8 percent of the JETS students' survey indicated that African tribes prefer to identify Christ with the name *Jesu/Yesu* and 99.6 percent of Kagoro students identified Jesus as *Yesu* or *Jesu*.

---

247. Samuel Waje Kunhiyop, *African Christian Theology* (Nairobi: HippoBooks, 2012), 136.

248. Veli-Matti Kärkkäinen, *Christ and Reconciliation* (Grand Rapids, MI: Eerdmans, 2013), 77.

The forum at JETS' summer school was a class of thirty-three Masters of Theology students from nine African countries and one Candian Korean. These thirty-three students were asked to write a three-page essay on the appropriate name to speak of Christ in their own dialect, since the research above has revealed that ancestor is not a favoured nomenclature and methodology with which to formulate the theology of Jesus in Africa. When the papers were turned in, the results were promising. In this class of thirty-three students, two were Kenyans, twenty-two Nigerians, one Tanzanian, one Ghanaian, one Liberian, one South Sudanese, one Sierra Leonean, two Gambians, one Malawian and one Korean from Canada.

All thirty-three students are either directors or highly placed staff of the International Fellowship of Evangelical Students (IFES) representing the Continent and Korea. These students are professionals from a full ramification of professions who came to JETS through the Post-Graduate Diploma of Theology track and proceeded into the master of theology class. The challenge that confronted me in this survey is the lopsided nature of the students since predominately they all came from the evangelical setting and faith. Be that as it may, the researcher is from this domain with the research itself tilted toward evangelical tradition.

To a large extent, the respondents reflect "grassroots" Nigerian and African Protestant Christianity. The term "grassroots" according to Palmer is not a precise term, but it suggests links with the typical Nigerian and African Christian.[249] The respondents are masters students, who are all halfway to completing a second degree in theology but who also have second degrees in other fields. But many of them have strong links with the rural, village churches; others have ties with both urban churches as well as cross-cultural experiences since they are IFES employees engaged with evangelical students from all over Africa.

It is striking to note that the results of the thirty-three essays on the subject of the appropriate African name for Jesus are breathtaking. In these essays thirty-one students without exception unanimously agreed that a proper African name for Jesus Christ which conveys a theological sense of his work of redemption according to traditional Christology and orthodox

---

249. Palmer, "Jesus Christ," 3.

Christian confession is *Yesu* or *Jesu*. There are, however, little dialectical variations in nuances among the tribes investigated as the survey reveals. Statistically, thirty-one students representing 99.8 percent exercised serious reservation calling Jesus by any name other than the transliterated Hebrew Yeshua and Greek Ἰησοῦς known by Africans as *Yesu* or *Jesu* our saviour while 0.2 percent indicate that Jesus bears some different name in their languages but which meaning has much to do with the person and work of Christ.

It is pertinent at this juncture for one to not only clearly state the reasons for such a universal acceptance of the African linguistic affinity name for Christ by the represented ethnic groups but also to inquire as to the grounds adduced. The following are some of the most common reasons advanced.

To start with, the thirty-three students faulted the ancestor Christology methodology and held that over against the ivory tower ancestor Christology formulated by some African theologians engaging inculturation methodology, which does not represent the opinion poll of grassroots Africans and also draws out explicitly the theological meaning of Jesus, African Linguistic Affinity christological methodology, which identifies Jesus as *Yesu* or *Jesu*, is most appropriate since it is not only generally the grassroots African name for Jesus Christ but also portrays him as the one who paid the price for sins and redeemed us from the curse of the Law. Another strong reason adduced by the thirty-three students against ancestor Christology is the African criteria for a man to qualify for an ancestor which when applied in the context of Jesus Christ he does not measure up to.

In light of the above, it is relevant for one to consider who an ancestor is in the traditional understanding of ancestor in the primal beliefs of African people and societies. For most ethnic groups represented in the survey, an ancestor is a man who lived to a ripe old age, who died a natural death and is given a befitting burial and who had children that celebrated his death. Anyone who meets these criteria is qualified for an ancestor. For many of the respondents, Jesus did not come close to meeting any of these requirements since he died as it were, a criminal death at the youthful age of thirty-three without children to celebrate his death.

More so, an ancestor in the African context is by consanguinity. For Jesus, therefore, to qualify for an ancestor of any community in Sub-Saharan Africa, he had to had come biologically from a particular clan and be its ancestor. This means that in the African context Jesus cannot be an ancestor of more than one family, group, and community since every African family, clan, and community have their ancestors unique to them. So, with this provision, how can Jesus be an ancestor of the entire African continent?

For the above reason, therefore, he is not qualified to be an ancestor to all Africans. Moreover, Africans have a linguistic flare for names that unites and makes sense to them. Accordingly, Jesus as *Yesu* or *Jesu* does not only reflect our linguistic affinity that unites and makes a lot of sense to us, but it does reveal our unity in diversity as having a common cultural heritage and Christian understanding that his death was a propitiation for our salvation as Africans. For this reason, he should be called *Yesu* or *Jesu* our redeemer and scapegoat while a theology to be formulated about him should employ African Linguistic Affinity methodology which identifies Jesus as *Yesu* or *Jesu* in continuation to biblical covenants and promises in the Old Testament as the conclusion is shown in their essays.

Besides, two Kenyan students who form part of the survey are in total agreement. The first student: a female in this people group writes, "In Kenya, the Kikuyu consist of the largest ethnic groups found in all parts of Kenya but concentrated in the Central highlands part of the nation near Mount Kenya." According to her, "Jesus is called '*Yesu*' – (Sacred One) in Kikuyu dialect which is a Bantu language." Elsewhere, she asserts, "*Yesu* was born of the Virgin Mary who died for the sins of mankind (*Muhonokia*, the Saviour)."

The second Kenyan student; a male held from the *Kamba* communities of the Bantu who live in the Eastern part of Kenya wrote, "The *Kamba* name for Jesus is *Yesu* which in many occasions is used with other names to show different offices and attributes of Jesus." For example, "*Yesumasia* is used to refer to Jesus the Messiah. In the community, *Masia* means one who helps in a crisis. *Yesu Masia Mwana wa Ngai* is used to mean Jesus the Son of God. *Yesu Mwovosya* is used in reference to Jesus the Redeemer. *Mwovosya* means one who cools down conflicts. *Yesu Mutaniie wa Andu* is used when referring to Jesus the Saviour of all."

The twenty-two Nigerians in the survey came from eighteen different ethnic groups in eleven states and the Federal Capital Territory making the twelve distributed as follows: two each from Igbos, Berom, Bura, and Esan;

and one each from Ngas, Mada, Hausa, Cham, Kono, Anaguta, Eggon, Kibaku, Kuteb, Igala, Waja, Fier, Gbagi and Mwaghavul. The eleven states and the Federal Capital Territory from which the twenty-two Nigerians came from were: six Plateau; three Borno; two Nassarawa, Edo, and Gombe; one Abia, Enugu, Kogi, Kano, Kaduna, Taraba, and the Federal Capital Territory.

From the ethnic distribution above, the two Nigerians who held from Abia and Enugu speak Igbo as their dialect. While the first person notes that "The name which the Igbos in South-Eastern Nigeria refer to Jesus in their language is *Jisos*," the second person states, "The missionaries' literal translation for the name of Jesus Christ in the Igbo language is *Jisos Kraist*." This is similar to the literal adaptation of the name in many other African languages. Elsewhere the first person also wrote, "The name itself implies salvation. Thus, when the Igbos call *Jisos*, it carries with it the sense of the incarnation, Lordship, redeemer, saviour and deliverer respectively."

The one Ngas man from that ethnic group reminds us,

> The name *Jesu* is the name of Jesus in the Ngas language. *Jesu* for us means that God is salvation. *Jesu* is understood as having a special mission of saving his people from their sins. When therefore the Ngas people adopted the name *Jesu* as the name of the Christ, they did that consciously and deliberately, adopting the same meaning and significance the name carried when originally mentioned in Matthew 1:21.

From the Berom ethnic group, a man claims,

> The name Jesus is *Hwei Dagwi* since in our primal beliefs "god" is *dagwi*, meaning "father of sun" Berom people believe that there is a Supreme Being that owns the sun. For this reason, when Christianity came to us, we accepted the faith and named Jesus *Hwei Dagwi* meaning Jesus the Son of God, the name has much significance in our lives as children of God.

Another Berom observes,

> The Berom has a specific name for Jesus known as "*Hwei Dagwi*," meaning "A Son of the Most High God." "*Hwei*" in Beron stands for "Son," "Da" stands for "Father" and "*Gwi*" means "the Sun, Sky, Moon, and Stars." For us, therefore, *Hwei*

Dagwi is the Son of God, the redeemer of the whole world. He is the God-Man of the Berom people who came into the world to save sinners.

In my investigation so far, it is only the Berom people of Plateau State that have literally d carried their African pre-Christian notion of the Supreme Being "*Dagwi*" into the Christian faith. This explains why Jesus is "*Hwei Dagwi*" from the Berom traditional idea of "*Dagwi*," supreme being and "*Hwei*" Son of the supreme being or God.

Of the two Bura men from Borno State, one of them maintained, "In Bura native language the name Jesus is called *Yesu*, meaning our saviour. In various usages, we call him by names that are descriptive of his nature and attributes such as *Yesu Bzir Hyel* means Jesus Son of God, *Yesu Mdir Mbanta* means Jesus is Saviour and *Yesu Mthlaku* means Jesus is Lord." The second man from Bura also responded, "*Yesu* is Bura native name for Jesus. The Bura use the name by his official designation Saviour that is, '*Ndar Mbanta.*'"

Too, a Mada respondent from Nassarawa state says, "Jesus is *Yɔso* in Mada language meaning the one who saves, and it is written '*Mkpechunwhor.*' The literal translation of '*Mkpechunwhor*' is 'take' and 'free.' *Yɔso* thus means deliverer from evil spirits, sickness, bad luck and giver of life." For a Hausa man from Kano Jesus is called, "*Yesu* among the Hausas and the name refers to the saving work of Christ for *Yesu* means one who is able to save."

Two respondents representing the Esan group of Edo State unanimously maintained that the name of Jesus in Esan is "*Jesu* (pronounced /jehsu/). *Jesu* came to be in the 15th century when Christianity was said to arrive in Esan land. History has it that it was based on the Missionary's explanation of the meaning of the name Jesus Christ to be the Son of God. Today's Esan meaning of Jesus (*Jesu*) is 'Owve-osanobua' literally means Son of the Supreme God."

Among the Cham people of Gombe State, Jesus is called *Yesu,* and it signifies Jesus's work as a deliverer. A respondent from this ethnic group states, "When the Cham people want to speak of Jesus' work, they say, '*Yesu Nijigiri*' meaning deliverer and remover of any form of oppression and calamity on the land and its people." A Kono man notes, "The name of God in Kono was *Gesilu* when Christianity came to Kono land, there was the need to have an indigenous name for Jesus. Since Jesus is the Son of God, the Kono people simply added the prefix '*Kon*,' meaning 'Son' to *Gesilu*, which is now '*KonGesilu*' Son of the Supreme Being." Based on the findings of this survey so far, the Kono ethnic group is second to the Berom language that has carried their African pre-Christian concept of the supreme being of the Christian faith. Thus, Jesus is *KonGesilu* from the traditional understanding of *Gesilu* – supreme being and "*Kon*" "Son."

An Anaguta man said,

> The Anaguta man strongly believes in African traditional religion which makes it very difficult to accept the gospel of Jesus Christ. For this reason, when the missionaries came with the gospel, they ran and hid in the hills, but when they came to understand Jesus, and because they came with traditional African belief, they called Jesus "*Yehsu*" meaning Son of God or the "breath of God" sent to the world. *Yehsu* among Anaguta means a healer, a protector and messenger from God.

An Eggon woman wrote,

> Names are important and convey special meaning to suit the occasion and circumstances of birth, hopes and desires of parents for the person so named. In view of the significance of the birth of Jesus, the Eggon word for Jesus is *Yesu* or *Eyesu*. This name evokes in the minds of Eggon people meaning that involves the person or attributes of Jesus Christ. He is someone who opens the eyes of people who hitherto were in darkness; he is the illumination or enlightenment.

A Kibaku man from Borno state said, "The name of Jesus in Kibaku is '*Yesu-Zhirhyel*.' '*Yesu*' means Jesus, while '*Zhir*' means a male child while '*hyel*' is God. '*Yesu-Zhirhyel*' is Jesus the Son of God." In traditional Kibaku Christian worldview, *Yesu-Zhirhyel* has three significant meanings: (1) *Yesu-Zhirhyel* is one who is sent to fight the enemies of the family, (2) *Yesu-Zhirhyel* is one who is sent to save or protect members of the family and (3) *Yesu-Zhirhyel* is someone sent into the family for a special task.

"*Yesu-Zhirhyel* in Kibaku language depicts a saviour, deliverer and protector." A Kuteb respondent from Taraba state asserts, "The name Jesus in Kuteb is '*Yesu*.'" According to him, "If one is to dissect the name '*Ye*' means 'hold' and 'Su' means properties. When such words are put together, they simply mean the one who holds all things. Thus, Kuteb speaks of '*Mbae na Rimam*,' – One who has the capacity to save humankind from condemnation since he holds them." An Igala man from Kogi state wrote, "Jesus is called *Jisos Kraist*. The translators were careful not to alter the meaning, the purpose and the efficacy of the name. For this reason, they retained the vernacular name-*Jisos Kraist* which designates, Christ as the Saviour (Matthew 1:21)." In Igala Christian confession, the purpose and significance of Jesus Christ are described as, "Enajadu, meaning, he who saves." Enajadu is further used as, "Ene Ujadu-Christ which is 'Kraist'-translated as 'Adokanya'-captain of warfare." A Waja man said, "Jesus is called '*Yesu*,' in Waja languages, a name we first heard from Baba Gelengu, a missionary from Portugal." When Baba Gelengu presented the gospel, he said, "*Yesu* has answers to all your problems, and he is the one to saves you from witches and wizards. So, in Waja, their fear of witches and wizards is less because of the first preaching of Baba Gelengu who introduced *Yesu* as one who gives life and protection."

A Fier respondent reminds us,

> The name for Jesus in Fier is *Yeso*, the use of this name is as old as the existence of Christianity amongst the people of Fier. This name which is not just particular to my language but it is used by many other languages in Africa, and some parts of the world is borrowed from the Hebrew language of Jesus which means saviour and within the tribe, no family has ever named their child "*Yeso*" because it is believed to be a sacred name for God who came to save us from the bondage of Satan.

A Gbagi man said, "The name of Jesus in Gbagi language is '*Jeisu*. *Jeisu* to a Gbagi Christian is not just a nomenclature, but it is believed to be the name of the Supreme God translated from the English name Jesus-a human embodiment of the divine idea. *Jeisu* is qualified with Chwashe nugnu-Jeisu Chwashe nugnu which translates-Jesus, Son of God."

A Mwaghavul woman said, "The name Jesus is *Yesu* in Mwaghavul language. The Mwaghavul hallows and reverence the name *Yesu* because having learned from Scriptures; he is the Son of God and God himself. The name is not given to children because it is regarded as sacred and meant only for Christ. It becomes a blasphemy for anyone to name his child *Jesu*."

From a survey of twenty-two Nigerian languages on the appropriate African name for Jesus, the statistics reveal the following: Jesus is called *Jisos* in two ethnic groups, Igala and Igbo, among the Berom Jesus is called *Hwei Dagwi* and Jesus is *KonGesilu* in Kono language. This means that only four out of the twenty-two Nigerian tribes call Jesus in their languages by a name other than *Yesu* or *Jesu* while the remaining eighteen languages are unanimous in calling Jesus *Yesu* or *Jesu*. For this reason, this study argues that in light of the widespread acceptance of Jesus as *Yesu* or *Jesu* among Nigerian languages, African Linguistic Affinity methodology is the most suitable model for the formulation of Christology in Africa.

It should be remembered that the twenty-two Nigerian ethnic groups are just but a cluster of the nine African nations and one Canadian Korean under survey. While two countries: Kenya and Nigeria have been considered, the remaining seven African nations and Korea would now be surveyed to ascertain the appropriate name they prefer for Jesus Christ.

A respondent from the Moro tribe of South Sudan writes,

> *Yesu* is Jesus name in the Moro tribe in the Republic of South Sudan. The first missionaries that arrived in Moro land were Anglican Missionaries, when they preached the gospel and translated the Bible into Moro language; they used *Yesu*. Thus, Jesus is known as *Yesu*. The name *Yesu* means: (i) just Lord Jesus, (ii) the anointed one (iii) Incarnate God, (iv) Mediator between man and God and (v) the Lamb of God who takes away the sin of the world.

A Tanzanian from the Zanaki tribe writes,

> The name Jesus in Zanaki is "*Yesu*" which was adopted as the missionaries reached Zanaki community, preached and taught that "*Yesu*" is the saviour. Not only that but he was born of the Virgin Mary by the power of the Holy Spirit. So, the Zanaki people adopted the name *Yesu* as the way they received the Gospel. For the Zanaki people, once they hear the name *Yesu*, they, therefore, understand it in the Christian way that it is the name associated with the faith of Christian religion.

A man from the Akan of Ghana pointed out that Akan is one of the largest ethnic groups in Ghana. The tribe has four main groups under it, namely, the Asante, Fante, Akyem, and Akuapen. Each of these groups also has under them, sub-groups. Mainly, they speak the Twi language with just one minor variation. All four languages are Semitic. This Ghanaian wrote,

> The name of Jesus in my tribe is "*Yesu*" sometimes expressed as "*Yesunyame ba*," literally translated "Jesus the Son of God." The etymology of the name Jesus in the Bible is not different from that in my tribe. *Yesu* means to my people a deliverer or rescuer from calamity. Songs about salvation from sin, deliverance from danger are hardly composed without the name *Yesu*. It's common to find people call the name *Yesu* when faced with a need so much so that, it means "help" sometimes too.

A hetero-lingual Liberian who came from the Bassa and Mano tribe of Liberia said, "In the Bassa tribe Jesus is called by several names. But two of those names have an implication of the meaning of the Hebrew Joshua which means saviour. That name sounds almost like the English one Jesus, but it is called '*Jezed*.' The other one is pronounced as '*A' Pou en yorn*.' This means the one who saves or my saviour." The Liberia further asserts, "In my Mano tribe, Jesus is also called '*Jezed*' as the name in my Bassa tribe, but there is another one that is called '*Uhn yeme*. This one talks about the one who 'rescues' or 'saves' from sin."

A Sierra Leonean of the Krio tribe maintained, "The name for Jesus in Krio language is '*Jiʒɔs*.' The name is a direct borrowing from the English – the Nova Scotians and the Maroons inherited from their Colonial Masters who taught them Christianity. '*Jiʒɔs*' in Krio language is not our ancestor; he is the Saviour and Lord we had come to know in the Christian religion." Of the thirty-three students, two (a male and a female) in the survey are from the Manjago tribe of Gambia. According to these students, "The Manjago are mostly found in Guinea Bissau which is believed to be their cradle. Their presence is also in their neighbouring countries of Guinea (Conakry), Senegal, and the Gambia."

Among the Manjago tribe, Jesus is called *Yesu*. One of them wrote, "The introduction of the gospel is perhaps the most probable explanation for the Manjago use of the word '*Yesu*.' To the Manjago, *Yesu* is known to be the Son of God, and the name conveys the idea of a Saviour which is complemented by the accompanying adjective 'na Boran.' 'na Boran' is basically a Manjago version and equivalent of the word 'Saviour.'" The last African ethnic group according to my survey comes from the Chewa tribe of Malawi. The person from Malawi wrote,

> In Malawi, 80% of our population are said to be Christians. As in any other Christians in the world, in Malawi, Christians name Jesus in their mother tongue as *Yesu Khristu*. Traditionally, if you ask many Malawians about who *Yesu Khristu* is, the answer you will get is *Yesu Khristu* is a Son of Joseph and Mary, born on December 25 many many years ago. *Yesu Khristu* is the name that is exalted above all names, and that is the only name, recommended name that has to be used when praying.

To some extent, the assertion from the Malawian student that *Yesu* is the Christian name the world over is substantiated and confirmed by the only Korean student in the forum surveyed. As a Canadian Korean, she wrote, "In Korean language, Jesus is '*Yesu*.' This name resonates with the salvific role of Jesus in the Bible. Not only Korean, but some other Canadian languages in Canada also call Jesus Christ '*Yesu*.' Significantly, '*Yesu*' means one who gives hope in the midst of modern ideologies sweeping the Western world."

The last survey to test and validate the reasons adduced for the rejection of Jesus as ancestor by some African theologians as well as the grassroots Christians in Africa is a two page essay given to fifteen international students comprising of both Masters and undergraduate students at the ECWA Theological Seminary, Kagoro, in the first semester of 2016 between August and December, on what name Jesus is called among their people group. It was shown that 99.6 percent of African tribes prefer to identify Christ with the name *Jesu/Yesu*.

At the forum of fifteen students, the national population distribution is as follows: Four – Cameroon; three – Chad Republic, and Ghana; two – Sierra Leon; one – Gambia, Malawi, and Liberia. Since the survey question: "What is the most appropriate African name for Jesus with which to formulate Christology," is the same for both the JETS and Kagoro students, two out of the three students from Ghana are from the Akan tribe while one is a Ewe. This means that the Akan response generated in the first survey of thirty-three JETS students suffices for this survey since the responses are basically the same.

Moreover, the only Ewe respondent in the survey reported, "We the Ewe address Jesus Christ as '*Yesu*,' a name which signifies our redemption for it means the redeemer of humankind." A Babanki-Tungo man from Cameroon strongly declared, "The Babanki-Tungo name for Jesus Christ is '*Nyiengon*.' This name is the translation of the name Lord for Jesus. Similarly, another Cameroonian from the Ewundu tribe wrote, "In Ewundu language, Jesus is known as '*Yesu*.' We prefer to refer to him this way because the name speaks of our adoption into the family of God." Still yet another Cameroonian from the Fulfulde tribe stated, "Jesus is called '*Yeesus*' in our dialect. This name speaks of the power and authority of Jesus to free from bondage and slavery. It also means the good shepherd who cares for the sheep." The last Cameroonian in this survey is held from the Yamba tribe. According to him, "The name of Jesus in our tribe is '*Monwi*' and is translated as 'Son of God.'"

Likewise a Via man from Liberia stated, "Jesus in Via language is '*Abi*.'" In the Chad Republic, the name for Jesus among the Ngambai and the Nbai is very similar. A Ngambai elder responded, "The Ngambai tribal name for Jesus is '*Jesju*.'" In the Nbai, a man wrote, "A Nbai name for Jesus is '*Jeju*.'" Interestingly enough, both "*Jesju* and *Jeju* stand for Saviour from sin and condemnation." An Arab man from the Chad Republic robustly remarked, "In our language, we call Jesus '*Yesuha* or *Issah–Almasihu*.' '*Yesuha*' is the Greek transliteration of 'Ιησοῦς which we employ to convey a sense of liberation and freedom from Satanic or diabolic manipulation." A Wolof man from Gambia pointed, "In my ethnic group, we have a tribal name for Jesus. In Wolof language, Jesus is called '*Yesu*', and the name stands for everything associated with Jesus Christ in the Christian Bible. For this reason, '*Yesu*' means for us the Christ of faith who went through apassion for us and for our salvation."

In the survey, the only student that represents the Lomwe tribe from Malawi keenly notes, "Among my tribe of Lomwe, we have a name for Jesus Christ which resonates with his biblical name. Jesus is '*Yesu*' in Lomwe language, and it means one who emancipated us from the fear of evil spirits and Satan." Finally, the fifteen international student survey at ECWA Theological Seminary in Kagoro is rounded up with the last two students who are Sierra

Leoneans but of course from different tribes. From the Menda, a respondent asserts, "Jesus is never known by any name other than '*Yesu*.' *Yesu* puts a smile on our faces because his coming to earth freed Sierra Leoneans from themselves and the Devil. Thus, *Yesu* is a freedom fighter and giver as our history reveals." The last but by no means the least Sierra Leonean student came from the Lemba tribe claims, "Jesus has a universally accepted name in Lemba language. He is '*Yissus*.' This name, when pronounced, wards off all misfortune and danger and brings absolute peace to one's mind and soul because '*Yissus*' did not only redeem us, but he also ensures and secures our security and even guarantees our future."

With a few exceptions like the Berom, Igbo, Igala, Kono, Babanki-Tunga, Yamba and Via, the consensus of this diverse ethnic groups is that an appropriate African name for Jesus Christ is *Yesu* or *Jesu*. It is this name that Africans recognize Jesus with as their saviour from Satan and sin and condemnation. *Yesu/Jesu* is the one who loved us and laid down his life for us. For this reason, this study argues that African Linguistic Affinity Christology methodology should be formulated in which Jesus is universally known as *Yesu* or *Jesu* the redeemer in Sub-Saharan Africa. This is since the grassroots responses suggests that Jesus as an ancestor does not clearly bring out the theological meaning of Christ the anointed one and long-awaited Messiah promised to the Jews but with universal import. For this reason, this study argues that ancestor Christology is not the ideal grassroots name for Jesus with which to formulate African Christology that Africans understand and accept. After all, ancestors are dead, but *Yesu/Jesu* is alive.

So, how can African Christians treat the dead on equal terms with the ever living Lord? After all, on the resurrection Sunday the angel who appeared to the women cautioned, "Why do you look for the living among the dead?" (Luke 24:5) So, why are African ancestor Christology theologians and biblical scholars looking for the living among the dead? Please, let us allow the dead to rest as we worship and reverence Christ. A key difference between Christ and African ancestors is the fact that the ancestors are dead, but Christ is living. Back in 1968, Sawyer said: "Unlike the ancestral dead of the Africans, Jesus Christ, once dead, now lives."[250] The living one is not

---

250. Palmer, "Jesus Christ," 7.

the same or similar to the dead ones to warrant theological comparison using an analogy by an ivory-tower scholarship. As Palmer asserts, "there is an incredible gap between the 'ivory-tower' scholarship of some of the academic professors and the experience of African students who are close to the 'grassroots.' The theology of Christ as an ancestor does not resonate with most of these respondents."[251] To concur with Palmer, contextualization and inculturation are good; they are necessary. The gospel must be related and incarnated in every culture. But care must be taken so that the contextualization and inculturation models are indeed relevant to the needs of the people at the grassroots. After all, Okey Jude Uche in his research on inculturation in the Roman Catholic Church in Igbo land had discovered clearly that inculturation as theological method was not working because it discussions have been one-sided and that people's traditional religious rituals have not been treated with respect and accorded the dignity they deserve through the method of inculturation.[252]

Consequent upon this Uche adds, "Every Igbo religious ritual has been condemned as evil and as paganism and a train therefore to hellfire. Consequently, the Igbo Christian is culturally and theologically handicapped by the present inculturation or adaptation approach. Therefore, every Igbo Christian needs liberation."[253] The best result inculturation as the theological method can offer the church according to Uche's research findings is, "The Church has directly or indirectly encouraged a life of deception, double standard, and hypocrisy and people do not know why they are and should be 'Christians.'"[254]

In the midst of this life of double standard, the Igbo Catholic appears triumphant and goes around proclaiming the *"theology of liberation as the good work of the gospel."*[255] It is obvious from Uche's conclusion that the inculturation methodology leads to dual church membership and religious syncretism since on Sunday people are Christian while Monday through to Saturday they are something else. Insofar as inculturation has failed, I would

---

251. Palmer, 7.
252. Uche, "Theological Analysis of Ikpu-Ala," 286.
253. Uche, 286.
254. Uche, 287.
255. Uche, 287.

like to suggest that the ancestorship of Christ causes too much confusion and does not meet the pastoral needs of the average African Christian.[256]

For the above reason, I proposed an appropriately universal African christological model that would meet the pastoral need of the average African Christian employing a linguistic affinity methodology which bridges the lacuna between the ivory-tower scholarship and grassroots Christians in Sub-Saharan Africa. When African Linguistic Affinity Christology methodology is religiously and judiciously followed, Jesus would be allowed to remain the Jesus presented to us in the Bible by the evangelists who wrote about him. The work of the evangelist became the basis upon which the early church fathers formulated the theological concept of the rule of faith as the norm for Christian theological articulation.

Summary

The New Testament furnishes the contemporary church with models with which to formulate a contextually acceptable theology that depicts the salvation work of Christ at Calvary. New Testament models were derived from the vocation of Jesus Christ and those of his followers. Who and what Jesus Christ did had lasting consequence in the life of those who were eyewitnesses of his deeds. The indelible memories of the Christ event and the extraordinary display of victory over nature and death and his victorious resurrection led ultimately to a radical transformation of the worldview of some of his contemporaries and context.

Out of the transformed experience came the understanding that what Christ did is in perfect fulfilment of messianic prophecies and promises. For this reason, Jesus's contemporaries saw him as the promised Messiah, high priest and mediator between God and man and the name of Jesus Christ came to signify these functions and achievements. This development made the name of Jesus to acquire a lot of global significance and sacred status in Christendom so much so that Christian parents are careful nowadays to name their children after Jesus because of its sacred nature and importance.

As the days of Jesus Christ, names are significant in Africa and carry a lot of meaning; names are given to signify who the bearer is and what they

---

256. Palmer, "Jesus Christ," 7.

do. For this reason, African theologians find it a great deal to retain and immortalize the memories of their forebears by formulating a theology that resonates with their pre-Christian past. With this, Christian theology is formulated with Jesus as an ancestor.

This work appreciates the significant contribution of African ancestor Christology proponents but however sees a severe pitfall of this construction since research has shown that such a methodology does not enjoy grassroots acceptance but rather, it is an ivory-tower Christology, formulated in African academic scholarship by innovative and erudite African minds, that does not reflect the theological meaning of Christ in keeping with God's covenant with Adam, Abraham, Isaac, Jacob, and Moses the patriarchs of the Jews.

The universal rejection of Jesus's ancestorship at the grassroots in favour of a universally accepted African name for Jesus as an eschatological deliverer demands that we chart a new course in formulating an African Christology. This accounts for why I proposed an African Linguistic Affinity Christology where Jesus is called *Yesu* or *Jesu* in keeping with the Hebrew, Greek and Arabic transliteration of the name Yeshua, Ἰησοῦς, and *Issah* that have the theological meaning of redemption in continuation with the Old Testament predictions, and consequent upon my research findings and the survey results conducted by Uche, Tennent and Palmer.

CHAPTER 8

General Summary and Conclusion

Summary of the Study

It is said that the journey of one thousand kilometres begins with a step. It is equally true to say that the journey of one thousand kilometres ends with a step. The veracity of this saying is mainly justified in this study as my readers might have established. The journey that began in chapter 1 terminates here. As I argued throughout the course of this work, the undergirding assertion of this study is that African ancestor Christology is born out of the solemn concern to immortalize the memories of the ancestors and thus make Jesus Christ relevant in the continent via the primal traditions of Africans by African theologians.

Uchenna A. Ezeh says it clearly, "It is . . . a religious and ontological duty to marry and procreate in order to leave behind those who would sustain one in personal immortality."[1] Geoffrey G. Parrinder confirms, "In Southern Ghana, in everyday life of the *Gā* the dead are very present."[2] Because the dead are believed to be very present, Africans find it very difficult to discard the memories of their beloved progenitors who, having gone into the ancestral realm, are now said to acquire supernatural powers with which to protect and mediate for their living kith and kin here on earth, as all the chapters of the study attempt to show.

To achieve the desired goal of this work, the first chapter layed the foundation by affirming African primal beliefs that hold, "those who are dead

---

1. Ezeh, *Jesus Christ the Ancestor*, 89.
2. Parrinder, *African Traditional Religion*, 57.

are never gone,"³ but "have survived death."⁴ The restatement of this ancient African belief prepares a soft landing ground for the chapter to investigate the relevance of memorials in people groups worldwide.

Indeed, memorials that celebrate antiquity and national or local leaders are common, but no people group the research had to discover ever employed the inculturation methodology to address Jesus as an ancestor in their context. Even within Africa at the grassroots, the ancestor model is strange. For this reason, the study proposes an African Linguistic Affinity Christology methodology that uses the transliterated Greek Ἰησοῦς to formulate *Yesu/ Jesu* Christology in Africa.

The central premise of this Christology is that it retains the main content and theological meaning of Jesus the Christ and thus allows for healthy and consistent continuity between African Christology and the Old and the New Testaments teachings about Jesus Christ according to promise/ fulfilment predictions. This proposal begun in this chapter, which is entirely developed in chapters 6 and 7, underscores the main contribution of the study to scholarship.

Building upon the argument of the first chapter, chapter 2 examines the genesis of ancestor Christology and contends that Africa's encounter with the Western superpowers: colonialism and the missionary movement of the eighteenth and nineteenth centuries that demeaned the African sense of personality and dignity as well as denigrated African culture and belief, engendered a reaction from African theologians. Consequently, African theology was born on which platform ancestor Christology is formulated as reviewed in the inculturation methodological works of Abbé Marc Ntetem, Bénézet Bujo and Charles Nyamiti on the ancestorhip of Jesus Christ in Africa.

Chapter 3 is the hinge upon which the study hangs since it calls for a return to the Roman-North African theological stance articulated by Tertullian and Athanasius in the third and fourth centuries against the heretics of their time. This was done by first reviewing the theological thought of the apostolic age from whence a transition is taken to the third and fourth centuries before a conclusion is reached.

---

3. Taylor, *Primal Vision*, 152.
4. Parrinder, *African Traditional Religion*, 58.

General Summary and Conclusion

Chapter 4 staunchly contends that ancestor Christology is formulated from the framework of the African worldview and traditional belief system. This accounts for why I asserted that ancestor Christology exponents employed African cultural categories of an ancestor and their perceived powers in the traditional religious practices to construct a contextual theology. Of course, the glaring metamorphosis from African ancestors to Christ as an ancestor in Africa speaks volumes. That apart, I have also pointed out that the Roman Catholic Church's practice of venerating the dead saints gave impetus to and adds colour to ancestor Christology since the ancestors in African primal traditions and the departed saints in Roman Catholic belief invariably occupy the same place in Roman Catholic thought forms and religious patterns.

The conclusion allows for a smooth transition to the fifth chapter which investigated the theological sources for African ancestor Christology. As I am convinced, it is from sacerdotal pronouncements of pre-Vatican II alongside the magisterial promulgation of Vatican II and post-Vatican II ecclesial doctrine of inculturation that Roman Catholic theologians drew inspiration to formulate theology around the pole of ancestrology. The church's adoption of the Italian's notion of *Aggiornamento*; a call for church "renewal,"[5] is the underpinning factor for the convocation of a Special Assembly for Africa of the Synod of Bishops to celebrate the communion and collegiality of the African Episcopate with Rome and the Universal Church.[6] The outcome of this Synod is the adaptation of Vatican II's doctrine of inculturation which has come to dictate the direction and tempo of Roman Catholic theology in Africa where the African pre-Christian model ancestor is being compared with the Christian model-Christ.

While chapter 5 deals strictly with theological sources from within the Roman Catholic Church, chapter 6 examined theological sources that are resonant of promise/fulfilment prophecies rooted in the Adamic covenant of redemption and the Abrahamic covenant of promise. I have proved in

---

5. Rahner, *Church after the Council*, 19.
6. Synod of Bishops, Special Assembly for Africa: The Church in Africa and Her Evangelizising Mission Towards the Year 2000—You Shall be My Witnesses. It should be recalled that I have defined *Lineamenta* as an "Outline," (cf. ch. 5). You may refer to Synod of Bishops, *Lineamenta*, vii.

this chapter that it was to wandering Mesopotamian nomads and animists that God first revealed himself and made an everlasting covenant of promise which would culminate in the birth of the Messiah (Gen 12:1–3).

Consequent upon this covenant Jesus Christ is born (Matt 1:21) in confirmation of God's promise. Given that the birth of Jesus fulfils the Jewish messianic expectation, I have suggested that African Linguistic Affinity Christology methodology finds perfectly a definition and a good fit since its source derives from a Jewish background and Christian theology. Against this backdrop, the study makes more apparent in this chapter and illuminates the contribution of the research briefly introduced in chapter 1 as would be entirely argued in chapters 6 and 7.

Chapter 7 explored the evolution of christological models in the New Testament and the significance of names in New Testament times and in the African worldview. The chapter highlights the encapsulating thesis vividly that inculturation as the theological method is not suitable for Africa. The fact of this conclusion has been established in several surveys conducted on the appropriateness of calling Jesus Christ an ancestor as well as the universally accepted African name for Jesus with which to formulate Christology. In April 2004, Timothy Palmer (a Professor of Theology at the Theological College of Northern Nigeria [TCNN]), Bukuru asked eighty students to write a two-page essay on whether it is appropriate to speak of Christ as an ancestor in their own culture.

When the essays were turned in, Palmer writes, "As one reads the 80 essays on this subject, one is struck by the almost universal rejection of the concept of Christ as an ancestor."[7] Similarly, during the 2016 summer school at JETS and the first semester of 2016 in ETS Kagoro, I conducted a survey on what name is appropriate for Jesus in Africa (see ch. 7). The results of these two surveys were stunning since the main theological meaning of Jesus is not only sustained, but the name shows continuity with the Adamic covenant of redemption and the Abrahamic covenant of promise.

The first survey revealed that 99.8 percent of students wrote that Jesus is known as *Yesu* or *Jesu* in their dialects. In the same vein, the second survey revealed that 99.6 percent of the students penned that Jesus is addressed as

---

7. Palmer, "Jesus Christ," 4–17.

Yesu or *Jesu* in their mother tongue. From the findings of the two surveys, I proposed an African Linguistic Affinity Christology methodology – an approach that seeks to be faithful to the Bible as it brings out the theological meaning of the messianic work of Christ and also leaned upon God's fundamental redemptive promises made to Jewish ancestors. This outlined the main contribution of this study to scholarship which then draws the whole work to a close as the present chapter has been positioned.

Pertinent Observations Derived from the Study

Belief in the ancestors in Africa is the most fundamental religious tenet governing religion, culture, customs, life, and meaning. Some refer to it as the "the 'cult of the ancestors' and speak of worship or veneration of the ancestors."[8] The traditional belief concerning the ancestors has two aspects: "(1) the memory of the dead through the name. They can be remembered through their names (memorial of the dead); (2) the spirits of the dead ancestors live on (ancestral spirit). In the first aspect, the descendants do many things in order to keep the memory of the dead. In the second aspect, it deals with rites and rituals relating to the spirits of the dead."[9]

Perpetuating the memory of the ancestors is one of the fundamental tenets and basis of African Traditional Religion. In light of the foregoing, some African theologians think that African traditional religion is preparatory to Christianity. For this reason, they argue that Christian theology should coexist side by side with African primal beliefs in order to allow for continuity between the two faiths.

In the course of this study, I have observed that the ancestor Christology model being vigorously pursued by Abbé Marc Ntetem, Bénézet Bujo and Charles Nyamiti is a passion taken in the frontier of African primal tradition. Unfortunately, because of the fluid and dynamic nature of human culture and changing societies, the conscious awareness of ancestral presence and influence are no longer the obsession of most Africans in the twenty-first century. For this reason, the ancestor category cannot be a relevant christological model with which to formulate Christian theology in twenty-first-century

---

8. Turaki, "Christianity and African Traditional Religion," vol. 1, 200.
9. Turaki, "Christianity and African Traditional Religion," vol. 2, 64.

Africa. It took off in 1979 when John Pobee wrote, "Our approach would be to look on Jesus as the Great and Greatest Ancestor–in Akan language *Nana*."[10]

Consequent upon this statement Charles Nyamiti published his monumental, "Christ as our Ancestor."[11] The ancestor model made for exciting reading, but theological issues are often very fluid and of course the ancestor model is a case in point. For this reason, twenty-first-century, post-colonial, post-missionary and post-independence Africa needs a current model relevant to its needs with which to theologize. This explains why I proposed African Linguistic Affinity Christology methodology as a contemporary approach to the study of Christ in Africa.

The observation raised above about the obsolete nature of the ancestor Christology model in twenty-first-century Africa demands that African theologians and biblical scholars look away from the ancestor model. In looking elsewhere, new models must necessarily show themselves by replacing the old model. Mostly, in this study, I have discovered some contemporary models proposed for this century. Victor Ifeanyi Ezigbo, for instance, proposes, "A Revealer Christology Model for the African context,"[12] and calls for, "Rethinking the sources of African Contextual Christology."[13]

Before now, Yusufu Turaki had earlier on maintained that "Christ came as a divine fulfilment of both the law and the Prophets and Christ's work had successfully made obsolete the role usually played by the ancestor."[14] In recent times Okey Jude Uche notes, "It is clear that inculturation has not been working."[15] Uche then concludes thus, "Therefore, there is need to try another method or model rather than inculturation."[16] The new method or model Uche proposes has been dubbed, "the dialogical approach."[17]

---

10. Palmer, "Jesus Christ," 5.

11. Palmer, 6.

12. Ezigbo, *Re-Imagining African Christologies*, 143–174.

13. Victor I. Ezigbo, "Rethinking the Sources of African Contextual Christology," *Journal of Theology for Southern Africa*, no. 132 (November 2008): 53–70.

14. Turaki, *Unique Christ*, 142.

15. Uche, "Theological Analysis of Ikpu-Ala," 286.

16. Uche, 286.

17. Uche, 285.

In April 2004, Timothy Palmer conducted a survey among eighty students at the Theological College of Northern Nigeria, Bukuru on the usefulness of calling Jesus their ancestor in the context of their own ethnic group. It was discovered that vast majority of these students outrightly rejected the idea of Christ as an ancestor in their culture.[18] Palmer's survey was validated by two research surveys I conducted in 2016 at JETS and EST, Kagoro on what is the appropriate African name for Jesus. The results were overwhelming as there was a universal concord at the grassroots that Jesus is called *Yesu* or *Jesu* in almost all African tribes (as shown in chs. 1, 6 and 7).

With the certainty of the stated results, I proposed an African Linguistic Affinity Christology methodology for present-day African theological enterprise since Africans at the grassroots prefer to call Jesus by his biblical names. In this study, one fact has been established. That is, African academics and scholars are apt to invent and articulate theological models within academic circles but are always unwilling to come to terms with the dynamic and fluid reality of human culture and language as is the case with the African ancestral cult – the category being employed to formulate the theology of ancestor in Africa.

For the above reason, the study implores for constant rethinking new and current ideas commensurate with Africa's changing times and situations we do theology. Throughout the study, I have observed that the ancestor Christology model starts and ends within Africa's theological environment since the grassroots never had genuine engagement with the notion let alone for it to excite them.

At the grassroots, Africans are excited when the name *Yesu* or *Jesu* is mentioned amidst them. A clear example is Madam Christina Afua Kuma's grassroots prayer in which she invokes, "Lord, I have come to hear what you have to say to me. I have been waiting and praying for a long time . . . I have come today, and my heart is very heavy. *Yesu Kristo*, you rose from the dead to give us life. Your blood gives us power and heals us."[19] The petition indicates that at the grassroots, *Yesu* or *Jesu* is the name that is universally accepted by grassroots Africans. In fact, even within African academic circles,

---

18. Palmer, "Jesus Christ," 1.
19. Clarke, "Towards a Post-Missionary," 5.

very few theologians and biblical scholars key into the ancestor Christology ideology while the most massive cluster says otherwise on the model.

A key and critical observation I have come to in the study is that a situation can generate any reaction whose footprints might be too difficult to erase. This is particularly true with African theology which was born out of a response to colonialism and imperialism thereby giving rise to the sincere concern to deconstruct Western theological hegemony and to offer an African voice afresh to the global theological enterprise.

Recommendations for Further Research

First, I have discovered that a lot of time has been devoted, and energy used in discussing the African ancestorship of Jesus in academic circles but care has not been indeed exercised to know for sure whether at the grassroots Africans will be comfortable and excited to call Jesus as their lineage ancestor. For this reason, exponents of African ancestor Christology need to rethink their methodology with a view to doing a thorough work in order to know what the grassroots opinion is with respect to Jesus's identity in the continent. My argument is that we cannot continue to formulate an ivory tower theology of ancestor without recourse to grassroots input. Therefore, a lot needs to be done in this area.

Second, from the study so far, there is no consensus even within African theological circles with respect to Jesus's ancestorship. Furthermore, the inculturation method used to explore ancestor Christology has been found to be grossly inadequate to reveal the mystery of the incarnate God who became flesh in the man Jesus of Nazareth. The becoming of God lays the foundation for Christology which itself is the fulfilment of Old Testament prophecies made to Adam and Abraham. The apparent disagreement on the appropriate model to employ to explore Christology in Africa necessarily calls for further probing into the issue.

Third and finally, it is the candid opinion of this researcher to recommend an in-depth exploration into Yusufu Turaki's model of "Christ as a divine fulfillment of both the law and the Prophets," Victor I. Ezigbo's "Revealer Christology Model" and Okey Jude Uche's dialogical approach which he believes is a convergent point for inculturation christological approaches and, of course, my African Linguistic Affinity Christology methodology which as I am convinced, is meaningfully faithful to the Bible and Christian theology.

My methodology that identifies Jesus Christ as *Yesu/Jesu* in continuation of the Adamic covenant of redemption, the Abrahamic covenant of promise and the Sinaitic covenant made to Moses all had the idea of redemption. For this reason, the Jews used the Hebrew word Yeshua to make sense of God's dealings with their ancestorsin the Old Testament era.

In the New Testament, the Greeks transliterated Yeshua as Ἰησοῦς to retain the covenantal and theological meaning of Yeshua. The simple logic of this argument is that the Old Testament's teachings were given and received in a Palestinian milieu and would have to be translated into a Greek milieu. Thus, the concept of Yeshua in a predominantly Jewish milieu became Ἰησοῦς in a Greek milieu. This study, therefore, argues that the life and mission of Jesus Christ climax the fulfilment of the redemptive plan and purpose of God and a primary means of making this point is in the frequent linkage of events in the life of Jesus to passages from the Old Testament (fulfillment formula – Matt 1:22).

The foregoing explains why the first verse of the gospel opens with four descriptive titles of Jesus: "Jesus the Son of David, the Son of Abraham" in fulfilment of God's promises and covenants to the patriarchs. Jesus is thus not just a given name without theological and covenantal significance. It is, by and large, a reference to the Adamic covenant of redemption, the Abrahamic covenant of promise and the Sinaitic covenant made to Moses. When he was given the name Jesus at his birth, it was a mark of continuation in the Christian tradition and theological formulation. Thus, Jesus became the Greek form of the Hebrew "Yeshua" – meaning "The Lord saves" (Matt 1:21), while "Christ" also became the Greek form of the Hebrew "messiah" – and means "Anointed One" or a person specially designated by God to carry out his will.

From the foregoing, this study argues that the notion of messiah is messianic and denotes an eschatological figure vested with kingly rule and authority descended from David with a rightful claim to Israel's throne while the son of Abraham applied to *Jesu/Yesu* reminds us that *Jesu/Yesu* was a Jew, a descendant of Abraham, the foundation of the patriarchs and Jews (Gen 12:3). In light of this, my approach calls upon African theologians mainly, Ntetem, Bujo and Nyamiti in the twenty-first century to formulate a theology that has continuation with Scripture, apostolic proclamation and Christian tradition in the early church the same way Tertullian and Athanasius formulated in the third and fourth century.

Bibliography

Aben, Tersur. "Ntetem on the Ancestorship of Christ." *TCNN Research Bulletin* 38 (August 2002): 32–38.
Abioye, Pius Oyeniran. "Christian Theological Literature on Ancestor Veneration in Africa: An Overview." In *Christology in African Context*, edited by S. O. Abogunrin, J. O. Akao, and Dorcas Olu Akintunde, 277–288. Biblical Studies Series no. 2. Ibadan: Nigerian Association for Biblical Studies, 2003.
Abogunrin, Samuel O. "Christology and the Contemporary Church." In *Christology in African context*, edited by S. O. Abogunrin, J. O. Akao, and Dorcas Olu Akintunde, 1–27. Biblical Studies Series no. 2. Ibadan: Nigerian Association for Biblical Studies, 2003.
———, ed. *Decolonization of Biblical Interpretation in Africa*. Ibadan: Nigerian Association for Biblical Studies, 2005.
———. "The Total Adequacy of Christ in the African Context." *Ogbomoso Journal of Theology* 1 (January 1986): 9–16.
Achebe, Chinua. *There Was a Country: A Personal History of Biafra*. London: Penguin Books, 2012.
———. *Things Fall Apart*. Oxford: Heinemann, 2008.
Adamo, David T. *Africa and the Africans in the Old Testament*. Benin City: Justice Jeco Press & Publishers, 2005.
———. *Reading and Interpreting the Bible in African Indigenous Churches*. Nigeria, Benin City: Justice Jeco Press & Publishers, 2005.
———. "What Is African Biblical Studies?" In *Decolonization of Biblical Interpretation in Africa*, edited by S. O. Abogunrin, 17–. Ibadan, Nigeria: Nigerian Association for Biblical Studies, 2005.
Adegbola, E. A. Ade. *Traditional Religion in West Africa*. Ibadan: Daystar Press, 1983.
Adeyemo, Tokunboh, ed. *Africa Bible Commentary*. Nairobi: Word Alive, 2006.
Ajah, Paul O. *African Traditional Religion*. Uburu: Truth & Life Publications, 2007.

Akinade, Akintude E. "'Who Do You Say That I Am?' An Assessment of Some Christological Constructs in Africa." *Asia Journal of Theology* 9, no.1 (1995): 181–200.

Akuezuilo, E. O. *Research Methodology and Statistics*. NUC/NBTE/NCCE Minimum Standard Edition. Abba: NuelCenti Publishers, 1993.

Amaladoss, Michael. *Beyond Inculturation: Can the Many Be One?* Delhi: ISPCK, 1998.

———. "Cross-Inculturation of Indian and African Christianity." *African Ecclesial Review* 32, no. 3 (June 1990): 157–168.

Amoah, Elizabeth. "African Christologies." In *Dictionary of Third World Theologies*, edited by Virginia Fabella and R. S. Surgirtharajah, 41–43. New York: Orbis Books, 2000.

Amobi, Charles Ekweozor. "The Development of Christo-Paganism among Igbo Christians of South-Eastern Nigeria." MA thesis, ECWA Theological Seminary, Jos, 2011.

Anderson, Allan H. *African Reformation: African Initiated Christianity in the 20th Century*. Asmara, Eritrea: African World Press, 2001.

Anderson, George W. *The History and Religion of Israel*. London: Oxford University Press, 1966.

Anderson, Michael John. *The Fall of Troy in Early Greek Poetry and Art*. New York: Oxford University Press, 1997.

Apel, Dean. "Towards a Samburu Christology." *Currents in Theology and Mission* 23, no. 5 (1996): 356–367.

Arrupe, Pedro. "Letter to the Whole Society on Inculturation." In *Other Apostolates Today: Selected Letters and Addresses of Pedro Arrupe*. Vol. 3, edited by J. Aixala, 172–181. St Louis, MO: Institute of Jesuit Sources, 1981.

Athanasius. *On the Incarnation*. Willits, CA: Eastern Orthodox Books, n.d.

Augustine. *The City of God*. New York: Modern Library, 2000.

Aulén, Gustaf. *Christus Victor: An Historical Study of the Three Main Types of the Idea of Atonement*. New York: Collier Books, 1986.

Austin, Bill R. *Austin's Topical History of Christianity*. Wheaton, IL: Tyndale House Publishers, 1983.

Aye-addo, Charles Sarpong. *Akan Christology: An Analysis of the Christologies of John Samuel Pobee and Kwame Bediako in Conversation with the Theology of Karl Barth*. Eugene, OR: Pickwick, 2013.

Ayegboyin, Deji. "Li Oruko Jesu: Aladura Grass-root Christology." *Journal of African Christian Thought* 8, no. 1 (2005): 11–21.

Ayres, Lewis. *Nicaea and Its Legacy: An Approach to Fourth-Century Trinitarian Theology*. Oxford: Oxford University Press, 2009.

Bae, C. S. "Ancestor Worship and the Challenges It Poses to the Christian Mission and Ministry." PhD thesis, University of Pretoria, 2007.

Bahnsen, Greg L. *Van Til's Apologetics: Readings and Analysis*. Phillipsburg, NJ: P & R, 1998.

Baillie, D. M. *God Was in Christ: An Essay on Incarnation and Atonement*. London: Faber & Faber, 1977.

Balcomb, Anthony O. "Narrative Epistemological Crisis and Reconstruction: My Story with Special Reference to the Work of Kwame Bediako." *Scriptura: International Journal of Bible, Religion and Theology* 97 (2008): 47–59.

Barclay, William. *Jesus as They Saw Him: New Testament Interpretations of Jesus*. London: SCM, 1962.

Barnett, Paul W. *Jesus and the Logic of History*. Downers Grove, IL: InterVarsity Press, 2000.

Barrett, David B. *Schism and Renewal in Africa: An Analysis of Six Thousand Contemporary Religious Movements*. Nairobi, Kenya: Oxford University Press, 1970.

Barr, O. Sydney. *From the Apostles' Faith to the Apostles' Creed*. New York: Oxford University Press, 1964.

Barth, Karl. *Church Dogmatics*. Vol. 1, *The Doctrine of the Word of God*. Edinburgh: T & T Clark, 1999.

———. *The Humanity of God*. Atlanta, GA: John Knox, 1978.

Barzun, Jacques, and Henry F. Graff. *The Modern Researcher*. Belmont, CA: Thomson/Wadsworth, 2004.

Bate, Stuart C. "Inculturation: The Local Church Emerges." *Missionalia* 22, no. 2 (August 1994): 93–117.

Bauckham, Richard. *The Bible and Mission: Christian Witness in a Postmodern World*. Carlisle, Cumbria: Paternoster, 2003.

———. *God Crucified: Monotheism and Christology in the New Testament*. Grand Rapids, MI: Eerdmans, 1998.

———. *Jesus and the Eyewitnesses: The Gospels as Eyewitness Testimony*. Grand Rapids, MI: Eerdmans, 2006.

Bauckham, Richard, and Carl Mosser, eds. *The Gospel of John and Christian Theology*. Cambridge: Eerdmans, 2008.

Baur, John. *2000 Years of Christianity in Africa: An African Church History*. 2nd edition. Nairobi, Kenya: Paulines Publications Africa, 2009.

Bavinck, Herman. *Reformed Dogmatics: Abridged in One Volume*. Edited by John Bolt. Grand Rapids, MI: Baker Academic, 2011.

Becker, Ernest. *Escape from Evil*. New York: Free Press, 1975.

Bediako, Kwame. "African Theology." In *The Modern Theologians: An Introduction to Christian Theology in the Twentieth Century*, edited by David F. Ford, 426–444. Malden: Blackwell, 2002.

———. *Christianity in Africa: The Renewal of a Non-Western Religion*. Maryknoll, NY: Orbis Books, 1997.

———. *Jesus and the Gospel in Africa: History and Experience.* Maryknoll, NY: Orbis Books, 2004.

———. *Jesus in Africa: The Christian Gospel in African History and Experience.* Akropong, Ghana: Regnum Africa, 2000.

———. *Theology and Identity: The Impact of Culture upon Christian Thought in the Second Century and in Modern Africa.* Oxford: Regnum, 1999.

Beegle, Dewey M. "Anthropomorphism." In *Evangelical Dictionary of Theology*, edited by Walter A. Elwell. Grand Rapids, MI: Baker Academic, 2001.

Beetham, T. A. *Christianity and the New Africa.* London: Praeger, 1967.

Benedict XVI. *Church Fathers: From Clement of Rome to Augustine.* San Francisco: Ignatius Press, 2010.

Benson, Bruce Ellis. *Graven Ideologies: Nietzsche, Derrida & Marion on Modern Idolatry.* Downers Grove, IL: InterVarsity Press, 2002.

Berkhof, Louis. *The History of Christian Doctrines.* Carlisle, PA: Banner of Truth, 2002.

Best, W. E. *Studies in the Person and Works of Jesus Christ.* Houston, TX: W. E. Best Book Missionary Trust, 1975.

Bettenson, Henry, ed. *Documents of the Christian Church.* 2nd edition. New York: Oxford University Press, 1967.

Bevans, Stephen B. *Models of Contextual Theology: Faith and Cultures.* Maryknoll, NY: Orbis Books, 2011.

Bird, Michael F. *Evangelical Theology: A Biblical and Systematic Introduction.* Grand Rapids, MI: Zondervan, 2013.

———. *Jesus Is the Christ: The Messianic Testimony of the Gospels.* Downers Grove, IL: InterVarsity Press, 2012.

Bird, Michael F., Craig A. Evans, Simon J. Gathercole, Charles E. Hill, and Chris Tilling. *How God Became Jesus: The Real Origins of Belief in Jesus' Divine Nature. A Response to Bart D. Erhman.* Grand Rapids, MI: Zondervan, 2014.

Boer, Harry R. *A Short History of the Early Church.* Ibadan: Daystar Press, 2003.

Boer, Jan H. *Missions: Heralds of Capitalism or Christ?* Ibadan: Daystar Press, 1984.

Bonino, José Míguez, ed. *Faces of Jesus: Latin American Christologies.* Maryknoll, NY: Orbis Books, 1984.

Borg, Marcus J., and N. T. Wright. *The Meaning of Jesus: Two Visions.* New York: HarperOne, 2007.

Bosch, David. *Transforming Mission: Paradigm Shifts in Theology of Mission.* Maryknoll, NY: Orbis Books, 2009.

Braaten, Carl E., ed. *Paul Tillich – A History of Christian Thought: From Its Judaic and Hellenistic Origins to Existentialism.* New York: Simon & Schuster, 1968.

Brandel-Syrier, Mia. *Black Woman in Search of God.* London: Lutterworth, 1962.

Bray, Gerald L. *Creeds, Councils and Christ: Did the Early Christians Misrepresent Jesus?* Fearn: Mentor, 2009.

———. *God Is Love: A Biblical and Systematic Theology.* Wheaton, IL: Crossway, 2012.

Brettenson, Henry, ed. *Documents of the Christian Church.* 2nd edition. New York: Oxford University Press, 1969.

Brettenson, Henry, and Chris Maunder, eds. *Documents of the Christian Church.* 3rd edition. New York: Oxford University Press, 1999.

Bright, John. *A History of Israel.* 4th ed. Louisville, KY: Westminster John Knox, 2000.

Bromiley, Geoffrey W. *Historical Theology: An Introduction.* Edinburgh: T & T Clark, 1994.

Brown, Collin. *Christianity and Western Thought: A History of Philosophers, Ideas & Movements.* Vol. 1, *From the Ancient World to the Age of Enlightenment.* Downers Grove, IL: InterVarsity Press, 1990.

Bruce, F. F. *New Testament History.* New York: Doubleday, 1980.

Brunner, Emil. *The Christian Doctrine of Creation and Redemption.* Volume 2. London: Lutherworth, 1952.

Bujo, Benézét. *African Theology in Its Social Context.* Nairobi, Kenya: Paulines Publications Africa, 2003.

Bujo, Benézét, and Juvénal Ilunga Muya, eds. *African Theology in the 21st Century: The Contribution of the Pioneers.* Vol. 2. Nairobi, Kenya: Paulines Publications Africa, 2006.

Bultmann, Rudolf. *Jesus Christ and Mythology.* New York: Scribner's & Sons, 1958.

———. *New Testament and Mythology: And Other Basic Writings.* Philadelphia, PA: Fortress, 1989.

Cairns, Earle E. *Christianity Through the Centuries: A History of the Church.* Grand Rapids, MI: Zondervan, 1996.

Calvin, John. *Institutes of the Christian Religion.* Translated by Henry Beveridge. Grand Rapids, MI: Eerdmans, 1989.

Carson, D. A. *Christ and Culture Revisited.* Grand Rapids, MI: Eerdmans, 2008.

———. *The Gospel According to John.* Grand Rapids, MI: Eerdmans, 1991.

Carson, Herbert M. "The Covenant of Grace." In *Basic Christian Doctrines: Contemporary Evangelical Thought,* edited by Carl F. H. Henry, 117–123. Grand Rapids, MI: Baker Books, 1979.

Catholic Secretariat of Nigeria. *Proceedings of the Bishops' Study Session on Inculturation Held at Sacred Heart Pastoral Centre, Jos, November 9-10, 1988.* Jos, Nigeria: Catholic Secretariat of Nigeria, 1989.

Cayré, F. A. *A Manual of Patrology and History of Theology.* Vol. 1, *First and Second Books.* Paris: Desclée, 1936.

Chatterji, Saral K. "Indigenous Christianity and Counter-Culture." *Religion and Society* 36, no. 4 (1989): 3–17.

Chester, Tim. *From Creation to New Creation: Understanding the Bible Story.* Carlisle, Cumbria: Paternoster, 2003.

Chidili, Barth. *Inculturation as a Symbol of Evangelization: Christian Faith Taking Root in African Soil.* Jos, Nigeria: Mono Expressions, 1997.

Chimeri, Dudzirai. "Interpreting Jesus from an African Context: A Critical Review of the Evidence from Zimbabwe." *Journal of African Christian Thought* 6, no. 2 (December 2003): 28–32.

Clark, David K. *To Know and Love God: Method for Theology.* Wheaton, IL: Crossway, 2010.

Clarke, Clifton R. *African Christology: Jesus in Post-Missionary African Christianity.* Eugene, OR: Pickwick Publications, 2011.

———. "Towards a Post-Missionary Oral Christology among African Indigenous Churches in Ghana." *Journal of African Christian Thought* 8, no. 1 (June 2005): 3–10.

Clines, David J. A. "The Image of God in Man." *Tyndale Bulletin* 19 (1968): 53–103.

Cock, John P. *The Transparent Event: Post-Modern Christ Images.* Greensboro, NC: Transcribe Books, 2001.

The Code of Canon Law. New revised English edition. Bangalore, India: Theological Publications, 2013.

Collins, Robert O., ed. *The Partition of Africa: Illusion or Necessity.* New York: Willey & Sons, 1969.

Composta, Dario. *History of Ancient Philosophy.* Bangalore: Theological Publications, 2008.

Cone, James H. *God of the Oppressed.* Maryknoll, NY: Orbis Books, 2015.

Cook, Robert W. *The Theology of John.* Chicago, IL: Moody, 1979.

Copleston, Frederick. *A History of Philosophy.* Vol. 1, *Greece and Rome.* New York: Doubleday, 1993.

Costa, Ruby O., ed. *One Faith, Many Cultures: Inculturation, Indigenization and Contextualization.* Maryknoll, NY: Orbis Books, 1998.

Cowan, Steven B., ed. *Five Views on Apologetics.* Grand Rapids, MI: Zondervan, 2000.

Crollius, Arij A. Roest. *Creative Inculturation and the Unity of Faith.* Rome: Centre "Cultures and Religions," Pontifical Gregorian University, 1986.

Cullmann, Oscar. *Christ and Time: The Primitive Christian Conception of Time and History.* Philadelphia: Westminster, 1950.

———. *The Christology of the New Testament.* London: SCM, 1983.

Culver, Robert Duncan. *Systematic Theology: Biblical and Historical.* Fearn: Christian Focus, 2006.

Cummins, S. A. "Divine Life and Corporate Christology: God, Messiah Jesus, and the Covenant Community in Paul." In *The Messiah in the Old and New Testaments*, edited by Stanley E. Porter, 190–208. Grand Rapids, MI: Eerdmans, 2007.

Cunningham, William. *Historical Theology: A Review of the Principal Doctrinal Discussions in the Christian Church Since the Apostolic Age*. Vol. 1. Carlisle, PA: Banner of Truth, 1994.

Dafwang, Istifanus. *Christians Are Politicians*. Benue, Nigeria: Vedan Biz Solutions, 2016.

Dapila, Fabian N. "The Importance of the Dagaaba Ancestors and Their Role in the Process of Inculturation." *Mission* 3 (1996): 91–122.

Dedji, Valentin. *Reconstruction and Renewal in African Christian Theology*. Nairobi, Kenya: Acton, 2003.

Dhavamony, Mariasusai. *Christian Theology of Inculturation*. Rome: Pontificia Università Gregoriana, 1997.

Dickson, Kwesi A. "The Theology of the Cross in Context." *Journal of African Christian Thought* 6, no.1 (2003): 10–14.

Dockery, David S., and Timothy George, eds. *The Great Tradition of Christian Thinking: A Student's Guide*. Wheaton, IL: Crossway, 2012.

Donald, G. Bloesch. *Essentials of Evangelical Theology*. Two volumes in one. Peabody, MA: Hendrickson, 2006.

Donovan, Vincent J. *Christianity Rediscovered*. Maryknoll, NY: Orbis Books, 2003.

Doriani, Daniel M., Philip Graham Ryken, and Richard D. Philips, eds. *The Incarnation in the Gospels: Reformed Expository Commentary*. Phillipsburg, NJ: P& R, 2008.

Dorries, David W. *Edward Irving's Incarnational Christology*. Fairfax, VA: Xulon Press, 2002.

Douglas, McCready. *He Came Down from Heaven: The Preexistence of Christ and the Christian Faith*. Leicester: Apollos, 2005.

Dowley, Tim, ed. *A Short Introduction to the History of Christianity*. Minneapolis, MN: Fortress, 2013.

Dunn, James D. G. *Christology in the Making*. London: SCM, 1980.

———. *The Theology of Paul the Apostle*. Edinburgh: T & T Clark, 2008.

———. *Unity and Diversity in the New Testament: An Inquiry into the Character of Earliest Christianity*. London: SCM, 1984.

Dunn, James D. G., and James P. Mackey, eds. *New Testament Theology in Dialogue*. Biblical Foundations in Theology Series. London: SPCK, 1987.

Dyrness, William A. *Emerging Voices in Global Christian Theology*. Grand Rapids, MI: Zondervan, 1994.

———. *Learning about Theology from the Third World*. Grand Rapids, MI: Zondervan, 1990.

Easton, Stewart C. *A Survey of Ancient, Medieval, and Modern History*. New York: Barnes & Noble, 1965.

Edgar, William, and K. Scott Oliphint, eds. *Christian Apologetics Past and Present: A Primary Source Reader, Vol. 1 to 1500*. Wheaton, IL: Crossway, 2009.

Edwards, James K. *Is Jesus the Only Saviour?* Grand Rapids, MI: Eerdmans, 2005.

Egbulefu, John. "Successful Inculturation of Christianity in Africa." *Seminarium* 32, no. 1 (1992): 102–120.

Ehrman, Bart D. *Did Jesus Exist?: The Historical Argument for Jesus of Nazareth*. New York: HarperOne, 2013.

"800 Killed During Post-Election Riots—Human Rights Watch." *The Punch*. Vol. 17, no. 208884, 17 May 2011.

Éla, Jean-Marc. *My Faith as an African*. Maryknoll, NY: Orbis Books, 1988.

Elioghae, Efe M. "Decolonizing Jesus in Africa: A Critical Evaluation of the Missionary Influence." In *Decolonization of Biblical Interpretation in Africa*, edited by Samuel O. Abogunrin, 307–321. Ibadan: Nigerian Association for Biblical Studies, 2005.

Enns, Paul Peter. *The Moody Handbook of Theology*. Chicago, IL: Moody, 1989.

Erickson, Millard J. *Christian Theology*. 2nd ed. Grand Rapids, MI: Baker Academic, 1998.

Etounga-Manuelle, Daniel. "Does Africa Need a Cultural Adjustment Program?" In *Culture Matters: How Values Shape Human Progress*, edited by Lawrence E. Harrison and Samuel P. Huntington, 65–77. New York: Basic Books, 2000.

Evans, Craig A. *Holman Quick Guide to the Dead Sea Scrolls*. Nashville, TN: B & H, 2010.

Everett, Ferguson. *Background of Early Christianity*. 2nd edition. Grand Rapids, MI: Eerdmans, 1993.

Ezeh, Uchenna A. *Jesus Christ the Ancestor: African Contextual Christology in the Light of the Major Dogmatic Christology Definitions of the Church from the Council of Nicaea (325) to Chalcedon (451)*. New York: Lang, 2003.

Ezigbo, Victor Ifeanyi. "Contextualizing the Christ-Event: A Christological Study of the Interpretations and Appropriations of Jesus in Nigerian Christianity." PhD diss, University of Edinburgh, 2008, PDF.

———. *Introducing Christian Theologies*. Vol. 1, *Voices from Global Christian Communities*. Eugene, OR: Cascade, 2013.

———. *Re-Imagining African Christologies: Conversing with the Interpretations and Appropriations of Jesus in Contemporary African Christianity*. Eugene, OR: Pickwick, 2010.

———. "Rethinking the Sources of African Contextual Christology." *Journal of Theology for Southern Africa*, no. 132 (2008): 53–70.

Fabella, Virginia, and R. S. Sugirtharajah, eds. *Dictionary of Third World Theologies*. Maryknoll, NY: Orbis Books, 2000.

———. *The SCM Dictionary of Third World Theologies*. London: SCM, 2003.

Fashole-Luke, Edward, ed. *Christianity in Independent Africa*. London: R. Collings, 1978.

Fee, Gordon D. *Pauline Christology: An Exegetical-Theological Study*. Grand Rapids, MI: Baker Academic, 2007.

Feinberg, John S., ed. *No One Like Him: The Doctrine of God*. Wheaton, IL: Crossway, 2006.

Ferdinando, Keith. "Christian Identity in the African Context: Reflections on Kwame Bediako's Theology and Identity." *Journal of the Evangelical Theological Society* 50, no. 1 (March 2007): 121–143.

———. *The Triumph of Christ in African Perspective: A Study of Demonology and Redemption in the African Context*. Carlisle, Cumbria: Paternoster, 1999.

Feuerbach, Ludwig. *The Essence of Christianity*. New York: Cambridge University Press, 2012.

Fisher, Robert B. *West African Religious Traditions: Focus on the Akan of Ghana*. Maryknoll, NY: Orbis Books, 1998.

Flannery, Austin, ed. *Vatican Council II*. Vol. 1, *The Conciliar and Post Conciliar Documents*. New Delhi, Mumbai: Rekha Printers, 2013.

———. *Vatican Council II*. Vol. 2, *More Post-Conciliar Documents*. Northport, NY: Costello, 1982.

Ford, David, F., ed. *The Modern Theologians: An Introduction to Christian Theology in the Twentieth Century*. Malden: Blackwell, 2002.

Fortes, Meyer, and G. Dieterlen. *African Systems of Thought: Studies Presented and Discussed at the Third International African Seminar in Salisbury, December 1960*. London: Oxford University Press, 1966.

Fotland, Roar. "The Christology of Kwame Bediako." *Journal of African Christian Thought* 8, no. 1 (2005): 36–49.

Frame, John M. *Apologetics to the Glory of God: An Introduction*. Phillipsburg, NJ: P & R, 1994.

———. "Christianity and Culture." Lectures given at the Pensacola Theological Institute, 23–27 July 2001. Available online, http://thirdmill.org/files/english/hall_of_frame/Frame.Apologetics2004.ChristandCulture.pdf.

———. *Cornelius Van Til: An analysis of His Thought*. Phillipsburg, NJ: P & R, 1995.

———. *Systematic Theology: An Introduction to Christian Belief*. Phillipsburg, NJ: P & R, 2013.

Fuller, Lois. *A Missionary Handbook on African Traditional Religion*. Plateau State: Africa Christian Textbooks, 2001.

Geertz, Clifford. *The Interpretation of Cultures: Selected Essays.* New York: Basic Books, 1973.

Gehman, Richard J. *African Traditional Religion in Biblical Perspective.* Wheaton, IL: Oasis International, 2012.

———. *Doing African Christian Theology: An Evangelical Perspective.* Nairobi: Evangel, 1987.

George, Francis E. *Inculturation and Ecclesial Communion: Culture and Church in the Teaching of Pope John Paul II.* Rome: Urbaniana University Press, 1990.

Gibbs, Philip. "Missionaries and Culture." *Verbum Svd* 41, no. 1 (2000): 91–104.

———. "Transforming Humanity from Within: Inculturation as a Challenge for Evangelisation in Papua New Guinea." *Compass* 33, no. 2 (1999): 16–20.

Gibellini, Rosino, ed. *Paths of African Theology.* Maryknoll, NY: Orbis Books, 1994.

Gibson, David, and Daniel Strange, eds. *Engaging with Barth: Contemporary Evangelical Critiques.* Nottingham: Apollos, 2008.

Gilkey, Langdon. *Maker of Heaven and Earth: The Christian Doctrine of Creation in the Light of Modern Knowledge.* Lanham, MD: University Press of America, 1959.

Gittins, Anthony J. *Gifts and Strangers: Meeting the Challenge of Inculturation.* New York: Paulist Press, 1989.

Glatzer, Nahum N. "What Are We to Do about the Ten Commandments?" In *On the Bible: Eighteen Studies by Martin Buber,* edited by Nahum N. Glatzer, 118–121. New York: Syracuse University Press, 2000.

Goba, Bonganjalo. "Three Christological Models in Third World Theology." *Theologia Evangelica* 15, no. 2 (1982): 60–67.

Goergen, Donald, J. "The Quest for the Christ of Africa." *African Christian Studies* 17, no. 1 (2001): 5–51. Available online, https://sedosmission.org/old/eng/goergen.htm.

Goguel, Maurice. *Jesus and the Origins of Christianity.* Vol. 1, *Prolegomena to the Life of Jesus.* New York: Harper Torchbooks, 1960.

González, Justo L. *A History of Christian Thought.* Vol. 1, *From the Beginnings to the Council of Chalcedon.* Revised edition. Nashville, TN: Abingdon, 1987.

———. *The Story of Christianity.* Vol. 1, *The Early Church to the Dawn of the Reformation.* New York: HarperOne, 2010.

Goudzwaard, Bob. *Idols of Our Time.* Downers Grove, IL: InterVarsity Press, 1984.

Government of Plateau State. "Armed Forces Remembrance Day and Emblem Appeal Week Launching." Circular to Government Boards and Parastatals. Ref no. MSDYS/ASS/294/550 of 8 January 1999.

Graigie, Peter C. "The Ten Commandments." In *Evangelical Dictionary of Theology*, edited by Walter A. Elwell. Grand Rapids, MI: Baker Academic, 2001.

Grant, Jamie A., and Alistair I. Wilson, eds. *The God of Covenant: Biblical, Theological and Contemporary Perspectives*. Leicester: Apollos, 2005.

Gray, John. *The Biblical Doctrine of the Reign of God*. Edinburgh: T & T Clark, 1979.

Grebe, Karl, and Wilfred Fon. *African Traditional Religion and Christian Counselling*. Wheaton, IL: Oasis, 2006.

Green, Garrett. *Theology, Hermeneutics, and Imagination: The Crisis of Interpretation at the End of Modernity*. Cambridge: Cambridge University Press, 2007.

Green, Gene L., Stephen Pardue, and K. K. Yeo, eds. *Jesus Without Borders: Christology in the Majority World*. Grand Rapids, MI: Eerdmans, 2014.

Grenz, Stanley J., and Roger E. Olson. *20th Century Theology: God & the World in a Transitional Age*. Downers Grove, IL: InterVarsity Press, 1992.

Grogan, Geoffrey. "New Testament Christology – Or New Testament Christologies?" *Themelios* 25, no. 1 (November 1999): 60–73.

Groothuis, Douglas. *Christian Apologetics: A Comprehensive Case for Biblical Faith*. Downers Grove, IL: IVP Academic, 2011.

Grudem, Wayne. *Systematic Theology: An Introduction to Biblical Doctrine*. Leicester: Inter-Varsity Press, 2007.

Gunton, Colin E. *The One, the Three and the Many: God, Creation and the Culture of Modernity*. Bampton Lectures, 1992. Cambridge: Cambridge University Press, 2004.

Hahn, Ferdinand. *The Titles of Jesus in Christology: Their History in Early Christianity*. London: Lutterworth Press, 1969.

Haight, Roger. *The Future of Christology*. London: Continuum, 2007.

Hall, Douglas John. *Thinking the Faith: Christian Theology in a North American Context*. Minneapolis, MN: Augsburg, 1989.

Hall, Stuart G. *Doctrine and Practice in the Early Church: A Companion to a New Eusebius and Creeds, Councils and Controversies*. 2nd edition. London: SPCK, 2005.

Hamell, Patrick J. *Handbook of Patrology: Concise, Authoritative Guide to the Life and Works of the Fathers of the Church*. Staten Island, NY: Alba House, 1968.

Healey, Joseph, and Donald Sybertz. *Toward an African Narrative Theology*. Maryknoll, NY: Orbis Books, 1996.

Hearne, Brian. "Christology Is Basic to Inculturation." In *32 Articles Evaluating Inculturation of Christianity in Africa*, edited by Teresa Okure and Paul van Thiel, 89–96. Eldoret, Kenya: AMECEA Gaba Publications, 1990.

Heick, Otto W. *A History of Christian Thought*. Vol. 1. Revised edition. Philadelphia: Fortress, 1965.

Hengel, Martin. *The Son of God: The Origin of Christology and the History of Jewish Hellenistic Religion*. Eugene, OR: Wipf & Stock, 2007.

Henry, Carl F. H., ed. *Basic Christian Doctrines: Contemporary Evangelical Thought*. Grand Rapids, MI: Baker Books, 1979.

Hesselgrave, David J., and Edward Rommen. *Contextualization: Meanings, Methods, and Models*. Grand Rapids, MI: Baker Books, 1989.

Hillman, Eugene. "Good News for Every Nation via Inculturation." *Louvain Studies* 25, no. 4 (Winter 2000): 336–347.

Hodge, Charles. *Systematic Theology*. Revised edition. Edited by Edward N. Gross. Phillipsburg, NJ: P & R, 1992.

Hoffecker, W. Andrew. *Revolutions in Worldview: Understanding the Flow of Western Thought*. Phillipsburg, NJ: P & R, 2007.

Horbury, William. *Jewish Messianism and the Cult of Christ*. London: SCM, 1998.

Houston, James M., ed. *The Mind on Fire: An Anthology of the Writings of Blaise Pascal*. Portland, OR: Multnomah, 1989.

Idowu, E. Bolaji. *African Traditional Religion: A Definition*. London: SCM, 1973.

———. *Toward an Indigenous Church*. London: Oxford University Press, 1965.

Ijatuyi-Morphé, Randee. *Africa's Social and Religious Quest: A Comprehensive Survey and Analysis of the African Situation*. Jos, Nigeria: LogosQuest, 2011.

Imasogie, Osadolor. *Guidelines for Christian Theology in Africa*. Achimota: African Christian Press, 1993.

John, Mark. "Senegal Unveils 'African Renaissance' Statue." *Reuters*, 4 April 2010, available online, https://www.reuters.com/article/idINIndia-47423520100404.

Jenkins, Keith, ed. *The Postmodern History Reader*. London: Routledge, 2001.

Jenkins, Michael. *Invitation to Theology*. Downers Grove, IL: InterVarsity Press, 2001.

Jenkins, Philip. *The New Faces of Christianity: Believing the Bible in the Global South*. Oxford: Oxford University Press, 2006.

Jensen, Irving L. *Jensen's Survey of the Old Testament*. Chicago, IL: Moody, 1978.

Jimoh, Shaykh Luqman. "Reincarnation: Re-Appraising the Belief of Yoruba Muslims within the Context of Islamic Orthodoxy." *Ilorin Journal of Religious Studies* 2, no. 1 (2012): 81–96.

Johnson, Alan F., ed. *God Speaks to an X-Rated Society*. Chicago: Moody, 1973.

Johnson, Terry L. *The Case for Traditional Protestantism: The Solas of the Reformation*. Edinburgh: Banner of Truth, 2004.

Jongeneel, Jan A. B. *Jesus Christ in World History: His Presence and Representation in Cyclical and Linear Settings*. New York: Lang, 2009.

Joy, C. I. David. *Christology Re-visited: Profiles and Prospects*. Bangalore: Asian Trading Corporation, 2010.

Juel, Donald. *Messianic Exegesis: Christological Interpretation of the Old Testament in Early Christianity*. Philadelphia: Fortress, 1992.

Kabasélé, François. "Christ as Ancestor and Elder Brother." In *Faces of Jesus in Africa*, edited by Robert J. Schreiter, 116–127. Maryknoll, NY: Orbis Books, 2005.

Kagabo, Liboire. "Alexis Kagame: The Trial of an African Theology." In *African Theology in the 21st Century: The Contribution of the Pioneers*. Vol. 2, edited by Bénézet Bujo and Juvénal Ilunga Muya, 13–43. Nairobi: Paulines Publications Africa, 2006.

Kaiser, Walter C., Jr. *The Messiah in the Old Testament*. Grand Rapids, MI: Zondervan, 1995.

Kärkkäinen, Veli-Matti. *Christ and Reconciliation*. Grand Rapids, MI: Eerdmans, 2013.

———. *Christology: A Global Introduction*. Grand Rapids, MI: Baker Academic, 2003.

Kasper, Walter. *Jesus the Christ*. New edition. New York: T & T Clark, 2011.

Kato, Byang H. *African Cultural Revolution and the Christian Faith*. Jos, Nigeria: Challenge, 1976.

———. *Biblical Christianity in Africa: A Collection of Papers and Addresses*. Achimota, Ghana: African Christian Press, 1985.

———. "A Critique of Incipient Universalism in Tropical Africa." PhD thesis, Dallas Theological Seminary, 1974.

———. *Theological Pitfalls in Africa*. Kisumu, Kenya: Evangel, 1975.

Kelly, J. N. D. *Early Christian Doctrines*. 5th edition. London: Continuum, 2007.

Kereszty, Roach A. *Jesus Christ: Fundamentals of Christology*. Revised and updated, 3rd edition. New York: St Paul, 2011.

Kibicho, Samuel G. "The Continuity of the African Conception of God into and through Christianity: A Kikuyu Case Study." In *Christianity in Independent Africa*, edited by Edward Fashole-Luke, 370–388. London: R. Collings, 1978.

Kim, Stephen S. "The Literary and Theological Significance of the Johannine Prologue." *Bibliotheca Sacra* 166 (2009): 421–435.

Kirwen, Michael C. *African Cultural Knowledge: Themes and Embeded Beliefs*. Nairobi: MIAS Books, 2005.

Klotsche, E. H. *The History of Christian Doctrine*. Revised edition. Grand Rapids, MI: Baker Books, 1979.

Knitter, Paul F. *No Other Name? A Critical Survey of Christian Attitudes Toward the World Religions*. Maryknoll, NY: Orbis Books, 2004.

Krieg, Robert A. *Story-Shaped Christology: The Role of Narratives in Identifying Jesus Christ*. New York: Paulist Press, 1988.

Kristeller, Paul Oskar. *Renaissance Thought: The Classic, Scholastic, and Humanist Strains*. New York: Harper & Row, 1961.

Kunhiyop, Samuel Waje. *African Christian Ethics*. Bukuru, Nigeria: ACTS, 2008.

———. *African Christian Theology*. Nairobi: HippoBooks, 2012.

———. *Christian Conversion in Africa: The Bajju Experience*. Jos, Nigeria: ECWA, 2005.

Kurewa, J. W. Zvomunondita. "Who Do You Say That I Am?" *International Review of Mission* 69, no. 274 (1980): 182–188.

Küster, Volker. *The Many Faces of Jesus Christ: Intercultural Christology*. Maryknoll: Orbis Books, 1999.

Kyeyune, David. "The Presence of the Triune God in the Church." In *Inculturating the Church in Africa: Theological and Practical Perspectives*, edited by Patrick Ryan and Cecil McGarry, 159–182. Nairobi, Kenya: Paulines Publications Africa, 2001.

Kähler, Martin. *The So-Called Historical Jesus and the Historic Biblical Christ*. Philadelphia, PA: Fortress, 1966.

Laryea, Philip T. "Mother Tongue Theology: Reflections on Images of Jesus in the Poetry of Christina Afua Kuma." *Journal of African Christian Thought* 3, no. 1 (2000): 50–60.

Lee, Francis Nigel. *The Central Significance of Culture*. Nutley, NJ: P & R, 1976.

Lee, Joongjae. "The Problem of Common Ground in Christian Apologetics: Toward an Integral Approach." PhD Thesis, Potchefstroom, North-West University, South Africa, 2014.

Léon-Dufour, Xavier. *The Gospels and the Jesus of History*. London: Collins, 1971.

Letham, Robert. *The Holy Trinity: In Scripture, History, Theology, and Worship*. Phillipsburg, NJ: P & R, 2004.

Lewis, Peter. *The Glory of Christ*. Carlisle, Cumbria: Paternoster, 2004.

Livingston, James C. *Modern Christian Thought*. Vol. 1, *The Enlightenment and the Nineteenth Century*. Second edition. Minneapolis, MN: Fortress, 2006.

———. *Modern Christian Thought*. Vol. 2, *The Twentieth Century*. Second edition. Upper Saddle River, NJ: Prentice Hall, 2000.

Lohse, Bernard. *A Short History of Christian Doctrine*. Philadelphia: Fortress, 1980.

Lonergan, Bernard J. F. *Method in Theology*. Toronto: University of Toronto Press, 2007.

Longenecker, Richard N. *The Christology of Early Jewish Christianity*. Vancouver: Regent College Publishing, 2001.

MacLeod, Donald. *Jesus Is Lord: Christology Yesterday and Today*. Fearn: Christian Focus, 2000.

———. *The Person of Christ: Contours of Christian Theology*. Downers Grove, IL: InterVarsity Press, 1998.

Macquarrie, John. *Christology Revisited*. London: SCM, 1998.

Magesa, Laurenti. *Anatomy of Inculturation: Transforming the Church in Africa*. Nairobi, Kenya: Paulines Publications Africa, 2004.

Maina, Willson Muoha. *Historical and Social Dimensions in African Christian Theology: A Contemporary Approach*. Eugene, OR: Wipf & Stock, 2009.

Maluleke, Tinyiko Sam. "In Search of 'True Character of African Christian Identity': A Review of the Theology of Kwame Bediako." *Missionalia* 25, no. 2 (August 1997): 210–219.

Mangalwadi, Vishal. *The Book That Made Your World: How the Bible Created the Soul of Western Civilization*. Nashville, TN: Nelson, 2011.

Marshall, I. Howard. "The Development of Christology in the Early Church." *Tyndale Bulletin* 18 (1967): 77–93.

———. "Jesus as Messiah in Mark and Matthew." In *The Messiah in the Old and New Testaments*, edited by Stanley E. Porter, 117–143. Grand Rapids, MI: Eerdmans, 2007.

———. *The Origins of New Testament Christology*. Downers Grove, IL: InterVarsity Press, 1990.

———. *The Work of Christ*. Devon: Paternoster, 1969.

Martey, Emmanuel. *African Theology: Inculturation and Liberation*. Eugene, OR: Wipf & Stock, 2009.

Mbiti, John S. *African Religions and Philosophy*. Second revised edition. Oxford: Heinemann, 2006.

———. *Bible and Theology in African Christianity*. Nairobi: Oxford University Press, 1986.

———. *Concepts of God in Africa*. New York: Praeger, 1970.

———. *Introduction to African Religion*. London: Heinemann, 1981.

———. *New Testament Eschatology in an African Background: A Study of the Encounter Between New Testament and African Traditional Concepts*. Oxford: Oxford University Press, 1971.

Mbogu, Nicholas. *Jesus in Post-Missionary Africa: Issues and Questions in African Contextual Christology*. Enugu: San Press, 2012.

McFarland, Ian. *The Divine Image: Envisioning the Invisible God*. Minneapolis, MN: Fortress, 2005.

McGee, J. Vernon. *Love Liberation & the Law: The Ten Commandments*. Nashville, TN: Nelson, 1995.

McGrath, Alister E. *Christian Theology: An Introduction*. 5th edition. Malden, MA: Blackwell, 2011.

———, ed. *The Christian Theology Reader*. Third edition. Malden, MA: Blackwell, 2009.

———. *Historical Theology: An Introduction to the History of Christian Thought.* Malden, MA: Blackwell, 2005.

———. *The Making of Modern German Christology: 1750-1990.* Eugene, OR: Wipf & Stock, 2005.

McGrath, James F. *John's Apologetic Christology: Legitimation and Development in Johannine Christology.* Cambridge: Cambridge University Press, 2004.

McManners, John, ed. *The Oxford Illustrated History of Christianity.* New York, NY: Oxford University Press, 1990.

Metuh, Emefie Ikenga. *Comparative Studies of African Traditional Religions.* Onitsha, Nigeria: IMICO, 1987.

———. *God and Man in African Religion: A Case Study of the Igbo of Nigeria.* London: G. Chapman, 1981.

Mofokeng, T. "Black Christians, the Bible and Liberation." *Journal of Black Theology in South Africa* 2, no. 1 (1988): 34–42.

Molnar, Paul D. *Incarnation & Resurrection: Toward a Contemporary Understanding.* Grand Rapids, MI: Eerdmans, 2007.

Morgan, G. Campbell. *The Ten Commandments.* Chicago: Bible Institute Colportage Association, 1901.

Morris, Leon. *Jesus Is the Christ: Studies in the Theology of John.* Leicester: Inter-Varsity Press, 1989.

Moule, C. F. D. *The Origin of Christology.* Cambridge: Cambridge University Press, 1984.

Mpolo, Masamba ma, and Kalu Wilhelmina, eds. *African Pastoral Studies.* Ibadan, Nigeria: Daystar Press, 1985.

Mugabe, Henry Johannes. "Christology in an African Context." *Review and Expositor* 88, no. 4 (1991): 343–355.

Mugambi, J. N. K. *Christianity and African Culture.* Nairobi, Kenya: Acton, 2002.

Mugambi, J. N. K., and Laurenti Magesa. *Jesus in African Christianity: Experimentation and Diversity in African Christology.* 3rd edition. Nairobi, Kenya: Acton, 2003.

Mununguri, Masumbuko. *The Closeness of the God of Our Ancestors: An African Approach to the Incarnation.* Nairobi, Kenya: Paulines Publications Africa, 1998.

Mushete, A. Ngindu. "An Overview of African Theology." In *Paths of African Theology,* edited by Rosino Gibellini, 9–26. Maryknoll: Orbis Books, 1994.

Muzorewa, Gwinyai H. *The Origins and Development of African Theology.* Maryknoll, NY: Orbis Books, 1987.

Naugle, David K. *Worldview: The History of a Concept.* Grand Rapids, MI: Eerdmans, 2002.

Ndung'u, Nahashon W., and Philomena N. Mwaura, eds. *Challenges and Prospects of the Church in Africa: Theological Reflections for the 21st Century.* Nairobi, Kenya: Paulines Publications Africa, 2005.

Needham, N. R. *2000 Years of Christ's Power.* Vol. 1, *The Age of the Early Church Fathers.* Revised edition. London: Grace Publications, 2002.

Neill, Stephen. *A History of Christian Missions.* London: Penguin, 1990.

———. *Jesus through Many Eyes: Introduction to the Theology of the New Testament.* Philadelphia: Fortress, 1976.

Neimark, Philip John. *The Way of the Orisa: Empowering Your Life through the Ancient African Religion of Ifa.* New York: HarperSanFrancisco, 1993.

Neve, J. L. *A History of Christian Thought.* Vol. 1, *History of Christian Doctrine.* Philadelphia, PA: Muhlenberg Press, 1946.

The New International Webster's Comprehensive Dictionary of the English Language. Encyclopaedic edition. Naples, FL: Typhoon Media Corporation, 2010.

Neyrey, Jerome H. *Christ Is Community: The Christologies of the New Testament.* Collegeville, MN: Liturgical Press, 1990.

Nichols, O. Samuel. "African Christian Theology and the Ancestors: Christology, Ecclesiology, Ethics and Their Implications beyond Africa." *Journal of African Christian Thought* 8, no. 1 (June 2005): 27–35.

Nichols, Stephen J. *For Us and for Our Salvation: The Doctrine of Christ in the Early Church.* Wheaton, IL: Crossway, 2007.

Niebuhr, H. Richard. *Christ and Culture.* Fiftieth anniversary expanded edition. New York: HarperCollins, 2001.

Nolan, Albert. *Jesus before Christianity.* Mumbai: St Pauls, 2010.

Norris, Richard A., Jr, ed. *The Christological Controversy.* Sources of Early Christian Thought. Philadelphia: Fortress, 1980.

Ntetem, Abbé Marc. "Initiation, Traditional and Christian." In *A Reader in African Christian Theology*, edited by John Parratt, 99–103. London: SPCK, 2001.

Nürnberger, Klaus. *The Living Dead and the Living God: Christ and the Ancestors in a Changing Africa.* Pietermaritzburg: Cluster, 2007.

Nwachukwu, P.N.D. *African Authentic Christianity: An Inculturation Model for the Igbo.* New York: Lang, 2000.

Nwaogwugwu, Cletus Chukwuemeka. *Ancestor Christology: A Christian Evaluation of the Ancestral Cult in the Traditional Religion of the Sub-Saharan Africa.* Bloomington, IN: iUniverse, 2011.

Nwigwe, N. S. "Johannine Christology: A Critical Analysis." In *Christology in African Context*, edited by S. O. Abogunrins, J. O. Akao, and Dorcas Olu Akintunde, 215–225. Biblical Studies Series, no. 2. Ibadan: Nigerian Association for Biblical Studies, 2003.

Nyamiti, Charles. "African Christologies Today." In *Faces of Jesus in Africa*, edited by Robert J. Schreiter, 3–23. Maryknoll: Orbis Books, 2005.

———. "African Christologies Today." In *Jesus in African Christianity: Experimentation and Diversity in African Christology*, 3rd edition, edited by J. N. K. Mugambi and Lauren Magesa, 17–39. Nairobi: Acton, 2003.

———. *African Theology: Its Nature, Problems and Methods*. Gaba Institute Pastoral Papers 19. Kampala: Gaba Publications, 1971.

———. *Christ as Our Ancestor: Christology from an African Perspective*. Gweru, Zimbabwe: Mambo Press, 1984.

———. "Contemporary African Christologies: Assessment and Practical Suggestions." In *Paths of African Theology*, edited by Rosino Gibellini, 62–77. Maryknoll, NY: Orbis Books, 1994.

———. "A Critical Assessment on Some Issues on Today's African Theology." *African Christian Studies* 5, no. 1 (1989): 5–19.

———. *Studies in African Christian Theology*. Vol. 1, *Jesus Christ the Ancestor of Humankind: Methodological and Trinitarian Foundation*. Nairobi, Kenya: CUEA, 2005.

———. *Studies in African Christian Theology*. Vol. 2, *Jesus Christ the Ancestor of Humankind: An Essay on African Christology*. Nairobi: CUEA, 2006.

O'Collins, Gerald. *Christology: A Biblical, Historical, and Systematic Study of Jesus*. 2nd edition. Oxford: Oxford University Press, 2009.

———. *Interpreting Jesus*. London: Mowbray, 1992.

O'Donovan, Wilbur. *Introduction to Biblical Christianity from African Perspective*. Ilorin, Nigeria: Nigeria Evangelical Fellowship, 1992.

Obaje, Yusufu Ameh. "Theocentric Christology as a Basis for a More Relevant Doctrine of Christ for the African Christian." *Ogbomoso Journal of Theology* 5 (1990): 1–7.

Oden, Thomas C. *After Modernity What?: Agenda For Theology*. Grand Rapids, MI: Zondervan, 1992.

———. *How Africa Shaped the Christian Mind: Rediscovering the African Seedbed of Western Christianity*. Downers Grove, IL: InterVarsity Press, 2007.

Oduyoye, Modupe. *The Vocabulary of Yoruba Religious Discourse*. Ibadan: Daystar Press, 1972.

Okure, Teresa. "Inculturation: Biblical / Theological Bases." In *32 Articles Evaluating Inculturation of Christianity in Africa*, edited by Teresa Okure and Paul van Theil, 55–61. Eldoret, Kenya: AMECEA Gaba Publications, 1990.

Okure, Teresa, and Paul van Thiel, eds. *32 Articles Evaluating Inculturation of Christianity in Africa*. Eldoret, Kenya: AMECEA Gaba Publications, 1990.

Oladunjoye, J. O. "Decolonizing Biblical Studies: An Opening Address." In *Decolonization of Biblical Interpretation in Africa*, edited by Samuel O. Abogunrin, 1–9. Ibadan: Nigerian Association for Biblical Studies, 2005.

Oliphint, K. Scott. *Reasons (for Faith): Philosophy in the Service of Theology.* Phillipsburg, NJ: P & R, 2006.

Olson, Jørn Henrik. "Contextualised Christology in Tropical Africa?" *Swedish Missiological Themes* 85, no. 3–4 (1997): 247–267.

Olson, Roger E. *The Story of Christian Theology: Twenty Centuries of Tradition & Reform.* Downers Grove, IL: InterVarsity Press, 1999.

Omoregbe, Joseph I. *A Simplified History of Western Philosophy: Ancient and Medieval Philosophy.* Vol. 1. Nigeria: Joja Press, 1991.

Onyenechechie, Thompson O. *Doing Incarnational Theology in Africa: A Christo-Centric Approach.* Aba: Assemblies of God, 2007.

Opoku, Kofi Asare. *West African Traditional Religion.* Lagos, Nigeria: FEP International, 1978.

Osuala, E. C. *Introduction to Research Methodology.* 3rd edition. Onisha, Nigeria: Africana First, 2005.

Ott, Craig, and Harold A. Netland, eds. *Globalizing Theology: Belief and Practice in an Era of World Christianity.* Grand Rapids, MI: Baker Books, 2006.

Palmer, Timothy. "Jesus Christ: Our Ancestor?" *TCNN Research Bulletin* 42 (2004): 4–17.

Pannenberg, Wolfhart. *Jesus – God and Man.* 2nd edition. Philadelphia: Westminster, 1977.

Parratt, John, ed. *The Practice of Presence: Shorter Writings of Harry Sawyerr.* Grand Rapids, MI: Eerdmans, 1996.

———, ed. *A Reader in African Christian Theology.* London: SPCK, 2001.

———. *Reinventing Christianity: African Theology Today.* Grand Rapids, MI: Eerdmans, 1995.

Parrinder, E. Geoffrey. *African Traditional Religion.* London: SPCK, 1962.

———. *African Traditional Religion.* 3rd edition. London: Sheldon, 1974.

———. *West African Religion: A Study of the Beliefs and Practices of Akan, Ewe, Yoruba, Ibo, and Kindred Peoples.* London: Epworth, 1978.

Pelikan, Jaroslav. *The Christian Tradition: A History of the Development of Doctrine.* Vol. 2, *The Spirit of Eastern Christendom (600–1700).* London: University of Chicago Press, 1977.

Peterson, Ryan S. *The Imago Dei as Human Identity: A Theological Interpretation.* Winona Lake, IN: Eisenbrauns, 2016.

Piper, John. *Contending for Our All: Defending Truth and Treasuring Christ in the Lives of Athanasius, John Owen and J. Gresham Machen.* Leicester: InterVarsity Press, 2006.

Placher, William C. *Readings in the History of Christian Theology.* Vol. 1, *From Its Beginnings to the Eve of the Reformation.* Philadelphia: Westminster, 1988.

———. *Readings in the History of Christian Theology.* Vol. 2, *From the Reformation to the Present.* Philadelphia: Westminster, 1988.

Pobee, John S. *Toward an African Theology*. Nashville, TN: Abingdon, 1979.
Pope Pius XII. *Evangelii Praecones (1951)*. Translated as *The Popes and the Missions: Four Encyclical Letters*. London: Sword of the Spirit, 1900.
Porter, Stanley E. "The Messiah in Luke and Acts: Forgiveness for the Captives." In *The Messiah in the Old and New Testaments*, edited by Stanley E. Porter, 144–164. Grand Rapids, MI: Eerdmans, 2007.
Quasten, Johannes. *Patrology Volume 1: The Beginnings of Patristic Literature from the Apostles Creed to Irenaeus*. Allen, TX: Christian Classics, 1995.
———. *Patrology Volume 2: The Ante-Nicene Literature after Irenaeus*. Westminster, MD: Christian Classics, 1995.
Radoli, Agatha. "Preface." In *32 Articles Evaluating Inculturation of Christiainity in Africa*, edited by Teresa Okure and Paul van Theil, x–xii. Kenya: AMECA Gaba Pubications, 1990.
Rahner, Karl. *The Church after the Council*. New York: Herder & Herder, 1966.
———. *Foundations of Christian Faith: An Introduction to the Idea of Christianity*. New York: Seabury Press, 1978.
Raj, P. S. "Inculturation." In *Dictionary of Mission Theology: Evangelical Foundations*, edited by John Corrie, 181. Downers Grove, IL: InterVarsity Press, 2007.
Ramm, Bernard L. *An Evangelical Christology: Ecumenical & Historic*. Nashville, TN: Nelson, 1985.
Ray, Benjamin C. *African Religions: Symbols, Rituals, and Community*. Upper Saddle River, NJ: Prentice Hall, 1976.
Renwick, A. M. *The Story of the Church*. London: Inter-Varsity Fellowship, 1966.
Renwick, A. M., and A. M. Harman. *The Story of the Church*. 3rd ed. Leicester: Inter-Varsity Press, 1999.
Richardson, Alan. *Creeds in the Making: A Short Introduction to the History of Christian Doctrine*. London: SCM, 1961.
Roberts, Alexander, and James Donaldson, eds. *The Ante-Nicene Fathers: Translation of the Writings of the Fathers Down to A.D. 325*. Vol. 3, *Latin Christianity: Its Founder, Tertullian*. Grand Rapids, MI: Eerdmans, 1980.
Robertson, O. Palmer. *The Christ of the Covenants*. Phillipsburg, NJ: P & R, 1980.
Robinson, John A. T., and David L. Edward. *The Honest to God Debate*. London: SCM, 1963.
Rodney, Walter. *How Europe Underdeveloped Africa*. Abuja: Panaf Publishing, 2009.
Runia, Klass. *The Present-day Christological Debate*. Leicester: Inter-Varsity Press, 1984.
Ryan, Patrick, ed. *Inculturation in the South African Context*. Nairobi, Kenya: Paulines Publications Africa, 2000.

Sacks, Stuart. *Revealing Jesus as the Messiah: Identifying Isaiah's Servant of the Lord.* Fearn: Christian Focus, 1998.

Samuel, Vinay, and Chris Sugden, eds. *Sharing Jesus in the Two Thirds World.* Grand Rapids, MI: Eerdmans, 1983.

Sanders, E. P. *Paul and Palestinian Judaism.* Philadelphia: Fortress, 1977.

Sawyer, Harry. *Creative Evangelism: Toward a New Christian Encounter with Africa.* London: Lutterworth, 1968.

———. "What Is African Theology?" In *A Reader in African Christian Theology,* edited by John Parratt, 9–22. London: SPCK, 2001.

Schaeffer, Francis A. *A Christian Manifesto.* Westchester, IL: Crossway, 1982.

———. *He Is There and He Is Not Silent.* Wheaton, IL: Tyndale House, 1972.

Schaff, Philip, ed. *History of the Christian Church.* Vol. 3, *Nicene and Post-Nicene Christianity: From Constantine the Great to Gregory the Great A.D. 311-600.* Grand Rapids, MI: Eerdmans, 1984.

———. *A Select Library of Nicene and Post-Nicene Fathers of the Christian Church.* First Series. Vol. 10, *Saint Chrysostom: Homily on the Gospel of Saint Matthew.* Edinburgh: T & T Clark, 1998.

———, ed. *A Select Library of the Nicene and Post-Nicene Fathers of the Christian Church.* First Series. Vol. 14, *Homilies on the Gospel of St John and the Epistle to the Hebrews.* Grand Rapids, MI: Eerdmans, 1983.

Schaff, Philip, and Henry Wace, eds. *A Select Library of Nicene and Post-Nicene Fathers of the Christian Church.* Second Series. Vol. 14, *The Seven Ecumenical Councils.* Grand Rapids, MI: Eerdmans, 1979.

———. *A Select Library of Nicene and Post-Nicene Fathers of the Christian Church.* Second Series. Vol. 4. *St Athanasius: Select Works and Letters.* New York: Charles Scribner's Sons, 1923.

———, eds. *A Select Library of Nicene and Post-Nicene Fathers of the Christian Church.* Second Series. Vol. 7. Grand Rapids, MI: Eerdmans, 1983.

———, eds. *Nicene and Post-Nicene Fathers of the Christian Church.* Second Series. Vol. 4. Grand Rapids, MI: Eerdmans, 1980.

Schineller, Peter. *A Handbook on Inculturation.* New York: Paulist Press, 1990.

———. "Inculturation and Syncretism: What Is the Real Issue?" *International Bulletin of Missionary Research* 16, no. 2 (April 1992): 50–53.

Schreiter, Robert J. *Constructing Local Theologies.* Maryknoll, NY: Orbis Books, 2003.

———, ed. *Faces of Jesus in Africa.* Maryknoll, NY: Orbis Books, 2005.

———. "Jesus Christ in Africa Today." In *Faces of Jesus in Africa,* edited by Robert J. Schreiter, vii–xiii. Maryknoll, NY: Orbis Books, 2005.

Schweitzer, Albert. *The Quest of the Historical Jesus: A Critical Study of Its Progress from Reimarus to Wrede.* New York: Macmillan, 1961.

Seeberg, Reinhold. *Text-Book of the History of Doctrines*. Vol. 1. *History of Doctrines in the Ancient Church*. Grand Rapids, MI: Baker Books, 1956.

Setiloane, Gabriel. "How the Traditional Worldview Persists in the Christianity of the Sotho-Tswana." In *Christianity in Independent Africa*, edited by Edward Fashole-Luke, 402–411. London: R. Collings, 1978.

———. "Where Are We in African Theology?" In *African Theology en Route*, edited by Kofi Appiah-Kubi and Sergio Torres, 59–65. Maryknoll, NY: Orbis Books, 1979.

Shelley, Bruce L. *Church History in Plain Language*. 3rd edition. Nashville, TN: Nelson, 2008.

Shorter, Aylward. *African Culture and the Christian Church: An Introduction to Social and Pastoral Anthropology*. Maryknoll, NY: Orbis Books, 1974.

———. *Toward a Theology of Inculturation*. Maryknoll, NY: Orbis Books, 1988.

Siollun, Max. *Oil, Politics and Violence: Nigeria's Military Coup Culture (1966–1976)*. New York: Algora, 2009.

Sire, James W. *The Universe Next Door: A Basic Worldview Catalog*. Downers Grove, IL: InterVarsity Press, 2009.

Smith, David L. *A Handbook of Contemporary Theology: Tracing Trends & Discerning Directions in Today's Theological Landscape*. Grand Rapids, MI: Baker Books, 2001.

Stinton, Diane B. *Jesus of Africa: Voices of Contemporary African Christology*. Nairobi, Kenya: Paulines Publications Africa, 2004.

Stott, John. *The Authentic Jesus: A Response to Current Skepticism in the Church*. London: Marshal, Morgan & Scott, 1985.

———. *The Incomparable Christ*. Downers Grove, IL: InterVarsity Press, 2004.

Strauss, David Friedrich. *The Life of Jesus, Critically Examined*. New York: Cosimo Classics, 2009.

Strauss, Lehman. *The Eleven Commandments*. Neptune, NJ: Loizeaux Brothers, 1975.

Strimple, Robert B. *The Modern Search for the Real Jesus: An Introductory Survey of the Historical Roots of Gospels Criticism*. Philipsburg, NJ: P & R, 1995.

Sullivan, Francis A. *Magisterium: Teaching Authority in the Catholic Church*. New York: Paulist Press, 1983.

Sullivan, Maureen. *101 Questions and Answers on Vatican II*. Mumbai, India: St Pauls, 2004.

Sundkler, Bengt G. M. *The Christian Ministry in Africa*. London: SCM, 1962.

Sykes, S. W., and J. P. Clayton, eds. *Christ, Faith and History: Cambridge Studies in Christology*. Cambridge: Cambridge University Press, 1978.

Synod of Bishops, Special Assembly for Africa. *Instrumentum Laboris: The Church in Africa and Her Evangelising Mission Towards the Year 2000: "You Shall Be My Witnesses" (Acts 1:8)*. Vatican City: Libreria Editrice Vaticana, 1993.

———. *Lineamenta*. Vatican City: Libreria Editrice Vaticana, 1990.
Synodus Episcoporum, Coetus Specialis pro Africa. *Nuntius, Relation Ante Disceptationem, Relation Post Disceptationem*. Vatican City: Libreria Editrice Vaticana, 1994.
Taylor, John V. *The Primal Vision: Christian Presence amid African Religion*. London: SCM, 1994.
Tennent, Timothy C. *Theology in the Context of World Christianity: How the Global Church Is Influencing the Way We Think About and Discuss Theology*. Grand Rapids, MI: Zondervan, 2007.
Thatcher, Tom. "Remembering Jesus: John's Negative Christology." In *The Messiah in the Old and New Testaments*, edited by Stanley E. Porter, 165–189. Grand Rapids, MI: Eerdmans, 2007.
Tlhagale, Buti. "Saints and Ancestors: A Close Look." In *Inculturation in the South African Context*, edited by Patrick Ryan, 27–38. Nairobi, Kenya: Pauline Publications Africa, 2000.
Turaki, Yusufu. "Christianity and African Traditional Religion: A Systematic Examination of the Interactions of Religion." Vols. 1 and 2. (Unpublished Manuscript).
———. "The Role of Ancestors." In *Africa Bible Commentary*, edited by Tokunboh Adeyemo. Nairobi: Word Alive, 2006.
———. "Techniques of African Pagan Spirituality." In *On Global Wizardry: Techniques of Pagan Spirituality and A Christian Response*, edited by Peter Jones, 115–130. Escondido, CA: Main Entry Editions, 2010.
———. *The Theory and Practice of Christian Missions in Africa: A Century of SIM/ECWA History and Legacy in Nigeria 1893–1993*. Vol. 1. Nairobi: International Bible Society Africa, 1999.
———. *Tribal Gods of Africa: Ethnicity, Racism, Tribalism and the Gospel of Christ*. Nairobi: Ethics, Peace and Justice Commission of the Association of Evangelicals, 1997.
———. *The Unique Christ for Salvation: The Challenge of the Non-Christian Religions and Cultures*. Nairobi: International Bible Society, 2001.
Turner, Harold W. *Living Tribal Religions*. London: Ward Lock Educational, 1971.
Tutu, Desmond. "Black Theology and African Theology – Soulmates of Antagonisits?" In *A Reader in African Christian Theology*, edited by John Parratt, 36–45. London: SPCK, 2001.
Tiénou, Tite. *The Theological Task of the Church in Africa: Theological Perspectives in Africa*. Ghana: African Christian Press, 1990.
Uche, Okey Jude. "The Theological Analysis of *Ikpu-Ala* as a Social Justice Value in Igbo Catholic Church (Nigeria)." PhD diss., South African Theological Seminary, June 2016.

Udeafor, Ndubisi Innocent. *Inculturation: Path to African Christianity*. Nigeria, Enugu: SNAAP Press, 1994.

Ukpong, Justin S. "Christology and Inculturation: A New Testament Perspective." In *Paths of African Theology*, edited by Rosino Gibellini, 40–61. Maryknoll, NY: Orbis Books, 1994.

———. "Rereading the Bible with African Eyes: Inculturation and Hermeneutics." *Journal of Theology for Southern Africa* 19 (June 1995): 3–14.

Urivwo, S. U. "Traditional Religion and Christianity Among the Urhobo." In *The Gods in Retreat*, edited by Emefie Ikenga Metuh. Enugu, Nigeria: Fourth Dimension Publishers, 1986.

van den Toren, Benno. "Kwame Bediako's Christology in Its African Evangelical Context." *Exchange* 26, no. 3 (1997): 218–232.

van der Walt, B. J. *The Eye Is the Lamp of the Body: Worldview and Their Impact*. Potchefstroom: ICCA, 2008.

———. *The Liberating Message: A Christian Worldview for Africa*. Potchefstroom: University for Christian Higher Education, 1994.

———. *When African and Western Cultures Meet*. Potchefstroom: Institute for Contemporary Christianity in Africa, 2006.

van Engen, Charles E. *Mission on the Way: Issues in Mission Theology*. Grand Rapids, MI: Baker Books, 1996.

Vine, W. E. *Vine's Complete Expository Dictionary of Old and New Testament Words with Topical Index*. Nashville, TN: Nelson, 2000.

Wace, Henry, and Philip Schaff, eds. *A Select Library of Nicene and Post-Nicene Fathers of the Christian Church*. Second series. Vol. 4, *St Athanasius: Select Works and Letters*. Grand Rapids, MI: Eerdmans, 1980.

Wachege, Patrick N. "Charles Nyamiti: Vibrant Pioneer of Inculturated African Theology." In *African Theology in the 21st Century: The Contribution of the Pioneers*. Vol. 2, edited by Bénézet Bujo and Juvénal Ilunga Muya, 149–160. Nairobi: Paulines Publications Africa, 2006.

Waliggo, J. M., A. Roest Crollius, T. Nkeramihigo, and, J. Mutiso-Mbinda. *Inculturation: Its Meaning and Urgency*. Kampala, Uganda: St Paul Publications, 1986.

Walls, Andrew F. *The Cross-Cultural Process in Christian History: Studies in the Transmission and Appropriation of Faith*. Maryknoll, NY: Orbis Books, 2002.

———. "The Gospel as the Prisoner and Liberator of Culture." In *The Missionary Movement in Christian History: Studies in the Transmission of Faith*. Maryknoll, NY: Orbis Books, 1996.

Walvoord, John F. *Jesus Christ Our Lord*. Chicago, IL: Moody, 1969.

Watson, Thomas. *The Ten Commandments*. London: Banner of Truth, 1962.

Wendland, Ernst. "'Who Do People Say That I Am?' Contextualizing Christology." *African Africa Journal of Evangelical Theology* 10, no. 2 (1991): 13–32.

Wessels, Anton. *Images of Jesus: How Jesus Is Perceived and Portrayed in Non-European Cultures*. Grand Rapids, MI: Eerdmans, 1991.

Westfall, Cynthia Long. "Messianic Themes of Temple, Enthronement, and Victory in Hebrews and the General Epistles." In *The Messiah in the Old and New Testaments*, edited by Stanley E. Porter, 210–229. Grand Rapids, MI: Eerdmans, 2007.

Wilken, Robert L. *The Myth of Christian Beginnings*. London: SCM, 1979.

Wilkinson, Michael B., and Hugh N. Campbell. *Philosophy of Religion: An Introduction*. New York: Continuum, 2010.

Willmington, H. L. *Willmington's Guide to the Bible*. Carol Stream, IL: Tyndale House, 1984.

Wood, Laurence W. *Theology as History and Hermeneutics: A Post-Critical Conversation with Contemporary Theology*. Lexington, KY: Emeth, 2005.

Wotogbe Weneka, Wellington O. "Christ as Our Ancestor." In *Christology in African Context*, edited by S. O. Abogunrin, J. O. Akao, and Dorcas Olu Akintunde, 289–298. Biblical Studies Series, no. 2. Ibadan: Nigerian Association for Biblical Studies, 2003.

Wright, Christopher J. H. "Biblical Ethics: A Survey of the Last Decade." *Themelios* 18, no. 2 (1993): 15–19.

———. *Knowing Jesus through the Old Testament*. Carlisle, Cumbria: Langham Preaching Resources, 2014.

———. *The Mission of God: Unlocking the Bible's Grand Narrative*. Downers Grove, IL: InterVarsity Press, 2008.

———. *Thinking Clearly about the Uniqueness of Jesus*. London: Evangelical Alliance, 1997.

Wright, N. T. *The Challenge of Jesus: Rediscovering Who Jesus Was and Is*. Downers Grove, IL: IVP Academic, 1999.

———. *Jesus and the Victory of God*. Vol. 2, *Christian Origins and the Question of God*. London: SPCK, 1996.

Yamsat, Pandang. *The Role of the Church in Democratic Governance in Nigeria*. Bukuru, Nigeria: Biblical Studies Foundation, 2001.

Young, Francis M. *From Nicaea to Chalcedon: A Guide to the Literature and Its Background*. Philadelphia: Fortress, 1983.

Young, T. C. "The Idea of God in Northern Nyasaland." In *African Ideas of God*, edited by E. Smith, 36–60. London: Edinburgh House Press, 1950.

Youngblood, Ronald. *The Heart of the Old Testament*. Grand Rapids, MI: Baker Books, 1998.

Zamoyta, Vincent. *The Theology of Christ: Sources*. Milwaukee, WI: Bruce, 1967.

Internet and Magazine Sources

"The African Renaissance Monument in Dakar, Senegal." Black History Heroes. http://www.blackhistoryheroes.com/2013/02/the-african-renaissance-monument.

Amanze, James N. "Globalisation of Theological Education and the Future of the Church in Africa: Some Critical Reflections Towards Edinburgh 2010 and Its Aftermath." *Missionalia* 38, no. 2 (2010): 294–306. Available online, https://journals.co.za/content/mission/38/2/EJC76141.

"Attorney General of Zambia v. Meer Care & Desai (A firm) & Ors." Casemine, https://www.casemine.com/judgement/uk/5b46f1f62c94e0775e7ef1bf.

"Corruption: The Cankerworm Eating Our Economy." *Countdown Magazine*. Vol. 4, no. 2, Information edition, 2011.

Craven, Jackie. "About the 2005 Berlin Holocaust Memorial: A Memorial to the Murdered Jews of Europe." Thought Co., https://www.thoughtco.com/the-berlin-holocaust-memorial-by-peter-eisenman-177928.

Danjuma, Johnny. "Violence in Lafia as Doma Is Arraigned." *The Nation*. Vol. 7, no. 1918, 19 October 2011.

Gale, Thompson. "Afrocentrism." *Encyclopedia of African-American Culture and History*. Encyclopedia.com, https://www.encyclopedia.com/history/biographies/historians-canadian-biographies/afrocentrism.

Gongloe, Tiawan. "Right and the Politics of Fear and Violence." The Perspective, http://www.theperspective.org/december2003/gongloe_un.html.

Iwerieblor, Ehiedu E. G. "The Colonization of Africa." African Age (website). Accessed 20 January 2016, http://exhibitions.nypl.org/africanaage/essay-colonization-of-africa.html.

Kimenyi, S. Mwangi, and Moyo Nelipher. "The Late Zambian President Fredrick Chiluba: A Legacy of Failed Democratic Transition." Brookings, https://www.brookings.edu/opinions/the-late-zambian-president-fredrick-chiluba-a-legacy-of-failed-democratic-transition/.

MacDonald, Carissa. "10 Festivals That Honor the Dead." Listverse. Posted on 19 January 2013. Accessed 1 August 2015. http://listverse.com/2013/01/19/10-festivals-that-honor-the-dead/.

Manwarren, Andrew. "Apollinarius: Know Your Heretics." Pastor Manwarren's Musings, https://pastorandrewmanwarren.com/2010/03/30/apollinarius-know-your-heretics/.

Njoku, J. Uzochukwu. "Reflecting on Assassinations and Destructions in Nigeria's Socio-Politcal Culture." *African Renaissance* 3, no. 6 (2006): 45–48. Available online, https://journals.co.za/content/aa_afren/3/6/EJC10240.

Oden, Patrick. "The Christologies of Apollinaris of Laoicea and Theodore of Mopsuestia." Dual Ravens. Accessed 17 June 2014, http://www.dualravens.com/fullerlife/christologies.htm.

Ritchie, Ian. "African Theology and Social Change: An Anthropological Approach." Phd diss., http://digitool.library.mcgill.ca/webclient/StreamGate?folder_id=0&dvs=1562851175221-663.

Sumitra. "Famadihana – Dancing with the Dead in Madagascar." OddityCentral. Posted 4 April 2012. Accessed 1 August 2015. http://www.odditycentral.com/pics/famadihana-dancing-with-the-dead.

"The Explosion of Christianity in Africa." Christianity.com. Accessed 7 December 2016. http://www.christianity.com/church/church-history/timeline/2001-now/the-explosion-of-christianity-in-africa-11630859.html.

"Trial of Ex-Governors: Another Offensive to Nowhere?" *TELL Magazine*, no. 42, 24 October 2011.

Virgil. "The Aeneid Book II." Translated by A. S. Kline. Poetry in Translation. Accessed 10 August 2012. https://www.poetryintranslation.com/PITBR/Latin/VirgilAeneidII.php#highlightaeneid.

"Visiting the Martin Luther King, Jr. Memorial in Washington, DC." Washington DC, https://washington.org/visit-dc/martin-luther-king-jr-memorial.

"War Against Corruption." *Countdown Magazine*, Vol. 7, No. 1; Anniversary Edition, 2011.

"Why Was Queen Elizabeth I Called Gloriana?" Answers. Accessed 13 November 2017. https://www.answers.com/Q/Why_was_Queen_Elizabeth_I_called_Gloriana.

Index of Names

A

Aaron 143, 306, 310
Aben, Tersur 24, 58, 80, 335
Abraham 8, 10, 23, 25, 27, 31–33, 92, 143, 183, 228, 230, 257, 258, 263–268, 270–272, 274, 275, 277–279, 284, 290, 306–309, 316, 339, 357, 366, 367
Achebe, Chinua 156
Adam 8, 26, 27, 31–33, 72, 84, 169, 192, 258, 261, 263, 270, 273, 276, 284, 288, 300, 308, 309, 357, 366
Adeyemo, Tokunboh 234
Ajah, Paul O. 137, 158, 167
Anderson, Allan 248
Anderson, George W. 257
Apollinarius 72, 84, 85, 128
Arius 15, 119–122, 124, 127–132, 147
Arrupe, Pedro 209, 255
Athanasius 7, 8, 12, 14, 15, 17–19, 21–24, 27, 29–31, 39, 55, 81–83, 96, 104, 107, 109, 110, 123–130, 132–134, 140, 141, 144, 145, 147, 193, 272, 335, 360, 368
Augustine, St 73, 116, 200, 301
Ayres, Lewis 81, 82

B

Baillie, D. M. 80, 81
Barclay, William 281, 282, 289–302, 304, 305, 308
Barth, Karl 85–87
Bauckham, Richard 92, 93, 265
Bediako, Kwame 23, 53, 212, 224
Benedict XV 190
Benedict XVI 107, 113
Bevans, Stephen B. 18, 189
Bingham, Roland V. 3
Bolaji Idowu, Edward 56
Bujo, Bénézet 1, 6, 16, 19, 23, 41, 55, 60, 61, 63–68, 70, 79, 80, 83, 86, 165, 166, 169, 239, 273, 335, 360, 363, 368

C

Calvin, John 301, 306, 332
Chidili, Barth 224–228
Clark, David K. 332, 334, 335
Copleston, Frederick 135, 136
Cullmann, Oscar 286, 307, 336, 337

D

da Vinci, Leonardo 2
Donovan, Vincent J. 38
Dunn, James D. G. 294–296

E

Edgar, William 109, 110
Enns, Paul Peter 33, 262, 264, 265, 270
Evans, Craig A. 287, 288

F

Fee, Gordon D. 295

G

Goergen, Donald J. 229, 252
Gowans, Walter 2

I
Idowu, Emmanuel Bolaji 1

J
John Paul II 202, 204, 205, 207, 256, 257
Johnson, Alan F. 324, 325
Johnson, Terry L. 335
John, the apostle 22, 30, 60, 68, 95, 292, 293
John XXIII 20, 191, 195–197, 199, 218, 222

K
Kato, Byang H. 19, 144, 212, 234
Kent, Thomas 2

M
Marcion 112, 114, 115, 117, 118, 133, 147
Mbiti, John S. 1, 55, 64, 138, 150, 152, 153, 156–159, 163, 174, 242, 245–247, 251, 311, 312, 317
Moses 10, 143, 183, 184, 263, 265, 266, 270, 274, 275, 279, 284, 288, 289, 301–306, 308–310, 325, 339, 357, 367
Mugambi, J. N. K. 158, 171, 176, 234, 244

N
Neyrey, Jerome H. 14, 283
Ntetem, Abbé Marc 6, 86, 165, 169, 237, 239, 273, 335, 360, 363, 368
Nürnberger, Klaus 2, 3, 18, 134, 142, 183, 239, 240, 246, 275, 313, 314, 330
Nwaogwugwu, Cletus Chukwuemeka 139, 151, 311, 341
Nyamiti, Charles 5, 6, 16, 19, 22, 23, 41, 51, 52, 55, 68, 69, 72–80, 83, 86, 96, 165, 169, 189, 236, 237, 273, 335, 360, 363, 364, 368

O
Oliphint, K. Scott 109, 110, 332

P
Paul, the apostle 22, 30, 58, 80, 89, 102, 188, 192, 224, 225, 256, 263, 271, 295, 341
Paul VI 20, 199–203, 207, 216, 222
Peter, the apostle 14, 19, 101, 271
Pius XII 20, 191–193, 195, 196
Plato 135–138
Praxeas 112, 114, 116, 118, 133, 147

R
Rahner, Karl 85, 86, 218, 225

S
Schweitzer, Albert 42, 98

T
Tennent, Timothy C. 8, 13, 341, 342, 357
Tertullian 7, 8, 12, 14, 17–19, 21–24, 27, 29–31, 39, 55, 94, 96, 105–107, 109–113, 115–118, 133, 134, 140, 141, 144, 145, 147, 187, 200, 214, 231, 235, 335, 360, 368
Turaki, Yusufu 33, 40, 41, 54, 138, 149, 153, 163, 234, 274, 277, 278, 314, 366

U
Uche, Okey Jude 6, 49, 75, 88, 208, 355, 357, 364, 366

W
Walls, Andrew F. 184, 185, 340
Wright, Christopher J. H. 92, 265, 266, 287, 289, 290
Wright, N. T. 287, 298, 331

Index of Subjects

A
adaptation 36, 179, 197, 198, 202, 210, 355
African Linguistic Affinity Christology 7, 9–11, 24, 25, 28, 29, 32, 36, 268, 270, 279, 280, 328, 336, 338, 345, 350, 354, 356, 360, 362–365, 367
African Traditional Religion 6, 53, 155, 164, 172, 175, 207, 234, 247, 327, 336, 348, 363
aggiornamento 20, 218
Akan, the 318
   cultural sources 60
   language 52
   traditional sources 60
analogies 75, 80, 226, 253, 328, 329, 332, 333
   African 321
   definition 333
   for Jesus 33, 70, 84, 226, 253, 277, 334
   for mystery of God 79
   human 281
   of proportionality 40, 75, 86, 333, 334
ancestors 5, 32, 33, 59, 63, 64, 66, 67, 69, 86, 87, 100, 133, 134, 139, 153, 155–159, 161–163, 165, 168, 172–174, 177, 185, 211, 223, 238, 243–246, 248, 249, 274, 275, 311–314, 345, 361
   African 24, 27, 33, 66, 71, 72, 76, 133, 134, 142, 144, 157, 171, 274, 311, 316, 319
   and Christ 19, 26, 34, 40, 59, 67, 75, 80, 83, 84, 86, 165, 190, 224–228, 237, 239, 252–254, 272, 273, 277, 278, 315, 316, 334–336, 339, 342, 354, 361
   and family 160, 162, 245
   and saints 148, 172
   as mediators 26, 163, 173, 240, 246, 275, 311, 315
   belief in 167, 170, 327
   character of 67, 138, 226, 248, 249
   cult of the 5, 10, 31, 34, 55, 56, 64, 79, 96, 107, 138, 165, 168, 173, 174, 237, 238, 243, 248, 252–254, 281, 310, 363, 365
   definition 40, 328
   functions of 161, 227, 240, 275, 315, 342
   God and 64, 239
   Hebrew 274, 276
   honouring of 24, 64, 239
   in African context 16, 229, 239, 240

in culture 223, 252, 253, 341
influence of 158, 159
in religion 55
Israel's 143, 266
Jewish 257, 263, 266, 268, 274, 277, 278, 280, 293, 363
memories of 16, 69, 160, 176, 359, 363
offerings to 241, 327
place of 65, 165, 166
power of 137, 138, 160, 170, 240, 249
protection 155, 243
relationship with 79, 138, 158, 314
reverance of 77, 170, 275
roles of 5, 33, 59, 60, 64, 148, 161, 162, 169, 172, 176, 240, 241, 243, 246, 247, 249, 254, 256, 268, 275, 277, 278, 309, 311
significance of 212, 233, 239, 241, 242, 340
traditions 229, 321
world of. See ancestral world
ancestral cult. See under ancestors, cult of the
ancestral realm. See ancestral world
ancestral world 69, 134, 137–139, 144, 155, 158, 159, 168, 226, 238, 338, 359
apologists 93, 96, 110, 145
  African 21, 22, 31, 109, 145
  early African 19, 110
  early church 91
apostolic age 95
Atsam, the 157

B
beliefs 238, 242
  African 41, 135, 137, 139, 144, 172, 201, 225, 234, 242, 338
  African primal 31, 35, 88, 185, 280, 309, 341, 344, 359
  African traditional 234, 238, 243, 328
  ancestor 83, 137
  ancient African 360
  Christian 12, 114, 129, 142, 185, 201, 220
    on communion 171
    traditional 96
  cultural 96, 190
  primal 165, 238, 363
  religious 41, 63, 69, 167, 190, 278, 283, 286, 288, 310, 312
  Roman Catholic 230, 361
  traditional 23, 49, 67, 144, 183, 223, 233, 234, 236, 242
  traditional African 31, 56, 80, 137, 148, 155, 156, 159, 167, 208, 245, 247, 248, 320, 348
belief systems 36, 267, 309, 326
  African 148, 155
  foreign 206
  heathen 193
  traditional 361
  traditional African 167, 245, 247
bishops
  African 207, 208, 256
blessings
  from ancestors 53, 162, 163, 168, 241, 246, 249
  from Christ 32, 264
  from God 265, 274, 290

C
Catechism 176, 227
categories 208
categories, cultural 17, 41, 255, 361

Index of Subjects

African 39, 49, 166, 174, 208, 224, 226, 236, 250
categories, religious 27, 41
  African 18, 24, 49, 50, 147, 207, 208, 226, 227
  Western 12, 48
Catholic 194
  Church 131, 206
  doctrine 15, 70
Catholicism 204, 206, 217, 219
  African 219
Chalcedon 15, 87, 147
Chawai, the 157, 242, 282, 311, 312, 320
  proverbs 257
Christ
  as high priest 28, 32, 33, 71, 305–307, 309, 312, 330, 341, 356
  divinity of 27, 87, 105, 130, 139
  essence of 27, 28, 121, 185, 189
  existence of 97, 121
  humanity of 15, 16, 60, 72, 93, 95, 105, 133, 140, 169
  identity of 8, 12–14, 39, 55, 68, 69, 80, 232, 253, 366
  image(s) of 20, 34, 188, 224, 225
  mystery of 101, 113, 256
  significance of 133, 185, 331, 340, 348, 349, 356
  the mediator 27, 28, 33, 34, 102, 247, 248, 278, 300, 305, 310, 312, 315, 356
  the Saviour 100, 115, 125, 253, 278, 345, 347, 349, 351
  work of 89, 93, 103, 166, 239, 250, 281, 284, 289, 310, 363
Christendom 25, 80, 97, 144, 225, 232, 356
Christianity 35, 186
  African 50, 173, 201, 230, 273, 339
  Africanizing 19, 200
  in Africa 13, 39, 41, 48, 107, 174, 175, 177, 179, 184, 200, 204, 247, 257, 281, 321
Christians
  African 11, 144, 237, 268, 354, 356
Christology 52, 62, 90, 95, 107, 140, 144, 229, 231, 234, 250, 276–278, 315, 338
  African 70, 167, 236, 360
  definition 236
  African context 86
  ancestor 18, 21, 24, 28–30, 35, 50–52, 55, 58, 63, 66, 68, 75, 83, 96, 100, 142, 144, 166, 172, 175, 177, 180, 198, 208, 212, 214, 215, 224, 230, 237, 238, 250, 257, 275–278, 321, 328, 338, 339, 344, 354, 357, 359–361, 363–366
  debate 53
  in Africa 69, 107, 165, 273, 350
  ivory tower 79, 344
  Marcion's 115, 116
  messianic 295, 296, 299
  New Testament 35, 283, 286
  orthodox 30, 31, 145
  Trinitarian 23, 39, 110, 147
  Yesu 284, 328
circumcision 57, 58, 264, 270, 274
clan 63, 65–67, 76, 152, 158, 159, 161, 169, 314, 344, 345
communities
  African 138, 149, 153, 162, 176, 240, 245, 314
  African Christian 96
  ethnic 229

non-Christian
  African 80
  west African 161
community 154
community-oriented life
  African 63
Constantinople 84, 104, 132, 140
context
  African 28, 49, 52, 169, 280, 334, 345, 364
  ancient Near East 260
  Arab 279
  cultural 57, 205, 210, 232
  Greek 269, 279
  Hebrew 279
  Jewish 33, 275, 295
  Old Testament 329
contextualization 19, 27, 32, 34, 41, 144, 179, 180, 184, 189, 190, 192, 205, 208, 209, 211–214, 230, 231, 273, 319, 321, 328, 342, 355
  definition of 213
cosmogony
  definition 152
cosmology
  African 154, 233, 239, 241
Covenant, New 307, 309
Covenant, Old 309
covenants 9, 11, 33, 272, 274, 279, 284, 308, 309, 367
  Abrahamic 9, 24, 26, 28, 31–33, 35, 102, 263–270, 272–274, 276, 278, 288, 297, 298, 303, 306, 341, 361, 362, 367
  Adamic 8, 24–28, 31, 32, 33, 35, 276, 277, 288, 303, 306, 341, 361, 362, 367
  Mosaic 266, 273
  of blessing 266
  of promise 8
  of redemption 266, 268
  Old Testament 10, 280, 338, 339
  Sinaitic 266, 270–272, 274, 303, 367
cultural values 190
culture 186, 188, 200, 210, 221, 228, 230
  African 41, 65, 70, 144, 166, 202, 204–206, 223, 224, 226, 236, 238
    traditional 41
  African primal 50
  Bantu 60
  Christ in 255
  civic 207
  diversity 109
  European 194
  gospel and 201, 213, 230
  host 18, 182, 189, 191, 195, 214
  non-Christian 49
  recipient 213
  Western 196

D

dead 354
  afterlife 28, 33, 135, 137, 142, 143, 155, 158, 161, 359, 363
  as intermediaries 247
  in the Bible 142
  living and the 142, 158, 168, 240, 245, 313
  memorial of 363
  raising the 66, 111
  remembering the 65, 363
  souls of the 136
  venerating the 361
disciples, the 12, 14, 67, 94, 97, 99, 100, 179, 184, 313
discourse 207
  christological 12, 18, 21, 26, 51, 68, 79, 93, 150, 180, 233
    African 31

theological 10, 25, 39, 55, 87, 175, 227, 235, 280, 329

E

early church 12, 14, 16, 17, 22, 35, 81, 84–86, 91, 94, 101, 102, 105–107, 109, 131, 141, 145, 214, 277, 278, 280, 281, 288, 289, 335
  belief 284
  creeds 22, 104, 105
  doctrine 166
  evangelists 280, 283
  fathers 21, 31, 91, 96, 105, 106, 108, 140, 356
  teaching 95
  tradition 268, 368
Ecumenical Council 132, 222
ECWA 3, 10, 192, 342, 352, 353
episcopate, African 219
ethics 135, 138, 241
etymology 29, 148, 285, 301
  of Jesus 351
Evangelical Church Winning All. See ECWA

F

family 138, 152, 158, 159, 161, 243, 246, 248, 311, 312
  African 87, 345
  deceased 242
  life 245, 330
  lineage 138
  protection of 348

G

gap and fulfilment 87, 233, 235, 278, 321
God
  as immanent 27, 33, 320
  as transcendent 27, 33, 301, 317, 327, 337
  as Trinity 113
  essence of 82, 87, 120, 121, 318, 331
  existence of 53, 331
  identity of 253
  image(s) of 125, 259–261, 325, 326, 328
  likeness of 261
  mystery of 83, 327
  of the Jews 265
  Son of 122, 220
  the Creator 100, 105, 111, 115, 124, 125, 150, 192, 193, 247, 273, 293, 299, 317, 319, 325, 332, 337
  the Father 8, 15, 23, 70, 76, 77, 82, 87, 105, 106, 108, 112–114, 117, 119, 121, 123, 126, 127, 130, 188, 253, 299, 330
  the Holy Spirit 8, 87, 112
  the Son 8, 15, 84, 122, 188
  Triune 33, 76
  unity of 129, 130, 139

H

heresies 107, 111, 112, 145
  Arian 39
  christological 147
  responses to 109
  Trinitarian 39
heresy 85, 110
  the Ebonites 108
heretics 14, 18, 39, 94, 106, 107, 110, 111, 116, 128, 141, 147, 360
heritage 204
  African 34, 45
  Christ's 298
heritage, cultural 345
  African 5, 70, 190, 200, 201

pre-Christian 20
heritage, religious
 African 5, 56, 201, 227, 231, 232, 250
 pre-Christian 220
Holy Spirit, the 7, 78, 108, 111, 132, 173, 204, 216, 231, 251, 296, 350
homoousios 15, 105, 129, 130

I

idolatry 278, 324, 325, 328
idol worship 33
incarnation 7, 11, 25, 28, 55, 83–85, 104, 109, 112, 124–127, 202, 216, 220, 221, 225, 254–257, 260, 295, 308, 316, 346
 as a symbol 86
 cultural 220
 mystery of 7, 55, 83, 87, 113, 255, 317, 322, 340, 366
 of Christian life 210
 purpose of 125, 126
 theology 80, 84, 95, 226
inculturation 34, 61, 195, 199, 205, 208, 209, 211, 213, 214, 216, 219–221, 228, 231, 255, 273, 342, 355, 362, 366
 and incarnation 255
 definition of 210
 doctrine of 230
 importance of 232
 methodology 7, 319, 321, 328, 344, 355, 360
 purposes of 230
 theology 191, 200, 201, 219, 222, 230, 235
interpretation
 African 244
 of Christ 107, 122, 288
 of the Bible 213
Issah 9, 268, 279, 353, 357

J

Jesu 8–11, 25, 27, 32, 33, 88, 176, 268, 273, 279, 280, 284, 321, 336, 338, 339, 342, 344–347, 349, 350, 352, 354, 357, 360, 362, 365, 367. See also Yesu
Jesu Kiristi 35, 315
Jesus
 death of 26, 32, 68, 71, 100, 101, 142, 167, 169, 212, 226, 277, 280, 294, 296, 308, 313, 315, 337, 345
 historical 42, 66, 98
 life of 89, 91, 93, 99, 103, 169, 284, 292, 308, 337

K

kin 1, 5, 26, 28, 76, 77, 134, 138, 170, 172, 248
kingdom of God 239, 286
kith and kin 2, 66, 86, 87, 159, 281, 311, 312, 319

L

language
 African 9, 10, 346
 Christian 300
 diversity 43
 for God 332
 Hebrew 349
 metaphorical 331, 335
 Nigerian 350
 religious 332
 Semitic 351
 theological 329, 335, 337
living-dead 1, 64, 85, 144, 159, 161, 162, 165, 229, 241–243, 246, 248, 311, 312, 338
living-memories 1, 64, 159
Logos 16, 40, 71, 72, 76, 79, 81, 84, 87, 105, 120, 122, 128, 130, 221, 293, 341

Index of Subjects

M

mediation 77, 247, 248, 275, 299–302, 305, 309–312
  African 314
  biblical 306, 314
  priestly 306, 310
Messiah, the 8, 27, 28, 33, 34, 73, 99, 115, 258, 267, 270, 272, 273, 276–279, 283, 284, 286, 289–293, 295, 296, 298, 299, 304, 309, 345, 354, 356, 362
metaphors 329–331
  ancestral 342
mission 54, 57, 230, 231, 287
  cross-cultural 265
  field 49
  theology of 278
missionaries 38, 43, 47, 49
  Lutheran 51
  Roman Catholic 191
  Western 18, 30, 38, 40, 41, 53, 54, 79
models
  ancestor 5, 11, 39, 41, 53, 85, 87, 95, 96, 147, 148, 167, 169, 189, 222, 226, 228, 278, 280, 314, 341, 360, 364
  biblical 106
  Christian 228
  christological 140, 250
  cultural 189, 223
  inculturation 88, 355
  New Testament 356
  pre-Christian 165, 224, 228, 361
  theological 365
mystery 14

N

names
  African 282
New Testament 14, 21, 89–91, 105, 141, 142, 184, 279, 304, 310, 313, 339, 341, 356, 367
  Christ 19, 21, 89, 91, 103, 115, 224, 227, 281, 283
  metaphors 330
  models 224, 280, 362
  teachings 90, 166
Nicaea 81, 82, 123, 132, 140, 147
Nicene Council 123, 131, 140
Nicene Creed 130, 331
Nigeria 46

O

Old Testament 90, 92, 111, 115, 171, 265, 275, 284, 303, 306, 308–310, 313, 330, 367
  belief 130
  metaphors 330
  prophecies 102, 280, 283, 284, 292, 303, 338, 339, 366
  Yeshua 268

P

patriarchs 26, 31, 106, 258, 278
  Jewish 257, 268, 269, 277, 284, 339, 357, 367
  of heresies 111
priesthood, Aaronic 33, 275, 307, 308
promises 9, 11, 279, 290, 367
  Abrahamic 92, 258, 263, 265, 267, 268, 277
  New Testament 8
  of God 257, 264, 266, 274, 277, 298
  of redemption 270, 273, 336, 363
  Old Testament 35, 280, 283, 284, 316, 345
  Sinaitic 288
prophecies
  Jewish 272, 309
Protestant 212

R

redemption 143, 221, 239, 247, 255, 263–266, 270, 275, 308, 315, 316, 353
  definition 266
  Israel's 283
  mystery of 72
  of bodies 276
religious categories
  African pre-Christian 59
religious concepts
  African traditional 22
religious consciousness
  African 165
religious system
  African traditional 151, 164
religious values
  traditional 190
resurrection, the 26, 32, 68, 71, 94, 99–101, 103, 104, 106, 115, 142, 212, 277, 280, 292, 295, 296, 301, 315, 337, 341, 354
rituals 63, 155, 160, 342, 363
  Igbo 36, 355
  offerings 74, 77, 78
  prayers 77
  religious 163, 355
  washing 57, 302
Roman Catholic 35, 73, 195
  accommodation 211
  Church 88, 174, 191, 195, 197, 206, 216, 218, 221, 222, 231, 361
  Church Magisterium 215
  liturgy 196
  Popes 199
  theology 208, 216, 217
  tradition 215

S

sacrifices 5, 150, 163, 173, 241–243, 248, 249, 306, 307, 311, 312, 327
  animal 300, 306
  New Testament 306
  of Christ 80, 308, 310, 312
  Old Testament 306, 307
  priests 305
saints 171–174
  Christian 148, 170
  Communion of 171
scholars 143, 167, 339
  African 40, 41, 164, 175, 236, 249, 319, 328, 334, 354, 364–366
  biblical 47, 48, 51, 56, 62, 69, 79, 251
  Eurocentric 251
Scriptures 33, 81, 82, 85, 90, 98, 121, 143, 184, 185, 212, 213, 226, 270, 272, 277, 278, 283, 304, 349, 368
  authority of 181, 213
  Christian 94
  Hebrew 268
  Jewish 143, 294
Second Vatican Council. *See* Vatican II
societies 182
  African 56, 58, 59, 62, 63, 68, 134, 138, 150, 152, 155, 161, 165, 177, 281, 311, 312, 338, 344
  ancient African 64, 85, 190
  Bantu 59, 60, 164
  Jewish 26
  modern 218
  religious 103
  secular 103

traditional 63, 64, 163, 223, 241, 275
tribal 241
Yoruba 170
Zambian 164
South Africa 38, 157, 164, 170, 249
Special Assembly for Africa of the Synod of Bishops 219, 361
Swahili 10, 157
Symposium of Episcopal Conferences of Africa and Madagascar 20, 200, 206

T

Ten Commandments 33, 183, 271, 301, 321, 323, 326–328
theologians 251, 339
  African 14, 30, 32, 33, 38–41, 47, 50, 51, 55, 56, 60–62, 69, 79, 86, 107, 133, 185, 223, 224, 226–228, 236, 237, 247, 249, 251–254, 257, 268, 273, 277, 278, 281, 309, 313, 314, 319, 320, 328, 334, 339, 344, 352, 354, 357, 359, 364, 366, 367
  ancestor 321
  evangelical 209
  French 218
  liberation 182
  postmodern African 17
  Protestant 209, 212
  Roman Catholic 208, 361
theology
  African 38, 40, 47, 49–55, 61, 62, 68, 69, 88, 95, 107, 172, 175, 185, 190, 205, 212, 224, 251, 253, 342, 360, 366
  definition 70
  African Catholic 61
  African Christian 30
  ancestor 61, 67, 144, 180, 221, 361, 365

  biblical 214, 338
  Christian 34, 88, 91, 142, 185, 189, 192, 201, 220, 234, 237, 250, 251, 254, 321, 328, 362, 363, 367
  contextual 13, 148, 182, 184, 203, 211, 361
  creation 274, 276
  cultural 208, 218
  in Africa 58
  ivory tower 366
  of Christ 355
  of power 249
  Roman Catholic 216, 217, 361
  salvation 199, 278
  traditional 91, 144, 318
  traditional Christian 30
titles
  for Christ 66, 176, 224, 227, 228, 230, 273, 281–283, 293
traditions
  African 56, 68, 95, 144, 165, 176, 232, 237, 250, 252
  African primal 50, 56, 63
  apostolic 95, 96, 104, 107, 111, 140, 144, 145, 214, 237
  biblical 68, 166, 338
  Christian 81, 172, 174
  evangelical 185, 343
  Jewish 102, 268, 286, 294
  orthodox 185
  primal 49, 214, 281, 312, 318, 321, 327, 338, 359, 361
  religious 4, 234
transcendence
  definition 317, 337
tribes 63, 158, 159, 161
  African 9, 10, 157, 170, 342
  cultures of 254
Trinitas 113

Trinity, the 75, 76, 78, 87, 112, 114, 118, 121, 308
  mystery of 72, 113

V

Vatican I 216
Vatican II 61, 170, 179, 191, 192, 195, 197–199, 204–208, 211, 214, 216, 218, 219, 222, 230, 231, 361
veneration 163, 165
  ancestor 33, 35, 51, 77, 143, 144, 164, 170, 175, 176, 229, 252, 275, 327, 338, 342, 363
  of gods 35
  of saints 175

W

world
  of forms 135, 138, 139
  of ideas 136, 139
  physical 134, 139, 149, 160, 164
  spirit 28, 155, 251
  spiritual 134, 149, 154, 164, 244, 311
  visible 155
worldview 79, 101, 139, 229, 238, 267, 356
  African 16, 35, 51, 58, 148, 149, 232, 236, 240, 361, 362
  cosmogony 31
  traditional 48, 56, 134, 150, 151, 153, 155, 233, 237–240, 243, 312
  Bantu 59
  definition 148, 149, 267
  Jewish 183, 286, 288
  Western 49
worship 323, 325–327
  ancestor 154, 163–165, 327, 328
  of idols 193, 325, 326

Y

Yahweh 143, 183, 184, 263, 266–272, 275, 277–279, 285, 286, 288, 294, 302, 310, 322, 323, 326
Yeshua 8, 268, 270, 273, 279, 344, 357, 367
  transliteration of 9
Yesu 8–11, 25, 27, 32, 33, 35, 88, 176, 268, 273, 279, 283, 284, 315, 321, 336, 338, 339, 342, 344, 345, 347–354, 357, 360, 362, 365, 367. *See also* Jesu
Yesu Kristo 11, 28, 250, 365
Yesu-Zhirhyel 348
Yoruba 10, 157, 160, 163, 170, 177, 327

Langham Literature, with its publishing work, is a ministry of Langham Partnership.

Langham Partnership is a global fellowship working in pursuit of the vision God entrusted to its founder John Stott –

> *to facilitate the growth of the church in maturity and Christ-likeness through raising the standards of biblical preaching and teaching.*

Our vision is to see churches in the majority world equipped for mission and growing to maturity in Christ through the ministry of pastors and leaders who believe, teach and live by the Word of God.

Our mission is to strengthen the ministry of the Word of God through:
- nurturing national movements for biblical preaching
- fostering the creation and distribution of evangelical literature
- enhancing evangelical theological education

especially in countries where churches are under-resourced.

Our ministry

Langham Preaching partners with national leaders to nurture indigenous biblical preaching movements for pastors and lay preachers all around the world. With the support of a team of trainers from many countries, a multi-level programme of seminars provides practical training, and is followed by a programme for training local facilitators. Local preachers' groups and national and regional networks ensure continuity and ongoing development, seeking to build vigorous movements committed to Bible exposition.

Langham Literature provides majority world preachers, scholars and seminary libraries with evangelical books and electronic resources through publishing and distribution, grants and discounts. The programme also fosters the creation of indigenous evangelical books in many languages, through writer's grants, strengthening local evangelical publishing houses, and investment in major regional literature projects, such as one volume Bible commentaries like the *Africa Bible Commentary* and the *South Asia Bible Commentary*.

Langham Scholars provides financial support for evangelical doctoral students from the majority world so that, when they return home, they may train pastors and other Christian leaders with sound, biblical and theological teaching. This programme equips those who equip others. Langham Scholars also works in partnership with majority world seminaries in strengthening evangelical theological education. A growing number of Langham Scholars study in high quality doctoral programmes in the majority world itself. As well as teaching the next generation of pastors, graduated Langham Scholars exercise significant influence through their writing and leadership.

To learn more about Langham Partnership and the work we do visit **langham.org**

www.ingramcontent.com/pod-product-compliance
Lightning Source LLC
Chambersburg PA
CBHW061703300426
44115CB00014B/2545